THE STORY OF SCANDINAVIA

Also by Stein Ringen

How Democracies Live: Power, Statecraft and
Freedom in Modern Societies, 2022

The Perfect Dictatorship: China in the 21st *Century,* 2016

Nation of Devils: Democratic Leadership and
the Problem of Obedience, 2013

The Korean State and Social Policy; How South Korea Lifted Itself
from Poverty and Dictatorship to Affluence and Democracy, with
Huck-ju Kwon, Ilcheong Yi, Taekyoon Kim and Jooha Lee, 2011

What Democracy Is For: On Freedom and Moral Government, 2007

Citizens, Families and Reform, 1997 and 2005

The Possibility of Politics: A Study in the Political
Economy of the Welfare State, 1987 and 2006

THE STORY OF SCANDINAVIA

From the Vikings to Social Democracy

STEIN RINGEN

WEIDENFELD & NICOLSON

First published in Great Britain in 2023 by Weidenfeld & Nicolson,
an imprint of The Orion Publishing Group Ltd
Carmelite House, 50 Victoria Embankment
London EC4Y 0DZ

An Hachette UK Company

1 3 5 7 9 10 8 6 4 2

A CIP catalogue record for this book is
available from the British Library.

ISBN (Hardback) 978 1 4746 2519 7
ISBN (Export Trade Paperback) 978 1 4746 2520 3
ISBN (eBook) 978 1 4746 2522 7
ISBN (Audio) 978 1 4746 2523 4

Typeset at The Spartan Press Ltd,
Lymington, Hants

Printed and bound in Great Britain by Clays Ltd,
Elcograf S.p.A.

www.weidenfeldandnicolson.co.uk
www.orionbooks.co.uk

The Scandinavians are magnificent writers of history. Their historians make up a community of dedicated scholars of the first order. I have absorbed their works and stand in humble admiration of their achievements. I dedicate this effort in synthesis in gratitude to the women and men of that community.

CONTENTS

PART FOUR: INTO THE MODERN WORLD

AUTHOR'S NOTE

Early on in the writing of this book, I found myself in Århus in Denmark. It was a fine spring day. I walked through that beautiful town, as idyllic as Scandinavia comes, whose history goes back to the Viking Age. I was reminded that here, a millennium ago, it was war of all against all, and death, destruction and misery everywhere. And then I was reminded that later on there came to the whole of Scandinavia more of the same: illness, plague, exploitation, wave after wave of war and war again, devastation and more devastation. Much of it was inter-Scandinavian, the peoples of the north destroying sometimes each other, sometimes themselves, in senseless violence. It has been an awful history.

Against that backdrop, against any historical awareness, Århus today is wondrous. The historical parts are maintained with skill and pride, the old quarters preserved and gentrified, the streets cobbled. The city is modern, with a superb university and the best of galleries and museums, the architecture splendid. It is orderly, clean, affluent, civil and friendly. It sits in a rich and well-governed country in which people live in comfort, safety and happiness. It is in a region of the world of well-functioning democracy and peaceful friendship and collaboration.

So I walked through the town – it could have been many a Scandinavian town – and I asked myself: how did it come to this?

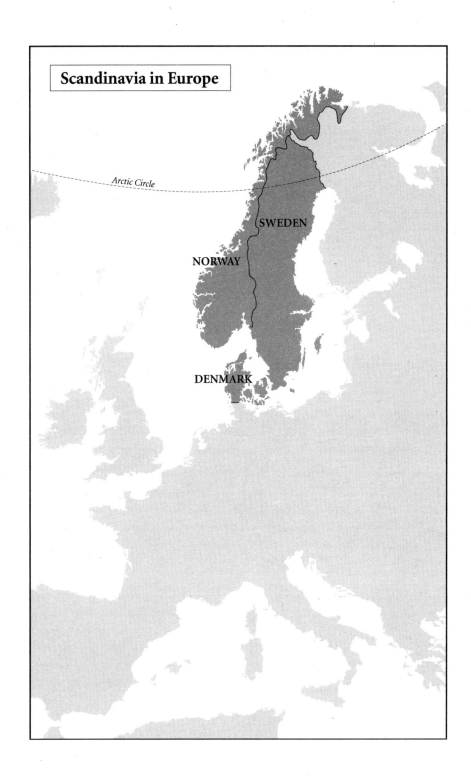

Scandinavia in Europe

LIST OF ILLUSTRATIONS

INTRODUCTION

Gudfred died in the year 810. He was murdered. Probably by one of his men – a soldier, a servant, a slave? Or it might have been an enemy assassin. What is known about him is from Frankish sources, which treat him as an upstart and a nuisance whom the Europeans might well have wished to be rid of. But it has also been said that he had betrayed a wife, who incited a son to revenge, who cut his father to pieces with his sword. He was not the first Dane to call himself king but was more so than any of the earlier pretenders.

All Norwegian schoolchildren learn that Norway was unified by Harald Finehair at the Battle of Hafrsfjord in the year 872 (or a decade or so later). He is called *Hårfagre* in Norwegian and often Fairhair in English, but that is a poor translation. He was honoured not for being blond but for having a lush head of hair, then as now a sign of male virility (which, the legend has it, he pledged not to cut until he had made himself supreme king). He probably did fight his way to the kind of control in Norway that Gudfred had in Denmark a century earlier. He is thought to have died in 931 at the age of about eighty, extraordinary for the time.

The Westrogothic Law is the first known written Swedish provincial law and the first known Swedish text in Latin. It dates from around 1325. Contained in it, as an appendix, is a list of Christian kings, which starts with Olof Skötkonung. He made parts of Sweden his domain around the year 1000. That's a century on from Harald and two centuries on from Gudfred. The kingdom was only a piece of today's central Sweden. His name could mean tax-king, or possibly minter of coins. Like other early Scandinavian kings he did mint coins (with his own image and the inscription OLUF REX in Latin). Coins were not general tender and were not minted in large numbers – these were not yet monetised economies. They were mainly to bring glory and standing to the king.

States were in the making, but slowly. It would be a thousand years of unruly history before Scandinavia settled into the contours we now know in which kingdoms have become nations.

European origins

Scandinavia, in this book, as in common parlance, comprises Denmark, Norway and Sweden; the broader region is Nordic. This is a history of three countries over 1,200 years.

If we think of European civilisation, as we should, as a set of ideas, inventions and influences that diffused west and north from their sources in the eastern Mediterranean – Mesopotamia, Egypt, Ancient Greece – Scandinavia is the final periphery. Population came late, as did agriculture, trade and further modernisations. Ideas and beliefs moved south to north: the mythologies, Christianity, Lutheranism, Renaissance, Enlightenment. The people in the north have been scrambling at the end of the European road to absorb and keep up with influences from civilisations ahead of them in a brutal process of rise and fall, collapse and restart. It has been a costly struggle of opportunities lost and gains reversed, of kingdoms aspiring to greatness only to collapse. It has been a struggle of high drama in the hands of sometimes great and complex men and women, sometimes petty and deplorable ones. A constant in this history, from the start, and as alive today as ever, is the European influence and the difficult question of how to be European.

People started to migrate into the area about 13,000 years ago. They came up from the south, some maybe from the east, if so later, possibly giving ancestry to the Sami people in the Arctic north. We are at the end of the Great Ice Age. The land was rising, forests spreading north, followed by animals, reindeer importantly, feeding off the growth, followed by people feeding off the animals. Within 7,000 years, only mountain glaciers remained of the ice. Within a further 3,000 or 4,000 years there was habitation all along the Norwegian coast to the far north.

The early people were hunters, fishermen and gatherers. Knowledge of agriculture started to reach southern Denmark two millennia ago, southern Sweden and coastal strips of Norway shortly after, then spread slowly north, back and forth depending on climate fluctuations. Agriculture became the way of life in the south while in the north the combination of hunting, fishing and gathering continued, in northern Norway and Sweden up to our time. From the sixteenth century, mainly non-agricultural economies in the inland north gradually adopted nomadic reindeer husbandry, still the way of life among some, but not the majority, of the Sami.

The Europeans were aware of the lands to the north. Phoenicians from Carthage had sailed out of the Mediterranean around 450 BC, reaching at least as far north as the British Isles, perhaps further. The geographer Pytheas, from the Greek colony of Massalia, present-day Marseilles, made a journey of discovery to northern Europe around 325 BC, to Britain, Ireland and the Arctic. He described polar ice and the midnight sun, possibly giving Norway the name of Thule, and may have entered the Baltic Sea. The first Roman contact may have been in a reconnaissance by a fleet up the western coast of Denmark in the year 5 AD. Later, during Nero's reign, around 60 AD, another fleet entered the Baltic Sea. Pliny the Elder, in his *Natural History*, written circa 70 AD, mentions Scandinavia, and Tacitus, in *Germania*, his work on the tribes outside the Roman Empire beyond the Rhine, written *c*.100, mentions the *Suiones*. Parts of Sweden were known as *Scania*, hence the name Scandinavia for the broader region. Cassiodorus, councillor to Theodoric, King of the Gothic Kingdom of Italy, wrote a history of the Goths around 500 in which he posited that they had their origin in Scandinavia (a myth revived by later Swedish nationalists). So says Jordanes in his *Getica*, written some thirty years later (Cassiodorus' books have been lost), who writes of a great island of *Scandza* and its various peoples, and mentions the *Dani* and the Swedes. The Byzantine historian Procopius, in his *Histories of the Wars*, written around the middle of the sixth century, mentions the Danes and the island of Thule, which again may be Norway. He writes of the midnight sun and of a people who were probably the Sami, whose way of life he compares to that of beasts. A Norwegian trader by name of Ottar (often called Ohthere in English texts) visited King Alfred of Wessex and said that he came from 'Nordveg', the land to the north, and spoke also of 'Denamearc'.

It seems pretty safe to assume that at the time our story begins there was awareness in Europe of lands in the north that formed an entity of sorts, referred to as some variation of Scandinavia, and that the main units of this entity were known by variants of the names of Denmark, Norway and Sweden. Scandinavia did not yet exist in the way we think of it today – far from it – but we will not go wrong by framing our story, from the beginning, around these labels and names.

Lands

Denmark is the smallest in territory, about 43,000 square km. The population is around 5.8 million, with another 100,000 in Greenland and the Faroes. It consists of a spit of land, Jylland (Jutland), that juts northward out of the European Continent with the North Sea to the west, the Skagerrak to the north towards Norway, and the Kattegat to the east towards Sweden. South of Jylland proper are Schleswig and Holstein. These are Denmark's troublesome borderlands with Germany, contested lands in which the German–Danish border has shifted restlessly, sometimes north, sometimes south. Holstein is now comfortably German, Schleswig divided between Germany and Denmark.

The rest of the territory is an archipelago between Jylland and Sweden, the biggest island being Sjælland (Zealand), on which sits Copenhagen, the capital, in and near which resides about a quarter of the national population. The land is flat, with not a single mountain, and hospitable: the climate is good, the soil fertile, the fisheries rich. Denmark has been and is still an agricultural economy. It has lent itself to large landholdings and a wealthy aristocracy.

Sweden is the biggest country: 450,000 square km with 10 million people. The south is flat-ish agricultural land, the north rugged and mountainous with deep forests. It has been a land of large holdings, aristocracy and concentrated wealth, and, eventually, a prosperous state. Agriculture is good in the south. It is rich in mineral wealth and is Scandinavia's most industrial economy. The capital is Stockholm with a population of about 2 million.

Norway has a territory of 385,000 square km and a population of 5.3 million, the Arctic archipelago of Svalbard adding a further 61,000 square km and 3,000 people. It is a long and narrow country of mountains and fjords. The distance from the south to the north is such that if you flip the country around on a map the northern tip would reach mid-Italy. It curves around Sweden and Finland to the Arctic Sea so that the easternmost city in the north, Kirkenes, is on the same longitude as Istanbul. The coast is long and the fisheries rich. The landscape is mountainous with little agricultural land; only 3 per cent of the area is arable. There has never been a class of rich landowners and never a viable aristocracy. The capital is Oslo, with a population just short of a million.

Conspicuous in the region's geography are the smallness of Denmark, the length of Norway and the solid land mass of Sweden. Scandinavia is thought of as small, but it is not: its territory is about the same as that of France and Germany combined. But its population is less than a third of that of France.

Denmark has no shared land border with the two other countries and to the south adjoins the Continent. It is a mystery why it became Scandinavian and not German, and often enough it was touch and go. Norway is rocky, cold and inhospitable. It is a mystery that it can sustain itself, and for a long time it could not. Sweden is locked in by its two neighbours, its back to the Norwegian mountains. It is a mystery that it could reach out into the world, and for long it was squeezed to operating eastward.

While Denmark was in control of southern Sweden, it also controlled the route into and out of the Baltic Sea, 'the Sound'. But the Baltic Sea is geopolitically a Swedish sphere. The Baltic question was long to poison Scandinavian relations and give rise to Danish–Swedish competition, conflict, warfare and mutual hatred. Norway stood aside from this quarrel, seen by the two other countries as an irrelevance. During most of the history covered in this book Denmark and Sweden were bitter enemies, both considering themselves big powers, both determined to outdo, sometimes destroy, the other, united only in contempt of little Norway. This enmity has not been resolved. Under the surface of collaboration there remain even today undercurrents of envy, contempt, pity, even hatred. An idea of Scandinavian unity was born early, but was for hundreds of years an utter failure, only to be realised to a limited degree late in the twentieth century. And even then, against those remaining criss-crossing animosities.

Peoples

The Scandinavians are mainly Germanic peoples. They have much in common in origin and culture. Danish, Norwegian and Swedish are dialects of a shared language. Danes and Norwegians read each other with ease, but may struggle in speech. Norwegians and Swedes understand each other easily in speech, but struggle in reading. Swedes understand Danes with difficulty, and Danes cannot easily distinguish between spoken Norwegian and Swedish. The Scandinavian alphabet has three more letters than the standard Latin one: æ (in Swedish ä), ø (in Swedish ö) and å (sometimes written with the double aa).

Language has been and is political. In Denmark, German was long a competing language, dominant at court and among élites, threatening to crowd out the use of Danish. Swedish royals and élites preferred French. Norway has two official language versions, *bokmål*, meaning 'book language', and *nynorsk*, meaning 'new Norwegian', and a bewildering array of dialects. In the valley of Gudbrandsdalen, which cuts north from Lillehammer in the rural heartland, the people in the north speak a light melodic dialect, more so the further north, and say 'us' for 'we', as in 'us will be home', while those in the south, only a few miles away, have a heavy drawl and use 'we' for 'we'. Other distinct dialects, within many variations, are the Danish-inspired *skånsk* in the south of Sweden, Finnish-inspired Swedish in northern Sweden, Swedish-inspired Danish on the island of Bornholm, and northern dialects in Norway and Sweden. Norway has the most diversity of dialects, Denmark the least.

There are three classical minorities: a Sami people in the north of Norway and Sweden (and Finland and Russia), a Finnish people in the north-east of Sweden, and a German people in the south of Denmark. These minorities mix with the majority populations in multiple ways, but their minority cultures, identities and languages survive and are now actively maintained. The Scandinavian people have been thought of as 'homogeneous' but were always mixed populations, and are certainly so today. Jews constitute an old, if small, minority, as do, after the Reformation, Catholics. There are big groups of other-country Nordics in all of the countries. Recent immigrations from Southern Europe, Asia and Africa have made the peoples of the north ever more mixed in ethnicity, race and religion.

The Sami in Norway number between 40,000 and 60,000, about half of whom live in the traditional Sami areas in the north. There are smaller subgroups, the Coastal Sami and the South Sami, and a South Sami language, which is different from the dominant Sami language and dialects. The Sami population in Sweden is about 20,000. Only 2,000 or so are reindeer herders. Many, perhaps most, do not use

Sami language or wear Sami costume. Their largest concentration is in Stockholm.

The Finnish minority in Sweden are the descendants of the Torne Valley people, who live along the River Torne on the border in the north between Sweden and Finland, and descendants living in other parts of Sweden and elsewhere, now some tens of thousands. Their origins in the area date from before the national border was drawn in 1809. They use a Finnish-influenced dialect of Swedish and a local dialect of Finnish. There is a National Association of Swedish Tornedalians that is active in matters of culture, language and civil society.

The German minority in Denmark consists of about 15,000 people, with their core domain in the border area near Germany. They have an association, the *Bund Deutscher Nordschleswiger*, refer to themselves as 'the German minority' (not 'German-speaking'), run their own kindergartens, schools, libraries and cultural institutions, have their own political party, *Slesvigsk Parti/Schleswigsche Partei*, and issue a German-language newspaper. Their area is in Danish terminology Southern Jylland, but they themselves refer to it as *Nordschleswig*.

In the Viking Age Sagas, those who were not kings or chiefs get only the briefest mention as 'small-folks'. That has been said to be biased, but was simply a reflection of reality. The small-folks were bypassed in the telling as they were in life. Scandinavian egalitarianism is new and has grown out of a long history of rigid class divisions. The small-folks have a constant presence in this history. There may be more to say about lords than about serfs, but there is a constant undercurrent concerning those less visible.

In the agricultural revolution of the 1200s, Scandinavia got its first taste of prosperity. With improvements in economy and government, we might think life would be better for the people. But it was not. Conditions for the small-folks instead deteriorated. In the Viking Age, men who were not slaves were free: not equals, not empowered, but free. Now they became property-less serfs and proletarians until, in the Age of Perpetual War, as of about 1600, they were reduced to fodder. Only with the end of royal absolutism, beginning in the eighteenth century, could the small-folks emerge from the shadows and start to matter. That will bring our story into a new world in which States serve people rather than people States.

Telling the story

This book has a simple ambition: to tell the story of how the Scandinavians have come to be as they are today. Our forebears have at times had some presence in Europe and the wider world, but as takers more than givers. Very recently there has been a turnaround. Scandinavia today is an entirely different reality from its historical personae: a better reality, a giver more than a taker.

In trying to tell this story, I have drawn on a great legacy of Scandinavian historiography. While the history of the Viking Age is Scandinavian, for the later periods the Scandinavians have written mainly national histories. I have wanted to bring back the all-Scandinavian perspective. There is, I have found, no national history in this region that is not also a Scandinavian one.

The writing of national history is, to put it carefully, difficult. Two tendencies are visible in much of the Scandinavian work. One is an inclination to look for interpretations that give rise to pride. The first Scandinavian historian, the thirteenth-century Dane Saxo Grammaticus, wrote to 'glorify our fatherland'. Modern historians do not do that: they write to tell what has unfolded. But a bias towards greatness remained long after Saxo. The Viking Age has been seen as one of impressive achievement. The period when Sweden was an imperial power in Europe is still known in Swedish historiography as *storhetstiden*, 'the Age of Grandeur'. This bias is less present in the works of today's historians, but probably lingers to some degree.

The other tendency is to look for continuity, as if there are straight lines from previous times up to today. This has been expressed in what has been called a Scandinavian continuity of freedom, running from the status of free men in the Viking Age to that of the free citizen in today's democracy. It has also been expressed in terms of a continuity of class struggle: the journey to modern nationhood has been one of the oppressed continuously rising in demand of equality.

What is true or not about greatness and continuity is not easily said. The Viking presence in medieval Europe was remarkable. But does that make it something we should celebrate? I doubt it. Of course, Scandinavian history, like any other, should be seen as a combination of continuity and change, but is continuity a defining characteristic of this history? I doubt that also.

To forge some order of my own into the story, I have made use of tools which I carry with me from my background as a social scientist. My approach is comparative. In trying to understand what Scandinavia looks like I have asked where Scandinavia stands against the broader European experience. My history is not a Scandinavian history of Scandinavia but a European history of Scandinavia, and hence also a slice of European history. My approach is one of critical scepticism. I am not at all non-judgemental, far from it, but I have tried, whenever up against what looks like some kind of established truth, in particular the pride narrative, to step back and ask: could it have been like that? In this, my method has often been to think in numbers and quantities. That starts in my understanding that the Vikings were small samples of small populations and that the whole enterprise could not have been bigger than the scant population numbers made possible.

These approaches have led me to what is perhaps a bias of my own on the two big questions of greatness and continuity. There is greatness in this story, but it was a long time coming and materialised only when the Scandinavians were able to cast aside the ambition of grandeur. In the balance of continuity and change, it is change that is conspicuous. I identify two big transitions: one in the thirteenth century and a second in the eighteenth to nineteenth centuries. Both were dramatic: the old up against failure and the new coming as fresh starts. With the second transition, a novelty emerged in which the Scandinavians might, perhaps, allow themselves to take some pride. Until then, the ambition had been for greatness at the expense of ever more and brutal exploitation of the small-folks. Only when that was left behind and the small-folks could start to claim recognition, very late in the long story, did we reach a time in which we might think of Scandinavia as a presence in Europe with a quality of its own.

A NOTE ON NAMES AND TERMINOLOGY

I borrow the term 'small-folks' from the Sagas to refer to the mass of mostly anonymous people at the bottom of the social order, those who for most of this history have counted for little and mattered for less. At the other extreme are small élites whom I often refer to as 'barons'. Not that they necessarily carried that title – formal aristocracies did not emerge until after the Middle Ages – but they were the ones with wealth and position.

I use mostly modernised Scandinavian names, hence King Knud rather that Cnut or Canute. But when honour names have meaning I use the English, hence Knud the Great rather than Knud den Store. But pragmatically, hence Harlad Hardrade, rather than Hard Ruler, because it sounds better. The big Danish peninsula is Jylland rather than Jutland, and the biggest island Sjælland rather than Zealand. But again pragmatically, Copenhagen rather than København.

I use capital letters liberally. A church is a house of worship but the Church the apparatus of institutions. A state may be a country but the State the administration that makes for governing. A crown sits on a king's head but the Crown is the position of authority that kings hold. The Social Democrats are the party, a social democrat a person of that persuasion.

Part One

Into Europe

In the Viking Ship Museum in Oslo is a vessel of such perfection in shape and proportions that it is a physical pleasure to stand still and behold it. It has twelve board-lengths on each side, each board overlapping the next, rising up at stern and aft to a great height, held together by iron rivets. The keel stretches the length of the ship, again rising at both stern and aft to be finished in delicately crafted spiralled serpents and snakeheads, decorated to below water level with fine carvings, as are the top sideboards. The sides bulge out to make space for a deck. The timber for the body is oak, with internal deck-boards, mast and oars of pine. It was powered by fifteen rowers on each side, and by a square sail. It would have been painted in bright colours.*

This is the Oseberg Ship, so named after the farm in the south of Norway where it was found in a burial mound in 1903. It was excavated the next year, removed from the mound with various other finds, and reassembled over the next twenty years. It had been built around the year 820, probably to be ceremonial, and may never have been to work at sea.

The other main ship in the Museum, the *Gokstad*, is built in the same gracious shape but without the elaborate decorations, and would have been a jobbing vessel before it too ended its days in a burial mound around 900.

The Oseberg funeral was in 834. Remains of two women were found in the grave, one seventy to eighty years old, having died of cancer, one fifty years old or thereabouts, cause of death unknown. At least one, probably the elder, would have been of high standing in her community: the wife of a chief, or perhaps herself a religious leader. The *Gokstad* was the grave of a male, probably a local chief who had died in battle.

The graves were lavishly equipped. Finds include clothes, some of silk, shoes and combs, ship's equipment, cooking utensils, farm and

* At the time of writing, the Viking Ship Museum is closed for rebuilding, to reopen as the Museum of the Viking Age in 2026.

fishing tools, ornate and working sleighs, carts, carved animal heads, beds, tents, horses, dogs, cows, various birds and much more.

Viking ships were built to be seafaring. They were supple, soft and fast, and could master rough seas although neither large not deep. The journeys would not have been comfortable, to put it mildly. There was space for cargo, sometimes cattle and horses, sometimes non-warrior followers, but no living quarters. The diet would have consisted of dried and salted fish and meat, with water, sour milk and beer. Ships like these carried Norsemen south to France, west to England, Scotland and Ireland, and further on to Iceland, Greenland and North America. They were shallow-bottomed, easily beached, and could float up rivers without much draught. Low and slender, they were difficult to spot from land and would come out of nowhere in surprise attacks. The mightiest ship described in the Sagas is Olav Tryggvason's *Long Serpent*, *Ormen Lange* in poetic Norwegian, built around the year 1000. It had a crew of sixty-eight rowers, twice as many as a standard ship, and was about forty-five metres long. (A ship uncovered in fragments in Roskilde in Denmark was built for eighty rowers.) The dragon heads for which the ships became known were mounted when they approached battle.

Viking ship finds in Norway, Denmark and Sweden tell stories of hierarchy, technology and capital. The men who built ships like these had skills and resources, and could get others to work for them. Those honoured by being buried in mounds were chiefs. They speak of strong beliefs. Men and women of power were equipped lavishly for their journeys to the afterworld. They tell a story of culture. The Oseberg is magnificently decorated; so are other finds, such as the ornate sleighs. The ships represent an extraordinary synthesis of function and beauty. There is a harmony of construction such that no detail presents itself to the onlooker with any disturbance. 'A ship', says the historian Michael Pye, 'didn't just show how rich or powerful or grand a man might be; it was his being.'*

Viking ships consisted of hull and sail, making them more than boats. The hull was a Scandinavian invention. These people had for ages used waterways for transport and had become steadily better boat builders, their boats getting bigger and eventually reaching ship proportions. The sail was a European invention, long having been used,

* For the sources of direct quotations see the Notes.

*The Oseberg Ship – 'an extraordinary
synthesis of function and beauty'*

for example, in the Mediterranean. It was by contact with Continental Europeans that the Scandinavians learned to use sails. They descended on Europe from the north with superior maritime skills, but it was in part through European influence that they had mastered those skills. If we have to give the Viking Age a beginning date it would be when they adopted the sail, around 750.

The ships were gracious – but they were also weapons of mass destruction. Their function was to bring warriors and conquerors to foreign shores. They were manned by men who were dedicated to their ventures and loyal to their chiefs. Those men were as merciless in battle as they were clever in navigation. Their method was to rampage, destroy, burn, kill, rape and plunder. The arrival of the Norsemen sent shivers of fear, deep fear, down the spines of more normal people.

1

The Vikings

In the early Middle Ages, something resembling 'social structure' (to use a modern term) emerged in at least parts of Scandinavia. Society (another term that would not have been understood) started to be stratified. A small tier of men drifted to the top. They could indulge the normal human passions for wealth and glory and press the humble masses into service for their designs. A catalyst was probably ecological calamities that afflicted Europe around the middle of the sixth century, caused by volcanic eruptions in the Americas. The north was hit badly due to its marginal agriculture. That led to a renewed increase in population as numbers caught up after the decimation, and a shift in land ownership upward. We arrive at the invention of class. A pattern of power and dependency was in the making out of which Vikings would present themselves as a recognisable force on the European fringe. Some of the bigger chiefs started to call themselves 'kings'. A Scandinavia of political entities was in the offing.

To Russia

It started to the east, with incursions into Russia – *Gardariki*, they called it, 'land of settlements' – mainly from Sweden, with a supporting cast from Denmark, Norway, Finland and the Baltics. These started around the year 800, about half a century ahead of the beginning of occupation and settlement in western Europe.

The advances into Russia were a continuation of established trades in the Baltic Sea and along Europe's northern shores. Fur from Sweden was a prized luxury in Constantinople in the sixth century, then traded through intermediaries. When their technology allowed it, the Swedes took on Russia. That technology was in ship-boats, solid enough to traverse the great Russian rivers and light enough to be hauled overland around rapids or from one river to the next. The main routes were from Lake Ladoga, just beyond present-day St Petersburg: one via the Dnieper to Kyiv and on to the Black Sea and Constantinople; and the other, the more lucrative, down the Volga to the cities of Bulghar and Atil on the Caspian Sea, on as far as Baghdad, and connecting with the Asian Silk Roads. The town of Staraya Ladoga was already established by the middle of the eighth century as a mainly Norse base. Centres like Novgorod ('Newfort'), Bulghar, Smolensk and Kyiv grew in part as a result of Scandinavian settlement. Constantinople, the Scandinavians' *Miklagard* ('the big place' – they did not have a word for town or city), was a destination for both trade and mercenary service.

The pattern was in some respects the same as is better known in the West: first raiding and trading, then settlement, then integration with the locals. This mixed population was known as the Rus, 'perhaps due to their distinctive red hair, or more likely their prowess with the oar. They were the fathers of Russia.' Kyiv became the early stronghold in the Russian lands, known as the Kyivan Rus, a stepping stone on the path to the Russian empire.

The routes were treacherous, long distances through difficult, dangerous and hostile lands. But it was worth it. The Norsemen connected with the economic centres of the known world, which held great resources of wealth and were thirsty markets for goods such as furs and had an insatiable demand for slaves. At the time it was in the east, in Byzantium and the Arab and Asiatic worlds, that there was serious wealth to be reckoned with. Silver was the currency that everyone craved, and the Norsemen brought 'an enormous influx' back home, *much* more wealth than was captured in the west. Evidence has been dug up in particular on the island of Gotland in the Baltic Sea, but also in sites across Sweden and Denmark and as far west as England: hoards of Arab *dirham*, not just the occasional coin but fortunes buried in the ground. Those finds speak of the magnitude of wealth coming back from the eastern trade and from how far afield the wealth trickled north. The historian Peter Frankopan describes it, in modern terms, as a 'multi-billion dollar industry'.

MYSTERIES OF SILVER

There is much about the Scandinavians and silver that escapes easy explanation. They wanted it and were successful at laying their hands on masses of it.

Much of the silver from the east remained in Gotland, multiple fortunes buried in the ground. It could have been for safekeeping in times of danger, but there is too much of it to be thus explained. Was there so much silver that inflation undercut its value? Why was it not moved on? Why was it spread out 'democratically' and not concentrated into a few big fortunes? Might it have had something to do with cults? Was it 'given' to the gods? According to the Icelandic political leader, poet and historian Snorri Sturluson (1179–1241), there was a pre-Christian belief that buried silver could be retrieved in the afterlife. Was silver from the distant Orient 'different' in people's minds to that from more familiar lands? Was it 'different' for having been obtained 'honourably' in trade rather than 'dishonourably' in extortion? The eastern coins were heavier that those from the west; were they held on to more tightly? The amount of eastern silver found in Gotland and elsewhere may even be greater than can be credibly explained by the known trade in goods, slaves and mercenary service.

More of the silver from the west seems to have been put back into circulation. That may have something to do with Denmark and Norway becoming kingdoms, whereas there was not yet a Swedish kingdom at the time of the great inflow of eastern silver. In England, the Scandinavians were out for land; some of the loot that was extracted might have been used to buy acreage from the same people who had been terrorised out of their silver.

Even some of the surplus English silver ended up in Gotland. Why? Gotland was far away from this route; it was mainly Danes and Norwegians who operated in England. Might it again have had something to do with cults? Or did Gotlanders have an 'expertise' as 'bankers' in silver management?

In the west the Vikings, says the historian David Abulafia, were 'sea-raiders and part-time traders'. In the east it was the other way round: they were traders and part-time raiders, in a rough trade to be sure, but predominantly trade nevertheless. A constant was the trade in slaves. As they manoeuvred up or down rivers they would take captives to be sold further on. According to the Persian geographer Ibn Rustah, writing in the tenth century, 'they would come in ships, go ashore, take prisoners, abduct them to the lands of the Kazaks and Bulghars and sell them there'. In Novgorod the slave market was at the intersection of High Street and Slave Street. By the middle of the tenth century Prague had become a major hub of Central European slave-trading, attracting both Viking Rus and Muslim merchants. The Arab geographer Ibn Khordadbeh, writing around 870, lists goods from the north including 'eunuchs, male slaves, female slaves, beaver- and marten-skins, and other furs'.

The trade depended on open routes deep into the eastern world and came to an end when those routes were closed by southern powers which squeezed out the northern invaders. The first route to shut was the easternmost one via the Volga to the Caspian Sea. By about 1070 the remaining route via Kyiv had been lost as well. The Scandinavian trading link to the east would survive, but in the main no deeper than into northern Russia-Novgorod, and then as a matter of 'normal' trade. The main commodities were now furs and grain, which would be part of what later became the Baltic trade under German-Hanseatic dominance.

To Normandy

He is called *Gange-Rolv* in Scandinavia, Rolf the Walker. It is through French chronicles that he was given the silly name now used in international writings: Rollo. He was called 'the Walker' because he was too big to be carried by horses. Too fat? Not necessarily. The Norse horses at the time were tiny. You can see their descendants in the small Icelandic ponies today, and in the *fjording* (fjord horse) of western Norway, small, blond and round-bellied, and even they are larger than their ancestors of a millennium ago. But the Norsemen did buy, and no doubt capture, better horses from the Franks. In 864, Emperor Charles the Bald prohibited, on pain of death, the selling of horses and weaponry to them, reiterating a ban that Charlemagne (Charles the Great) had imposed three-quarters of a century earlier, again apparently with little success.

He was the maker of Normandy. The Norwegians have claimed him for themselves as part of the nationalistic narrative of Viking greatness and have raised a statue in his glory in the town of Ålesund on the west coast, but he may well have been Danish. He took a European name when he converted to Christianity and is known also as Robert of Normandy.

Raiders from the north were operating on the Continent from the early ninth century. There had been raiding before that, but it was now taking on new dimensions. In 834 a Danish force attacked Dorestad, a trading centre on the Rhine about 100 km inland from the Dutch coast, slaughtering at will, laying waste to the surrounding regions and coming away with much booty and large numbers of slaves. In 845 a Danish fleet of, it has been said, 600 ships sacked Hamburg and burned it to the ground, destroying the church and its school and library, but sparing the bishop, Ansgar, who was able to escape with some of the holy relics. They were active in southern Europe from around the same time. In 844, from a base at the mouth of the River Loire, they mounted raids on the Iberian peninsula and reached Seville, looting as usual, killing men and enslaving women and children.

They arrived in the town of Rouen in the Seine valley in 841. Four years later they extracted their first ransom from Paris, 7,000 pounds in silver. 'Between 856 and 859 various Norse armies burnt Paris, Bayeux, Chartres, Tours, Blois, Lyon and Amiens.'

They followed the pattern of first coming for plunder, then settling, then assimilating. Charlemagne's empire was disintegrating and the Norse were able to gain firm control of Rouen and its surrounding areas by the 870s. Sieges of Paris followed in 885 and 886, and again in 911. Rollo had risen to leadership (and in the process abducted and married the beautiful Poppa, daughter of a Frankish chief, from a raid on Bayeux). From his success in Paris he went on to lay siege to Chartres, but had now overreached and met resistance from a coalition of French barons. The following stalemate resulted in the Treaty of Saint-Clair-sur-Epte between Charles III and Rollo. Not a bad treaty for Rollo. He was given territory in fief in return for a pledge of loyalty to the French king, the end of raiding, and conversion of the Norse settlers to Christianity.

Peace did not prevail. Rollo reneged on his pledge of loyalty, resumed raiding, and killed the next French king, Robert the Strong. A new treaty was struck with yet another French king, Rudolph, securing more territorial concessions for Rollo.

Normandy was the most consequential of Viking conquests, although by the time those consequences materialised the Normans were no longer Norsemen. It was not where the Viking business started, or the most important in financial terms – that was in Russia – but nowhere else were there similar long-term political ramifications.

Rollo died around 930, leaving a solid duchy to his successors. From here, the Norse ingredient thoroughly diluted, the Normans would take England in 1066 under William the Conqueror, the great-great-great grandson of Rollo – Snorri, and others, called him William the Bastard. Even today, the King or Queen of England is also the Duke of Normandy, by force of which he or she is head of state of Jersey and other Channel Islands, known previously as the Isles of Normandy. The Normans who invaded England were French. The language they brought with them was French, laying the foundations of today's rich spoken English with its combined Germanic and Latin roots. William never spoke the native tongue of the country he invaded and was, like most rulers of the time, illiterate.

The Norse ingredient may have been diluted, but possibly not extinguished. In the Bayeux Tapestry, which commemorates William's conquest, the Normans are recognisable in part by their distinctive hairstyle, short and high at the back, known in eleventh-century England as the 'Danish cut'. The 700 or so ships which William had built for the conquest were of the Viking style with high bows both fore and aft. The invasion was a masterclass in navigation. Only two ships were lost. One of them carried the expedition's soothsayer. 'No great loss,' said William, 'he could not even predict his own fate.'

Again from the 1060s, Normans would also conquer southern Italy and other Mediterranean territories from the Arab Muslims. Norman nobles had more sons than they could provide for at home and sent some to adventure in the south, in which they excelled. Robert, of the d'Hauteville family, captured southern Italy. His brother, Roger, took the campaign to the Emirate of Sicily and became the first Count of Sicily in 1071. By 1091 he had won control of all the island. That same year he invaded Malta, an event which was welcomed there as liberation from Muslim rule and in remembrance of which Mass is still said once a year in the Cathedral of Mdina. His descendants continued to rule Sicily until 1194, when the Norman line died out.

Upon his death in 1101 the title passed to his son, Roger II, who had himself elevated to king by the pope in 1130 when the island and other territories in southern Italy became the Kingdom of Sicily. He established a splendid and tolerant court to which he attracted artisans, artists and scholars from all corners of the known world – Greece, Byzantium, the Arab countries, England, a few Normans as well – and made Palermo a leading centre of learning and culture in Europe. Roger raised the Cathedral of Cefalù and built the Palatina Chapel in the royal palace in Palermo, and his grandson William II the Cathedral and monastery of Monreale in the hills overlooking the city, all decorated with magnificent mosaics depicting biblical narratives. Monreale, splendidly preserved, stands as their crowning achievement in architectural and artistic prowess and devotion to the faith, and as one of the most glorious monuments anywhere in all of Christendom.

Normans had come to the Mediterranean before the arrival of Robert and Roger, from the beginning of the eleventh century as mercenaries for Lombard and Byzantine powers. There had also been raiders directly from Scandinavia. A Viking incursion is said to have occurred around 860 under the leadership of a Swedish chief known as Björn Ironside, raiding along both the African and European coasts, up the Rhône, across the Balearic Islands and possibly laying siege to the city of Pisa. A legend has it that they reached Egypt. It must count as a great maritime and military achievement to have brought a force from the north along western Europe and into the Mediterranean and escaped laden with booty. But this venture, however fearsome at the time, was to be of no lasting consequence. The Viking story is indeed a story of conquest, but also one of overreach.

To England and beyond

A monastery of the Celtic Church had been established in the year 634 at Lindisfarne, on the coast of Northumbria, close to today's border with Scotland. Its most revered bishop was Cuthbert, later St Cuthbert, who died in 687 and was buried there. When it was laid to waste, the surviving monks fled and took St Cuthbert's body with them. After seven years of wandering they received a sign that the saint wished to rest on a mount in what was to be the city of Durham. A stone church was raised on the site of what is now Durham's imposing cathedral, within which is St Cuthbert's tomb (and also that of Venerable Bede, the father of the writing of English history).

On 8 June 793 Lindisfarne was attacked from the sea by a force of Norsemen. There is much one would want to find out about this terrible event. Just who were the attackers? How many and from where? Did they know of Lindisfarne, and how did they find it? They might have been Norwegians who came upon the monastery by chance while exploring from bases in the Orkneys and Shetlands, but this is uncertain.*

The assault has been described by various Church scholars, including Simeon of Durham in his *Historia regum Anglorum et Dacorum*, composed in the early twelfth century: 'They laid everything waste with grievous plundering, trampled the holy places with polluted steps, dug up the altars and seized all the treasures of the holy church. They killed some of the brothers, took some away with them in fetters, many they drove out, naked and loaded with insults, some they drowned in the sea.' It was an act of unspeakable barbarity. What was of value, including people, was plundered; what could not be taken was destroyed.

News of the raid spread throughout Europe and shook all of Christendom. The Norsemen had demonstrated the power of their wrath. One might think it was their way of warning others to respect their intentions. Possibly so, but not necessarily. Later, when raiding became business, there was a plan to it, but in this early assault most likely there was no strategy, no design, no project. The raiders were just a gang. The monastery was undefended, a remote religious community dedicated to study and contemplation. The holy men were killed because they were there, others captured because they were useful. The Norsemen came from the sea, took what they wanted, slaughtered as was their pleasure, made away with slaves, desecrated for the hell of it and left richer and happier. In an age of outrage, it was rightly seen as outrageous in the extreme. They came out of the blue, unprovoked, without warning, and left behind as much destruction as they could.

* Recent scholars, such as Cat Jarman in *River Kings*, think it likely that the raiders knew of the monastery and its location and that there were already established connections across the North Sea. But this happened very early, only a few decades into the Norsemen's use of the sail, which was a condition for cross-ocean travel. They had come to the south of England earlier, but that would have been possible without ocean sailing.

They came back the next year for the monastery of Jarrow and would have done it again had they not lost their leader and some of their ships to storms. Monasteries continued to be targeted – obviously, they had valuables; obviously, they were undefended. In 794 the monastery at Donemuthan in Northumbria was plundered. The year after, they reached the island of Iona on the west coast of Scotland and sacked the monastery of St Columba, the first site of the Celtic Church of Ireland in Britain, killing (then or in a later raid) the abbot and sixty-eight monks. Whitby monastery, then known as Streoneshalch, on the North Yorkshire coast was plundered, destroyed and laid to waste in successive raids in the 860s. Repton Abbey, a monastery of both monks and nuns, was destroyed in 873 by the 'Great Heathen Army', which established winter quarters there before completing the conquest of Mercia, the dominant central kingdom, the next year. The raiders of what became Normandy started with attacking monasteries and churches, as did others elsewhere in France, and in Germany, Spain, Britain and Ireland. Their readiness to raid churches and monasteries was part of what gave them a comparative advantage in barbarity. The holy places were easy takings because it was accepted by Christian kings and chiefs that they should have peace. Later Christian leaders from the north came to adopt that convention, but the early heathens were not restrained by such worries. Monasteries at the time were centres of learning. Much of their treasure was in manuscripts, then precious works of art. They were nothing to the Norsemen, except that they could be ransomed. An ealdorman of Surrey, Ælfred, is known in the mid-ninth century to have paid a Viking band pure gold 'for the love of God and the good of our souls so that these holy books should no longer be in heathen ownership'. (That same manuscript is now known as the *Stockholm Codex Aureus*, having been acquired from Spain for the Swedish Royal Library in 1690.)

In this way, western Europe entered the Age of the Vikings, an era that has subsequently been glorified by Scandinavian nationalists and also by many a historian. But the experience of being on the receiving end of the Viking venture was devastation, destruction, murder, rape, enslavement and robbery, and the threat thereof. They became known, deservedly, as killers who spared no one – not women, not children, not the old.

*

The Norsemen first arrived on southern English shores in 787, in three ships, six years before the rape of Lindisfarne. The guests gave a taste of what was to come. They were invited to meet the king but slew the messenger.

After the first horrors, raiding was taken up in north-eastern England in a regular way from around 830, 'Gradually it became clear that the Danes were set on the colonisation of England. From 834 onward barely a year passed without a record of raids, and a crescendo of attacks climaxed in 866, when, having wintered in East Anglia, a Danish army broke into York and took over the city, putting their own puppet (an Englishman) on the throne. The Scandinavians were in England to stay; they made war on the powerful kingdom of Wessex and nearly defeated its greatest king, Alfred. In 876 they settled in Northumbria and in the years that followed gradually took over the kingdoms of Mercia and East Anglia. North and east of a line drawn from London to Chester they held sway in a series of loose petty kingdoms and misty political groupings, in an area which became known as the Danelaw. They ruled York, which they called *Jorvik*, for about a hundred years. Alfred, with his son-in-law Æthelred and formidable daughter Æthelflæd, began to rebuild the English kingdom, and, although Alfred had many setbacks, by his death in 899 the English were ready to start the painful re-conquest of the Danelaw.'

While Alfred was gradually able, by and large, to establish control of southern England, the Danes crushed the kingdoms up north. That later enabled the unification of England when the Danes, about a century later, lost control of their part. A lasting Viking influence in England, then, paradoxically, was the creation of England itself.

What was the Danelaw? The name sounds good, suggesting that civilised Scandinavians brought Danish law to the unruly English. But none of it. What they brought was not peace but plunder. There was no Danish law to bring to England. Denmark at the time was a patchwork of law districts, laws were made locally and kings were neither lawmakers nor law enforcers. 'Under Danish law' meant Danish overlordship and the payment of taxes to Danish masters. English land was confiscated and given to Danes, previous owners and users dislodged, in an early ethnic cleansing.

The Danelaw was not a kingdom or in any real meaning a political entity but, exactly as described above, a patchwork of misty group-ings without any central organisation to hold it together. The English re-conquest was steady and gradual, chipping away at Danish fiefs slice by slice. By 920, most of the Danelaw south of the Humber was back in English control, by 954 the rest of it up to York. The first Danish period in England was over.

But the English were not rid of the Norse. Treasure from the east was drying up and, says the archaeologist Barry Cunliffe, 'the Scandinavians, still avid for silver, had to look elsewhere, particularly to Britain and Ireland, where there was plenty of silver to be had for the price of a raid and the spilling of a little blood'. From about 980, Vikings were again raiding the south of England and from 'then on until 1016, the Chronicle contains almost annual accounts of great calamities caused by Viking armies'.

The leading marauders were the father-and-son duo of Svend Forkbeard and Knud, soon to be 'the Great'. Svend mounted a full-scale invasion in the summer of 1013 and declared himself King of England. Knud, although barely out of his teens, took part in his father's invasion as one of his commanders. Svend returned to Denmark later in 1013 to secure his control there, leaving Knud in command of the English conquest, but died on arrival.

In England, Knud was overpowered and also fled back to Denmark. He was defeated by King Æthelred, who had earlier been beaten by the Danes and fled the country, but now returned to take up battle again, assisted by Olav Haraldsson of Norway, the future St Olav, with a large following of Norwegians. (Danes and Norwegians fighting each other, then; nothing unusual as long as the money was good.) They made their way up the Thames to London, where the Danes held the fort, which they defended from a bridge over the river. Olav, so the story goes, devised a way of undermining the bridge so that it collapsed under the weight of the soldiers who were amassed on it. The English captured the fort and the Danes gave up London. From this episode, legend has it, originates the English nursery rhyme 'London Bridge Is Falling Down'. True or not, there is no other recorded instance of London Bridge collapsing.

Back in Denmark, Knud and his brother Harald struck a deal that Harald would hold the Crown at home and Knud lead a new invasion of England. A formidable force was raised in the summer of 1015. It landed on the southern shore, not far from where the Normans would invade fifty-one years later. A year of relentless warfare followed. Wessex crumbled, the campaign moved north with devastating brutality, subduing Mercia and Northumbria, and turned south again to wreak havoc through Gloucestershire and other territories and lay siege to London. The English king, now Edmund, signed a treaty with Knud – we are in 1016 – in which England north of the Thames would, again, be Danish, as would the rest of the country on Edmund's death. He obliged by dying later in the year, murdered probably. Knud was King of England, crowned in London by the Archbishop of Canterbury, about twenty-five years old.

A favourite method of Viking plunder was by large-scale protection racketeering: pay us and we will not kill you. The method is as old as Viking raiding. From the first extortion in France of 7,000 pounds in silver in 845, Frankish sources record payments over the years of a total of 700 pounds in gold and 40,000 pounds in silver. In England the loot became known as *Danegeld*, 'Danish money'. David Wilson, then Director of the British Museum, writes: 'In 991, Olav Tryggvason (a rather wild Norwegian chieftain who built up a fortune by raids in England) took the first in a regular series of payments from the English: a colossal sum of 10,000 pounds in silver. When Svend joined Olav in 994 they shared 16,000 pounds and, as Olav returned to Norway in that year, the sorry story of the Danes in England is told in the pages of the *Anglo-Saxon Chronicle*. Under Svend, the *Danegeld* rose in size from 24,000 pounds in 1002 to 36,000 pounds in 1007 and 48,000 pounds in 1011.'

The biggest extortioner of them all was Knud the Great. On being crowned King of England he extracted 82,000 pounds in silver from his new subjects, of which 10,500 pounds came from London alone, most of it to pay off various Norse chiefs who had helped him in the conquest.

Knud ruled England for nearly two decades. In Denmark, Harald died and brother Knud took over that Crown as well. He then turned to fighting off Norwegian and Swedish pretenders and declaring him-self to be king not only of England and Denmark but also of Norway and 'some of the Swedes'.

This was the summit of Viking power. And it was recognised as such in Europe. Knud was the first Norse lord to be 'admitted into the civilised fraternity of Christian kings'. In 1027, he was an honoured guest of the pope in Rome to witness the accession of Conrad II as European Emperor.

It did not last. Knud died in 1035; he was buried in the Minster in

Winchester and his bones, or some of them, now rest in Winchester Cathedral, or so we must believe. In England, the Danish kingdom dissolved. Back in Scandinavia, Knud's sons fell out with each other and died out within a decade of their father's death. The empire, it turned out, had not been an empire at all. Once the emperor died, it vanished like a puff of smoke.

But the ambition of a great northern kingdom did not die. The revered father of Danish history, Saxo Grammaticus, had claimed that both the Danish and English royal houses stemmed from a joint ancestor, one Dan. Scandinavian kings clung on to the notion that the English throne was theirs by right. In 1066, Harald Hardrade of Norway invaded. Thus started the events of that year that would change English history forever.

Harald sailed for England in August, gathering up additional forces in the Shetlands, Orkneys and Scotland, landed on the north-eastern coast and ravaged his way inland, in, says the Danish historian Ole Fenger, a 'foolhardy' enterprise. Harold Godwinson had taken the English Crown earlier in the year (an offence since he, although the richest man in England, was not even of a royal family). His brother, Tostig, wanted the Crown for himself; he was banished from England (to Flanders), but returned in May, landing in Sandwich on the south coast. He worked his way north and teamed up with Harald of Norway for the first of three great battles of the year, at Fulford on 20 September. They were victorious. Their force then moved on to meet England's Harold himself at Stamford Bridge on 25 September. Here they were defeated. Harald was killed, hit by an arrow in the throat, aged fifty, as was Tostig. The remains of their army fled. The English had fought off the first invasion of the year. Thus ended not only the attempt to restore Knud's empire but also the Viking Age in England. Indeed, the Viking Age full stop.

Harold Godwinson's victory was costly. His army was seriously depleted. In the south, William of Normandy was preparing for the second invasion of the year. Harold had to march south to meet William in less than three weeks, virtually raising a new army on the way. They met at the Battle of Hastings on 14 October. The English were defeated and the Normans occupied England. This turned out to be a different kind of occupation. The pattern of the Vikings had been to settle and assimilate. The Normans did not assimilate. They took over and remade England in their own image.

The Battle of Fulford, as envisaged in the thirteenth century 'Life of King Edward the Confessor'

It could have been different. William's intention had been to invade England six weeks earlier than he did, but the winds were against him and he was unable to cross the Channel. Had he been able to launch as planned, Harold Godwinson would have met him with the full force of his army and would likely have prevailed. It was touch and go that he was beaten in October, even with his depleted army. Had he defeated William in early September, he would have had to march north with a shattered force, and would have met Harald with less capacity than he in fact did. The Battle of Stamford Bridge was also touch and go. Had Harold had a weaker army he would probably have been defeated there rather than in the south. Harald of Norway might well have formed a Norwegian-English kingdom, in due course adding Denmark, and re-established the empire of the north. Both England's, in due course Britain's, history, and Scandinavia's, would have unfolded in entirely different ways.

It is said that Vikings founded Dublin, but there were people settled in the area when the Vikings arrived. They, under the leadership of a man with the un-Nordic name of Turgeis, of unknown origin, occupied the settlement in 836.

There was a natural highway of the seas from Norway via the Faroe Isles, the Shetlands and Orkneys and the north and west of Scotland, leading into the Irish Sea. Raiding had started towards the end of the eighth century, becoming constant from the mid-830s, around the same time that it took off in earnest along the western edge of the Continent. They targeted monastic communities as usual, such as the wealthy monastery at Armagh, whose abbot was patriarch of the Irish Church, which was sacked in 832. Christian worship had reached Ireland in about 400, giving rise to a decentralised monastic culture around the Irish Sea in which Latin learning was preserved and cultivated. For this culture the Vikings represented mayhem, says the writer Delisle Burns, 'destroying the great tradition of learning and piety in Ireland, which had for some centuries before illuminated western Europe'.

There was a difference between the Norwegian and Danish Vikings. They were all after plunder, but the Norwegians were more desperate for land. They had very little of it at home, the result being population surplus despite its paucity of inhabitants. And even without overcrowding, it is not difficult to understand, if you travel through western Norway today, that migration for better land elsewhere would be tempting. At home they could scrape out a single meagre harvest on small patches of fields. Abroad they could find easy-to-work land that would yield two harvests a year.

What the Vikings brought to Ireland was, for a while, international trade. They had the connections and the ships. There had long been Irish-on-Irish slave-taking and this activity now increased with the opening up of access to international markets. Dublin was made a centre of regional slave trade, possibly the biggest slave market in western Europe. Raiding through England and Scotland, for example, the Vikings would take slaves with them and bring them to Dublin, from there to sell them on further afield.

Otherwise their conquest did not amount to much. Nothing like the Danelaw was established there. If Turgeis in any real sense captured Dublin, he was soon enough, in 845, deposed by an Irish pretender and drowned in a nearby lake. Nor did settlement succeed on any significant scale. The ninth century was a period of never-ending, unresolved and criss-crossing warfare, sometimes between invaders and the Irish, sometimes between competing Viking factions. That came to an end in 902 when an alliance of Gaelic lords attacked Dublin and expelled the last Norseman pretending to be king, one Ivar, who fled to Scotland. The Norse presence was reduced to a few scattered settlements.

But there was not to be peace. In 914 Viking fleets returned, starting another century of incessant warfare. This has been called the Second Viking Age in Ireland, but that is a faulty description. The invaders were now mainly from across the Irish Sea, some possibly of Norse descent but now more British. People who could in some sense be called Norse fought on all sides, fought each other, and did not make up any unified or even identifiable faction. By around the end of the century, the Vikings were no longer Vikings and the Norse threat was no more.

To Iceland and beyond

Iceland is unique among the world's nations in having its entire history written down. We therefore know that Ingólfr Arnarson was the first settler. He was a refugee from Norway, running away from a blood feud. He had been told about the island from earlier explorers and set off to find it and settle with his wife, a brother and some Irish slaves. He let destiny decide where to take him and landed in the bay which was to become Reykjavik. It was in the year 874.*

Others soon followed and a Norse community was in the making. The brother, Hj□rleifr, was not to see it. He was killed by his slaves, whom he had mistreated, in the first of several slave rebellions. Iceland was uninhabited except for some Irish monks, who are said to have left, not wanting to live among pagans, or who may have been forced to leave or killed.

Further settlement followed, mainly from Norway, but also by slaves and freemen from Ireland and Scotland, who may have constituted as many as half of the settlers. The supply of women in the original population was predominantly Gaelic. The settlers first ruled themselves, but the new nation gradually succumbed to Norwegian and then Danish overlordship.

From Iceland, the migration continued west to Greenland, under the

---

* Recent archaeological finds suggest that there may have been seasonal settlements of Scandinavians from possibly as early as around 800, but it is likely that Ingólfr and his flock were the first to arrive with the intention of settling permanently.

leadership of Eirik the Red, and from there on to America (as it was to become) under Leif Eirikson. Leif probably grew up in Greenland, probably did *viking* service – meaning to 'go raiding' or 'go to other lands' – in his early years, and probably saw the land he was to call *Vinland* for the first time when blown off course on his way back to Greenland. He was probably not the first Norseman to make it to the American continent, but may have been the first to try to establish a settlement there, tempted by supposedly having seen fields of wild wheat and grapes. We are at the beginning of the eleventh century.

At least two parties of settlers set off from Greenland, mostly men but with a few women, bringing livestock, aiming to stay. A child was born to the settlers, a boy whom they called Snorri, the first Euro-American. Settlement building works were unearthed by archaeologists in the twentieth century, proving the Norse presence. It may have lasted ten years or so but did not work. The settlers ran into trouble with both native Americans and each other, and gave up. The settlement back in Greenland, while it lasted, continued to use the American coast as a source of timber. They called some of it *Markland*, 'the forest land'.

How do we know?

We have no archives of stored information. The oldest known Scandinavian manuscript of any kind is a letter of 1085, in Latin, from Knud the Holy to the bishopric of Lund in which he bequeaths it various privileges and properties.

The most important written sources are the Icelandic Sagas and other Icelandic manuscripts, compiled later. The technology of pen and ink came to Scandinavia with Christianity. It was in Iceland that these tools were put most energetically to use. The Sagas – there are about 700 of them, small and large, the earliest ones from the 1100s – are of debatable reliability for many reasons, including that many were written 200 or 300 years after the events and penned by Christians about a pagan world. But they deal with real events and people and are the most comprehensive sources we have.

Ahead of the writing of history there was an oral tradition of poetry, that of the *Edda*. Poets told stories of the cosmos, origins and contemporary events. They were held in high esteem, as myth-tellers, carriers of memory and tradition, and as men and women of wisdom, priest-like, doctor-like. In one mythological story a god shows himself to be the strongest of all, but that is not enough. 'I may be strong,' he says, 'but to be a poet is the finest calling.' The poetic form was used to assist memory in the passing-down of ancient beliefs and events. Some of this was put into written form, again in Iceland. The *Elder (Poetic) Edda* is a collection of early poems that deal mainly with mythology. Works known as 'skaldic' poetry praise the deeds of great doers in heroic style, some in the form of elegies to lament heroic or tragic death, but they also retell ancient myths. The *Prose Edda* (*Younger Edda*) is a thirteenth-century handbook for the composition of poetry in the skaldic style, in which is retold much of the mythology from the *Elder Edda* as well as recording more contemporary verse.

The towering personality in the preservation of this historical and mythological material is Snorri Sturluson. His *Kringla Heimsins* ('Circle of the World'), completed shortly before he died in 1241, is a survey of Scandinavian history, specifically of the Norwegian kings, from mythological origins down to his own time. He is also the author of the *Prose Edda*, which has been called 'a North European equivalent of Aristotle's *Poetics*'.

The Norse poetry recounts the history of the cosmos from its origins to the destruction of the world in the *Ragnarök* – the lives of the gods, various other mythologies and beliefs, but also real-life events. The Sagas – the word means epic story – are of two kinds: the Sagas of Icelandic families and the lives of Norwegian kings. The typical Family Saga is an idealised account of the doings and adventures of young Icelandic men of good family, usually efforts to gain fame and win wealth in foreign lands. The finest of these is *Njál's Saga*, culminating in the account of how the heroic Njál and his sons burn to death in their smouldering house. In *Egill's Saga*, Egill Skalla-Grímsson makes plundering expeditions, fights on the side of an English king, and escapes capture at York with courage and nobility.

The most referred to source is the *Kringla Heimsins*, usually called, as it will be here, simply 'Snorri'. From this we know of Harald Finehair and the Battle of Hafrsfjord, of the bringing of Christianity to Norway, of many events around the Battle of Stamford Bridge in 1066, and much more. He based his history, he says, on sayings of Norse chiefs, 'as knowledgeable men have told'. On one occasion he interrupts his telling, although there are more great deeds that would merit being told, 'because we have not wanted to put to book stories that do not come from firm evidence'. He has drawn on family histories of kings and nobles, and on poetry passed down the generations. He does present myths as truths, and later editors have discovered not a few mistakes of fact, but there is also an eerie accuracy to it. When he recounts the young Olav Haraldsson's journeys through Norway to spread the Christian faith he is mostly correct, down to geographical detail. He comes to Gudbrandsdalen in central Norway (which happens to be my ancestral homeland, and is an area we will revisit many times in this history) and passes through villages and neighbourhoods mentioned in their right order according to the names they still have. He mentions the farms of local chiefs which still bear the same names. One such farm is Steig in the village of Fron, 'of the mightiest man in the northern valley', a farm that enters indirectly into my own family story, as we will see in due course.

What the Scandinavians of the time themselves left in writing is on rune-stones, raised stones with brief inscriptions. Upward of 100 survive in Norway, 400 in Denmark and 2,000 in Sweden. The runes were an alphabet of (eventually) sixteen symbols used by the pagan Scandinavians. It was not an alphabet that lent itself to much writing, but rune-stones and runic graffiti have been found all over the Viking territories, from the British Isles to Greenland, Iceland, Russia and Byzantium, as far as to Piraeus, the port of Athens. Most of them give the names and a little information about men who are otherwise unknown, some a bit of historical substance. The inscription on the older of two stones at Jelling in Denmark, erected around 950, reads: 'King Gorm erected this memorial in honour of his wife, Thyra, restorer of Denmark.' Is the husband honouring his wife as 'restorer'? Another translation is 'Denmark's adornment'. At least we see that women at the time were not totally anonymous. On the larger stone the inscription reads: 'King Harald had this monument made for his father Gorm and his mother Thyra, that Harald who won all Denmark and Norway and made the Danes Christian.' The longest known inscription is on a stone at Rök in Sweden. In transliteration it has about 800 characters in about 170 words, around a quarter of a book page.

Rune-stone at Jelling, Denmark

Many of the rune-stones tell of heroic deaths in battle. Falling in battle was honourable since it gave you entry into paradise, the home of heroes. Some were raised by women in celebration of the deeds of husbands and sons. Some also give the name of the man who carved them, suggesting that runic carving was enough of an art to be worth commemorating. One of the most elaborate is also the most distant: the one in Piraeus. The runes were etched into the Piraeus Lion, the pride of the port, sometime in the second half of the eleventh century, most likely by Swedish mercenaries in the service of the emperor in Constantinople. They probably (the deciphering is questionable) celebrate the conquest and looting of the port and the success of the etchers in making themselves rich in imperial service. The Lion now sits in Venice, having been looted from Piraeus in 1687 during the Great Turkish War, in front of the gate to the Arsenale, the old shipyard, now the main venue of the alternate art and architecture 'biennales'.

If they did not leave much writing, they left stuff submerged in the ground, later to be uncovered as archaeological evidence, from houses and household goods via coins and jewellery to skeletons in graves and buried animals and harnesses, and on to weapons, ships with various contents and whole settlements, forts and towns. Viking archaeology has made strides in recent years, both in Scandinavia and foreign lands where the Norse operated, and has contributed to creating a more solid base of knowledge than was available only a decade or two ago. Two recent syntheses, *The Children of Ash and Elm* by the British-Swedish scholar Neil Price and *River Kings* by the Norwegian-British scholar Cat Jarman, are tributes to the force of archaeological analysis.

A source much referred to is Master Adam of Bremen, a fascinating if unreliable chronicler: among the Scandinavians he knew of people with one eye, with their heads growing out of their chests, who moved by hopping on one foot, who hunted monsters in the sea (probably right if you do not know what whales and walrus are), women who grew beards, and many who practised black magic. He was a German cleric-scholar, writing in the second half of the eleventh century, hence nearer in time to the events than the Icelandic Sagas (but he certainly knew less than Snorri of the geography). He was charged by the Archbishop of Hamburg to write the history of the bishopric, whose domain included Scandinavia, wherefore his *Gesta Hammaburgensis ecclesiae pontificum* ('Deeds of Bishops of the Hamburg Church') covers the northern area as one of four parts. He learned about Scandinavia from various sources, including during a stay at the court of King Svend Estridsen, and compiled information about geography, beliefs, religious practices and more.

We know of the Scandinavians in Normandy from *De moribus et actis primorum Normanniae Ducum* (Concerning the Customs and Deeds of the First Dukes of the Normans), written by the cleric Dudu around the year 1020. Events in Ireland are described in the *Cogadh Gaedhel re Gallaibh*, written in the twelfth century ('The War of the Irish against the Foreigners' – a work of crude political propaganda, says Else Roesdahl, the eminent Danish historian of the Viking Age) and the fifteenth-century *Irish Annals*. Viking adventures through Russia and in the area of today's Ukraine are described in the *Primary Chronicle of Nestor*, written in Kyiv in the twelfth century, and also in Arab and Persian chronicles. There are fewer sources about the Vikings in the east than in the west, which is why the east often gets less treatment in the literature, although it was the more important for the accumulation of Norse wealth.

We know a good deal about the Vikings in England from the *Anglo-Saxon Chronicle*, a record of English history compiled mostly in the reign of Alfred the Great. From here we read of the first Norse arrival in England and the raiding that followed, and the burdens of *Danegeld* extortions. We learn of the Norwegian Ottar, who arrived at King Alfred's court around 890 and told the English about Scandinavia. Since those Scandinavians did not leave anything in writing about their world (except little runic scripts), his tellings in the *Chronicle* are the nearest we have to a contemporary Scandinavian written source. Although the mightiest chief in the north of Norway, he was not a big player and not a warrior – a trader mainly. He told of expeditions to the White Sea in northern Russia for whales and walrus and their tusks, hides and oil, much in demand in Europe, and of annual trade ventures to the south. He would be in Hedeby in southern Denmark most years to trade in furs, feathers, ivory, rope and other goods. He said that on his travels he would carefully hug the coast all the way, not sailing from the south of Norway to the northern tip of Denmark but taking the long route along the Norwegian coast to Kaupang (at the entrance to today's Oslo Fjord) and then south to Denmark along the Swedish coast. The journey from Kaupang to Hedeby would take him five days, from his home in the north a month. He could travel only in the summer, when weather, light and temperature allowed it.

The *Royal Frankish Annals* are a chronology of events around and during Charlemagne's rule, the most detailed about his military campaigns. Here we learn, for example, about Gudfred of Denmark, seen through Frankish eyes. Alcuin of York was an English theologian who spent much of his adult life at the court of Charlemagne as Charles's 'favourite scholar' among the many he gathered around him. York was then a powerhouse of learning in Europe and Alcuin brought with him, to a receptive Charles, the idea of broadly based education. He maintained a frequent correspondence with other scholars and from here we have one of several accounts of the assault on the monastery at Lindisfarne (when he happened to be temporarily back in Northumbria): 'Never before has such terror appeared in Britain. Behold the church of St Cuthbert, splattered with the blood of God's priests, robbed of its ornaments.' Among his achievements was to edit a single-volume edition of Scripture, written to be user-friendly. Capital letters started new sentences, words were separated so as not to run into each other, and the question mark used to indicate doubt. Another Frankish source is the *Life of St Ansgar*, Archbishop of Hamburg-Bremen, the one who escaped the Danish assault on Hamburg. His life was written by a pupil and contains, among much else, a description of missionary travels in the north and of life in the town of Birka in Sweden. The Bayeux Tapestry contains a wealth of information, in much detail, about Norman weaponry and other battle equipment, such as the dreaded Viking axe which the English warriors carried into the Battle of Hastings, having taken them, one imagines, from the defeated Norsemen at the earlier Battle of Stamford Bridge.

Saxo Grammaticus ('the Learned') was the Danish historian whose history, *Gesta Danorum* ('The Deeds of the Danes'), in sixteen books, was written to 'glorify our fatherland' and completed around 1215, about twenty years before Snorri finished *Kringla Heimsins*. From about the same time we have some written versions of early regional law, first maintained only orally.

It adds up to quite a bit, considering that we are looking at least 1,300 years back in time. It is all biased in various ways. The archaeological material is evidence of those who had something to leave behind. The written material was composed retrospectively, by Christians or foreigners, for many of whom the Norse were barbarian enemies. The information that can be gleaned from these and other sources has over the years been debated and assessed in the vast literature that keeps flowing to satisfy the never-ending fascination of historians and the reading public with the vicious Vikings. Speculation is unavoidable in the telling of their stories, but it is informed speculation.

The quest for capital

The curtain goes up on the Viking drama as class divisions lift some men high enough to reach for greatness. There were many motives: greed, glory, adventure, emigration. Fame, achievement and honour were prized values in the Vikings' culture. Their religion told them that combat, violence and death were honourable, and imposed on them no moral bonds of restraint. It instructed them that their world was justly divided into masters and servants, with servants bound in loyalty to masters. There were more people than could find satisfaction at home, certainly more young men. Chiefs took many wives, leaving lesser men unable to find any at all. Property was inherited by primogeniture: the oldest son took all. What were younger sons to do? The Europeans and Orientals were rich and sophisticated, their worlds beckoned.

Their own countries were without the resources needed for greatness. Those who wanted power needed capital, but their lands yielded few resources and had next to no wealth to dig out of the ground, no silver, no gold. They were able to scrape together some surplus from their economies, but not in any quantity. They could tax, but poor farmers did not have much to give up. Kingships in the making rested on such riches as could be taken home, one way or another, from sources in other lands.

Chiefs, eventually kings, needed capital to work with, and a great deal of it. 'Power was visible in the Middle Ages. Powerful people needed to look the part.' If you were to be king, you had to surround yourself with 'glittering splendour'. You would not be respected unless you could show it. Chiefs required ships and weapons. They had to display generous hospitality and distribute gifts and rewards. They wanted halls for lavish banquets (the largest known one measured eighty metres in length). They and their women were obliged to wear jewellery, fine clothing and other luxuries. Kings needed more of these things than others, and chiefs as much as they could muster.

Kings had to have armies, and armies consisted of men who were loyal to the degree that they were rewarded. Without a bigger army than others you would just be a chief, and without the ability to reward better than others your army would desert you. Theirs was a culture of gift-giving, says the Swedish historian Anders Winroth: loyalty flowed to the most generous giver. Armies depended on ships, and a constant supply of them; they wore down fast and were lost when put into service. Shipbuilding was no small matter. Trees had to be felled and prepared for sideboards, keels, masts, oars and internal fittings, tar needed to be burned. A standard ship would take 200 to 300 kilograms of iron in rivets, and perhaps 500 litres of tar. Sails had to be woven and ropes tied, ships and sails decorated. A sail required the wool of at least fifty sheep, more for bigger sails on bigger ships, and might require about the same amount of work as was going into the ship itself. The crew had to be equipped with robust clothing, shields and weapons. This was a continuous industry of more, better and bigger. All of it had to be paid for.

Their ambitions were in need of what their own economies could not generate. Solution: what you cannot raise at home, you must get from elsewhere. They could steal from each other, but if three kings fight over their treasure they do nothing to increase the joint stock. Solution: take it from others.

In the history books the Vikings are traders, and indeed they were. But, for the purpose of raising capital, there was only so much trade they could do. A man from the north goes south with furs. He meets a man from the south with silks. They exchange, and both go home better off with something they appreciate more for having given up something they appreciate less. The value added in this exchange is in standard of living, but with little profit in capital.

He might instead have sold his furs for silver and taken that home with him, as many did. But it would be hard to return with much surplus. Take the trade into Russia. The men from the north would first have to gather together goods with which to barter. Land transport was difficult, there being hardly any roads. Coastal transport by boat was easier, but slow. Sailing up the Russian rivers, only possible in the summer season, they could take no more goods than could be carried against the currents and in small boats light enough to be hauled overland. The distance to the markets down south was long and the journey rough. Even after profitable exchanges, a good deal of the surplus would be absorbed by paying for the expeditions. It was a dangerous business. On the way back, the trader with silver in his boat would be at risk of shipwreck or robbery. Some would get through without harm, but much would unavoidably be lost.

The cost could be reduced by picking up goods en route. Instead of bringing furs all the way from Scandinavia, they could be had from hunting in the Russian forests. But that would take time, and time is money. Or they could trade their way along, selling and buying and selling and buying again, and with skill come home richer than when they had left.

All these forms of trade were undertaken, and with many kinds of goods, not only furs but also ivory, hides, rope, feathers, amber and more. It would have been a profitable business, otherwise the effort and risk would not have been worth it. These exchanges no doubt generated some capital, but not much; the profit would have been mainly in foreign goods and luxuries.

For serious capital, the Vikings had to turn to a different form of trade: using other people's goods. If you trade in your own goods, you can make some profit. If you sell goods you have taken from someone else, you return home with a profit of 100 per cent. The Vikings did this in three or four ways: plunder, extortion, slavery and mercenary service. This was immeasurably more profitable than 'ordinary' trade. The Norse needed to go abroad to raise the capital they required at home, and to do that they had to reach beyond conventional trade to enterprises that, although dishonourable in our eyes today, were profitable. Their wants at home made them raiders abroad. In the history books the Vikings, in addition to being traders, are also pillagers. They were both, but it was as pillagers that they could underwrite their ambitions.

Men, women and slaves

The most reliable estimate available, by the historical demographer Ole Jørgen Benedictow, sets the Norwegian population towards the end of the Viking Age at about 185,000 people, in 25,000 to 30,000 households, with an average of six or seven household members, including a slave or two. These people were predominantly farmers, most of them poor. They cultivated oats, barley, rye, peas and in some places wheat, had cattle, pigs and poultry for meat, dairy and eggs and sheep for wool, all supplemented by fishing, hunting and gathering.

The rich might have had a varied and appealing diet, or so suggests a reconstruction of Viking cooking. They were 'creative in the kitchen', says the historian Neil Price. But for the common folk the mainstay was porridge and gruel. Animals and humans did not live separately. Arab chroniclers who encountered Vikings in Russia were repulsed by the filthiness of their way of life. The non-farming population was tiny. There were Sami in the north, at this time living as hunter–gatherers and not yet reindeer nomads (although Ottar told King Arthur that he owned a herd of domesticated reindeer).

Similar estimates of population size are not available for Denmark and Sweden, but since these were richer lands it is thought they had more inhabitants. If the Swedes were 200,000 or a bit more and the Danes about 400,000, we are looking at 800,000 to 900,000 Scandinavians in around 150,000 or 160,000 households. The Scandinavian populations grew during the Viking Age. Earlier on, when *viking* was at its most active, they would have been fewer.

Life expectancy was low. Those surviving into adulthood could not expect to live to more than about forty. Health was poor, largely due to grossly unhygienic living conditions. Attaining the age of fifty was unusual, and sixty or more exceptional. Over one in four children died in infancy, another one in four before the age of fifteen. Women typically married between the ages of fourteen and sixteen, very few later than in their teens. Adulthood would come early. Harald Finehair gave his favourite son, Eirik, five ships when he was twelve and sent him raiding.

From these populations came the subgroup known as Vikings. How many were they? We hear in the chronicles of large Viking armies and of marauders described as hordes. There *were* imposing armies and navies. This is confirmed, for example, by archaeological excavations in England. But how large and how common were big contingents? The demographics set limits. The home populations continued to grow through the Viking Age. Those going *viking* could not have been more numerous than small populations could afford to dispense with without declining.

There are reasons to think that the number of Vikings was later exaggerated in the written sources. The Sagas were compiled to celebrate the deeds of Viking grandees and might have tended to maximise their glory. Some of the information came from defeated people; it would have been in their interest to stretch the numbers to reduce the humiliation. For example, the story of the assault on Hamburg with 600 ships – that would have meant 20,000 men or more – is utterly implausible. This was early on in the Viking experience, too early for such a fleet to have been assembled. Hamburg was not a city but a settlement or small town, and no such force would have been needed to take it. Nor would it have made any sense; there would not have been enough booty to pay off so large a contingent. The archaeological evidence too needs to be interpreted with care. There are many excavations, and there have been many more in recent years; but, as is known from sampling theory, an increase in the number of samples does not in itself improve their representativity. The bigger the group of people, the more likely they are to leave remains. Finds by excavators and detectorists at and near Torksey and Repton in England, for example, where the Great Heathen Army overwintered from 872 to 874, show that these were indeed units of some proportions. But such finds cannot tell us exactly how big they were, nor how usual it was to deploy similar armies elsewhere. Did the overwintering Great Heathen Army consist of more or fewer than 1,000 warriors? The archaeological evidence cannot give us the answer, or even establish that it was anything like a single army. All considered, it is plausible and prudent to think that big forces were the exception and that the usual contingents would have been no more than bands. Snorri describes a 'formidable force' of four ships.

An army or navy at the time was a coalition of bands, each under their own chief, held together by loyalties – warriors loyal to their chief and to each other. Bands would come and go, sometimes team up with each other, sometimes operate on their own. An army today could be dispersed tomorrow. The unit that spent the winter at Repton split up the next year, one part moving north and others west and south to complete the conquest of Mercia. Bands could team up with other bands, sometimes with those who were enemies yesterday. Vikings in England sometimes joined up with English chiefs, sometimes fought other Scandinavians. They could consist of warriors from several countries, and perhaps foreign mercenaries and captured enemies pressed into service. They could be contingents of warriors and family members, perhaps in the process of emigration, with 'civilian' traders and craftsmen who might well be Continental Europeans. Those overwintering at Repton and Torksey, for example, were not only warriors but also families and followers, including children, probably with non-warrior non-Scandinavian hangers-on.

If households had an average size of six or seven people, it is unlikely that they on average could spare more than one man per generation for non-domestic service. That's not much, considering that the Viking Age came and went in fifteen or so generations. Slaves would mostly stay put; they were kept back for farming and other hard work at home and were not reliable for raiding. Most of the women and girls would remain at home, grown women making up the permanent core of farm management. The paterfamilias, if still alive by the time his sons were grown, might have been out raiding in younger years but would soon be too old. It was a young man's game. If there were two sons, one would have to stay to look after land and property; menfolk were needed to control the slaves and keep them working. Many households were poor and small, with no surplus men for adventuring, and lived disconnected from Viking adventures. Non-poor farming households would have possessed a few slaves and might have been able to provide a son or two. The rich had larger households, the men typically having several wives, concubines and slave mistresses, and children with all of them. It was from this (small) class that the majority of Vikings were recruited.

Those going into non-domestic service had much to do. There were the constant and never-ending feuding and civil wars in their own districts and countries and within Scandinavia. They had to man the militias of local chiefs, and the kings' guards once there were national rulers. They had to tend to the non-martial trade; someone had to transport the goods. Trade was carried out by ships designed for the purpose and unsuited for raiding, and those working them would not be available for warfare. Some would venture east down the Russian rivers, some south along the Baltic shores and into Continental Europe, some to Normandy and beyond, some west to England, some to Scotland and on to Ireland, and some to the Atlantic isles, Iceland and further afield. If the pool of Scandinavian Vikings was 150,000 men per generation, or even 200,000, which would be a very generous guesstimate, that's not many per year, and, except in exceptional circumstances, the number of men active at any given time in any of the theatres would hardly constitute an army. They might recruit non-Scandinavians into their service, but then Scandinavians too would desert or go into foreign service. Some would abandon the battle to settle abroad, become farmers and integrate with their new neighbours. Many of those who went out would soon vanish, often quickly. Some who went seafaring would drown. Their ships might be good, but they would be no match for storms in the North Sea or other oceans. 'Of the three ships that had gone out,' says Anders Winroth of a raid, 'only one came back, and that was without their leader, who had fallen when the Frisians had unexpectedly fought back.' A man called Gudrød, says Snorri, was warned against setting off in bad weather but did; his ship went down and all drowned. Eirik the Red set off from Iceland to Greenland with twenty-four ships; only fourteen arrived. A ship Olav Haraldsson sent to the Faroes on taxation duty never made it. Many would be killed in battle, others taken captive and themselves end in slavery. The Sagas are orgies of Vikings killing each other and being killed; you read them and think it a miracle that there were any left standing. Those who follow kings, says Snorri, 'put their lives at risk'.

So the demographic truth behind the Viking Age is that those who made it were remarkably few.

They did not call themselves Vikings. The Sagas use the noun *viking*, but retrospectively. They did not call themselves anything. They were not preoccupied with identity. They were doers, and what they did was much what their forebears had been doing: journeying, trading, fighting, looting, taking slaves. Nothing remarkable about that, except that they were getting better at it. Nor did others call them Vikings. In England they were mostly known as Danes, or 'the heathen', or sometimes as 'North-Men', whether they came from Denmark, Norway or Sweden. Elsewhere in Europe they had many names, none of them 'Viking'. That label was not used much, either in Scandinavia or elsewhere, until the nineteenth century, when the Viking adventures became nationalistically useful.

The term 'Viking Age' is unavoidable but misleading. Most of the people at the time had nothing to do with being Vikings. The farmers and fishermen were not Vikings, they were farmers and fisher-men. The traders were not Vikings, they were traders. Ottar traded and journeyed far, but evaded fighting and was not a Viking. 'Most Scandinavians lived comparatively unaffected by the dramas of the age. They concentrated on winning a livelihood for themselves and their families, and from time to time they heard exciting tales of the conquests. Many owned a few objects imported from the great world outside, perhaps a quern for grinding flour, or some beads.'

Vikings were of two kinds: kings and chiefs after wealth, honour and conquest, and freelancers after land, adventure and booty, or on the run from persecution at home. 'They appeared in many guises: as pirates, traders, extortionists of tribute, mercenaries, conquerors, rulers, warlords, emigrating farmers, explorers and colonisers of uninhabited regions.' They were mobile: a man could be in England one year, in Russia the next.

What they were getting better at was harassing others, stealing from them and taking over their territories. Nationalists later turned this into a story of achievement, a story that has taken hold, so that these people we now call Vikings are getting a steadily better press as settlers and integrators. But glory was not their game. No need to be romantic about it: they were, says Kevin Crossley-Holland, an authority on Norse mythology, 'gangsters'. So were others, but the Norsemen were getting the upper hand.

They had good ships, good weapons and organisational ability. They were supreme in their time in maritime technology: not in sea battle, which they avoided if they could, but in seafaring and in getting themselves to shores where they could deploy their fighting ability on land. They were masters of the surprise attack and quick escape.

They had some capital to work with. From the early Middle Ages gold and silver started to trickle north. Raiding paid off. There were solid economic reasons for those who had the means to invest in better and bigger ships and in the best weaponry.

In the eighth century came the breakthrough in maritime technology that made ships seaworthy. The Vikings now learned to shape hulls better and build the sides of ships higher, to make stronger keels that could bear the weight of masts and sails. They could set out across the high seas and find their way to their intended destinations. From Denmark or southern Norway to eastern England was about a week's sailing, or less in good winds; from the west of Norway to the Shetlands could be twenty-four hours. The historian Peter Sawyer estimates that Ottar sailed from Kaupang in Norway to Hedeby in Denmark at an average speed of 5 knots, and that one Wulfstan, an English trader, sailed from Hedeby in Denmark through the Baltic Sea to Truso in present-day Poland in seven days at an average speed of

2.5 knots. (A modern passenger ship on high seas holds a speed of 20 to 25 knots.)

They had good weapons. One of the privileges of being a free-man was the right to bear arms. The prized weapon was the sword, owned by men of standing, while common warriors used the battleaxe and spear. All carried personal knives as tools in work and arms in fighting. Their weapons were of good quality, the best ones made by Frankish smiths and imported, their swords decorated and often given personal names, say to honour a father or fallen brother. The god Thor's hammer was called Mjølner, 'the crusher'. The horned helmets belong to later fairy tales. The ones used in battle were unglamorous, except that chiefs might have bronzed or gilded helmets for effect.

They had social hierarchy: lords, farmers, slaves. Their cultures were honour-bound: if you were not a lord your duty was to obey and serve. Such economic surplus as there was sat at the top. The combined effect of class and loyalty was to enable collective effort.

And they had another indispensable capacity that compensated for their small numbers. Charlemagne, himself no pussycat – 'autocratic, imperial, a tycoon of the slave trade and aggressively brutal to his neighbours' – was nevertheless in the end successful at war because he made sure he had a bigger army than his enemies. Not so the Vikings; they did not have that luxury. What they had instead was uninhibited ruthlessness. Their cruelty was legendary. They lived in brutal times, but even so they were soon known and feared for their unforgiving viciousness. Master Adam says of the Danes, 'so true is this that they have no faith in one another, and as soon as one of them catches another, he mercilessly sells him into slavery either to one of his fellows or to a barbarian. None of these points appears to me worth discussing, unless it be that they immediately sell women who have been violated and that men who have been caught betraying his royal majesty or in some other crime would rather be beheaded than flogged. No other punishment exists than the axe and servitude, and then it is glorious for a man to take his punishment joyfully. Tears and plaints and other forms of compunction, by us regarded as wholesome, are by the Danes so much abominated that one may weep neither over his sins nor over his beloved dead.'

And further, although no doubt influenced by a desire to stimulate missionary zeal: they were an 'exceedingly fierce race' and a 'piratical people' living in a 'land of horror' as 'ferocious barbarians'. When

Knud, not yet 'the Great', was ousted from England in 1014, he disembarked, as he had promised, his English hostages, but only after
having their hands, ears and noses cut off. When he came back and
conquered England anew, it was thanks to violence and the credible
threat thereof that he prevailed. It should not have been. The English
were the more wealthy and advanced and should have been expected to
turn back the aggressor, but were unable to withstand. The Norsemen
subdued the English, and others, by their prime asset, which was fear.
To be effectively feared, they had to be more fearsome than others. If
it had not been for their ability to create exceptional fear, there would
not today be anyone known as Vikings and we would not have been
aware of any Viking Age.

Did they use rape as a weapon of war? They did; their reputation in
this is deserved. Harald Hardrade equipped ships and sailed towards
Denmark; the poet, in praise it would seem, mentions the 'fear you
brought to Danish women'. Men were killed and 'fair women captured
and bound, chains biting into beautiful bodies'. Danish maidens made
light of marauding Norwegians, but when they saw ships approaching,
then 'laughing not many do'. Chroniclers in Christian Europe, Master
Adam and others, make repeated mention of Scandinavian men violat-
ing women such as captured women before selling them on as slaves.
The Arab chronicler Ahmad ibn Fadlan encountered Swedes in Bulghar
who were there selling slaves and recounts how they had uninhibited
intercourse with slave women, many at a time, in sight of potential
buyers. A slave woman who was to be buried alive with her master
was raped by half a dozen men before going to her destiny. In their
mythological world, into which they projected their lives and habits,
even Odin, the god of gods, is in praise of force. 'How did you win
them, your women?' asks Thor. 'They welcomed us with good grace.
And they were well advised to do so, for they could no more have
escaped us than make ropes of sand. I slept with seven sisters, and each
one gave me ecstasy.' Another time: 'I turned the head of a linen-white
maid. I aroused that lady, and then I enjoyed her. I could have done
with your help to hold that white maid down.' Thor in reply: 'I wish
I'd been with you. I'd have been only too ready.'

They lived in violent times and were themselves violent. Historians
of the Vikings have left it at that: they did as others did. But even in
violent times, not all are the same. We know that today: before our
eyes, Putin of Russia has adopted a military strategy of excelling in

shockingly brutal death and devastation. Through history, even among
barbarians some have been more barbarian than others. The Roman
historian Livy, writing in a time as violent as any, said of a tribe on
the margins of the empire that they made their living out of 'their
talent for inspiring terror'. From the fourth to the sixth century, the
Huns ravaged the Caucasus and into Europe. Like the Vikings, they
had a technological forte: the Vikings were master mariners, the Steppe
people were horsemen like no others. Their invention was to 'democ-
ratise' cavalry warfare by making the horse, elsewhere a prerogative
of the rich, available to all. Like the Vikings, they came out of the
edges of the known world and had the same ability for unrestrained
violence. In the early thirteenth century, as the Viking Age was coming
to an end in the north, the Mongol warrior Genghis Kahn established
a conquest more extensive than that of Alexander 1,500 years earlier.
He dominated by abiding by no rules to limit his use of force. 'Peaceful
submission was rewarded; resistance was punished brutally.' In one
city, 'every living being was butchered as the order was given that
not even dogs or cats should be left alive. All the corpses were piled
up in a series of enormous pyramids as gruesome warnings of the
consequences of standing up to the Mongols.' His scale was bigger
than that of the Norsemen, but the ways were similar. The Vikings
dispensed ruthlessness, and then used the threat of more to extract
submission. Even in their brutal times, they were known throughout
Europe by various names depicting them as 'the violent ones'. That's
how they prevailed in spite of being few. They were perhaps strategic in
the use of violence, dispensing no more than was necessary to prevail
in a violent age. But if they were not violent for the sake of violence,
they were at least generous in giving the gift of wrath.

Where did their ruthlessness come from? We need not think they
were inherently, by nature, more vicious than others; they were as
they were out of necessity. If they were to come home with bounty,
they would have to take it. If they were to appropriate other people's
land, they would have to fight them off. They had to manage in spite
of being, often, inferior in numbers. Even if we grant that they were
not primitives who were violent for the sake of evil, they were totally
dependent on infusing others with fear.

But it did help that they came out of cultures that celebrated violence and were shallow in empathy. Their laws did not prohibit killings,
only killings that were not justified or were cowardly. Infanticide was

usual, of children who did not have the promise of strength or who were just not wanted. Life was not precious. Snorri says approvingly of men that they were great 'mankillers'. A Norwegian king takes care of disobedient locals by 'killing their leader and many more, and breaking and paralysing others'. Of an earl who had not shown the king respect, the king said to Ivar, 'You go kill him.' Which Ivar did, in church, to the king's praise: 'Well done.' Says Kevin Crossley-Holland: 'The natural disposition of the Vikings, adventurous and aggressive and scornful of death, must have given added momentum to the impulse to raid, conquer and colonise.' It was in their experience, and in their beliefs, that might is right and that might grows, if not out of the barrel of a gun, as Mao Zedong was to say a millennium later, then from the sword and the axe and the happiness to use such arms in anger. They did not use means that others denied themselves but they were better than others in being violent. Not always – there were Viking defeats, many of them – but for a good while the Vikings were successfully violent in a violent world.

Women have much presence in the Sagas. Some get honourable mention as eminent men's wives or sons' mothers; a Gunnhild was known as 'mother of kings'. Others are there by force of themselves. A man called Gunnar slaps his wife in the face during an argument. You will regret that, she says. Later, Gunnar is fighting off enemies from their house. His bowstring breaks, he begs her to fix a new one, she refuses, reminding him of his slap, and lets him die. King Agne's wife was Skjålv, so Snorri tells the story. One evening he was celebrating with many men and the drinking was heavy. Skjålv persuaded him to guard a golden ring by wearing it round his neck. (Neck rings of gold and silver were used to display wealth.) When he fell asleep, she hung him dead by the ring and neck, and Skjålv and 'her men' boarded their ships and rowed off. A Swedish chief Alv was of peaceful, or cowardly, sentiment and did not go raiding. His wife Bera was more beautiful than other women. His brother Yngve was a great adventurer and Bera liked his company. Alv told her to come to bed with him, but she replied that a woman would be glad to have a man like Yngve. One evening while drinking, the two brothers killed each other with their swords, leaving Bera the survivor. Another Swedish king, Ingjald, was said to have killed twelve other kings, all by deceit. He gave his daughter, Åsa, in marriage to King Gudrød in Skåne. She was like her father. She made Gudrød kill his brother and then had Gudrød himself killed. A Gudrun was of high family. Her second husband, Atli, killed her brothers for their gold. She took revenge by killing her two sons by Atli, mixing their blood with ale and carving their flesh into steaks, all of which she fed her husband before killing him as well and setting his hall on fire. Early in his career, Harald Finehair sent his men for the beautiful Gyda. But she told them to go back with the message that she would not waste her virginity on a man who did not even rule a country and that she would only wed him if he subdued all of Norway. She would have been fifteen or sixteen years old! Harald's men thought that such an arrogant woman should be taken by force, but Harald paid her the respect that she had made him see what he had not previously thought. He did subdue the country and did get Gyda, although he had/married other women in the meantime and would have/marry more later, nine in all it was said. One was Ragnhild, called 'the Mighty'. She was the mother of the favourite son Eirik, and a master schemer in his advancement.

Women *could* rise to significance – although no woman made it to becoming queen in her own right.* Olav Haraldsson in Norway was distracted by trouble from Sweden. Messengers went between him and Ragnvald and his wife Ingebjörg in Sweden. 'By her persuasion', Ragnvald was brought over to friendship with Olav and the two agreed to peace. Others in Sweden did not like it and held it against Ragnvald that he had let a woman mislead him. Astrid was the wife of King Tryggve in Norway. When he fell, she escaped with treasure and the help of 'the faithful men she had'. She hid her pregnancy and gave birth to a son. The hunt was on, led by another woman, Gunnhild, who sent men and 'equipped them well with weapons and horses', but the resourceful Astrid escaped again, now to Sweden. Olav Tryggvason was raiding along the Baltic shores when he had to seek shelter from bad weather. Where he landed, it was Geira the king's daughter who 'ruled and had the power'. The leading man, Diksin, 'had influence'. Olav stayed the winter, the two liked each other 'very much' and were married. Olav gained charge over these lands 'together with her'. He stayed three more years until Geira died, when he went off again,

---

* But it was later said of Gunnhild, consort of Eirik Bloodaxe, that she for a brief stint ruled as queen in Norway. When Knud the Great conquered Norway in 1028, he installed a consort, Alfiva, and her son, Svend, as co-regents.

eventually to England where he finally reached the Scilly Isles. There a fortune-teller saw that he would be a great king and do great deeds. He returned to England where Gyda, a royal widow, 'had the country' after her husband. She said, 'Since he died, I have ruled here. Men have proposed to me but none I have wanted.' She and Olav talked the matter over and agreed. Olav wed Gyda.

Sigrid ('the Haughty' she is mostly called, 'the Ambitious' says Else Roesdahl) was the widow of King Erik the Victorious in Sweden and owned many estates. She had two suitors burned to death at a feast, as a warning to others to be left alone. Olav Tryggvason wanted her for a wife. He asked her to let herself be baptised but she refused to give up the old religion. He intended to force her, but she refused again and said to his face that this could be his death. The king had to slink home without a wife.

The strategy for a woman who wanted to matter was to be of good family and to marry well, preferably both, and then to be of strong will. Men of the gentry wanted women for their position and beauty, which is to say for the benefit they brought them in repute and property. Men were away much of the time, leaving their women to run households and property, thus ceding domestic power to them. The matriarch was in charge indoors and the holder of the keys. The women were the guardians of the oral heritage, the stories of kinship and mythology, and their domain included the (unmanly) rituals of grief over the dead. In widowhood, and many survived several husbands, women could become landowners. Women had the right to respect. It contributed to the downfall of King Håkon Sigurdsson in Norway that he accumulated enemies among the barons by being too free with other men's wives and too cavalier in the way he cast them aside when used.

Might there have been women fighting? There are stories of women commanding men, as we have seen, and a few graves have been excavated of women buried with warrior paraphernalia. In Greenland, Leif Eirikson's sister, Freydis Eiriksdottir, is said to have fought off hostile natives, sword in hand. Shield-maidens are prominent in the mythologies, but only there. Women (and children) did accompany men on raids and to settlements, and it is not to be ruled out that some participated as warriors, but there are no firm records of women fighting alongside the men. Saxo Grammaticus wrote of women who dressed like men and devoted themselves to war, but in such a way as to put down women who were not properly female. Neil Price, who likes his Vikings to be progressive, thinks it likely that there were female warriors, even if the hard evidence is yet to be found.

The forceful women of the Sagas were, however, few and far between. In general, women were outside public life. They did not, except extraordinarily, have property, and even if they did they could not engage in transactions without the consent of male guardians. A dowry would follow daughters into marriage, and marriage might be confirmed, among the rich, in an endowment, possibly of land, given to the wife by the husband as her property, at least nominally. Marriage was usually arranged between families, in part as a financial transaction, and did not require the consent of the bride to be. Adultery, standard among men, was punishable for women. Mothers were charged with the care for and raising of children, but the father's authority was absolute, including in the question of whether newborns should live or die. Women had no political rights, except sometimes to speak at *thing* (an assembly) alongside a male guardian, and no rights to prosecute in law unless it was done by male guardians on their behalf. Men had many women and several wives, 'princes an unlimited number', says Master Adam. They took their sexual pleasure where they could, 'in their sexual relations with women they know no bonds', according to Master Adam again. Their language had a word, *frille*, for a (slave) woman or girl who served the pleasure of a man of the household. Rape of low-born girls is a casual matter in the Sagas.

Women did the housework. Among the men, drinking and getting drunk was part of social life. In Norse mythology heavy drinking is manly and glorious, no less among gods than men. The festive drink was mead, based on honey. The rich drank from elaborate beakers made of horn and with silver decorations, or cups of glass, a prized luxury from abroad. At feasts honoured guests were given the biggest beakers and the strongest drink. There was a trickle of imported wine, of terrible quality we must think, but with the merit of being strong in alcohol. The daily drink was beer. It was not storable and brewing was a continuous, permanent and burdensome chore for farm women, as it was to be for centuries to come.

Another arduous female chore was the weaving of wool for sails. A mainsail for a standard ship would take two, three or more person-years of weaving and making, much of it done in the dark and cold of winter. In families involved in the *viking* business, it was a never-ending industry of back-breaking, eye-destroying and lung-infecting labour, left to slave women, no doubt, where possible.

So if we consider the women of Scandinavia at the time, all things considered, we must conclude that life, for most of them, was hard, dreary, miserable and unremarkable. 'Sexually active and fertile women were likely pregnant, suffering miscarriages, healing from childbirth and/or nursing for much of their life between puberty and menopause.' Mostly, says Jóhanna Friðriksdóttir in her fine book *Valkyrie: The Women of the Viking World*, the world of the Sagas was one in which 'men were in the company of other warriors, and women seldom appear except to admire them'.

A story is told about Gregory the Great, by none less than the Venerable Bede. Bede was the Benedictine monk-historian whose *Ecclesiastical History of the English People* was completed around 730. Gregory was the Pope of the Church in Rome from 590 to his death in 604, and is revered in England for having sent Augustine to bring them the gospel, establish the monastery at Canterbury and become the first archbishop of the Church of England.

Gregory saw fair-skinned, blue-eyed Anglo-Saxon boys being sold in the slave market in Rome and asked: 'Who are these people?' 'They are Angles,' was the reply. '*Non Angli sed Angeli*,' replied Gregory. 'Not Angles, but Angels.' British children are told this tale about the agreeable and witty Gregory. But the sting in the story is obviously this: there were slave markets in Rome where children from England were bought and sold. It was part of daily life, nothing out of the ordinary for a pope. The children traded there came from afar. How had they reached Rome? Who had sold them in the first place? We cannot know, except that they were part of a trade in human beings that criss-crossed the known world. Slavery and slave-trading were normal and standard in the world the Vikings became part of. Alcuin, writing about the rape of Lindisfarne, mentions 'the boys' who were taken hostage by the pagans.

Slaves come into the Viking story in two ways: as labour and as commodities. The Scandinavian economies of the time were slave ones, with the 'forced exploitation of human beings always a central pillar of their culture'. Where Vikings operated they took slaves, both for their own use and for sale to others. Usually, a prize of raiding would be people. 'The great recruiting grounds were war, piracy and trade.

They came in great numbers from the British Isles, either caught in the dragnet of the Viking raids and invasions or as straightforward objects of commerce; they came from all other countries where Viking power reached.' The eastern Vikings profited monumentally, according to Peter Frankopan: 'nowhere was there greater demand, nowhere was there greater spending power than the buoyant and wealthy markets in Atil that ultimately fed Baghdad and other cities in Asia, as well as elsewhere in the Muslim world, including North Africa and Spain. Beautiful women were particularly highly prized, sold on to merchants in Khazaria and Volga Bulghar, who would take them even further south.' The very word 'slave' originates from 'Slav', which was used in Moorish Spain as a term meaning slaves of European origin, as opposed to African. The trade was in women and children as well as men. 'Human beings were probably the commonest commodity the Vikings dealt in, both as traders and raiders. Treasure in metals and jewels might easily be missed in an attack; provisions, tools and utensils might have relatively small value; but people were to be found everywhere and always had value, ransom from kinsmen or cash from the slave-trader.' In *Cogadh Gaedhel re Gallaibh*, the history of Viking battles in Ireland, it is told that after the sack of Limerick in 967 every captive 'that was fit for war was killed, and every one that was fit for a slave was enslaved'. They took slaves from each other. The Baltic Sea, criss-crossed by raiding through the Viking Age, was a 'slave-sea'. Wherever there were markets, says Snorri, there would be slaves for sale. As without ships no Vikings, and without violence no Vikings, without slaves no Vikings.

The slave populations increased during the Viking Age with an increasing supply from raiding abroad. At its height, between a third and a fifth of the populations were slaves. A good-size farm might have up to five, a lord's estate thirty or more – in Sweden, says the historian Dick Harrison, there were on average three to eight per household. It was a matter of status to have both domestic and out-of-house slaves to do the heavy work and a sign of distinction to avoid work; it was 'dishonourable and cowardly to gain by sweat what could be won by blood'. Standards of living were maintained or rose during the Viking Age in spite of population growth thanks to an increasing supply of cheap slave labour. They made up the workforce at home that enabled the release of manpower for raiding abroad.

Slaves were chattel, bought and sold as property. They had no rights.

Marriage between unfree partners had no legal standing. Slaves were born of slaves. The children of slaves were themselves slaves, also, but not in Swedish law, children of a slave mother and a free father. Sexual abuse of enslaved women was standard. Men who could not find wives at home took women from elsewhere into sexual slavery. If a slave was injured, it was the owner who should have recompense. Slaves could be killed off, including infants, because of old age or disability, for falling ill, and by being buried ceremonially with a deceased owner. A man called Klerkon, says Snorri, was given a gift of a slave he thought too old to be of use and killed him.

The trade in slaves was foul – as always, the act of being made a slave dehumanises the victim, and the trade dehumanises the trader. It met with objections, and from these we know something about it. One source of grievance was that Christians were enslaved by heathens. The complaints were at first more about the trade than slavery as such. 'And it is terrible to know what too many do often, those who for a while carry out a miserable deed, who contribute together and buy a woman as a joint purchase between them and practice foul sin with that one woman, one after another, and each after the other like dogs that care not about filth, and then for a price they sell a creature of God into the power of enemies.' So writes Wulfstan of York in an eleventh-century homily known as *Sermon of the Wolf to the English* (*Sermo Lupi ad Anglos*).

A second Wulfstan, Bishop of Worcester, also eleventh-century, was credited with getting the trade shut down in Bristol, a late outpost of slave-trading in England because of its direct contact with Ireland. (Bristol, interestingly, would later again become a major city to profit from slave-trading, in the Africa-to-America slave trade.) His *Life* was written by William of Malmesbury about fifty years after his death and contains this dramatic rendering of the misery: 'they would buy up men from all over England and sell them off to Ireland in hope of a profit, and put up for sale maidservants after toying with them in bed and making them pregnant. You would have groaned to see the files of the wretched roped together, young persons of both sexes, whose youth and respectable appearance would have aroused the pity of barbarians, being put up for sale every day. An accursed deed, and a crying shame, that men devoid of emotions that even beasts feel should condemn to slavery their own relations and even their flesh and blood!'

Slavery lasted until around 1200 in Denmark and Norway, a century more in Sweden. Attitudes evolved during the Viking Age, much under the influence of Christianity, in a gradual easing of the harshness of conditions and treatment. But when it did come to an end, it was because it had become impractical. 'Christian antipathy, the falling-off of supplies, new means of livelihood offered by internal colonization and the growing fishing industry, stronger monarchical government, foreign influence, all contributed to bringing slavery to an end.' Laws against slavery followed later.

THE SLAVES AND THE HISTORIANS

Slavery and the slave trade have been a difficult matter for Scandinavian historians. Dick Harrison, in his Swedish history – he is also an authority on slavery in general – gives the slave dependency of early Scandinavia the full treatment, as does also Neil Price in *The Children of Ash and Elm*. But Harrison also makes the point that slavery has not been a priority in Scandinavian historical research, the slave trade even less than slavery itself. In earlier standard texts it tends to get some mention in passing, but often no more than is unavoidable. In writings in the Scandinavian languages, the term 'slave' has tended to be avoided in favour of *trell* (thrall), which refers more to their hard work than the unfreedom part of their status. In Claus Krag's volume in the most recent collective history of Norway, covering the period from 800 to 1130, slaves, or *treller*, get a one-page treatment in which the trading of slaves is just touched on, with four other brief mentions. But in the next volume of the same history, for the period 1130–1350, Knut Helle observes that it was earlier the view among historians that slavery was not a matter of much importance in these societies and that the tendency more recently has been to interpret it as of greater economic and social significance, in part due to the influence of modern comparative research on slavery. Peter Sawyer, in his Danish history from 700 to 1050, gets himself into a twist by having to touch on a matter he would seemingly have liked to avoid. 'There is no basis for describing Viking Age Denmark as a slave society,' he writes in the short page he devotes to the topic – then going on to describe both Denmark proper and the Danelaw in England as slave societies, complete with the underlying trade in chattel.

The law

The Vikings came out of cultures of violence. But, paradoxically, they also came from lands of law. The early Scandinavians were prolific lawmakers. And they were democratic in the way they did it. They agreed laws at *thing*. A *thing* was an assembly of free men, or free men of (some significant) property. Local *thing* could be regular events. Higher-level *thing* might convene once a year, or when called together by a chief or king, and sit for a few days, agreeing laws, sealing contracts, dispensing justice, sometimes staging religious rituals. They consisted of free men, of course – not slaves, not the poor, not (usually) women, but were still, in principle, assemblies of the people.

The holding of *thing* has come to be seen as a Norse heritage, but that is not correct. It was a Germanic convention, already described by Tacitus in Roman times. Just as the Viking ship was, in part, a product of European influence, so also was the *thing*.

In societies as rigidly class-divided as the early Scandinavian ones, there would not have been equality among those who could attend *thing*. Only at very local *thing* could all men meet. Other *thing* would be made up of representatives, *thingmen*. In Danish regional law, a *thing* would be constituted with at least twelve men meeting. One one occasion when Olav Haraldsson was touring the country to restore Harald Finehair's unity and needed local backing, tells Snorri, he first conferred with the barons for their consent, and 'after this' convened the *thing* to get what had been agreed rubber-stamped.

The purpose of law is to make it possible for people to live with some security and predictability and to settle disputes in an orderly manner. The strange thing about early Scandinavia, however, is that although there were quite sophisticated laws, widespread lawlessness was not avoided, nor was resorting to blood feud to settle grievances. The laws were not written down. 'The law' was what was agreed, and the agreement was entrusted to a 'lawspeaker', whose responsibility it was to remember the laws that had been agreed and to re-announce them at the next *thing*. Laws were not written down, both because the early Scandinavians were not writing folk but also because most people, who could not read, did not trust those who could write to do so honestly. The law was still the law, even if it was not written down, but it would have been ambiguous to appeal to.

The early laws were local, hence the Westrogothic Law in Sweden. A *thing* would be an assembly of local people and the rules they agreed would apply to their locality; if you crossed into another locality, other laws might prevail. When the law differs depending on where you are, it is not clear what the law is. And even if you feel a duty to obey the law in your own locality you might not feel bound by that of another, which after all would not be your law.

And while the early Scandinavians did make laws, they had not yet established institutions with which to uphold them. Kings had no authority over law. There were no police. The *thing* would serve as a court of justice in some matters, for example inheritance, but if your neighbour was invading your land and claiming it for himself, it would not do you much good to wait until the following year and bring your complaint to the next *thing*.

The making and administration of law evolved from the end of the Viking Age to gradually deal with these shortcomings. Laws started to be written down when the Scandinavians learned to write: the Westrogothic Law again. Then lawmaking started to be centralised. The first step was to shift authority from local *thing* to super-*thing* that covered broader territories. In Denmark, the main law districts became Lund for the Danish areas in what is now southern Sweden, Ringsted for Sjælland and associated islands, and Viborg for Jylland. In Norway, the country was divided into four super-*thing* by the early eleventh century.

Then lawmaking was centralised further to the – in some senses – national level. National rulers started to claim the right to make laws that applied to all of the land and to put the law in writing. That came at a price: the *thing* became obsolete for lawmaking, which was taken out of the hands of the people and turned into a royal prerogative. In Norway, Magnus Lawmender, king from 1257 to 1280, put a code of law into writing as a *landslov*, 'law of the land'. His law built on existing regional laws but smoothed out differences into a single system, an early case in Europe of a centralised national code of law. In Sweden national law was first codified about a century later; in Denmark, technically, even later again. Only in the outer settlements of Iceland, the Faroe Isles and the Isle of Man were national *thing* constituted as lawmaking assemblies. Thus it came about that Iceland did not become a monarchy. Elsewhere, the beginning of national lawmaking was the end of democratic lawmaking.

Taxes

The early kings may not have known much about statecraft, but they knew about taxation. What ruling a territory meant at the time was to tax the people who lived in it. When they fought each other over territory, they did so for the right to tax. When Norwegian and Swedish kings confronted each other over borderlands it was the tax base they were fighting over.

Taxes were extracted in many forms: some in cash, if there was any; the always attractive silver; more usually in kind – agricultural produce such as wool, timber and furs. But most importantly in manpower. What made a chief a chief was his ability to command the loyalty of men, and hence their labour. Under national rulers, districts were obliged to provide men and equipment for the king's guard and fleet. Of each seven men, one would be liable for service, with such equipment as was needed to be a soldier on land or a rower at sea. And in land: a king or chief might confiscate your land, possibly to give it as a reward to a more deserving servant, or add it to his own property. There would be nothing you could do about it unless you were ready to take up your sword against the king – which you would not be able to do since the reason why he, not you, was king was that he had more force. Fines for crimes were a source of royal revenue, often in the form of land again, frequently so heavy that the extended family would have to pitch in. Fortifications along Denmark's southern border with Germany, known as *Danevirke*, first built in the eighth century, possibly even earlier, are evidence of chiefs' ability to mobilise resources and workforce. The construction of the mature wall would have taken 30,000 oak trees and the shifting of 80,000 cubic metres of soil and gravel. Some of the workforce were no doubt slaves, but this was still labour extracted from agricultural work at home. Kings travelled their countries and local barons had to provide for them and their retinues. Locals were obliged to build and maintain the compounds the king wanted on his various estates. Fishermen paid a tax in fish and tradesmen a toll. In towns there were property and business fees to pay. Ships in foreign trades were obliged to reserve space for the king's use. With the Christian Church came the tithe, which enabled the building and maintenance of churches and cathedrals to God's and kings' glory. Local barons would be obliged to build parish churches and provide for priests. Taxes were extracted in layers: the king taxed barons and barons farmers. When Harald Finehair installed earls in the Orkneys and Shetlands, it was for them to tax the islanders against the duty to be taxed by him.

Taxation was ruthlessly exploitative but also notoriously ineffective. Not only were most people so poor there was not much to take, but kings had no administration yet to collect what little there was. The practical power of barons over underlings was limited, and anyway the barons would keep what they could and pass on no more than they had to. Early kings knew nothing about tax accounting.

How heavy might the tax burden have been? Harald Bluetooth in Denmark was a builder king, of roads, bridges and forts. That required him to extract heavy taxes, to such a degree that the burden might have contributed to rebellion against him and resulting civil war. His son, Svend, was more cautious, but at the cost of his father's works falling into decline. When that same Svend claimed the Norwegian Crown (in the year 1000) he brought with him, says Snorri, new laws, harder than those in Denmark. A man could not leave the country without the king's permission; if he did his property would fall to the king. The punishment for murder was to forfeit land and property. Annually, at year's end, each farmer would owe the king a quantity of beer, meat and butter, and as much woven linen as could be held within the longest fingers.

In the welfare state of today the Scandinavians shoulder a heavy load of taxes, but there is nothing new in that. So they did a thousand years ago. The best way of putting it is probably that kings then taxed as much as they were able to extract.

And so they would do over the following centuries. Today we pay taxes which we may well feel to be heavy, but which we can still by and large afford; this is a novelty of the twentieth century. Until recent times the small-folks were poor, with little to spare, and still the State would come for their meagre funds again and again, constantly, ruthlessly. The rich, the aristocracy, were exempt from most taxes, in theory in return for a duty to serve as military commanders. It was the poor who had to pay up, for most of the time in provisions and manpower but also in cash and valuables. As we move on in this story, we will see an astonishing power to extract massive taxes from poor populations.

Who were the Vikings?

Their lives were dramatic: fighting, warring, thieving, marauding. They hired themselves out to fight other people's wars, they took captives whom they held as hostages or sold as slaves. They laid waste to holy places and desecrated holy texts. They confiscated land and sent former owners packing. They tortured prisoners and blinded and mutilated them. Wherever they operated they made away with valuables but brought and gave nothing. At home, men betrayed wives and wives killed husbands. Fathers killed sons, sons fathers, brothers brothers. Kings terrorised their subjects, murdered their enemies, and won loyalty with bribes. Barons betrayed their lords and signed up in treachery with foreign invaders.

We have seen what they *did*, but what did they think of it, who *were* they? The Sagas have little or nothing to say about how their adventures affected them. Some were victorious; were they humble? Some failed; were they desolate? Did any of them have doubts? Were any tormented? Were they haunted by their deeds and desires? Those who sold slave women in Bulghar and raped them while waiting for custom, were they troubled? Was there such a thing as a bad conscience? Were they able to empathise with others, with those who were not of their own kind? Did they do battle with their own worries over right and wrong? Did husbands have love for wives, and wives for husbands?

Was there homosexuality? There must have been because there always is, and because male bonding was strong in a masculine way of life in which the awareness of sex was omnipresent. It was dishonourable and is hence not mentioned in the Sagas except for purposes of insult, but we know of it from homosexual acts being crimes punishable by outlawry in early law. It was common encampment banter for bored warriors to berate each other with suggested homosexuality.

Was there prostitution? From ancient times in Europe, 'brothels were full of women who, as infants, had been abandoned by their parents'. In a Norse mythology story, a mason strikes a contract with the gods to build them a wall in record time in return for Freyja to be his wife. He finishes the wall but not in time and is refused his prize. 'Tricked,' he rages, 'by a gang of gods and a brothel of goddesses.' In another story, Thor has lost his hammer, stolen by the giants as it turns out. It will be returned if Freyja is brought to the king giant to sleep with him.

She refuses: 'Everyone would say the same. A whore! Just a whore!' (The other gods then dress up Thor in drag to trick the giants out of his hammer, with which, once in hand, he crushes the king giant's skull and fells the other giants and giant women as well.)

If the human spirit is constant we must suppose that the Vikings, like others, must have thought about what they were doing. Their actions were the stuff of Greek tragedies; there must have been tragedy in their lives. In Ancient Greece, husbands killed wives and wives husbands, and brothers brothers – and they fought battles with themselves against personal demons over uses and abuses of power, over fidelity and treachery, over honour and shame. This we know because the Greeks left us both histories and literature, the latter notably in the Athenian theatre, which, says E.F. Watling in his Introduction to Sophocles' *Theban Plays*, 'fills out the factual narratives of the historians'. For the Vikings we have the historical accounts, left to us by Snorri and others, but we are not without other legacies to 'fill out' those narratives. The histories are recounted. What might the other sources add about the human condition in Norse life?

There is the mythology and the old faith (as retold by Kevin Crossley-Holland in *The Penguin Book of Norse Myths*, which is referred to here). The early Scandinavians held on to stories about creation and the universe. The cosmos emerged when ice and fire met to engender life. The first beings were a giant and a cow. The cow licks out of the ice a creature who begets gods. The giant is killed and from his body nine worlds are created. These worlds are ordered in sections, the *Asgard* with the worlds of the gods, the *Midgard* with the worlds of giants, dwarfs and elves, and the underworld, *Hel*, the world of the dead. The cosmos moves through time, from the creation to the *Ragnarök*, when all things end in decadence and battle between gods, men and monsters, when Odin himself dies, when the dead are separated into those who rise and those who go down, and out of which finally new life is born.

In the anticipation of *Ragnarök*, men and women live their lives as best they can under the influence of the gods and spirits above, who have power over them and whom they need to satisfy. In the mature mythologies there are twelve gods, the major ones being Odin, the allfather, Thor, Odin's son and the god of strength and war, whose anger was volcanic, Freyr, the god of plenty, Heimdall, the watchman of the gods, Tyr, the god of battlefields, Loki, the evil one, and Balder, another son of Odin, whose death will release the *Ragnarök*. There are as many goddesses but only Freyja, the goddess of womanhood who uses her sexuality as an instrument of power, has much presence of her own. She is, perhaps, Odin's equal, in command of her own hall in the afterlife, Sessrúmnir, as Odin is in command of Valhalla, and the two of them share slain heroes from battlefields. Frigg was the wife of Odin, an earth goddess perhaps, of maternity perhaps. The Valkyries are female supernatural beings who decide who will live and who will die on the battlefield, and by extension who will have the good fortune of being taken care of by Odin and Freyja and feast with them while they wait for the final reckoning. Who of the men, that is. Where women went when they died we do not know; the mythologies are silent.

The gods and goddesses live recognisable lives in their *Asgard* worlds, with scheming, greed, fighting, drink, sex and so on. There is no harmony in their world. With the end in sight they fall out horribly with each other. In an orgy of infighting, the evil Loki lets loose. To Idun: 'I know no woman as wanton as you. You even wound your white arms around your brother's murderer.' To Gefion: 'I know who seduced you – that boy offered you a sparkling neckless [necklace] and you, you straddled him.' To Frigg: 'You were born a whore. You may be Odin's wife but you've shared your bed with his brothers.' To Freyja: 'You've slept with every single god and elf gathered in this hall, and the gods caught you in bed with your own brother.' Paradise is the Valhalla where dead heroes reside, fighting and killing by day, arising from the dead to feast by night, only to resume fighting the next day. The gods' most dangerous enemies are the giants in their *Midgard* world of the *Jotunheim* (still today the name of the wildest mountain range in Norway). The mythologies evolved and developed over time – Loki, for example, started his life as a mischievous trickster but ended as an evil demon – to the form that was passed down from the beginning of the Viking Age.

Is this mythology an original Norse conception? Some of it, perhaps, such as creation being formed out of the melting ice, as was indeed the way human life came to these regions. But for the most part it is adopted. The Lithuanian cultural historian Marija Gimbutas calls it 'Germanic'. It became known as Norse when the Germanic tribes converted to Christianity and left the old beliefs to their northern brethren, and it was in the north, in Iceland, that it was converted from oral to written memory. Mythological beliefs spread geographically up from Europe, as would Christian beliefs later. Those that settled are recognisably early Germanic, Indo-European, Iranian and Greek, with links to Christian legend and Celtic mythology. When Loki reproaches Idun for winding her 'white arms' around a murderer he is using language that goes back to Greek mythology, specifically to Homer, one of whose epithets for women was 'white-armed', meaning beautiful, innocent and rich – able to live protected from the sun. We have seen earlier that Odin boasted of having turned the head of a 'linen-white' lady. Not just any woman was raped, then, but a young virgin of standing whom he made his in such a way as to destroy her bodily and socially. Were the tellers of these Norse stories aware that they were using language and images handed down to them from afar in time and distance? Probably not.

There is the art. The early Scandinavians created wood carvings, jewellery and runic inscriptions. This art has originality, although again with recognisable Germanic and further European influences. A core feature is the constant presence of snakes and monster dragons, tangled and intertwined, as serpents were plentiful in their world of myths. The elaborate runes on the Piraeus Lion, for example, are contained in the bodies of twisting serpents. These lands were not, and are not, ones of snakes or many dangerous animals but their people absorbed motives of fear from earlier European mythologies. If we can read meaning into it, the art suggests mainly fright. It looks into an unknown world of 'forces' in which 'creatures' are entangled and imprisoned in incomprehension and fatalism, and tells a story of artists who were haunted by horrors which they could sense but not understand.

And there is the vast, mostly Icelandic, literature, both the historical accounts and the poetic narratives. The Sagas recount the doings of kings and great Icelanders. The poetry transmits the mythological legacies and adds heroic tales to those of the Sagas, but also gives us a body of Eddic elegies with a different content, more from the world of feeling than that of doing.

The Norse mythology is gripping, but when looked into as a belief system it is vacuous. The notion of 'sin and guilt', says Ole Fenger, 'came to Denmark' with Christianity. The art, such as in jewellery, has character, but the range of artistic expression is narrow. The literary corpus is immense, but heavy on the heroic and light on the reflective. 'The classical literature of medieval Scandinavia is primarily one of "doom and gloom" within a strict and austere form.' In looking into the available material for elements that might fill out the factual narratives, what strikes us is how much is *not* there. The author Marie Arana has said, in praise of the Greek myths, that there 'you will find just about everything you need to know about love, war, power, honor, cowardice, valor and frailty'. Might we say the same about Norse mythology? Hardly – war, power and cowardice, yes, but less about love, honour, valour or frailty. In the poem *Håvamål*, in which Odin dispenses advice on life and wisdom (including how to seduce women), it is good to value friendship and hospitality, but above all to win fame through bravery. Life is predetermined; death will come as it is given and is not to be feared. What you should make for yourself is reputation, because a good name is all you can hope to remain after you are gone.

Their gods were men writ large, with the vanities and defects of earthly humans. It is difficult to see why they should be believed in at all, except for the fear that if you did not honour them they would, petty and vengeful as they were, thwart your ambitions. They set no example, conveyed no morality. And why were there not more of them, and why were they not more intriguing? It is difficult to understand, for example, why there was no deity associated with the sun, as in so many early religions. These are lands of winter darkness that are, with the regularity of the seasons, reborn into days of eternal light on which today's Scandinavians, on the first warm day of spring, take to the fields, strip what they can and embrace the warm rays with ritualistic fervour. We are on the European fringe, on the edge of civilisation, in cultures with limited ability to handle the influences that pushed up against them.

Artistic expression was limited to jewellery and carvings; other pictorial forms seem to have been unknown. A millennium and a half after the Greeks invented the sculptural form that is still the standard of classicism; the Norse had no idea. The mythologies do mention, although sparingly, song and dance, but hardly musical instruments. They did have instruments: horns made of wood, bronze and rams' horns, flutes and harps. Master Adam mentions 'shameful' songs to accompany pagan sacrificial rituals, but earlier the Anglo-Saxon poem *Beowulf* holds song and harp-playing in high esteem. Would there have been entertainment in the halls of the rich? Perhaps myth-telling and the recital of poetry, perhaps choral-style singing, but hardly anything like performance. The rich built halls, glorified drinking dens really, of wood and mud, without windows, dark and smoky, in which feasters sat on benches, were not what one might call buildings with what we know as furniture. At a time when Charlemagne built his magnificent church in Aachen, the splendour of which can be admired today as the core of the now grander cathedral, there was in all of Scandinavia not a single building of any architectural or artistic value. Four millennia after the Celts built vast burial monuments which captured the rays of the sun at the solstice and directed them to the centre chamber, as can be seen for example at the site of Newgrange in Ireland, and three millennia after the Egyptians built the pyramids, the Scandinavians built nothing. Five hundred years after the Goths in Ravenna built a mausoleum for King Theodoric, still standing, the roof of which is a single slab of stone weighing 300 tons – it is still a wonder how they got it into position – the Norse got as far as making burial mounds of dirt which could be thrown up with shovels, 'exceedingly simple, primitive and cheap'. At Stonehenge in England is a monument 4,000 or 5,000 years old made of 30–40-ton stone slabs that had been hewed into shape and transported down rivers and hauled over meadows to their present site. The Norse got as far as upending stones and etching brief self-congratulatory boasts into them with their little alphabet. They did have temples. The most important one, at Uppsala, gets a mention by Master Adam as being 'very famous' and 'decked out in gold'. But the idea of building for the glory of God came only with Christianity, in time finding its expression in churches and cathedrals when there was enough wealth to draw on.

The Norse literature has a deserved reputation for a lack of emotional display, but is not entirely emotionally barren. The Sagas are dry and factual, those of the kings in particular, but not void of emotion. There are displays of anger, pride, frustration, achievement, friendship, betrayal. Perhaps anger in particular. So also in the mythology. Thor, the favourite god, is renowned and revered for his wild temper, but also for not letting anger last and for being merciful, in a Norse way. On one journey he is cheated on a petty matter by a farmer: 'His eyes burned like orange flames and the family thought their days had come to an end.' But when he saw their panic, the blood stopped racing in his body and he reassured the farmer that he would only take his sons as servants. 'And that's the end of the matter.'

The mythological world had goddesses of love, Sjofn and Lofn, but the meaning of love is elusive. It could be lust, or marriage, but tenderness is not much in evidence. The Sagas are full of sex and matchmaking, and for the most part leave it at that, but even Snorri cannot fully evade the matter of adoration. When Olav Tryggvason lost Geira, he grieved over her so much that he could no longer live in their home and pulled himself together by going raiding again. The young Harald Finehair wanted Gyda 'because she was beautiful', but when she refused him he took other wives; and when he did get her there was not much to it, except that they had five children. Later he wed Snøfrid, whom 'he loved to delirium', so much that he neglected 'all other things'. When she died he sat with her body, believing that she would rise again, and mourned her for three years; others worried that he had gone mad. The story is told, however, not in celebration of the power of love but as a warning against the loss of self-control. But very occasionally, even the hardened historian in Snorri lets his guard down. A Swedish Ingegjerd 'went all red' at the suggestion that she might wed the Norwegian king. This beautiful if careless little allusion to young, innocent and blissful love is unique and surprising in an otherwise hard history.

The emotional repertoire that this part of the literary canon allows itself is harsh and narrow: anger, pride, shame, humiliation, hate. As we move through the literature, though – to the heroic Sagas, to the poetry and to female voices – it become more inclusive of softer emotions, if still guardedly. This journey of emotionality is analysed beautifully by the Icelandic scholar Sif Rikhardsdottir in her *Emotion in Old Norse Literature*. The *Saga of Egill Skalla-Grímsson* is 'a prime example of the objective narrative style' with 'limited emotional content'. A brother's reaction to a killing in the family is to be 'unhappy', and a wife's to the death of her husband to be 'upset'. But at the death of his son Bodvar, when Egill remains a model of composure, the story moves on to let the reader sense that there is more to it. The father's grief that cannot be expressed in words is observed in his behaviour, 'quite literally as the body strains to contain the emotions evoked by the loss'. We get a glimpse of the softness of soul that lives under the hardness of flesh. After the burial of Bodvar, at home and beyond public gaze, Egill's daughter Thorgerd saves her father from his death wish by inviting him to compose a poem in Bodvar's memory. He does, and now, in the protective format of poetry and with female influence, he is better able to articulate the agony he has previously suppressed, revealing 'gestures of mourning that the prose text adamantly avoids', although keeping his guard up to remind himself that 'deep as my sorrow is I must keep it to myself'.

King Håkon Håkonsson of Norway, king from 1217 to 1263, and his queen Margrete were ambitious monarchs who wanted Norway and their court to be part of the European cultural community. To that end they had major works of French and English literature translated into Norse, such as the twelfth-century courtly romances of *Tristan and Iseult* (Isolde) and *Yvain, the Knight of the Lion*. This was to bring works of emotional intensity into a culture of emotional repression, a mission that proved fraught. 'Many of the Norse translations of French material reveal cultural adaptations in the behaviour of characters.' Those adaptations were radical, some material being omitted and some being modified, adding up to a loss of 'emotional life'. In *Tristan*, the emotive language of passionate love is 'significantly curtailed' to a shift in focus to 'the negative social consequences of unrestrained passion' and other 'negative emotions'. Missing in the Norse translation is 'any reference to the joy of love and the physical pleasure derived from the enactments of those desires so prevalent' in the original. Perhaps the translator was unable to absorb the range of emotion in the European texts; perhaps he (they) though it beyond the reach of Norse readers; perhaps it reflected royal expectations.

The literature gets nearer to emotional softness when it allows female voices to speak. A group of Eddic poems, of a class described as elegies to separate them from the heroic poems, have a Gudrun as their main protagonist. The first one deals primarily with the emotional effects on Gudrun of the death of her husband. Although Gudrun will 'not lament, nor beat her hands, nor wail as other women', the poem is a litany of deep grief. A recital of female voices assumes the form of a chant – 'Gudrun was unable to cry, she was so overcome' – that builds emotive suspense and guides Gudrun to a cathartic gesture of affection: 'Look at your beloved, lay your mouth on his lips, the king you used to embrace when still alive.'

So there *was* emotional imagination in the Norse world. The hard emotions are easy to deal with and therefore plentiful: satisfaction in one form or other with designs gone well, anger about ventures that have failed. The soft emotions are difficult and as a result restrained, repressed and hesitant. Love tends to take the prosaic form of convenience rather than the emotional form of longing. Grief is dangerous, to be avoided. But just what is being avoided? The Norse were supposedly fierce adventurers of courage who were afraid of nothing. One Högni laughs when his captors cut out his heart. A Gudrun smiles as a killer uses her shawl to wipe the blood off the weapon that had killed her husband. (But revenge is already brewing behind her enigmatic smile. She waits until her sons are sixteen and twelve years old and then sends them to kill the murderer of their father.) Displays like these are masking what must be there but cannot be shown. What they are telling us, we may suppose, is that men and women who outwardly fear nothing are inwardly stymied by fear. There is an echo here of Norse art. When they set out to design beauty, they took their inspiration not from life and joy but from the dangerous unknown. In their emotional repression they stand before us as men and (to a lesser degree) women who were unable to deal with the complexities of human living, with an emotional imagination that was narrow in range and shallow in depth. Perhaps, in the end, their lives were so raw that it would have been impossible for them to open the door, more than a crack, into a contemplation on decency, meaning and worthiness. Master Adam must have been right that 'tears and plaints and other forms of compunction' were abominated, but only half right. They did mourn and lament but were economical in the extreme in showing it. Regret, yes; but shedding tears was not the Norse way.

In contrast, let us return to the earlier Greek mythology, and take the story of Orestes as told by Euripides. He kills his mother Clytemnestra to avenge her killing of his father, Agamemnon. While Agamemnon was away fighting the war in Troy she had taken a lover, betrayed the husband and despoiled the conjugal bed and family home. When Agamemnon returns unexpectedly she has the lover kill her husband, debasing even further the family's honour. Orestes' act was just and sanctioned by the gods – but he goes mad when, after the deed, he is riven by furies that tear at his soul. He had done what a son should do as a matter of right and honour, but is crushed by his own torment over an act he could not have avoided. Here is a man who does what he should and is successful in his undertaking, but who is self-destroyed by the tragedy that has befallen him.

Can we imagine this story in the Norse world? It would seem out of character and beyond the Norse emotional capacity. We started this history with the death of Gudfred and his possible killing by a son enticed by a wife-mother, not unlike the story of Orestes. Say that story were true. Would we then expect to see the mother or son dragged down into agony and torment? Not if we go by the Sagas we wouldn't.

However, there is a paradox. Look again at their gracious ships. These people may have had a limited repertoire in art and literature, but they clearly had a yearning for creativity which they were able to follow through when the opportunity arose. They invested their ingenuity where they had to invest it, in the ships. They had some skills, but they were limited and needed to be rationed. They could not waste what flair they did possess and were obliged to use it where it was most needed. Their existence depended on the ships. They had to keep building ships and they had to be good. It was shipbuilding that they put their hearts into, and in his ships the Viking found 'his being'. Other things that richer kings could indulge in would have to wait. It is a sad observation, perhaps, that Scandinavian grandees, in their desire for impact, were doomed to invest their emotional ability in the instruments of terror on which their existence depended.

What came of the Viking Age?

They traded. By trading they were able to bring back valuables such as jewellery and silks that helped kings to be kings and chiefs chiefs.

They raided, which is to say taking valuables rather than buying them. That enabled them to bring more profit home and pay for projects such as building ships and raising armies. But it was success at a cost. They depended on violence and could not avoid the stigma of being regarded as barbarians by people who thought themselves better.

They settled and colonised. In this they were more influential than powerful. They were influential towards the creation of Russia. They had an impact in the cultures in which they assimilated. That is still recognisable in England, for example, in its language and place names. Mostly, they were rapidly absorbed into the populations among whom they settled. Only in Iceland and the Faroes were lasting cultures created.

They conquered. There is no clear dividing line between settlement and conquest, but if we think of conquest as taking over someone else's territory and making oneself its master, there were only three: the conquest of what became Normandy and the two invasions of England (although the first one, the Danelaw, was at best a quasi-conquest).

These were of consequence, clearing the way, inadvertently, for the unification of England and the making of Normandy, and the further conquests from there in Italy and again in England.

If these were the Vikings' achievements, big or small depending on how you see it, there were also failures. Gudfred might have wished to take on Charlemagne, but that was hopeless. Rollo wanted more of France than he was able to take. Conquest eluded them in both Ireland and Russia, as did the maintenance of conquest in England. These failures were inevitable given the backwardness of their cultures. They trusted power too much, fighting where they could not win, overreaching, shedding energy and resources. Even Knud the Great's story was delusional. He thought he could have an empire but had no capacity to make it stick.

In some ways, the Viking Age went nowhere. Notably so in trade. The Scandinavians remained content to exchange goods for goods and failed to evolve to conduct trading operations with organised teamwork, finance, records, accounts and the like. That goes some way to explaining why their trade into Russia came to an end so rapidly. They were outcompeted by more organised operators from the south who had capabilities the Scandinavians were unable to emulate. Much of their success rested on their mastery of maritime technology, but when the time was up for the Viking ship they were unable to move on and adopt new technologies, and control of shipping passed to others. These failures were to be of lasting consequence. When serious trade took off across the Baltic and North Seas from the thirteenth century, the business fell into the hands of those who were better in technology and organisation, the German Hansa, and eventually the Dutch and the English. For 300 years and more, they lost economic surplus to the Germans and had to tolerate the Hansa as a fourth state-like force in their home areas.

Here again, failure is explained by cultural backwardness. Not only in Europe but also at home in Scandinavia, everyone fought everyone else, shedding social energy. The proud builders and users of Viking ships did not have the drive to renew their ways. The goods-on-goods traders in Russia and elsewhere were unable to learn more sophisticated techniques from those they dealt with. Central to this backwardness was the failure to take up the use of writing, essential in any civilising project and also for basic trading techniques such as correspondence and book-keeping. In *The Children of Ash and Elm*, Neil Price thinks the Scandinavians were satisfied with runic writing and 'rejected books and the distinctive literary culture that came with them... because it gave them nothing they wanted'. But their problem was that they were unable to want what they needed. 'If we were to point to a single and decisive innovation,' says Ole Fenger, 'it is the skill of writing. The transition from a society without writing to one that uses the written word is an event of profound consequence. When writing takes hold in a society, that society is transformed once and for all.' In Scandinavia that transformation had to wait until after the Viking Age.

The Scandinavians were latecomers. The Viking Age was a race to catch up with Europe, exhausting, relentless – but not achieved.

2

The First Modernisations

For all the shortcomings of the Viking venture, it did clear the way for a new era. The men who ravaged Europe brought north seeds of modernisation. They found a new and superior faith and took it home, out of which would grow Church organisations. The most successful fighters became kings and started to acquire a new understanding of politics, out of which would emerge early State structures. It took time, but the order they passed on to their successors would be more robust than the one they themselves had inherited. Where there had been a Scandinavia of warriors, there would be a Scandinavia of Church and kingship.

The coming of Christianity

The Christian conquest of Europe followed a pattern. Emperors, kings and nobles would convert, mostly for reasons of political expediency. They would try to carry with them their subjects, but those people would be reluctant to accept the new. Some of the converts in positions of power would become fanatical and force the new faith on the populace, sometimes by violent means. People would convert, but hedge their bets by preserving what they could of the old. Late Viking Age coins typically had a Christian cross on one side and Thor's hammer on the other. But then later, the further north, common folk would turn from reluctant converts to true believers, and the Christian faith would, by 'its establishment of a community of feeling and experience among all men, women and children', take on a force of such strength that it is difficult to fathom for those of us who have lived for generations in the age of reason.

Christianity came slowly to Scandinavia, paganism's final outpost in Europe (along with the Viking playgrounds in the Baltic and Russia). The new faith was present and tolerated in Denmark and Sweden from at least the middle of the ninth century, in the sense that priests could preach and baptise. Pagan forms of burial were no longer practised in Denmark by the end of the tenth century, but Uppsala in Sweden, the most enduring centre of the old cult, was not won over for another century. The first Christian king in Norway was Håkon the Good, from around 935. He had grown up in England and brought priests with him back to the old country, but met determined resistance and died having failed to convert his people and seen churches pulled down again. The final conversion was still sixty or seventy years off, and was to be violent. 'So in Denmark and Sweden Christianity sifted in quite peacefully, in Norway the newly converted kings used the sword to force the new religion on the people.'

The reluctant conversion was accomplished by the year 1000, in the sense that Christianity was the religion of royal approval and that active resistance was coming to an end. An organised Church then imposed itself with speed while the transition among common folk, in which old and new beliefs and practices lived side by side, would last for two or more centuries, longer in the peripheries, such as among the Sami in the north, and on the island of Gotland.

The first recognised missionary was one Willibrord, an eighth-century monk and later Frankish bishop. His concern was the Frisians, of whom the Danes, for him, were an extension. According to Alcuin of York, he visited 'the wild Danish tribes' around 710 and tried to convert a Danish king. He failed and nothing came of it, except that he returned to Utrecht with thirty boys to be raised in the Christian faith, possibly with the intention that they would go back north again as emissaries; it is unlikely that they did. A century later, Ebbo, Archbishop of Reims, was in Denmark and may have succeeded in baptising some Danes. Ansgar, Ebbo's assistant, whom we met earlier as Bishop and Archbishop of Hamburg-Bremen, travelled to Hedeby in Denmark in 827 and to Birka in Sweden around 850 and built the first churches in both Denmark and Sweden. He has been known as 'the Apostle of the North', misleadingly says Else Roesdahl. The foreign mission, such as it was, was of little consequence. The bringing of Christianity was the Scandinavians' own doing.

The project was political. It was a way of strengthening royal authority, in which 'few worried particularly much about beliefs'. Norsemen encountered Christianity abroad and were impressed by the wealth and splendour they saw, and by the respect the Christian faith commanded. By converting, the former pagan kings would make themselves equals of allies and adversaries alike, could deal with Europeans on an equal footing and be accepted as members of what was understood as civilised culture. Kings could not be European kings without being Christian, and when kings were Christian barons could not be barons without following suit.

Once the new faith was 'official' in the sense of having established royal backing, a Church organisation would emerge and take hold around permanent bishoprics, cathedral-churches, parishes and ordained priests. The Churches gradually made themselves more independent of lay authority and claimed various privileges, such as independence from secular jurisdiction and freedom from taxation. Bishops took on the authority to bestow God's blessing on kings. The Christian faith, says Delisle Burns in his study of medieval Christianity, was the force 'through which moral authority was infused into political and economic institutions'. It was the victorious religion under an international Church and ever stronger papal leadership. It does not take much explanation as to why it made it to the north.

All the more so since the faith that gave way was without morality. Doing right by the old gods was a matter of satisfying them. They were not worshipped but called on. They were given silver and gold, and food to eat. They were sacrificed to. The normal sacrifice was animals: calves, cattle, oxen, horses – sometimes dead meat. These pre-Christians had a thing about blood. In their ceremonies, blood was collected from animals or humans and sprinkled on the participants and inside houses. Battlefields were soaked in 'blood-rain'. The Valkyries separated the dead from the living by weaving fabrics of entrails, dripping in blood. Their sacrifices did include people, men, women and children, which is not in dispute although the extent of human sacrifice is not clear. Master Adam said that there were sacrificial ceremonies at Uppsala every nine years, for nine days, with human sacrifice – but of the ceremonies he remarked that they were unseemly and that it was best to keep silent about them, except for a mention that both beasts and men were suspended in a holy tree and left to rot. A tapestry from the Oseberg grave mound contains an image of a tree with a row of men hanging from it, in what appears to be a ritual ceremony. Snorri says that the Svears at Uppsala once blamed their king for years of bad harvest and killed him in sacrifice (whereupon the harvest was good). The humans who were sacrificed were often slaves, but not necessarily.

A King Aun in Sweden, says Snorri, sacrificed eight of his own sons in a pact with Odin for a long life. This may not have been the literal truth, but it is told as not being unbelievable. When in one encounter Olav Tryggvason was asked to revert back to the old faith and to confirm it by conducting a sacrifice, he retorted that if so it would be nothing less than human sacrifice and that those sacrificed would not be 'slaves and others worthless' but the local chiefs themselves. As late as around 1000, a German Bishop Thietmar tells of a festival celebrated at Lejre in Denmark every nine years on New Year's Day. Here were sacrificed, he says, ninety-nine men, ninety-nine horses, ninety-nine dogs and ninety-nine cocks. Against this, the bearers of the new faith brought with them a gospel of faith, mercy, peace, the liberation of slaves and help to the poor, all of which would have seemed remarkable to pagan Scandinavians. The old faith just could not compete.

Christianity was the official religion in Denmark from the year 965, by decree of Harald Bluetooth. Over the next two centuries nearly 3,000 parish churches were built, mostly under local patronage. Already by 1070, there were churches in half of the places that have churches today. There were eight bishoprics. These were soon to hold land in ownership, eventually about four of every ten acres. By 1200 there were about sixty monasteries, sharing in the ownership of land. In 1104 an archbishopric was established in Lund in Skåne, ending the authority of Hamburg-Bremen. The tithe was introduced as the first regularised national tax, certainly by the early 1100s, in principle awarding the Church 10 per cent of all production. By the thirteenth century the ecclesiastical class comprised about one in every 300 of the population.

The Norwegian conversion had to wait for the two Olavs. Olav Tryggvason, who had, like Håkon the Good, been baptised in England and come back with priests and made himself king (in 995), gathered his chiefs and told them that he would convert all of Norway – or die! He set off through the country to command reluctant people to accept the faith. His method, as Snorri tells it, was simple: he told the people to convert or fight. Those who spoke against him he punished; some he killed, some he mutilated, some he drove out of the land.

Olav Haraldsson, king from 1015, followed in the same fashion.

He had also been converted abroad, in his case baptised in Rouen in Normandy. When he learned that people in Trøndelag held on to their heathen ways, he went up the fjord with five ships and 300 men, killed the local chiefs and many more as well, held others hostage, and, in Snorri's telling, 'converted all of the people to the right faith'. When he came through Gudbrandsdalen he was met by a local chief called Gudbrand – *Dale-Gudbrand*, 'Gudbrand of the Valley' – who did not much heed Olav's god, 'whom we cannot even see'. Our own god, he explained, is there in our temple, big and strong and with a hammer in his hand; we offer him gold and silver and feed him to eat every day. This god-statue was carried out of the temple for the intruders to behold. Olav arranged for one of his men to crush it. It fell apart, and 'mice as big as cats' fled from the wreckage. It's just folly, said Olav, take the Christian faith or fight me here today. 'We have suffered much damage to our god,' said Gudbrand, 'but as he still could not help us we will now believe in the god you believe in.' Thus happened much of the Norwegian conversion, the old gods being proven to have no wrath to bring down upon even violent intruders.

This Olav became St Olav by virtue of miracles after his death. His face remained clear and fresh, as if he were sleeping. Blood from his body healed the wounds of those who cleaned it. A blind man could see again. Where his body was hidden there was a sheen of light in the night. It was buried in secrecy. It was exhumed, buried again at a church, and then exhumed once more after a year. His face was still fresh. His hair and nails had grown as if he had been living, and hair that was cut from the corpse would not burn. A source sprang from where his body had been first buried, with healing water. His official decree of canonisation was to list twenty-five miracles. At his first burial site was built a chapel, then a church and eventually the splendid Nidaros Cathedral.

NIDAROS CATHEDRAL

The finest cathedral in Scandinavia was raised in the most peripheral of the early archbishoprics, in Nidaros (meaning estuary of River Nidar), today's Trondheim. Other cathedrals are in Lund, Roskilde and Uppsala, grand as well, the one in Uppsala the biggest, but it is Nidaros that has the feel of a cathedral to match the most imposing European ones. It is Catholic in appearance but now a house of the Evangelical Lutheran Church.

Building started in 1070, forty years after Olav's death, and it was finished in its first incarnation by around 1300. St Olav's remains were contained in a silver casket behind the high altar, which was looted from the church by the Danish King Christian II (king until 1520) in order for the silver to be melted down, the saint's remains being buried in an unknown place under the cathedral floor.

As the Kingdom of Norway declined, so did its first church. It was neglected during the period of Danish overrule and damaged by fires in 1327, 1531, 1708 and 1719. During the Seven Years War (1563–70), it was used as a stable by Swedish armies. In 1689 the tower collapsed, destroying much of the structure. Reconstruction started as a national project in the 1800s.

It is a cruciform church in Romanesque Gothic style, with a now imposing façade, the West Front. This had deteriorated to near-destruction, making its reconstruction, undertaken between 1905 and 1983, difficult and controversial. The façade has three rows of sculptures above the entrance level, fifty-six in all, arranged around an image of the Crucifixion. The sculptures depict Old Testament prophets and kings, New Testament scenes and theological virtues, and, on the lower level, a parade of apostles and saints, St Peter and St Paul flanking the Crucifixion scene. From the original front only five sculptures had survived, now preserved as museum pieces. All the present sculptures on the West Front are from the restoration period. In the middle of the façade is a large round rose window of stained glass with themes from biblical stories, and on each side imposing bell towers.

There was a final controversy over the central tower: with or without spire? A spire had been erected in the early phase of restoration but it had long been criticised by architects and historians. The debate became intense and raged for years. *Stortinget* (Parliament) in 1971 decided to have the spire removed, but the decision was scuppered by a parliamentary faction which was able to prevent the appropriation of funds. The spire survived, as a historical mistake but to the pleasure, mostly, of the people of Trondheim.

Nidaros Cathedral, the West Front

By about 1100 Norway had three bishoprics, Nidaros, Oslo and Bergen, and fifty years later two more: Stavanger and Hamar. Monasteries were being established, at first with imported monks, mainly from England. The tithe started to be collected from the early 1100s. Nidaros was made an archbishopric in 1152 (or 1153 or 1154), again ending the authority of Hamburg-Bremen, with an area of responsibility including the Shetlands, Orkneys, Hebrides, the Isle of Man, the Faroes, Iceland and Greenland. By the coming of the Big Death there were 1,300 churches and a clerical class of 3,000 persons. As in Denmark, the Church owned 40 per cent of the land. Income from land rent was about equal to that from the tithe. The clerical class was rich and its members lived well and in comfort.

Olof Skötkonung in Sweden converted around 990, probably baptised by an emissary from England. By the end of the next century Sweden had become predominantly Christian, not without at least two missionaries having been slain as martyrs and a king, one Inge, having been driven out of his kingdom for refusing to officiate at sacrificial ceremonies – but taking revenge by returning and tearing down the old temple at Uppsala and building a church in its place. The Church became established during the twelfth century, with four bishoprics by the time Uppsala became an archbishopric in 1164. As in Denmark and Norway, the establishment of a Church organisation was followed by the building of cathedrals, monasteries and parish churches, with cathedrals and monasteries becoming landowners, and the tithe a regular tax.

The first churches were of wood and have mostly disappeared, except for some surviving 'stave' churches, all but two in Norway. At least 2,000 were built in that country alone, though now only twenty-eight remain. They are so called because the structures rest on wood rather than stone pillars. The earliest ones disappeared when their pillars rotted. Those that still stand were built with better technology: the pillars were petrified so as to be resistant to rot and woodworm. This was done by identifying the trees that would serve as pillars and cutting off their tops and branches, then leaving them on root for another five to ten years. They continued to suck sap from the ground which had nowhere to go and thus solidified in the trunk. The church builders learned to set the pillars on dry-stone foundations rather than directly in the ground.

The early churches were often built on sites with previous pagan temples – although some historians think that the old religion did not have many temples, or temples of much note – and there was a great deal of continuity, some of which is visible in remaining churches. They were originally dark with only small slots for light to come in; windows were put in later, as were pews. Their decorations go back to pre-Christian Norse styles, with dragon heads and the foliate ornaments of twisting serpents and monster-like animals. Some builders carved pagan symbols and figures in dark corners, as, one imagines, insurance in case the new faith might not prove supreme.

With Church organisation came various new skills and ideas. One, as we have seen, was writing, and the common European language of Latin. For a couple of centuries all writing, including that on behalf of kings, was in the hands of churchmen.

Another new, related idea was education and study, again initially a Church prerogative. It was the partnership of State and Church that enabled the revival of learning in Europe. In 789 Charlemagne decreed that cathedrals and monasteries establish schools. The first cathedral school in Scandinavia opened in Lund in 1085. Cathedrals ran schools for the preparation of new clergy. The recruits would mostly come from wealthy families, but could also be other promising young men whom the Church would co-opt. They would undertake studies, be ordained, train for some years as junior priests, then take up posts. Some, but very few, went on to further studies abroad, sometimes in the theological or other sciences, such as mathematics or astronomy, sometimes in philosophy, sometimes in law. Universities were in operation in Bologna, Paris and Oxford from around 1200, colleges earlier. The clergy was the first class of educated men.

Yet another novelty was poor relief. There had been some provisions for care of orphans in early law – although unwanted children were also susceptible to being set out to die. With Christianity came the idea of a duty to help the poor, even an idealisation of the poor – Jesus had himself been poor, after all. Poverty as we think of it now did not exist since almost everyone was poor, but there were beggars without family who were reduced to wandering for mercy. Itinerants could turn to churches and monasteries for at least some help.

Kings – and kingdoms?

With Gudfred in Denmark, we are at the beginning of the beginning of what in time was to become kingdoms and, eventually, nations. Early on there were chiefs in regional domains. During the Viking Age, dominant chiefs started to claim national authority. By the end there were countries and kingdoms, if still wobbly ones.

Gudfred had gained control over what is today's Denmark, southern parts of present-day Sweden, and areas up the Swedish coast and into the south-eastern regions of Norway. The Danish claim to territories in Swedish and Norwegian land persisted through and beyond the Viking Age in what would be a lasting source of Scandinavian conflict. He probably also dominated parts of the Continental coast to the Baltic Sea, where he destroyed Slavic trading centres and had the trade moved to his own port of Hedeby in southern Denmark. He ravaged the Frisian coast to the west in what was becoming the Viking way.

He did not in any modern sense govern a country, but just claimed superiority over other barons. Kings were in control as long as lesser warlords were unable to revolt and as long as they accepted the king's authority by paying him tribute – taxes, that is – and providing him with soldiers and crews for raiding and warfare. Anyone could call himself king who was, says Neil Price, the first and most able of entrepreneurs. Successful ones had to maintain their superiority with

force, against constant challenge. Warfare was the order of the day –
internally against rebellious barons and often relatives, typically uncles,
brothers and sons, often egged on by wives and mothers, externally
against enemies eyeing up the king's territory. Gudfred's territorial
control did not survive him. As was to happen again and again, when
the king went his sons took to the sword against each other. It was
to be centuries before kingship shifted from control to governance,
and further centuries again before governance made warfare obsolete.

Gudfred was an ambitious king who thought highly of himself and
his powers, a madman, the Franks thought. The big enemy to the south
was none less than Charles the Great, emperor from 800 to 814 of what
would later be the Holy Roman Empire, to whom Gudfred may have
thought himself equal. Gudfred protected himself against the Franks
by waging war on them, but with little success. His territory was in
the main not occupied, probably because it was not worth Charles's
trouble. He only once went after the Danes in anger, in 808, when
Gudfred's army had entered Frankish territory and Gudfred 'boasted
that he would march to Aachen, dethrone Charles, chase the Franks back
across the Rhine and stamp out Christianity'. As soon as he was rid of
Gudfred, Charles settled the northern problem in a pact with a nephew
of Gudfred, at a treaty-meeting in 811 of twelve *primores* on each side.

Up against the southern enemy, Gudfred improved the *Danevirke*
walled fortifications to control the ancient land route (later knowns as
the *Hærvej* in Danish, 'the army route') leading into Jylland north from
Germany. Those fortifications had been established before his time and
were to be a lasting line of defence, put to use finally more than a thousand years on, in the Danish–Prussian War of 1864, when little Denmark
was to meet the cynical wrath of Otto von Bismarck of Prussia.

In taking on Charlemagne, Gudfred inaugurated what was to be and
has remained a Scandinavian preoccupation with being powerful, with
being of impact, with being noticed, heeded and respected. The urge
to glory was one of many motivations driving first the Vikings and in
later centuries Danish and Swedish kings to play the game of being
big powers in Europe. The Danes of the 1860s were as vainglorious
up against Bismarck as was Gudfred against Charles the Great. The
main instrument of this preoccupation was for centuries to be warfare,
but the quest for eminence has outlasted the Scandinavians' claim
to martial strength and is visible today in their habit of presenting
themselves to the world as a 'model' for others in good governance,

peace-making and welfare state excellence.* Olof Palme, Prime Minister of Sweden during the 1970s and 1980s, and king of social democratic Scandinavia, was no less assertive of Swedish–Scandinavian excellence and in wanting to stand up to the superpowers of the day than were his big-power predecessors.

About thirty kings followed Gudfred during the next two centuries, most of them unknown to history except for some of their names. Gorm the Old claimed the title from about 936 to 958, and may have been able to hold on to a good deal of Danish territory. His son was the Harald Bluetooth who claimed, on the rune-stone he raised at Jelling, that he 'won for himself all of Denmark and Norway and made the Danes Christian'.

Notable kings of the Viking Age, with approximate years of reign

Years	Denmark	Norway	Sweden
800	Gudfred 804–10		
850			
		Harald Finehair 872–931	
900			
		Eirik Bloodaxe 931–34	
	Gorm the Old 936–58	Håkon the Good 935–61	
950	Harald Bluetooth 958–86		
		Harald Bluetooth 961–80	
	Svend Forkbeard 986–1014	Olav Tryggvason 995–1000	Olof Skötkonung 995–1022
1000		Svend Forkbeard 1000–13	
	Knud the Great 1019–35	Olav Haraldsson 1015–28	Anund 1022–50
	Hardeknud 1035–42	Knud the Great 1028–35	
	Magnus the Good 1042–47	Magnus the Good 1035–47	
1050	Svend Estridsen 1047–76	Harald Hardrade 1046–66	Edmund 1050–60
	Knud the Holy 1080–86		
1100	Niels 1104–34		

---

* I myself, for my sins, am the co-editor (with Robert Erikson, Erik Jørgen Hansen and Hannu Uusitalo) of a book on Scandinavian social policy under the title *The Scandinavian Model*.

If Gudfred had been in control of Denmark and Harald later 'won' it, had it in the meantime been lost? A later king, Svend Estridsen, king from 1047, said to Adam of Bremen that kingship had indeed collapsed. It is thought that a German army captured at least a good deal of Danish territory in 974, but lost it back to Harald again in 983, wherefore he could rightly boast that he had won 'all of Denmark'.

Harald was killed fighting a rebellion by a son, that Svend Forkbeard who finally, if only for five weeks, also called himself King of England. He won the southern part of Norway by defeating Olav Tryggvason in the Battle of Svolder, in southern Sweden, where Olav was said to have jumped overboard from his ship and vanished in the sea.

He was followed by Knud the Great, who was followed by Hardeknud, on whose death in 1042 (he died of a stroke during heavy drinking) the royal line from Gorm died out and Denmark fell into disorder and civil war. The Crown was taken over by Magnus the Good of Norway, whose reign lasted five years until it was reclaimed by Svend Estridsen. He in turn managed to hold the kingdom together until he died in 1076, leaving at least twenty children by many women. Five of his sons followed as kings over the next fifty-eight years. The most notable of these was Knud the Holy, king from 1080 to 1086, later to become patron saint of Denmark, ambitious, intent on strengthening the power of the Crown, but in the process giving rise to resistance for heavy-handedness with taxation. When he made plans to retake England he provoked a rebellion which he failed to put down, took refuge in a church, and was killed there along with a brother and various of his retinue. These events were followed by crop failures, which were interpreted as divine punishment for the slaying of a pious king. Miracles were seen around his grave. A brother and later king lobbied the pope for canonisation, which was achieved in 1101. The last of the sons was Niels, who held the throne for thirty years, from 1104 to 1134, by the end of which period Denmark collapsed into another civil war of succession.

Hafrsfjord is in the south-west of Norway, near the city of Stavanger, now the country's petroleum capital. If you visit what is thought to be the site of the battle you will find a memorial of national pride in the shape of three mighty swords, of unclear symbolism, stuck into a rock.

Norway at the time was a patchwork of chiefdoms, some of which were Harald Finehair's domains. He started to claim kingship while still a teenager, travelling the country and extracting loyalty from local chiefs as he went. Those not brought to heel formed an alliance and mobilised a joint force which met up at Hafrsfjord, where Harald was waiting with a force of his own. The two sides engaged in battle, which Snorri describes as 'long and hard', and out of which Harald came victorious. Many of the challenger chiefs were killed, as were many of their men, and survivors fled in all directions. Harald proclaimed himself King of all of Norway and claimed the right to collect taxes from a broad swathe of territory, although he did not bring the northern parts under his control, nor (decisively) the south-eastern parts traditionally claimed by Denmark. His rule lasted until about 931. After his death his kingdom disintegrated in feuding between his sons, of which he is said to have had about twenty and upon most of whom he sought to bestow dignity and position. Another embryo of nationhood, then, but again only an early and unfulfilled yearning.

Of Harald's sons, Eirik, known as Bloodaxe, claimed the throne from 931 to 934, killing various half-brothers in the process (hence his honour name), gaining few friends and many enemies, only to be deposed by another brother, Håkon the Good. Eirik for a while clamed also to be King of Northumbria, and when deposed fled to England where he engaged in more fighting and died in 954, probably killed by one of his own men. Håkon's reign was tenuous, dominated by fighting Bloodaxe's sons, who finally prevailed when the king was killed in battle in 961. Another Harald, son of Eirik, claimed the kingship from 961 to 970, but was not in control of territory beyond western Norway. Harald Bluetooth of Denmark claimed for himself the Norwegian Crown, also in 961. The Norwegian Harald was in due course lured to Denmark and killed in a plot arranged by a Sigurd Håkonsson, whose son, Håkon Sigurdsson, was installed as Bluetooth's proxy king in Norway. He ruled, after a fashion, until 995 when, during a rebellion, and hiding in a pigsty on a farm, he was killed by a slave.

Grasping the opportunity offered by chaos, another pretender to the Crown, Olav Tryggvason again (who claimed to be the great-grandson of Harald Finehair and who had been enriching himself by raiding far and wide in both eastern and western Viking areas, most profitably in England) returned to Norway and was received as king by some of the barons, thanks to the bribes in silver he was able to pay them. He stimulated the rebellion against Håkon and pledged a reward to anyone who would kill him. Håkon's slave, hiding with him in the pigsty, responded by cutting off his head and presenting it to Olav for the reward, only to have his own head cut off, being a mere slave. Olav was the first Norwegian king to mint coins, with himself as king on one side and Christian iconography on the other. He built a huge fleet, including the legendary *Long Serpent*, and set off to subdue more territory in Denmark and along the Baltic shores, but was eventually trapped and defeated at Svolder.

After Olav Tryggvason had been eliminated, Danish kings held sway in Norway until the arrival of the next Olav, the one who was to be saint, Olav Haraldsson. He was born around 995 and was not more than twelve years of age when he embarked on the expected career of raiding and pillaging, first around the Baltic Sea and then on to England, where he rented himself out sometimes to Danish armies fighting the English, sometimes to English armies fighting the Danes. In 1015, aged twenty, he landed on the western coast of Norway with only two ships, and fought and bought his way to controlling by the next year the territories up to Trøndelag in mid-country. He is now revered as a good king: lawful, fair, bringer of Christianity, but it did not go well for him at the time. The Norwegian barons turned against him, probably as a result of aggressive land confiscation, and he forfeited the support of common folk – 'if he ever had it', says the historian Claus Krag. The Danes took revenge, in the form of a large fleet under Knud the Great. He landed in Norway in 1028, bribed his way to loyalty from eager barons and proclaimed himself king. Olav fled through Sweden and took refuge in Novgorod at the court of Yaroslav, known as 'the Wise'.

Yaroslav tried to dissuade him from any further Norwegian ambition, offering him instead (as kings at the time would do) a land of Bulgaria, where the people were still pagans and where he could enrich himself as he wanted. But in early 1030 Olav nevertheless mobilised to return to a divided Norway, where he had some allies but more enemies. He marched through Sweden raising troops as he went, 'an assortment of unidentifiable riff-raff [highway robbers, according to Snorri], many of them heathens'. His enemies raised an army of perhaps 14,000 men, unprecedented at the time (and probably a later exaggeration), while he himself had no more than between 3,000 and 4,000. They met at the Battle of Stiklestad on 29 July, where Olav was defeated and killed and from the ashes of which would rise the future

King Harald Hardrade, of Stamford Bridge 1066 fame. The 29th of July remains celebrated in Norway as *Olsok*, when each year the epic battle is re-enacted in a festival at Stiklestad.

Although Olav personally failed, his cause prevailed. Norway was won for Christianity. Olav was sainted and his grave became the most important Christian pilgrimage destination in Scandinavia, as it remains to this day. (The main pilgrims' route passes below the ancestral farm of my family in the village of Tretten in Gudbrandsdalen, where each summer a trickle of pilgrims move north. As in previous times, accommodation is arranged in farms and inns along the route.)

Knud and two sons, and a consort, ruled in Norway until 1035, when the tables turned and Magnus the Good, the illegitimate son of the second Olav, was proclaimed king at the age of eleven, and in 1042 also King of Denmark. Magnus had been taken by his father into refuge at Yaroslav's court, where he grew up. From there Norwegian barons opposed to the Danish rule brought him back home when they were able to depose the Danes. He became a fierce and successful warrior king, reunited the Norwegian and Danish Crowns, probably intended to re-establish Knud the Great's combined rule of Norway, Denmark and England, but died in 1047, stumbling off his ship and drowning aged twenty-three. Norwegian claims to the Danish throne were never again effective.

Harald, to be Hardrade, was born in 1015, the son of a minor chief and the half-brother of the saintly Olav Haraldsson. In 1030, aged fifteen, he fought with Olav in the Battle of Stiklestad, where he was wounded in the defeat. He first hid in Norway to recover, then made his way into exile at the court of Yaroslav (now in Kyiv), where he served in the guard and learned the art of warfare and command.

After a few years, and with a force of fifty men, he moved on to Constantinople and went into the service of Emperor Michael IV in the élite Varangian Guard. He fought on various fronts, throughout the Mediterranean, in Africa against 'the bluemen' and into Asia Minor, perhaps making it to Jerusalem, perhaps as far as Mesopotamia, rising to positions of command. When Michael died he became embroiled in court infighting, may have been imprisoned and may have escaped in heroic circumstances.

In the emperor's service Harald amassed a huge fortune in silver and gold, partly from the spoils of war and probably also court plunder, booty he was able (miraculously) to ship back to Yaroslav's court for safekeeping (miraculously) and eventually bring back (miraculously) to Norway. He arrived laden with silver and gold in such quantity that the ships could barely manage. The Norwegian throne had now been restored to Magnus the Good. Harald used his booty from Byzantium to buy from Magnus, who was broke, a position as co-regent, thus making himself one of two Norwegian kings, until Magnus died the next year, 1047, and Harald was sole king.

But not as big a king as he throught he should be. He set about recapturing the Danish throne and set his sights on restoring Knud the Great's empire of the north. That resulted in almost constant warfare against the Danes from 1050, raiding for fifteen years running, in a relentless campaign of terror. The town of Hedeby, Denmark's trading centre and Scandinavia's largest town, was looted, burned and destroyed, never to recover. But, for all his ruthlessness, he failed to bring Denmark under his control. In 1066, as we have seen, he attacked England, failed again and was killed.

From then on, for another seventy years, Norway had kings who were sons of Harald and sons of sons etc. down to Magnus the Blind. The line stopped with him in an orgy of infighting when he was defeated in battle by a co-regent uncle, who was himself killed the next year in his sleep by yet another pretender, Sigurd Slembe, 'the Bad'. The murder, however, did not work. Instead of becoming king, Sigurd was captured and tortured to death. Magnus became known as 'the Blind' when, on his defeat, he was not only dethroned but also castrated, amputated of one foot and blinded. Norway had now descended into a century of civil war.

Olof's reign in Sweden was from about 995 to 1022, but what he reigned over is much in dispute. He probably died of natural causes, unusually at the time for men in power, but another legend has it that he was killed somewhere near what was later to be Stockholm for refusing to respect pagan gods.

The territory that at the time might have been thought of as in some sense Swedish was much less than later became Sweden. Areas towards the north were either empty and uninteresting or Norwegian, or both. The southern parts, Skåne and nearby lands, were under Danish control, as were coastal lands to the west towards the Kattegat. (Danish territory in south Sweden comprised roughly three counties, what are now Skåne, Halland and Blekinge, but which are here for convenience usually referred to as simply Skåne or Skåne-lands.) Only in the thirteenth century would a corridor to the Kattegat come under Swedish control at the estuary of the River Göta, where today sits the city of Gothenburg. In the territory he did hold, however, Olof introduced something new in Sweden: kingly control of the kind Gudfred had brought to Denmark.

The core regions in this early version of Sweden were the lands of the *Svear* (around Lake Mälaren, inland from what is now Stockholm) and of the *Götar* (to the south thereof). The lands of the *Götar* were divided into Western and Eastern Götaland (not to be confused with the island of Gotland). Olof Skötkonung was the first king to control both these lands, as well as the lands of the *Svear*, and may have been able to claim tribute from areas across the Baltic Sea in what are now Estonia and Latvia.

Olof was described as a peaceful king by Adam of Bremen, but that would have been unlikely at the time and was probably to put a Christian gloss on an inevitably barbarian story. His reign was, as it had to be, dominated by conflict and war with other barons in Swedish lands, with the majority pagan population who resented his Christianity and his tearing down of their temples, and with Danish and Norwegian chiefs, and no doubt Baltic ones, who laid claim to lands he also wanted.

Getting to be a king in early Scandinavia was a complicated matter. You obviously needed enough power to dominate others who also aspired to be kings or who wanted territory you intended to control. But there was also procedure. Kings were elected or proclaimed at *thing*. It was helpful, but not necessary, to be an heir, near or distant, to an earlier king. Svend Estridsen claimed the right to the Danish Crown by inheritance but still took care to have his claim confirmed and reconfirmed at *thing* across the realm. For more than 200 years kings in Norway claimed legitimacy by belonging to Harald Finehair's line. In Sweden the hereditary principle mattered less and kingship was more elective. A convention was emerging that kings should be accepted on a journey from county to county, and finally anointed and crowned in Uppsala Cathedral.

Olof was succeeded by two sons (by different mothers), Anund from about 1022 to 1050 and Edmund from 1050 to 1060. The kingdom, if that is what it was, did not flourish, and with Edmund the royal line, if that is what is was, died out. More men followed to call themselves kings, none of quality, and so ended the Viking Age in Sweden. The project, the making of a kingdom, had been running for over a century but had not come far. There was no Sweden, and even the smaller part of it that Olof had subdued was in the chaos of civil wars and wars with outsiders.

These early kings were little more than successful gangsters. As a rule, they held on until they were killed and their departure was followed by violent anarchy. The story of kingship in the Viking Age is a story of failures. They wanted more. They wanted to secure power and pass it on. But almost none of them managed.

Even Knud the Great, the most eminent of Viking kings, created nothing that could last. He did not know how. When the Romans occupied England in the second invasion under Emperor Claudius in the year 43 AD, a thousand years before Knud, they incorporated England as a province of their empire by imposing their whole State structure. They brought laws and coinage, established capital cities, built roads, operated a postal system, maintained links of transport to the Continent, kept records and accounts and had an organised army under orderly lines of command. As a result, their rule in England was not dependent on kingly personalities and would last 400 years.

The reason why Knud's empire failed is that he had no knowledge of state-building. Nor did most other Scandinavian kings. They ruled by control exercised through local barons. Control depended on the standing of the king personally. Knud was a forceful leader and an impressive man, tall, strong and handsome. He brought in loyal barons and bought the loyalty of others. But he wrote no laws and created no institutions. When he died, there was no State in place to maintain continuous rule and the edifice just fell apart.

The early exemption from the rule of ignorance was Harald Hardrade. With him something new entered into Scandinavian kingship: a foretaste of State formation. As a human being he was of the worst sort: treacherous, deceiving, double-crossing, not to be trusted on his word, without loyalty, a terrorist, a mass murderer, a rapist. But he had possibly learned something about governing in the service of the emperor in Constantinople. He would have only a single second-in-command at a time. He proclaimed laws to apply nationally. He regulated royal succession. He minted coins from the treasure he had brought with him from Byzantium (first valued at the silver they contained but gradually, as the silver ran out, diluted to lesser value and giving the Norwegians an early taste of inflation). Importantly, he centralised power by emasculating local barons, making them dependent on him rather than he on them. That was possible in Norway because local barons there were neither rich nor strong. Those who mattered and who had some sense of autonomy were in Trøndelag, mid-country, the most prominent of whom was a legendary Einar Tambarskjelve, meaning 'strongbow' or 'big belly'. He might have been able to stand up to the tyrant. Harald solved the problem in the strongman way: he had Einar killed, and killed a son as well for good measure.

None of this adds up to a State, but not a single one of the men we have met so far who wanted to be kings understood that if rule is to last it must rest not only on their personal prowess but on institutions and structures that have some durability of their own.

We are in much the same predicament as with trade. There was organised trade out there, but the Scandinavians were unable to copy it. There was organised kingship out there, but the Scandinavians were mostly unable to learn from others. Why? How was it that they could not move on from gangsterism? The answer must be, again, that they were latecomers. They were scrambling to catch up, but never quite getting there. They wanted, they tried, but better ways eluded them. The best we can say, perhaps, is that they must have been learning. There was to be kingship of some quality down the road. Perhaps the Vikings were paving the way and making possible in the future what they themselves could not achieve.

But were they Scandinavians?

The Roman Empire in the west had collapsed, leaving a vacuum that predators could exploit: Muslim Arabs from the south, Magyars from the east and Norsemen from the north. Vikings could start their incursions into Russia and their land grabs in the west that were to become Normandy and Danish England.

The Byzantine Empire in the east flourished, with Constantinople the new Rome, presenting itself as a source of wealth and glory to traders, adventurers and mercenaries from Scandinavia. In a gallery in the Hagia Sofia in what is now Istanbul there is a runic piece of graffiti (one of several, some of which are in the shape of Viking ships) – 'Halfdan carved these runes' – from the ninth century, evidence of the Norsemen's early arrival in the distant metropole.

After the Romans withdrew from Britain around 400, groups of Germanic peoples from north-west Europe and southern Scandinavia migrated across the North Sea. In the year 367 Saxons overran still-Roman Londinium, establishing their city of Lundenwic – meaning 'port' or 'market' – and soon settled parts of southern and eastern England. A new English-Anglo-Saxon culture emerged and eventually became dominant, encouraged by long-established links between coastal England and coastal north-Continental Europe, notably Frisia, and stimulated by existing two-way exchanges across the North Sea. This culture was linked to that of Scandinavia by common roots and similarities in language, beliefs and habits. Old Norse and Old English were in the same language family of Germanic origin. Vikings from Scandinavia arriving in England could possibly have understood the local language. Ottar spoke with Alfred, or a scribe of his, and told him about his life and travels; there is no mention that they used interpreters. Scholars disagree about how close the languages might have been, and there were dialects within Old English as in Old Norse. Later on, the English and Norse languages probably grew closer when language in England had been influenced by the presence for some time of Norse settlers and rulers. Snorri tells of an escapee from the Battle of Stamford Bridge who asked a farmer if he would sell him his fur coat, which the farmer refused, because 'you are a Norseman, I recognise you from your language'.

On the Continent a Frankish kingdom started to make itself dominant, consolidated under Charlemagne. He built not only an empire but also a State with a reasonably well-organised central and local administration, co-opted the Christian Church, and with its help revived education and the use of writing. (Charles was himself eager to be literate, but never mastered Latin reading and writing, at least not beyond the rudimentary and not until late in life.)

This greater European area was one of interlinked and connected cultures and peoples in continuing migration and trade. Archaeological finds in Scandinavia have revealed coins, jewellery, glass drinking vessels and other luxuries from across the Continent and beyond, dating back to Roman times. Christian belief might have been present in Scandinavia well ahead of the official conversions. The Scandinavians were interacting with eastern, southern and western Europeans before the Viking Age. They used iron. Theirs was of low quality, bog ore smelted in small-scale farm-based production, but they may perhaps have learned to extract it in sufficient quantity to have been able to export it from the seventh or eighth century. Walrus was valuable both for the ivory and for high-quality rope made from the hides. Ottar said of his team that they captured sixty walruses in two days. The Norwegian trade in dried fish started during the Viking Age. Eventually, when Scandinavia became integrated in Christian Europe, it grew to a scale that explains the emergence of Bergen as Norway's biggest and richest city.

They exchanged skills in iron-working, to make tools and weapons, and fashioning gold, silver and copper to make jewellery. The Sutton Hoo find in southern England, dating from the early seventh century, before the arrival of the Vikings but hardly before English-Norse trade, revealed a mound in the Scandinavian style over a rich burial, with a longship loaded with tools and luxuries to accompany probably a king of East Anglia on his voyage to the next world. In *Beowulf*, the oldest written English epic poem, possibly committed to vellum in the eighth century, the protagonist is a Geat, meaning Dane, and the story, says Anders Winroth, 'entirely Scandinavian'.

The Scandinavians who were entering the European stage as Vikings were shaped by the lands they inhabited. They were rural people and lived in dispersed settlements. Slaves did the hard work. Freemen were mostly farmers, but some part-time craftsmen such as boat-builders, blacksmiths and gold- and silversmiths. The nobles either did warfare or practised for it. They were honoured with more names than others. All were known by their given name, say Svend or Astrid, and by a second name of lineage, say Gudbrandsdottir. Men of high standing might also have a name of honour, such as 'the Good' or 'Finehair', but not all honour names were all that honourable, as for example 'the Lisp and Lame' for a Swedish King Erik, or in *Njál's Saga* a warrior called Ulf the Unwashed. Family names did not start to come into common usage until the fifteenth century, in Denmark being made obligatory for the nobility by royal decree in 1526.

They were of the same kind and looked alike. They had a shared ancestry, shared conventions in art and poetry, and in costume and building works. They had a common language of Germanic origin. They had a great deal of interaction, both peaceful and warlike, with much intermarriage among nobles. Kings in whatever country belonged to families that extended throughout Scandinavia and beyond. Viking armies and fleets could be made up of ships and crew from all three lands. They were makers of fine jewellery, of silver and gold and other metals, decorated in shared and distinctive styles. They were master woodcarvers. They had a religion and believed in many gods, goddesses and spirits. 'A culture finds the gods it needs', observes Kevin Crossly-Holland, 'and the Norse world needed gods to justify the violence that is one of its hallmarks.' When the early Vikings set off on western raids they were pagans attacking Christians, and there was an element of religious war to it.

There were towns that served as centres of trade. The most eminent of these was Hedeby in Denmark ('town of heathens'), which flourished from the ninth to the eleventh century as a centre of trade between Europe, Scandinavia and the Baltic. Its permanent population might have reached about 1,000 people. The town of Ribe, on the western coast, operated as a settlement of artisans and traders from around a century earlier.

The first town of note in Sweden was Birka, on an island in Lake Mälaren. There had previously been a trading post nearby, at Helgö ('holy island'), and there might have been others now forgotten. Lake Mälaren was then level with the Baltic Sea and easily reachable by ship. Birka might have been established as a royal concession and source of royal trade revenue around 750 and functioned until it was abandoned about 200 years later, for unknown reasons. Its population was possibly somewhere between 500 and 1,000.

Gotland was a centre for the Baltic trade, with Visby becoming a town from around the year 900. Unlike Hedeby and Birka, Visby has continued to flourish to our time.

Kaupang in Norway was the only trading town of any size in Viking Age Norway (the name means 'trading town', as would later Copenhagen). It was situated at the entrance to the Oslo Fjord and was in operation from around the 780s until it was abandoned in the early tenth century when larger vessels could not enter its bay. The population might have reached about 500. Bergen started to emerge as a trading town towards the end of the eleventh century.

There were differences. Denmark was early in modernisation, Sweden late. Both Adam of Bremen and Snorri single out Norway as the poorest of the lands. We must suppose that Gudfred had awareness of a land of Denmark and Harald Finehair of Norway. When the *Danevirke*, or 'Danish fortification', became known under that name is uncertain. Perhaps already in Gudfred's time. King Gorm etched the name Denmark on his stone at Jelling. Ottar said he was from Norway. But whether Olof Skötkonung's domain was Sweden is less clear; the *Svear* were the people of one of his provinces.

What they did not have is what we now know as countries and borders. Territories were what kings could control. At times, Danish kings controlled Norwegian and Swedish territories, Norwegian or Swedish ones Danish lands, and so on in ever-shifting constellations.

As to the majority of common people, of whom next to nothing can be gleaned from the sources, we cannot know at this distance what their thinking was regarding nationality. Would they have said of themselves that they were Danes or Norwegians or Swedes, and were they in their own minds Scandinavians? Probably not. Even the early Vikings presented themselves abroad as men of their region, say of Hordaland rather than of Norway. They would primarily have belonged to family and clan. They were by nature local and would not have known much of the world outside their community. 'They had no notion of loyalty to a state or fatherland.' The concepts of country, state and nation did not exist.

If a nation is made up of a people with, in some sense, a shared identity, under a set of reasonably stable State institutions and within reasonably defined borders, we are very far from that at this stage of the story. Denmark had started the journey first, but an early start turned out to be no advantage. It was the leading and most prosperous power, and had built itself up to imperial ambition, only to collapse into chaos. Soon enough, by about 1300 the Danish Crown simply ceased to exist for a while as a result of excessive big-power ambition and resulting bankruptcy. Norway had followed, with a relatively strong royal State for a short while in the thirteenth century, but not a lasting one. Instead Norway would be subsumed by a recovered Denmark and cease to exist as a kingdom. Sweden, the latecomer, eventually fared the best. Here a strong and durable State emerged, one that would endure, even through much further trouble and turbulence. It would take a long time to establish what territory and what peoples this State should preside over, but the bedrock of the State was there that would render the late developer pre-eminent over the earlier starters.

Were they Europeans?

The great French historian Fernand Braudel insisted that history needs to be understood in the *longue durée*, but in Scandinavia there is not that much long perspective to draw on. To understand the Viking Age we need to accept the unpalatable truth that these lands were scrambling on the edge of Europe to catch up with the rest. Denmark, says Ole Fenger, started to become a partner in Europe only during a period of some stability after 1050.

The Scandinavians were agricultural, but at a low level of sophistication. They had the wheel, but without roads did not get much use out of it and it did not become an instrument of war for them. They had horses but depended on the Franks for quality. Travel was mainly by water. In time-distance, England and Norway were 'closer than an overland journey of thirty or forty miles'. The Norse built some fortifications, but neither forts nor palaces, only compounds behind ramparts of timber and earth. The Romans had invented concrete around 200 BC; a thousand years later the Scandinavians knew no other building materials than wood and earth. Stone churches had to wait until well into the Middle Ages, the first ones being built in Denmark (Roskilde) and Danish Skåne in 1035 and 1060 respectively, and only towards the end of the century did they start to be common. They traded but could not keep it up. They did not use currency, except silver by weight, sometimes in the form of coins of their own minting, sometimes as ingots. There was no merchant class and they had nothing resembling banking or insurance. The Romans, a millennium earlier, had large cities and administrative capitals, a flourishing literature, education and the remarkably successful Roman Law, complete with jurists as legal advisors and barristers. In England, Alfred the Great had his own history recorded in the *Anglo-Saxon Chronicle*; Knud the Great knew of nothing like it (but he did donate a confraternity book to Winchester Minster, complete with his own portrait and that of his wife, Emma of Normandy, whom he had taken on when she was widowed from King Æthelred of England, whom he had previously been fighting for the kingdom). In Denmark it was not until the late twelfth century that the keeping of some historical records started. There are 164 surviving charters issued by Charlemagne (who died in 814, it will be remembered); the earliest known Scandinavian royal charter is that of Knud the Holy from 1085. Charles governed with a constant flow of documents, accounts, lists, letters, statistics and written orders; nothing like it would be known in Scandinavia until 400 years later. They had laws, but not much by way of law enforcement, and only after the Viking Age national law, Hardrade's attempt notwithstanding. There were some trading towns but no cities, and therefore not the division of labour, industry and intellectual inventiveness that cities enable. They had nothing but the skimpiest notion of poor relief, in part because only with the late coming of Church organisation were there institutions in place which could take on the duty of charity. Charlemagne, in response to a famine of 778-9, had been able to call on the Church and issue instructions for alms and other reliefs for 'the starving poor', with some success. The Vikings would make themselves felt in Europe, but in spite of resource paucity rather than thanks to resource plenty. The peoples of the north would be aggressive, out of necessity, and go on to invade others, but it says much about who they were that no one took any interest in invading them. Danes had much to gain from raiding in England and Norwegians in Scotland and Ireland, but there was nothing to attract the peoples of those countries to counter-raid the lands of their tormentors.

It is heart-wrenching – there is no better term for it – to look back to the Scandinavia of a millennium ago. Those people who ventured out into Europe came from the fringe of the known world, as latecomers economically and culturally. It was not their fault that their homelands were at the end of the road and that their civilisation was rough around the edges when they were able to engage with the Byzantines, the Franks, the English. It was not their fault that they were small in number and poor in resources when they took on the big powers, and had no choice but to compensate with brute violence. But their underdevelopment goes a long way to explaining their reputation as barbarians. Abroad, they *were* fiercer than others for their disinterest in mercy. At home, they could have done with some peace and collaboration, and might have made something of themselves. They were small tribes, similar to one another in every way, yet wasted their potential in senseless, counterproductive and incessant inter-Scandinavian warfare. All they achieved from all that stupid fighting was to incur massive losses in the few resources they had.

Historians before me have wanted to tell the Viking story in the grand style, as one of conquests, wealth, empires and civilisation, of the great traders of the north. They have installed Knud the Great in the pantheon with Alfred, he who made England a going concern, with Charles, he who ruled almost all of Europe and who *governed* his empire to boot. The Vikings, it has been said, 'conquered the world'. But this is to overtell the story. There were achievements. If the project at home was to build kingdoms, that work had started. With the adoption of Christianity, the integration into the European community had also begun. But if we imagine ourselves back to around 1100 and gaze out over the Scandinavian landscape and the lands afar in which the Vikings operated, not much remains and a great deal has collapsed. Scandinavia itself fell into a century of chaos and civil wars. The Norse colonies of Iceland and the Faroes were unable to defend their independence. Greenland and America had been a reach too far. The Shetlands and Orkneys would be Scottish. In Ireland the Norse were Irish, in England English, and in Russia Russians. In Normandy they were French, the memory remaining only in the name. Vikings were successful as long as they stuck to what they knew, the combination of trade and pillage; but when they became ambitious and wanted empire they reached beyond their powers. Kingship and civilisation based on plunder from others could not last.

Excursion

Neighbours West and East

On 21 April 1971, a Danish naval ship arrived in the port of Reykjavik in Iceland. Much of the city's population was there to receive it, and many from other parts of the country. It was carrying a cargo of manuscripts, the original vellums of the *Codex Regius* (*Konungsbók*) and the *Book of Flatey* (*Flateyjarbók*). The *Codex Regius* is made up of forty-five vellum leaves of Old Norse poems. The *Book of Flatey* consists of 225 vellum leaves, richly illustrated, and is the largest book of remaining Icelandic medieval manuscripts. It contains the Sagas of a range of Norse kings, the histories of the Greenlanders, the Orkney and Faroe Islanders, an account of the Vinland settlement on the American continent and Eddic poetry.

One of the achievements of the settlers in Iceland was to write up their history and preserve the Norse heritage of oral poetry. Most of the medieval manuscripts had been removed from Iceland, some being sold and some taken by Danish royal decree to be preserved in Denmark. An Icelander, Árni Magnússon, was an early Professor of Antiquities at the University of Copenhagen and Secretary of the Royal Archives. He amassed a large collection of books and manuscripts, including as many Icelandic texts as he could find. On his death in 1730 he left his collection to the University of Copenhagen, which established the Árni Magnússon Collection for the preservation and study of ancient manuscripts.

In the Icelandic struggle for independence, the demand arose for the return of the classical manuscripts from Danish collections. In 1961, the Danish *Folketing* (Parliament) passed legislation to transfer a substantial proportion of these manuscripts to Iceland. Due to resistance in Denmark, its implementation was delayed and only settled by the Supreme Court in 1971. The *Konungsbók* and the *Flateyjarbók* were the first two manuscript compilations to be returned. A tangible national identity was being brought home.

From the first settlement in the late ninth century, Iceland's population grew to between 10,000 and 20,000 in the first century, by the eleventh century to possibly as many as 40,000, perhaps 60,000 a century later again.

The economy was fragile. Like other Atlantic islands, Iceland was dependent on imports, of grain in particular. To finance imports it needed exports. Wool soon became a major commodity. The Scandinavians used (and use) *vadmel*, a heavy thick-woven woollen cloth, stiff but warm and water-resistant. The Icelandic wool was well suited and became sought after, and remains an important export today. When the Norwegian Crown was able to tax Iceland, as of 1262, each taxpayer was liable for twenty lengths of *vadmel* a year.

Iceland was ravaged by epidemics in the fifteenth century which wiped out half of the population, and by a series of later famines. Official statistics start in 1703, recording a population of 50,000 which has subsequently grown to 350,000. This population growth has been assisted by Iceland's geology, which makes the land more hospitable than it should be by geography. There is access to naturally heated water, which both keeps the cold at bay and now enables the growing of fruit and vegetables in tracts of greenhouse agriculture.

The settlers established themselves without kingship in what has been called a commonwealth, with a unique political organisation. The *Althing*, 'Assembly of All', operated from about 930 at Thingvellir, the meadowlands near Reykjavik, in the bottom of the canyon where the Atlantic crack cuts through the country from south to north, causing the land mass to expand east and west by an inch or two per year. In addition, there were four regional and many local *thing*, and a network of elected chiefs known as 'good men'. These constitutional arrangements, along with Ancient Athens, count as original inventions of direct democracy.

The glory days were, however, short-lived. Due to economic decline and internal conflict, the Icelanders were unable to resist pressure from Norway for supremacy. In the 'Old Covenant' of 1262, their commonwealth was reduced to a Norwegian possession, soon converted to a Danish possession when Denmark absorbed Norway. Not until 1944 would there again be an independent Iceland, then reborn as a republic, again rejecting the Scandinavian tradition of monarchy. The Second World War enabled Iceland to break free from Denmark, formalising its independence with a 97 per cent referendum majority. Iceland fought on the Allied side, after the war joined NATO and entered into a pact with the United States in which the USA took responsibility for military defence from a base on the island, lasting until 2006. Iceland now defends itself with a Coast Guard – most recently in warlike action in the 'Cod Wars' with Britain over fishing rights, concluded in 1976 with a British climbdown – but has no standing army.

Since the settlement the Icelandic population has evolved from its own stock, with next to no 'alien' immigration. That has enabled various continuities. One is the Icelandic language, a variant of Old Norse, different enough now from the Scandinavian languages for them to be foreign to each other. With the preservation of language comes the preservation of name usage. Icelanders are known by their given name. The standard second name ends in –son or –dottir and denotes the paternal parentage of the person. Hence a woman with the glorious name of Vigdís Finnbogadóttir was the first female president. Some Icelanders, though, for historical reasons do have family names which are inherited down the line, such as the author Halldór Laxness, who was awarded the 1955 Nobel Prize in Literature. New given names can only be used if approved by an official naming committee.

Because of its homogeneity, the Icelandic population constitutes a unique laboratory for genetic research. That potential has been utilised by a private research organisation, known as deCODE, which has created a databank of DNA material of about a third of the population, and rising, which it uses for research of its own and by others on a commercial basis. This is controversial in Iceland, possibly because of the commercial element, but has contributed to enhanced knowledge about the population, such as its mixed origin from Scandinavian and Irish-Scottish roots.

The Norse settlement in Iceland spilled on further west. Eirik the Red was exiled from Iceland for murder. (His father had come to Iceland from Norway, also exiled for murder.) This was around the year 982, when he was about thirty years old. He had sent some of his slaves to a neighbouring farm; the farmer killed the slaves and Eirik killed the farmer. He sailed west to the land he was, in a propaganda trick, to call Greenland and explored for the duration of his exile, before going back to Iceland to persuade some of the lumpenproletariat to move west with him again.

The colony grew to perhaps 5,000 inhabitants. It was subjugated under the Norwegian Crown from 1262, and under the Danish Crown when Norway fell to Denmark. The settlement did not last and by the fifteenth century was no more.

The other migration to Greenland was by Inuit people from the north-west, most likely before the time of the Norse arrival. There was probably contact between the Norse and the Inuit, possibly conflict, and this might finally have contributed to the Norse abandonment of their settlements.

In the seventeenth century Denmark started to take an interest in Greenland again, sent expeditions to locate the old Norse settlements (unsuccessfully), asserted sovereignty over the island, and started to build a new Nordic settlement known as Godthåb – 'good hope' – in the south-west.

In one of the most bizarre happenings in Nordic history, Norway in 1931 tried to occupy a slice of eastern Greenland as a colony of its own, within the Danish colony, calling it Eirik the Red's Land (although it was in a part of the island where Eirik and his flock had never set foot). A governor, or *sysselmann* (a title of old Norse origin), was appointed in the person of Helge Ingstad, a buccaneering Arctic explorer and adventurer who later, in the 1960s, with his wife Anne Stine Ingstad, was to direct the excavations in L'Anse aux Meadows in Newfoundland which proved that Norsemen had made it to the American continent around the year 1000. This clumsy act of mini-imperialism was brought before the Court of International Justice in 1933, which easily ruled against Norway, which backed off its claim. With that ruling came also final international recognition of Denmark's sovereignty over all of Greenland.

In the Second World War Greenland was under protective occupation by the United States, which established air and naval bases and meteorological stations there. After the war, President Truman offered to buy Greenland from Denmark. That came to nothing, but American military bases continued. In 2019, in another bizarre case of hapless mini-imperialism, America's President Donald Trump again floated the idea of the United States buying Greenland from Denmark, to bewildered bemusement in Greenland, Denmark and elsewhere. The comedy turned to tragedy, of sorts, when President Trump, having been refused, cancelled a planned state visit to Denmark. The episode was summed up thus in an editorial in the *New York Times*: ' "I want to buy Greenland," said President Trump. "No way," said the Danes and Greenlanders, who share control over the giant frozen island and its rich mineral treasures. "Then I'm not going to visit your queen," shot back the self-proclaimed master of the real-estate deal, who can't stand being rebuffed.' 'Is this some sort of joke?' tweeted Helle Thorning-Schmidt, a former Danish prime minister, speaking for everyone. It was. But if you reflect on it, it is perhaps not entirely a non-joke that little Denmark, a small country in Europe, 'owns' big Greenland, the world's largest island (not counting the continent of Australia), snug up against the American continent, with an almost entirely Inuit population.

In 1953, Denmark ended Greenland's status as a colony. The island was made a Danish county, was then granted home rule in 1979 and as of 2008 extended home rule cum semi-independence. Greenland was at first included in Denmark's membership of the European Union, but in 1985 cancelled its EU membership.

In recent years China has taken an interest in Greenlandic affairs. Chinese companies have invested in uranium, rare earth elements and iron ore mining, and have been vying for participation in airport and other infrastructural investments. In 2016 a Chinese company attempted to buy a former US military base, a deal stopped only by the government in Copenhagen.

This seemingly strange Chinese reach into the cold north is not as odd as might appear. China also takes a keen interest in Iceland. The two countries signed what was the first Chinese free-trade agreement with any European country. In 2011 a Chinese businessman, one Huang Nubo, a real-estate tycoon and former Chinese government official, sought to acquire 300 square km of windswept barren wilderness in north-east Iceland where, he said, he planned to build an eco-tourism resort, golf course and nature reserve. The deal came to nothing, and to nothing again when he tried anew in 2013. He has also sought to acquire land in Norwegian Svalbard purportedly for the same purpose, and was again refused.

Behind China's interest in the Arctic north lies the prospect of the opening-up, by the effect of global warming, of the North-East Passage north of Russia from the Pacific to the Atlantic for commercial trade, a route that would cut 40 per cent off the sea transport distance. Plans are unfolding, under the brand of an 'Arctic Corridor', for a mega-port at Kirkenes in northern Norway and high-capacity rail links through

Finland and Sweden to eastern and western Europe. The opening-up of the North-East Passage is in the process of changing Scandinavia's geopolitical situation in the world.

The Shetland and the Orkney Islands became Norwegian Viking Age possessions – Harald Finehair considered their annexation part of his unification of Norway – and Danish possessions when Denmark subjugated Norway. In 1469 Christian I of Denmark pawned them to James III of Scotland on the marriage to him of his daughter, twelve-year-old Margrete, in lieu of a dowry which he was unable to raise. When Christian wanted to release the pawn James refused to return the islands, since when they have been a part of Scotland and eventually Britain and the United Kingdom.

The Norse influence remains in language, place names and music. The islanders consider themselves apart in Scotland and Britain. In the Scottish independence referendum of 2014, Orkney and Shetland led the vote against independence: better a distant overlord in London than a near overlord in Edinburgh.

During the Second World War, the link that had been the Norwegian Viking highway over Shetland was restored as a transport enterprise, organised under the British Special Operations Executive, mainly by fishing boats between Shetland and western Norway, undertaken by Shetlanders and Norwegians alike, bringing partisans and equipment in for the Norwegian resistance and taking escapees out – later commemorated by David Howarth, one of the British leaders of the operation, in his book *The Shetland Bus*, published in 1951.

The Faroe Isles, comprising about eighteen islands and innumerable islets, were like the Shetlands and Orkneys first annexed by Norway and later passed to Denmark, but unlike them have remained Nordic. The population was and remains Norse, and the language continues to be a variant of Old Norse. The Faroe Parliament today is the *Løgting*, 'the law assembly', and the capital city Thorshavn, 'Thor's port'. The economy is fragile, dependent on fishing and the export of quality wool and woollen products.

In the Second World War Britain secured the islands, which did not see action during the conflict. When Denmark became a member of the European Union in 1973 the Faroes decided against and are therefore, although part of the Kingdom of Denmark, not a member of the European Union. An independence movement emerged during the nineteenth century. A referendum in 1946 was indecisive and, after a failed declaration of independence, union forces prevailed. From 1948, the islands have had home rule with extensive local autonomy. The question of independence remains unsettled.

Habitation came to Finland, as to the rest of the Nordic area, after the last Ice Age. Finnic language arrived later, about 4,000 years ago, and took root in the eastern Baltic area around what is now the Gulf of Finland. The Finnish language is totally different from the Scandinavian languages and is of the Uralic family, close to Estonian, related to the Hungarian and possibly to Sami languages. Finland was part of the Nordic battleground during the Viking Age, squeezed between Scandinavia to the west and Russia to the east.

From the end of the Viking Age, Finland fell increasingly under Swedish dominance. This was driven by Swedish traders who established settlements along the Finnish coasts, followed by Christian activity against the heathen Finns, followed by military campaigns. In 1323 Sweden and Novgorod-Russia concluded a formal pact in which the southern part of Finland was to be Swedish and the eastern and northern parts Russian, a fuzzy demarcation that was soon pushed north and east for all of Finland to be absorbed as an integral part of the Swedish realm. It was to be six centuries before Finland could be Finland. When that happened, says Dick Harrison, for the Swedes it was not just that Finland was lost but that the *rike* (kingdom) 'cracked in two' (thus leaving it ambiguous whether he is speaking of Swedish sentiment at the time or of lasting contemporary sentiments).

Until the end of the twentieth century, Finland was to be on the receiving end of one of Europe's most devastating histories. Swedish rule amounted to ruthless colonial repression and economic exploitation, followed by poverty, famines and periods of population decline. Swedish war prowess in Europe in the sixteenth and seventeenth centuries was enabled by armies filled with Finnish conscripts. In the eighteenth-century wars between Sweden and Russia, Finland was caught in the middle and suffered extremes of destruction. During the Great Northern War (1700–21) Russia attacked Sweden through Finland, in campaigns in which both sides used scorched-earth tactics that physically destroyed the country. Russia held Finland from 1714 to 1721, in another period of uninhibited plunder and devastation, in the end returning what was left to Sweden, except for a slice at the south-east. In the War of Finland in 1808–9 the Swedish era came to an end. Finland was taken over by Russia and made into a semi-autonomous grand duchy within the Russian Empire.

From 1917, Finland was caught up in the Russian Revolutions and plunged into civil war between the Reds, supported by the Soviets, and the Whites, supported by Germany, a war of extremes of barbarity even in the annals of such wars. The outcome was Finnish independence from 1919, under a republican constitution. In the following border treaty with Russia, Finland won a port in the north in the Arctic, Petsamo, inserting a strip of Finnish territory between Norway and Russia.

In the Bay of Bothnia, the archipelago of Åland forms a bridge of islands, about 300 of which are inhabited, between mainland Finland and eastern Sweden towards Stockholm. It is now a province of Finland, constituted as an 'autonomous region' with a population of about 30,000, with Swedish the popular and official language. It came under Russian rule in 1809. A Russian fort was attacked and destroyed by British and French forces in 1854, as an offshoot, believe it or not, of the Crimean War. Swedish troops entered in 1918 during the Finnish Civil War in an attempt to reclaim the islands, but gave way to German forces at the request of the Finnish government. After the war a movement on the islands worked for unification with Sweden. The matter was brought before the League of Nations, resulting in the Convention of Åland in 1921, in which the islands remained under Finnish sovereignty with guarantees regarding Swedish language and culture, and as a demilitarised zone. Åland was neutral territory during the Second World War.

At the beginning of that war, Finland fought the Winter War of 1939–40 against invasion by Soviet Russia, another war of utter horror, holding Russia to a truce. Finland then aligned with Germany until switching sides at the end of the war, fighting German retreating forces. In treaties with Soviet Russia in 1947 and 1948, Finland was forced to accept reparations, restrictions on its autonomy, and territorial concessions. The port area of Petsamo reverted to Russia, now as Pechenga, re-establishing the Russian–Norwegian border. Finland lost territories at the bottom of the Gulf of Finland to the north-west of St Petersburg (then Leningrad) and some territories further north on the border. In these settlements, seemingly humiliating, Finland with great skill escaped being absorbed into the Soviet Union. It was to be the country's destiny in the twentieth century, so says the Finnish historian Matti Klinge, to hold back the Bolshevik Revolution and the Russian Empire from westward expansion. During the Cold War the country held steady as a neutral power and established itself as a Nordic welfare-state democracy, in close collaboration with the other Nordic countries. In 1995 she joined the European Union and in 1999, unlike Denmark and Sweden, adopted the Euro as the common currency. After Russia's war on Ukraine in 2022, Finland renounced neutrality and the next year joined NATO.

The Finns are said to be a melancholy people. Perhaps so, but then they have much to be melancholy about.

Part Two

Progress, Death and Restoration

Sverre was king in Norway from 1184 to 1202. He is a romantic figure who has attracted massive interest and admiration from historians, mainly for his swashbuckling successes as a warrior. He engaged a scribe to get his life written up as he wanted it remembered, in a magnificent piece of propaganda, the *Saga of Sverre*. Here and in another document, *A Speech Against the Bishops* (he chased them out of the country), he left records for later generations to attract their interest and shape their interpretations.

He grew up in the Faroe Isles, fostered by a bishop, was an educated man and an ordained priest. He arrived in Norway aged twenty-four, claiming to be of royal descent, an assertion probably supported by forged documents (not unusual at the time). He gathered around him a flock of roaming bandits that he turned into a formidable fighting force. He was a commander of superb ability, had the best imported weapons and was the first in Norway to use foreign (English) mercenaries. He fought more than sixty battles against seven competing chief-kings, most of them victoriously, a record he turned into boasting evidence that he had God's favour. The final competitor was one Magnus, whom Sverre fought for five years across the country, ending with a showdown in a sea battle at Fimreite, deep into the Sogne Fjord. Sverre had fourteen ships against Magnus's twenty-six, but outsmarted his opponent by deploying an original guerrilla strategy of spreading his ships out to hit the enemy at sides and aft. Magnus and at least 2,000 of his men perished. The victor elevated himself from outlaw to king. He would never be in control of more than parts of the country, never have peace, and never get the Church's backing.

The Viking Age had imploded. There was to be progress, but not until the peoples in the north had suffered a century or so of chaos and civil wars. From the gangster-infused wasteland, men of stature arose. Sverre's attempt at state-building was to kill off – 'slaughter', says the Norwegian historian Kåre Lunden – leading men across the country, thereby weakening the old class of barons. Harald Hardrade had done much the same more than a century earlier. It had not worked for him, nor did it for Sverre. His Saga concluded that 'even those who were not his friends said that there had not come a comparable man to Norway in their time'. True, but it was not enough. The old times of raw power were over. Before there could be a new kingship, there had to be a new society.

3

The Great Transformation

The 1200s, with a half-century head start in Denmark, were a watershed in which economic, religious and political life were all remade. The domestic economies started to generate surplus. The Church made itself super-rich. Landowners became aristocrats. Tenants sank into subjugation. Trade flourished. Over the next two or three centuries, the Hanseatic League became a fourth power around the three Norse kingdoms. Its profits accumulated into monetary capital that presented itself to kings as a source of credit. In Sweden, the bargain with the Germans was capital for privileges, which worked for both parties. In Denmark, it was capital for security in territory, which bankrupted the State. A genius queen pulls the three kingdoms into a union under a shared Crown. Lesser men pull it apart again. A mad Danish king commits war-rape on Sweden in an orgy of mass murder. The Reformation reshapes Church and State. Norway ceases to exist as a kingdom. Sweden and Denmark ready themselves to take on the world in war and imperialism.

Property and class

It was the plough that made the difference, another European invention that was adopted in the north after having proved its usefulness in the south, a strong plough of heavy iron, replacing the old hook plough which had, by comparison, only scratched the surface – 'the most important innovation in agriculture in the Middle Ages', says the Danish historian Kai Hørby. Existing land was made more productive and new land added to the arable territory.

Other improvements seeped in as well. More, and more varied, grain could be grown, generating more energy than grass for hay and shifting agriculture from cattle husbandry to more intensive and marketable cereal cultivation. Twice-yearly seeding was introduced, reducing the risk of crop failure. Horses replaced oxen as draught animals. Better spades and axes came into use, as well as improved scythes and sickles. The heavy iron spade, designed to be pushed into the ground by a foot, was an innovation, enabling more effective ditching. Wind- and watermills were built, one result being the grinding of more flour and a change of diet from porridge to bread. Apple and pear trees were introduced from the south. Progress was assisted by climate change, making for shorter winters and warmer summers.

Land became valuable. It could feed people, pay taxes and generate produce for trade. The Church, the barons and the Crown secured its ownership. Farmers were reduced to working land held by those in power. For that privilege, they had to pay. And there we have an ingenious arrangement. The right to use land gives the user enough produce to live and survive. The combination of rent, tithe and tax sees to it that the surplus floats to the top. Kings can rule, barons be aristocrats, Churches build and do good work. There was an explosion of creativity. Forts and castles rose, cities emerged, all of society's upper crust came together to build churches. Masons and artisans were brought in from Europe and came as teachers of many crafts: stonework, leadwork, bell-founding, brick-making, church art.

A qualification is needed. In Norway there was not enough good land to enable the kind of modernisation that was seen in particular in Denmark. Low agricultural output combined with population growth made for poorer standards than in Denmark and (southern) Sweden. The same rush of activity emanated, for a while, from Crown and Church, but was not supported to the same degree by agricultural surplus. That overreach goes some way to explaining why the Norwegian Crown would soon collapse.

With new property relations came new class divisions. Ownership shifted 'upward' to create wider divides of inequality. It became possible for landlords to live from rent rather than work. Land could more readily be bought and sold, or given away.

The Church became the biggest owner. It had the ability to persuade people that they would do God's bidding by gifting property to its institutions. By papal influence, European law on property was softened to extend the right of owners to give away their land, or some of it, unbound, or less bound, by the consent of those who stood to inherit. Massively, land flowed to the Church, often as bequests in wills. Bequeathers 'bought' the Church's goodwill, for example by purchasing Mass to be said regularly for their own souls. Farmers in debt to the Church, such as in unpaid tithe, could clear their dues by giving up land. Others relinquished ownership voluntarily for more security as tenants, something the Church encouraged by offering lifelong tenancy.

It also acquired land from bequests by Crowns that needed the Church's goodwill. In Knud the Holy's royal charter of 1085, the king gives to the archbishopric of Lund various tracts of land. The bequest specified that the bishopric would have the income from the land, but the king retained the right to fines that tenants might be liable for.

Most Church land was held by bishoprics and monasteries, in holdings of different sizes and patterns. Bishops were barons who ruled large domains as princes. Some land was put in the hands of parish priests. For each parish a parish farm, usually a substantial property with tenancies under it. The Church, then, was landowning, from top to bottom, with the proviso that the priest at the bottom was often a local man, the first man in the community but still in class terms a farmer rather than a landowner.

The Crown had land that previous kings had been able to grab during the long periods of unruly civil wars, personal kingly property now becoming Crown property. It acquired new land in various other ways. It could take it, which it would do by persuading owners that it was in their interest to cede ownership, for example if they were in debt to the king for back taxes. Fines might be paid to the Crown in the form of land. In serious matters Church and Crown had the power to outlaw delinquents, whose families, however, could save them from banishment by paying a fine to the Crown, which could be rendered in land. Fines were becoming a more important source of Crown revenue.

'Civil' landowners had the land that was not in Church and Crown possession, typically about half, the same as Church and Crown combined. Their holdings were of different kinds and sizes. An estate might consist of a husband's holdings and those of a wife which she brought with her at marriage (and which might revert to her family if she died ahead of her husband). A landowner might add to his estate by leasing additional land, which would then be under his control but not his ownership. Or he might lease out some of his own estate to a subcontractor, who would run it as his own fief against rent to the owner. Over time estates might split up, be sold or given away, or fall apart and be no more. Smaller landowners were big farmers, some of whom might work their own farm and have rent from a modest, or not so modest, number of tenancies.

Tenancies also were of different kinds. In Denmark and southern Sweden, peasants mostly lived in villages and worked fields in the surrounding area. In Norway and northern Sweden, habitation was dispersed in tenements spread over the landscape. Some tenancies were long-term, others short-term. It was a complex and shifting pattern with much variation. But through this complexity a basic structure emerged: land was worked by people who did not own it. Landlords (outside of Church and Crown) were sometimes big – we can now refer to this class as 'the aristocracy' – and sometimes not so big – we might call them 'squires'.

The basic conditions of tenancy – although conditions varied a great deal both in form and burden and over time – were that tenants paid a rent and had a duty of work. The rent was usually estimated as a fraction of the expected produce from the land, typically 5 to 10 per cent. That put the risk of bad harvest on the tenant; the rent would be given irrespective of yield. It also brought tenants little joy from rising prices as it was the landowner who traded surplus goods. Rent would usually be paid in the best produce, such as grain or butter. The duty of work was primarily to maintain the property under tenancy so as to preserve its capital value, and usually also to work directly for the master. In Denmark, where livestock was an important export, tenants might have a duty to rear cattle on behalf of the landlord. Over time, population growth led to increasing demand for land and thereby to an increasing rate of rent; in Norway by 1300 it was between 10 and 20 per cent. Big estates might be managed by a steward or stewards, who moved around and inspected the tenancies; in Denmark they were known as a *ridefoged*, 'riding-steward', after their mode of transport: the toffs came on horseback. There was an obligation for tenants to house and feed them during their inspections. They expected comfort and the best foodstuffs, and oats for the horses.

If the Church might offer lifelong tenancy, other landowners were inclined to time-limited contracts. These could be short, say for three years at a time, sometimes less. Gradually tenancies were extended, by the late Middle Ages typically to ten to twenty years, although again with much variation. In the Danish Landlaw of 1522, tenancy was regulated to a minimum of eight years. Along with extended tenancies came additional duties of work for the landlord. Sometimes tenancy was inheritable, presumably at the discretion of the landowner.

By around 1300, the agricultural revolution had transformed Scandinavian society. There being surplus, the Crown invented new methods of taxation, such as fees to local officials and courts, city taxes, more tolls on trade and duties of work, such as maintaining an emerging network of primitive roads. The Church instituted new forms of illegality in detailed rules about obligatory fasting, church attendance and other forms of religious behaviour, extending the system of fines paid to both Crown and Church. It all meant more wealth at the top and proletarisation at the bottom.

This is the place to pay tribute to the late Kåre Lunden, historian *extraordinaire*, who explained the resulting political economy with admirable detail and clarity. He did that not only by meticulous analysis but also by presenting that analysis in the wondrous medium of numbers. The case is Norway, the poor cousin in the family.

His guesstimate for population size around the year 1300 was about 460,000 people, resulting from a population increase over the last 300 years of about 145 per cent. That makes for less population growth than in Denmark, the most affluent of the countries, but even so a more 'overpopulated' economy relative to resources.

The national product (to use modern language) came mainly from farming and fisheries, with cities as yet contributing very little. Lunden estimated the amount of produce and found that the average standard of living in the common population, as measured by available consumption, was about 2,000 calories per person per day, similar to that of, for example, India in 1960.

In terms of land ownership, the Church held about 40 per cent (in about fifteen to sixteen holdings per churchman), about the same as we have seen previously for Denmark, the Crown about 7 per cent. In land rent the Church was the big taker, way ahead of the Crown. On top of that again, the tithe gave the Church at least twice as much revenue as other taxes gave the Crown. The Crown was the major recipient of revenue from fines, about five times as much as the Church, with fines contributing as much Crown revenue as did land rent. All together, Church and Crown revenues were split at about 80 per cent Church and 20 per cent Crown.

These estimates are rough approximations. There were no accounts; not until the sixteenth century did any semblance of State account-ing come into use. Population numbers can only be guessed at. But Professor Lunden's numbers give as good a picture of the shape of the economy as is possible.

He concluded by adding it up. Transfers upward from the population to the Crown and Church, what today we would call 'the tax burden', constituted approximately 25 per cent of net production value, total transfers to Crown, Church and other landowners, including rent, approximately 33 per cent. That makes for a level of extraction, from a poor population, not much less than today's affluent populations experience in modern taxation. Indeed, it was in reality a much heavier burden. Most of the taxes paid today go back to the population in public services, of which there were then next to none.

In addition to the burden on the small-folks, what is striking in these figures is the weakness of the Crown. The Church was wealthy. The Crown was by comparison a small landowner with small rev-enues. That was the case not only in Norway but equally in the two other countries, and was to be the case for a long time to come. In Denmark and Sweden, the aristocracies were wealthy. Kings were increasingly ambitious, both in domestic governance and foreign policy (i.e. warfare). They never had enough revenue. That meant borrowing, sometimes from foreigners, sometimes from domestic barons. Debt is dependency. Power-hungry kings would have to bend to the will of the money-men. The fiscal problem was a constant.

In the transition into the new economy, ordinary men had their social standing drastically slashed. The small-folks, who in the Viking Age had been poor but free, were reduced to an underclass, divided into some who had land in tenancy and a landless lumpenproletariat at the bottom of the pecking order. Others rose, some to constitute a *Mittelstand* of owner-farmers, some the class of landowners who would be the new aristocracy. In the emerging cities, a small middle class of urban traders and craftsmen was in the making.

In Norway, class relations worked out differently from those in Denmark and the dominant agricultural regions of Sweden. Working farmers were reduced to peasants, but the upper class was to be made up of mainly owner-farmer squires. There was not sufficient wealth of land to support more than a handful of serious landowners. Norway would never have a viable aristocracy on anything like the scale of Denmark and Sweden.

One might think a class system dominated by big landowners harder than one in which there is less distance between top and bottom, as in Norway, but that has not been the case, not in direct social relations. Where there is distance, those at the top and those at the bottom live separated from one another. There is ruthless exploitation, but also a genteel order. Where there is less distance, those at the top depend on protecting their status in daily interactions with those lower down. A high nobility can take its domination as the normal order of things. Those who are only squires must affirm their superiority day in and day out. It must be established and re-established that 'we' are the ones who count and that 'you' owe us obedience and respect. That affirmation comes not simply from structure, from ownership and wealth, but must also be sought in the conventions of daily life, such as an understanding that 'you' take off your cap when 'we' walk past. Aristocrats can afford to be mundane about their elevation; those who are less elevated cannot relax a moment in claiming their turf and making others accept their own station of inferiority. Where there is proximity between exploiters and exploited, class relations become personal.

This Norwegian rural class system came into being during the thirteenth century and then stayed put, only starting to be modified from the eighteenth century. The language has a word for the members of the squire class; they were, and are, *odelsbønder*. An *odelsbonde* is a farmer (*bonde*) who holds *odel*-land. That is land that is in the ownership of the *ætt*, a term that means family collectively over the generations. The owner at any given time is a custodian, and it is understood that the land will pass on down the family line. It applies to land of some significance; an *odel*-farm would have tenancies under it. *Odelsbønder* were not rich by landowner standards but would be intensely aware of themselves as the upper class, as was the way others saw them.

THE ENDURANCE OF CLASS

On 14 January 1951, at 5:05 in the morning, a man died in a hospital bed in Oslo. Three days earlier he had taken an overdose of barbiturates and fallen into a coma. He was found by two friends who broke down the door to his room and had him taken to hospital. On a sheet of paper near his bed was a poem the friends had not seen before and that he must have written in his last days. It starts, 'I owned not love.'

The man was Tor Jonsson, an author who had broken through to popular and critical acclaim and seen himself praised as one of the most significant poets of the land. He was productive and had a mass of material awaiting publication. He was thirty-four years old.

He was as tortured a soul as a man could be, unable to find peace with himself and with others, unable to experience intimacy and love, unable to protect himself from self-hate. In the same poem he says of his life that it had betrayed everything. He was indeed a failure in love, and that was the catalyst of his suicide, but only the catalyst, not the cause.

He was born and grew up in the village of Lom in Gudbrandsdalen. Here, the class structure of *odelsbonde* dominance is crystal-clear in the landscape to this day. The imposing farms are on the flat valley bottoms and the soft eastern and northern slopes with good sun and long seasons, the tenancies in the steeper and darker hills. The main highway ran along the eastern side of the river to serve the good farms. Even today road signs point across the river to a place called *Baksida*, the 'Back Side'.

His father was born in poverty but did well. At about age forty, he returned to the village with money in the bank and an ambition to make something of himself. He took a tenancy under the vicarage in the same year that Tor was born with the expectation of being able to buy it and join the class of property-owners, if not as an *odelsbonde* at least as an owner of land. But he failed. When he had improved the property through eight years of hard work another claimant presented himself and the Jonsson family was evicted. The man who had been on the threshold of rising to respectability was demoted to a day labourer, and soon died. He had been forward in letting it be understood in the village that he was on the rise, offending the social order of who 'we' were and who 'you' were.

> The young Tor had been given to understand that the property was his inheritance. In his mind, when that did not happen he and his family had been crushed by a conspiracy of old owner-farmer families, with the connivance of the vicar and others in authority. He thought of that conspiracy as *bygdedyret*, 'the village beast'. The man from below who aspired to property was denied access and the family found the door to community membership slammed in their face, in a case of unforgiving class dominance that could draw on a pedigree six or seven centuries old.

Schooling was for the select few, in the hands of the Church, hence not a 'public' concern. Pupils, a few boys from upper-class families, would learn reading and writing, some Latin, some numeracy, and the Bible, the religious calendar and liturgical song. They were taken through what we today would think of as elementary or middle school. Further education was conducted on the job for those who went on to the priesthood or a career as monk-scribes.

The Church's monopoly on schooling was not totally unchallenged. In the emerging cities, an ambitious middle class wanted respect. They needed their sons to be skilled. They joined together in guilds or similar associations which could muster agreement and money for joint projects. The first city school in Stockholm dates from 1315 and in Malmö from 1406, in Visby (then a Hanseatic city) from 1220. These schools were not much different from the Church schools in what they taught, but they made schooling available to sons of the parvenus who had means but not standing. This is not unique to Scandinavia: in Britain, today's old élite and very selective schools are known as 'public schools'.

The many had no formal education and were illiterate. But it would be wrong to think that they were ignorant just because they did not read Latin. It was by being held down that they were downtrodden, not because they were unable. They had many sources of knowledge and carried with them the wisdom of experience. They started work early and would soon know about the soil, about fishing rivers and seas, hunting and gathering, domestic and wild animals, about cleaning, weaving, spinning, sewing and cooking, about the weather and the seasons, about crafts and trades. In the family, they learned about themselves and about identity and history, and about kin. To this day, country folk are more knowledgeable about kinship relations than their 'modern' city counterparts, for example by instinct who are whose cousins down the line and at what remoteness. They would inherit folk knowledge, such as how to deal with illness and the use of natural remedies. They knew the intimacies of life from birth to death, from much of which we moderns are sheltered.

Tenants acquired knowledge from their dealings with landlords. They paid rent in produce which they brought to the masters. They did work for them, some periodically, some permanently as farmhands or in domestic service. They knew how those 'up there' lived, who in turn had no secrets from their small-folks.

They gained knowledge from strangers coming and going. There was much mobility across the land, as would be seen shortly from the rapid spreading of the Big Death plague. Goods were traded and had to be transported, by horse or carriage overland or by boat at sea. Help would be needed locally with fetching and loading and local folk would hear from traders about affairs elsewhere in the country.

There were regional *thing* which men of good standing could attend, and local assemblies down to the village level. These met regularly, the most local ones as often as weekly. Information would flow, politics and economics be discussed, and pressure from above and influence from below exchanged. A system of local officialdom was in the making and the king's representatives would educate the people in the law and in other expectations of the high-ups. Perhaps something from the emerging literary cultures at court, bishoprics and monasteries trickled down and out into the lands.

And there was the Church. Children were baptised, the young confirmed and married, the dead buried. Attendance was obligatory, or at least expected, and the Church's truths, understandings and world views were preached with heavy authority week in, week out, and with super-authority during the many Church holidays. Services brought together the high and the low and were educational: it was the responsibility of the vicar to teach his flock the gospel. You were required to know the Creed, the main prayers, and the wording of emergency baptisms of newborns who were in danger of dying before being brought to church.

Not much is known with any measure of certainty about social conditions and conventions. From what can be read in the sources, these look in some ways to have been well-ordered societies: people worked the land and got on with life, their betters governed. In fact, however, they were all but well ordered. There was population growth, soon outstripping the increase in food production. Not only was there much chaos at the top, with long periods of bloody feuds; at the bottom the combination of misery and exploitation gave rise to peasant revolts all through the Middle Ages, directed against both Crown and Church and their taxes and against landowners for their demands on rent and work. These were, as we would think of it today, developing-country economies in which masses of people lived from hand to mouth in constant destitution.

A typical tenancy would provide a livelihood for a man and wife and their children. If there were four or five surviving children, a tenancy could support only two of them in the next generation. This left a surplus of two or more children from that generation who would have to find their livelihoods elsewhere. A very few might migrate to the emerging but as yet small cities; a few might take up a craft, say as smiths, baker-women, weavers or shoemakers, but for most the option was agricultural labour or domestic service. The lucky ones had more or less permanent posts; others made do as itinerants and day labourers scraping out a living, or not, as best they could.

Daily life for most women was much the same as it had been: toil, chores, pregnancy, childbirth. But Church regulation of family life did come with some improvement in the social standing of women. In Church teaching, marriage was a sacrament which should depend on the consent of both man and woman. Women were less susceptible to being married off against their will. The banning of divorce and the strict distinction between legitimate and illegitimate children strengthened the position of women in marriage and family. Wives could not easily be cast aside by husbands, and the children of the family were *her* children. Husbands were still in charge of family property, but wives obtained more say. Sons remained first in line in inheritance, but daughters gained some new rights of inheritance and property.

Marriage remained a practical matter and was arranged by the families. Among the rich it was, as it had long been, about property and alliances. A few upper-class daughters who might not want to marry or had poor prospects could take holy orders – the first convents were aristocratic institutions. Among ordinary folk, men needed wives to run the tenancy with them, and women needed husbands to provide for them. There was hardly any concept of the young meeting up in search of love and companionship, in part because there was nowhere for them to get together, no schools, no clubs, no parties, no dances. At church perhaps, but then with glances across the pews. Church attendance was, one would think, welcome – however long and tedious the sermons might be. The Sunday was a day off work (if not off female chores), and a chance to get away from the daily drudgery and enjoy togetherness with friends and neighbours.

Social life came within the orbit of Church Law. The core of a family was a married couple, and a proper couple were properly married when they were formally wed in church. As divorce was banned, unless it turned out that the marriage had been in contravention of Church Law, and a sharp line was drawn between legitimate and illegitimate children, only legitimate children had right to inheritance. The Scandinavian languages were, and are, brutally harsh. Children who in English are 'legitimate' are there 'real' or 'genuine', otherwise 'ungeniune'.

A constant, and losing, struggle for the Church was the imposition of sexual discipline. The preaching of abstinence was more a 'high' Church matter, the remit of bishops and the like who lived removed from congregational life. Priests on the ground accommodated themselves to life and habits as they were, often living in disregard of official morality, sometimes with 'housekeepers', sometimes simply married.

Those who went into service lived in unprotected conditions. Farm maids slept in cowsheds and stables, farmhands in barns or sheds, city labourers anywhere. Family daughters were looked after by their parents but maids left to themselves. They would be sought out by young men for togetherness, and might welcome it, although often not.

What happened to 'fallen' women? And to children of fallen women? Some were taken care of by family or masters, some might find refuge in a monastery. But many would be rejected and left to their own devices. The faith that preached help to the poor was unforgiving of sinners. Would fatherless children, some born in secrecy, be baptised? Some perhaps, others not. Life expectancy was low and death a problem-solver. The setting-out of children was unlawful, but continued. As late as in Knut Hamsun's masterpiece *The Growth of the Soil*, set at the dawn of the twentieth century, the early story evolves around a mother who lets a newborn daughter with a deformity die, in a 'solution' that is seen to be not unusual.

In cities and at market, and elsewhere, there was trade in sex. Cities attracted migrants, including abandoned women and children from the countryside. Many could only with difficulty find decent livelihoods, some fell into beggary. Prostitution was rife. When, during the Norwegian civil wars of the thirteenth century, a bishop set Bergen alight, causing six churches to burn, he defended the outrage by claiming the churches had been desecrated and were no more holy that 'whores' huts'. Around 1300, the city had at least 200 working prostitutes, one of the more numerous city trades in a population of no more than 5,000. When the German Office (the Hansiatic enclave) was established as a community of men only, fraternising with outsiders was forbidden. But young apprentices would be in want of sex which 'gate women' at the fence were there to provide.

Was there, for ordinary folk in the ordinary business of life, enjoyment and fun? No doubt: people are as they are. Then, as now, people just liked being together. A wall painting in Ørslev church in Denmark from around 1325 shows a party of women and men making merry and dancing. A Middle Ages drawing from an archaeological find in Aalborg in Denmark shows a lively party with music, dance and drink, in the middle a naked man sports a prominent phallus. Those who could afford to gathered at feasts on festive occasions, the grander the better. In towns people lived and worked in close proximity and would enjoy each other's company as part of daily life. Drinking was togetherness, in taverns where men met. Where habitation was dispersed, as in much of Norway, the scope for daily socialising outside the family and household was perforce more limited. Even today these are communities in which the institution of the inn or tavern is absent. People were neighbours and neighbours get together, to help each other, to celebrate, to maintain social bonds and for merriment and gossip. They also fight – local life everywhere is vicious – but even that is part of the making of community.

Slavery ended with a combination of less supply and less demand. The end of Viking raiding abroad spelled the end of foreign slaves. In the new ways of agriculture, slave labour was less productive. With population growth there were tenants enough.

Once new slaves were not recruited, existing ones would die out. But a considerable number progressed from slavery to freedom, normally by buying their freedom from their masters, usually in instalments. Some might transition into real freedom, for example by clearing new land. But many remained in continuing dependency on their previous masters. They and their children did not have freedom of economic transaction, could not give or receive inheritance, could not marry without the master's permission, and had a duty of work for him. The master might allocate a piece of land to the former slave for him to tend, out of which produce he would buy his liberty. The process from enslavement to freedom could last several generations.

Were they serfs? In Norway and much of Sweden, the peasantry retained its status of being legally free – in dependency, certainly, but not in legal unfreedom. Not so in Denmark: 'The long periods of political unrest up to the first half of the fourteenth century', says the historian Eljas Orrman, 'made it increasingly difficult for the peasants to defend themselves against infringements of rights and property.' Tenants had nowhere to turn in legal matters other than to landlords, who were the holders of an ancient right-duty to protect their dependants. They used the increasing dependency to tighten the grip. This was facilitated by the Danish structure of landownings being predominantly large. From around 1300, tenants could no longer represent themselves in court but had to be represented by the landowner or his representative. Gradually, landowner authority broadened, such as to the right to subject tenants to trial and collect fines from them. That was not always to the tenants' detriment, as they were spared from being embroiled in higher-level protracted and messy court proceedings, but it still meant deeper subjugation. From the end of the century, tenants were not permitted to move without paying the landowner compensation, which could amount to six months' rent. Soon, in parts of the country, the right to move was abolished. A monastery in Sorø, in a dispute with their bishop in the 1490s, argued that 'from old, the monastery's peasants had been bound to their place of birth so that in certain circumstances escaped peasants could be forced back, and [that] even the monastery could sell its peasants, which has often been done'. Serfdom in Europe ranged from 'hard' near-slavery, such as in Russia, eastern Europe and Spain to 'soft' in some other areas. In parts of Denmark, the standing of the lowest peasantry deteriorated into at least soft, and sometimes hard-ish, serfdom. From the fifteenth century peasant circumstances gradually improved, at least in law, but the burden of tenancy remained heavy, involving ever more work for the benefit of the landlord. Only with land reforms at the end of the eighteenth century was the burden of exploitation on the peasantry alleviated.

The poor were their families' responsibility; that was the tradition, it became Church teaching. But families were hard pressed to cope. It was the Church's duty to bring peace to those who could not manage for themselves: paupers, widows, orphans. A quarter of the tithe was devoted to the poor. Churches and monasteries distributed alms and provided some shelter. At sites of pilgrimage and in cities they ran hospices to accommodate pilgrims and shelter the ill and the helpless, institutions that with time would evolve into poorhouse hostels and hospitals.

In Denmark, non-family poor relief became the exclusive responsibility of churches and monasteries, with guilds also gradually taking some responsibility. The Code of Jylland of 1241, the most advanced early written law, makes no provisions for 'public' poor relief. In Norway and Sweden, some early forms of 'public' assistance came into being outside of the Church. There was care by rota. A specified circle of farms or city properties were charged with the care of one pauper, who was to be accommodated from house to house, spending a night or a week in each, if necessary by being carried en route. Rota participation was a duty and failure to comply might incur a fine. In Magnus Lawmender's laws of 1274–76 the destitute had a right to protection, so that if, for example, a pauper was found dead, responsibility attached to those who could have prevented it. He who was deprived of his livelihood through no fault of his own had a right to get the payment of debt deferred. A man who carried a beggar's stave – a signal that he was worthy, whereby he gave himself an advantage on the beggars' market – forfeited his rights if it turned out that he was able to work or had family he could have turned to.* All pretty

---

* The beggar's stave was a signal that the carrier was worthy. It appears that it was a personal decision to 'take the stave'. Those who did were known in Swedish as *stavkarlar*, 'stave men'. The provision on the matter in Magnus's law was to prevent abuses of the bond of sympathy. The stave was a known symbol of honourableness through the ages. In Sophocles' *Oedipus Rex*, a rich man is reduced to begging, 'stick-in-hand'. Pilgrims today on the route to Nidaros and St Olav's shrine, and no doubt elsewhere, make themselves recognised as such by carrying a long stave.

raw in our eyes, but there was at least a recognition of poverty and a 'public' duty to help.

Life, compared to how we know it, was different: in look, in feel, in smell. Filth was omnipresent, hygiene absent. Not until the twentieth century were anything like modern habits and standards of cleanliness known, aided by the increased use of two distinctly modern commodities: affordable soap and toilet paper. Until then, life was thoroughly dirty, ravaged by illness and contagious disease, contributing to high rates of mortality, in particular at birth and in childhood.

Through the Middle Ages, people and animals lived in close proximity and mingled intimately, in towns and cities as much as on farms. Shit, to put no gloss on it, was everywhere, dragged around by foot, inside as well as outdoors. The idea that defecation is done in private is new. The usual way of cleaning oneself afterwards was with a hand, which itself could not be cleaned except by being wiped on something, perhaps the back of a trouser or frock. A wooden or some other tool might be used, which, if you were not rich, would be reused and shared. Moss and other natural materials were utilised, but the regular collection of moss was expensive. Food was eaten by hand, from common dishes. In Europe, the table-set of knife, fork and spoon was an innovation of the eighteenth century.

Dug latrines had been used from the Viking Age, but the privy, a designated closed-off place for defecation, was not in regular use, except possibly by the rich, until the nineteenth century, at least in Norway. As late as the 1960s, on my uncle's farm, where I spent my childhood summers, the paper in the privy across the yard was shreds of old newspaper.

The concentration of dirt was dense in towns and cities. Waste was left where it fell or thrown where it could be got rid of, eventually into water. Rivers downstream were thick with muck. A lucky city like Stockholm, which has much water running through it, could wash refuse out to sea, but in a city like Copenhagen, on flat land, it would stay put and accumulate. Once privies came into use, the profession of 'nightmen' emerged. They worked as scavengers to collect human excrement to be mixed with other refuse and sold to farmers as fertiliser, not as a city service but a business. The building of sewers in major cities commenced around the 1850s. The first sewer cleansing plant in Oslo started operating in 1911. Water closets did not begin to become usual until well into the twentieth century.

Body and clothing went unwashed. Water was in short supply and hot water an expensive luxury, town and city water contaminated. On my uncle's farm again – and this was a well-to-do farm – there was inside running water but neither water closets nor baths. After a day in the fields, my uncle might take me, a proud little farmhand, perhaps after the shorter Saturday shift, to shower in a waterfall in a nearby river, cold then, impossible most of the year.

Change of clothing was rare, as was the changing and cleaning of bed linen. In the nineteenth century, it was said, rich ship-owners in Norway sent their linen to London for laundry. People slept in blankets or skins, many together. Mice, rats, lice, fleas and worms were standard, with flies everywhere, feeding off the filth. The dirt and peril in and after sexual intercourse does not bear thinking about. Anal sex was an established technique of pregnancy prevention in Europe in the Middle Ages. Abortion was practised in horrendously dangerous ways. Communal saunas and baths were known of but were a luxury, or brothels in disguise. City bathhouses were discontinued across Europe with the arrival of syphilis in the sixteenth century.

Trade

What the strong plough did for agriculture, cheap salt did for trade. The traditional exports were, from Denmark, then as now, agricultural produce such as butter, meat and livestock. From Norway came dried fish, hides and gradually timber. Exports of iron and copper from Sweden grew from modest beginnings to about 300 metric tons by around 1370 and upward of 1,000 tons a century later. The main imports were malt, flour, honey, fabrics and luxuries such as wine, and, certainly to Norway, grain. Norway was not (and is still not today) self-sufficient in food. In the Viking Age, part of the problem was solved by exporting people, as would happen again in later emigrations; now it is done by importing nutrition. A previously important trade that had ceased was slaves. But it had not ceased forever. When the opportunity returned with the Atlantic slave trade the Scandinavians would embrace it again, with no more compunction against the buying and selling of human chattel than they had in the Viking Age.

The old trades were low-level. The volume increased with the coming of economic surplus as of the 1200s. A first upturn came from increasing Crown and Church revenue. Rent, tithe and other taxes were paid mostly in goods, some of which were traded for necessities from abroad.

The big upturn came with the trade in fish. Not a new trade, but one that now took on new proportions. The supply side was herring from the Baltic Sea and the shores between Denmark and Sweden. The demand was created by the Church, which from its command post in Rome was fortifying its power by issuing dogmatic rules about behaviour to its flock. Fasting was imposed, and strictly – not only in the great holidays but regularly, every Wednesday and Friday: fasting days would take up about a third of the year. The miracle for the Nordic trade was that fish was permitted, hence the gigantic market for it throughout Europe.

At just the right time, the supply of herring surged and the price of salt fell. In the Swedish and Danish waters, herring were so thick in the seas that they could be hauled directly on to land or into boats with hand nets. Salting had not been the traditional way of preserving fish; it had been too expensive. But new finds changed that. The biggest mines were in Lüneburg, from where the salt was traded via Lübeck. The Scandinavians had the fish, the Germans the salt. The match was made.

The question was, who was going to do the trading? The Germans, it turned out. They had not only salt but also ships, finance, skills and organisation.

The German lands were a loose confederation of fiefdoms which owed allegiance to the emperor but practically managed themselves. Some of the fiefdoms were self-governing cities that had grown up around trade. A network of cities along the Baltic shores and routes south and west, more than 200 at its peak, formed an alliance, the Hanseatic League, in which they collaborated, although not always harmoniously, and merged enough force to defend their interests, with army and navy might when necessary. The League was not a state but was sufficiently organised to be able to deal collectively with states on an equal footing, for example to forge treaties and negotiate trading laws. It operated from around 1200, branching out from Lübeck, embracing Visby on Gotland and setting up 'offices' under Hanseatic law and management in cities like Copenhagen, Stockholm, Bergen,

Novgorod, Bruges and London. The office in Bergen became permanent during the 1350s (after the Big Death, the Germans benefited from the city being on its knees), eventually to make up about a fifth of the city's population. After 200 years or so, the League started to slip into slow decline. The Novgorod office closed in 1494 and the London office in 1598. In the end it was reduced to three member cities – Lübeck, Hamburg and Bremen – and held its last general assembly in 1669. The Bergen office survived the League and continued to trade until around 1760. The premises were destroyed in a city fire in 1702 but were rebuilt in the old style in the *brygge* (harbour) that survives today.

Visby town, Middle Age image, a Viking, Hanseatic and Danish trading city on Gotland, Swedish from the seventeenth century

The Scandinavians resented the Germans for making themselves rich at their expense, but were unable to do much about it. They were reliant on them to manage the trade they needed, and were anyway outgunned. For the next two centuries or so, the Hansa held a near-monopoly on trade between Scandinavia and Europe and in and out of the Baltic Sea. It was costly, but the Scandinavians got their trade done while they waited for the day when they would be able to take care of it themselves.

The German traders, similarly to the Norse Vikings earlier, but not using pillage, started by coming and going for the trading seasons, then semi-settling over the winters, then establishing themselves with permanent settlements. From early on the Germans had a quota of members in Stockholm's city council, where they constituted about a third of the city's burghers by the fourteenth century. Thanks to the fish trade, the lands of the north had become valuable enough to be of interest for 'conquest'.

A concern for the Crowns in international trade was to tax it. Trade was located in designated cities and stations where fees and tolls could be collected. Denmark controlled the Sound in and out of the Baltic Sea and could charge fees of passage. By the end of the fifteenth century there were around 3,000 passages annually, giving a hefty income to the Danish Crown. A continuing trade from Denmark was in live cattle and horses, in particular from Jylland south into Germany. The north–south road between Germany and Denmark, usually known as the *Hærvej*, was also known as the Ox Route. In principle, goods were to be exchanged at border stations where Crown tolls could be collected.

The herring trade came under Danish royal regulation and was largely located on a small spit of land that juts out into the Sound from the south-eastern tip of Skåne, the Skanör and Falsterbo market. Here, Swedes and Danes, and some Norwegians, provided the herring and the Germans the salt, the men doing the trading and their women the preserving and barrelling. A wild community grew up for a few months in the second half of the year – not only Scandinavians and Germans selling and buying herring, but Scandinavians selling anything, and other Europeans trading the prized herring in return for textiles, for example.

Accommodation was in crowded shacks or tents. People were packed tight, herring gutted and rinsed in the millions, live animals brought – think about the sticky, smelly filth of it all. Locals offered provisions, food and drink. The Germans brought their own prostitutes to supplement the local supply. Danish officials, in addition to collecting tolls, tried to preserve some order, but with modest success. It does not take much imagination to know it inevitable, in a transient community where everyone is away from home, where men and women mix, where money flows, where crooks crowd in, that life would consist, in addition to business, of drinking, fighting and whoring, which indeed it did. Still, the market operated under a Christian regime and, as awful as it was, Christian authorities extracted from it a surplus to build churches, the beautiful Skanör and Falsterbo churches that are still there today in their splendour.

Church

In medieval Europe, says Tom Holland in his history of the Christian faith, the Roman Church held a 'total monopoly' in the understanding of the divine (save for the occasional community of Jews) in a way that defined the entire rhythm of life, so that women and men 'absorbed its assumptions into their bones'. It was thought true and obvious, by high and low alike, that God's hand was everywhere and in all doings and happenings. It was both impossible practically and unthinkable in people's minds to live outside the regime of a Church that dictated the norms of life from birth to death and morning to night.

Christianity was the sanctioned religion of the Roman Empire from 312, when, during a series of civil wars, Constantine rose to be sole emperor. He had seen a cross in the sky and been visited in a dream by the Saviour, and ascribed his victory to Christ's blessing. From that base arose the institution that became the Roman Church. The combination of faith and organisation in due course helped the Europeans to pull themselves out of the chaos that followed the fall of the old empire in the west and in the creation of a new empire, eventually known as Holy Roman. That construct sat on a dual base of State and Church power, an alliance that was consummated when the pope crowned Charlemagne emperor in the year 800. When Viking kings brought Christianity to Scandinavia it was organisation, as much as faith, that they brought with them. The faith was the enabler, the organisation the doer.

The Church organisation was like nothing else at the time or ever before. It had the legitimacy of the only valid faith and hence the authority to bestow God's grace on commoners, lords and kings alike. It redefined kingship, imbuing it with the dual responsibility of protecting the faith and ruling the land. It dominated narratives and mindsets as much as practical affairs. It brought with it a rhythm of life – Sabbaths, days of fasting, ceremonial holidays, church attendance, confessions, baptisms, confirmations – and rules of obedience to fortify the unity of faith and life. It was Europe-wide, imposing a universal written language, Latin, with an institutional network spreading out from the papal seat in Rome of archbishops, bishops, priests and monks, and their cathedrals, churches and monasteries. It ran what schools there were and was in charge of much of civil justice. It was the sole provider to the Crown of educated men, hence of recording history, drafting charters and treaties, maintaining archives. Church councils were taken as models for later Crown councils. The priests in the parishes were teachers, guardians and captains of morality and local order. Their churches were sites of belonging and togetherness. When people asked themselves about truth, reason and purpose, they had nowhere else to go for answers than to the Church.

Secular power depended on Church sanction and services. As beliefs were, kings could not be kings without being seen to be God's servants. They needed the Church's anointment, typically by being crowned by a high cleric. They were in need of skills under Church control, the art of writing and documentation again. They could not afford to have bishops or popes against them, or even in only reluctant collaboration.

The Church had the organisational strength to extract a price for its collaboration. It made itself rich in property and revenue. When Charlemagne was crowned, that looked to be enough: the Church was dependent on his protection and he was able to use the Church as his apparatus of governance. Soon, however, the Church was not content with being only equal to the Crown. It came to see itself as the superior partner. It wanted autonomy for itself. It wanted to appoint its own bishops, who would then not be beholden to kings. It wanted to be in charge of its own jurisdiction. It wanted protection from State taxation.

All these things would be achieved, but not without difficulty. On the Continent, State–Church relations came to a head in a clash between Pope Gregory VII and Emperor Henry IV, culminating in their meeting at Canossa in 1077. Henry insisted on retaining the authority to appoint bishops and issued an order for Gregory to relinquish the papacy. Gregory responded by excommunicating Henry. It was the pope who prevailed and the emperor who had to concede, finding that without the pope's backing he was bereft of standing. He saved himself by crawling (literally, on his knees) to Canossa, begging the pope's forgiveness and being readmitted to the community of the faithful. Their conflict did not end and Henry was later to chase Gregory out of Rome, but the Church had secured its autonomy. When the pope had crowned Charlemagne, he had confirmed a reality: now it was popes who would make and unmake emperors.

The Church was late in being established in Scandinavia, and came with the expectation of autonomy. That was the reason for the conflict between Sverre and the bishops more than a century after Canossa. Sverre – he is known in Norwegian historiography as the courageous king who stood up even to Rome – denied the Church the price it demanded, shut down its activity and drove the bishops into exile. But soon it was Sverre who was gone and the bishops who were back, and the Church had its autonomy confirmed.

The powerful Church never had it easy. Emperors and kings conceded more than they wanted and resented the Church, on which they were dependent, a resentment waiting in the wings when the curtain went up for the Reformation. Another difficulty was internal. Rebels thought a Church that sought power and wealth had allowed itself to be corrupted. Opposition theologians worked towards a theology of purity. New monastic orders emerged which renounced property, and whose members committed themselves to lives of poverty and service and to spreading the true gospel by way of assisting the needy.

An extension of the Church's claim to supremacy was the doctrine of the pope's power, and of his clergy in his place, to absolve sin. Was salvation, it was now asked, in the gift of the Church and did it depend on obedience to Church authority and doctrine, or was it a matter between the believer and his God? In 1517, a German monk and professor of biblical studies in the town of Wittenberg, Martin Luther, nailed a list of ninety-five theses on a church door, the gist of which was a denial of the Church's claim that there was no salvation other than through priestly grace. In many of the German lands, and certainly in Scandinavia, it turned out that princes who had been held back by Church counter-power were more than happy to cut that Church down to size when it had weakened itself with obscene wealth, abusive control and internal discord.

When Scandinavia was pulled into the embrace of the Church of Rome, that Church was in the grips of Crusader mania. The Crusades started with a call by Pope Urban II in 1095 for Christians in Europe to go forth with military strength to liberate Jerusalem and the Holy Land from the Muslim infidels. The First Crusade set off in 1096, and was followed by at least eight more (thirteen depending on how you count them) in the Mediterranean area in the next two centuries. The First Crusade reached and captured Jerusalem, but only temporarily, and in the end the Crusades failed to conquer the Holy Land. They were political-religious ventures of mixed and complex causes, and disorganised campaigns of horrible and arbitrary violence, meted out not only to the Muslim enemy in the east but also to Christian lands and peoples both at home and on the way. Constantinople, the centre of Orthodox Christianity, was sacked in 1204. Jewish communities came under attack, both in Europe at the initiating end and in Palestine, where there were assaults on Jewish towns, including Haifa. Jews fought and died alongside Muslims in the defence of Jerusalem against the intruders.

Most of European Christendom became involved. The First Crusade was followed by a Norwegian Crusade, from 1107 to 1111. It was led by King Sigurd, then about twenty years old, who became the first European monarch to go to Jerusalem. At the outset it comprised 5,000 or so men, fighting their way along the western coasts of Europe and through the Mediterranean until reaching Jerusalem in 1110. (They were received with brotherly welcome in Norman Sicily. Roger II, not yet king, was fourteen years old; tolerant ruler that he would become, he refused to join the Crusades.) Later Scandinavian kings would commit as well, but evade or pay themselves free, or have their own local wars labelled Crusades.

Sigurd was a young man, there was adventure to be had and fame to be won. A Crusader chief by name of Baldwin held Jerusalem. Sigurd joined him in subduing the coastal town of Sidon, in a siege lasting forty-seven days, made possible by the Norse fleet barricading the town's sea routes. Job done, Sigurd and his men left for Constantinople from where the king returned north overland, bringing with him a splinter of the True Cross for St Olav's burial site, and, as Norse chiefs craved, repute and honour.

Crusading swept through Europe itself in a large number of wars across the continent that were given dignity by being fought under the banner of the cross. (Only now did the term 'Crusade' come into use; later historians have also used it retrospectively for the early armed pilgrimages to the Holy Land.) Not only kings but also commoners felt the pull. A Gislo Petersson in Sweden made a will before he left for Palestine in about 1250, donating his farm to a monastery, and probably perished. A Nils Sigridsson, also in Sweden, says in his will that he reached the Holy Land and brought back a small golden cross, which he gifted to his church.

Various campaigns along the continental fringe of the Baltic Sea and into the lands of the Orthodox Church in Novgorod and elsewhere in Russia called themselves Crusades, but had little success. During the thirteenth century (possibly starting in the twelfth century with a Crusade later said to have been led by the future Erik the Saint of Sweden) three Swedish and two Danish Crusades, so called, were waged on Finland, under papal encouragement and authority, presumably to prevent the Finns from falling under the Orthodox Church, of which the lasting result was the Swedish conquest of Finland.

State

A new Scandinavian kingship was taking form, similar to Middle Age developments elsewhere and earlier in Europe. It had some basic components that can be outlined quite easily. It did not take exactly the same shape in all three countries, things did not unfold on the same schedule, it did not all last, not all reforms were equally effective: some would be contested and at times ignored, officials would be crooked and corrupt, kings and pretenders fight and kill each other in bursts of warfare – but things were changing in a consistent manner. By 1300, says Dick Harrison – writing of Sweden, but the same could be said of the others – there was a country with reasonably clear territorial configurations, a political system, a central State, established Crown and Church, an emerging nobility and city bourgeoisie, a tax-paying population and national laws.

Kings became holders of 'the Crown', heads of state. That in part grew out of more stringent rules of succession. Kingship had been elective; one way or another kings had been accepted and given dignity at *thing*. The bloodline had not been decisive but had mattered. Anyone who could claim kinship to an earlier king had a claim, be he near or distant, legitimate or illegitimate. As a result there were often many pretenders, there was no clear order, endless fighting, sometimes shared kingships, lands divided. To forge some order, the understanding shifted towards kingship being hereditary, down the male line, the legitimate line, the oldest legitimate son being the heir. The Church insisted that hereditary rights were limited to legitimate offspring since any equality between legitimate and illegitimate children was against Church teaching. The hereditary principle was accepted in theory in Denmark by the mid-twelfth century and in Norway by the mid-thirteenth (in Sweden only later), but only in a limited way: kings should have hereditary legitimacy but still be, as previously, proclaimed. That power was moved out of more or less democratic *thing* into new councils of leading men, primarily bishops and big landowners, soon known as *rigsråd* (*riksråd* in Swedish). Barons and churchmen did not want to give up their control over who would be king. Kings would be anointed in return for a commitment, set down in a written pact, to respect 'the people', meaning Church and aristocratic privileges.

The way of being king changed. Kings took to residing. Cities were emerging and it was better, more comfortable and effective to establish a firm base and stay put. They built forts where they could live in safety, comfort and splendour. They did not have capital cities as we now think of them and still moved around a great deal (as do governors today), but they took to staying for much of the time in their favourite palaces.

One reason why kings became more stationary was that new State institutions were coming into being. There were the councils, the forerunners of today's national assemblies. In stable times it was for the king to decide who would be included, obviously from among leading men in the Church and aristocracy. They were, however, soon sufficiently institutionalised to be able to convene themselves, as might happen in critical situations, not only for the anointment of a new king or to take charge in interregnums when there was no king or the king was underage, but also, for example, to rebel against a sitting one, typically in matters of warfare. Councils would meet not infrequently, sometimes yearly, sometimes more often. What exactly they did was fluid – for example, whether they or the king made laws – but governance now emanated from some form of king–council collusion.

Another new institution was a king's committee, a sub-council if you will, a smaller circle of leading men who would work with the king on a more permanent basis, the embryo of what would later be governments.

To buttress the new form of governance there would furthermore be an office of scribes and experts. Governance was being exercised in writing; someone had to do the writing and someone else scrutinise what was being written down. The king would have advisors and, in foreign policy, ambassadors. There would be a chancellery, a civil service in the making, and a chancellor, a prime minister in the making.

And a final new institution came in the form of permanent regional officials, both in cities and country districts, moving local affairs into the hands of royal appointees who would answer to the Crown. Kings built royal mansions, eventually castles, at strategic locations around the country and installed in them loyal commanders with garrisons as regional governors. They, and appointed officials on lower levels, exercised the king's governance locally and were in charge of Crown property, as well as justice and order, and, importantly, tax collection. They would work side by side with assemblies of 'the people' which carried the authority of the *thing* tradition, and which both facilitated and constrained royal governance.

Soon, it was through the castles that political and regional control was exercised. They became fought over, sometimes answering to kings, sometimes to *rigsråd*, depending on the flow of power. The way for Danes to take Swedish territory, or Swedes Danish territory, was to capture strategic castles and instal their own officials in them.

We are at the dawn of law being recorded. The Church was influential through its own law, which made up half of the total legal burden that weighed down the populace, and by shaping the codification of secular law to bring it into conformity with Church doctrine. Canon law had been combined into a first single consistent code by the Bolognese scholar Gratian in the 1140s, and was taken throughout Christendom as the authoritative guide for the compilation of written law. Kings became lawmakers (under varying degrees of council oversight) and the exercise of law was centralised. Local *thing* continued to operate as courts in the first instance, but higher and appeal courts came under Crown authority, with the king himself the ultimate appeal judge. In that capacity he had further lawmaking authority by creating laws through judgments in matters not covered by written codes.

Further developments were in taxation and defence. A core form of taxation had been a duty on locals to provide men for the king's guard and ships and equipment for his fleet. A weakness of that arrangement, seen from the king's side, was that it made him dependent on baron underlings for physical power. If they refused him men, ships and equipment, which happened often enough, there was not much he could do. And even if they did provide men, they were still *their* men, not his. Kingship that is not in command of arms is inevitably weak. As a solution, taxation was shifted from a duty of provision to paying in kind: tax was not paid in money, at least not in most cases, but in goods. That worked for the king since there was now trade. He could put taxed goods on the market and get revenue in return. Moreover, defence was professionalised and placed more directly under royal command.

The downside was that professional defence forces are expensive. It was a lasting problem in the new kingship that tax revenues were not sufficient to cover costs, certainly not the cost of warfare. To make matters worse financially, defence technology was shifting from infantry to cavalry, to soldiers on horseback. A soldier with horse, weapons and armour is an expensive piece of kit. To remedy this problem again, the old system was partly retained: provide and equip cavalry soldiers and you will get tax exemption in return. That would be possible only for the rich, the result being a class of élite soldiers recruited from the economic upper crust who would be knights. There was an element of European chivalric romanticism involved. The knights had the right to call themselves, and be called, 'Herr', the equivalent of the English 'Sir'. This was to be another element in the emergence of a formal aristocracy: the nobles who served militarily were, in the language of the day, 'salvaged'. In another downside, a handful of knights does not make an army. To fight wars, kings became dependent on hired mercenaries. That again was expensive, contributing yet further to the Crowns' permanent financial distress.

Out of these institutional changes emerged a new system: monarchs with hereditary legitimacy, a resident (more or less) king, council, committee, chancellery and a network of royal officials. The leading men who filled these institutions served the king in return for rewards, typically tax-exempted land. Not only kingship became more hereditary, but also noble and court position. Next to the new Crown sat the Church, with a power base in its elaborate organisation. Where there had been kings and barons, there were now kings, barons and churchmen. The Church sat in the middle of the new order, asserting power upward on the Crown and giving itself presence in ordinary daily life.

These developments unfolded in Denmark from around 1160 to 1200, and in Norway between 1240 and 1280. Sweden was working itself through a string of ineffective kings and was able to turn to reform slightly later again, from around 1250 to 1290.

Denmark had order, more or less, once the relentless onslaught by Harald Hardrade was over, for sixty years under Svend Estridsen and five of his sons. That came to an end on 7 January 1131, when one pretender to the Crown, another Knud, was ambushed and killed by a half-brother, who in turn was killed in battle three years later, all of which was followed by twenty-six years of civil war.

A week after Knud was killed, his wife gave birth to a son. He was given the name Valdemar and a share of the divided kingdom. He grew up to want the rest. So did two other pretenders. The three of them arranged to convene at Roskilde on 9 August 1157, in what was supposed to be a meeting of friendship. It became a bloodbath. In an ambush one pretender was killed, his head cleaved. Valdemar escaped and vanquished the second pretender when the two met in battle. Valdemar was King of all of Denmark.

He is known as Valdemar the Great. That may be on the generous side. It is no small thing to restore a small kingdom, but it was hardly enough to elevate him to the rank of, say, Charlemagne, or even Knud the Great. He did, however, set in motion the redefinition of kingship which we have visited above. The Scandinavian quest for nationhood had started in Denmark. Now, state-building started there as well. It made sense that this began in the most prosperous and populous of the three countries, nearest to the Continent and to European influences.

Thus opened a new chapter in Denmark's political history, known as the Valdemar period, which was to last a short century – under Valdemar himself until 1182, his son Knud VI until 1202, and a second son Valdemar II (also called the Victorious, in spite of having very little victory to his name) until 1241.

Notable kings of the high Middle Ages, with approximate years of reign

Years	Denmark	Norway	Sweden
1100		Sigurd Crusader 1103–30	
			Sverker the Old 1130–56
1150	Valdemar the Great 1157–82		Erik the Saint 1156–60
	Knud VI 1182–1202	Magnus V 1161–84	Magnus II 1160–61
		Sverre 1184–1202	
1200	Valdemar II 1202–41	Håkon III 1202–04	
		Håkon Håkonsson 1217–63	
	Erik IV 1232–50		Erik Lisp and Lame 1234–50
1250	Abel 1250–52	Magnus Lawmender 1257–80	Valdemar 1250–75
	Erik Klipping 1259–86	Erik 1280–99	Magnus III 1275–90
	Erik Menved 1286–1319	Håkon V 1299–1319	Birger 1290–1318
1300	Christoffer 1329–32	Magnus Eriksson 1319–55	Magnus Eriksson 1319–64
	No king 1332–40		
	Valdemar Atterdag 1340–75		
1350		Håkon VI 1355–80	
			Albrekt 1363–89

From this period, two notable documents survive which give some insight into the new form of governance, one that goes under the name of *Kong Valdemars Jordebog* – literally 'ground book' but in English said to be a 'Census Book' – and one known as *Kong Valdemars Lovbog* or the 'Code of Jylland'.

The *Jordebog* is a collection of miscellaneous documents, mainly lists – lists of lands, islands, borders, dates, kings and kingdoms, popes, Crown properties and incomes, taxes, townships, cultivated fields in selected areas by number and size, a mysterious list of Knud VI's 'brothers' (215 of them, meaning unknown), of the royal retinue's consumption while travelling the country, and more. They were compiled later, in copies, around 1300 – someone must have thought it important to preserve these documents. They are for the most part connected in some way with the exercise of administration and the use of writing. It is difficult for us today to imagine a world in which business depended entirely on memory, with nowhere to look things up. How would kings know their land, how it was laid out, what parts it consisted of, who was who? How would they know who other kings were and whom they were married to, who was related to whom? How would they know when things occurred, such as religious ceremonies through the year? How would they know who had paid taxes and who not, and how much? How would they know what was traded in cities and what tolls were due and collected? They were supposed to be in charge but had no way of knowing, in any detail, what they were in charge of. What the *Jordebog* shows is the monumental difference between kingship with and without writing. The new kingship could not have happened without writing.

The *Lovbog* is from the very end of the Valdemar period, the first comprehensive written code of law in Scandinavia. The thinking was that 'the law' existed in society, as an amalgam of tradition and Church learning. The writing-down was a matter of putting into letters, words and sentences what already existed. The law was said, in the *Lovbog* Preface, to be 'gifted by King Valdemar and received by the Danes', meaning that the king was bringing to the Danes the law that was theirs. However that may be in theory, with written law kings (in collusion with Church and nobles) would be lawmakers. 'The law' would be what was written down.

This first code consisted of three slim 'books', one dealing with property and inheritance, one with judicial process, and one with crime and punishment. Its opening words, in the Preface, are 'Let lands be built by law' (*Med lov skal land bygges*), which remains today an honoured slogan in Scandinavian jurisprudence. It also explains the need for law: 'Where there is not law in the land, then he would have most who could most take.'

Once Valdemar had a grip on Denmark, he wanted his country to be a big power. He could well follow that ambition since both Norwegians and Swedes were preoccupied with fighting themselves and represented no threat. Enemies from the south had been raiding Danish shores from a stronghold on an old Viking station on the island of Rügen, on the German north coast. In 1169, Valdemar struck back and subdued the island. In this he was much encouraged by the Church. Rügen was a centre of pagan cult. Valdemar was on a Crusading mission. Warring continued eastward under his sons, to capture more German and Polish (as they are now) coastal territories, and further on to present-day Estonia. Fifty years after Valdemar had restored the kingdom, Denmark was again a big power, at least on Europe's northern fringe.

Kong Valdemars Lovbog, *aka King Valdemar's Code,*
The Code of Jylland

Or so it looked. But it soon turned out that the Danes had been able to grab German lands only because of disorder there, and that once the menace from the south got its act together, Danish big-power ambition was in vain. All it took was for an obscure baron in a fief that was supposedly Danish, at what was supposed to be (again) a meeting of friendship at the king's invitation, to simply lock up the king, the second Valdemar, and his son in a fort in Mecklenburg. The Danes had to accept a treaty in which they gave up their German possessions and paid the upshot baron a ransom in silver, gold, horses and equipment for the release of the man who called himself king after two and a half years in an underling's prison. An attempt by Valdemar two years later to regain some of his lost territory resulted in another defeat, the king only just escaping imprisonment again (and suffering the loss of an eye).

It was to get worse. Valdemar II died in 1241. His son Erik IV was king but fell out with his brothers. The country was plunged into civil war again. Erik got the upper hand, his brother Abel sued for peace, they met up to celebrate – they never did learn, did they? At the feast Abel's men killed Erik (and threw his body in a river, from where it was later fished out and buried honourably). The year was 1250. Abel the brother-killer lasted two years. Then followed years of uneasy tug-of-war between Crown and Church and Crown and barons to chip away at the Crown's powers. This came to a head in the enforcement by the barons on the king of a charter known as *Håndfæstningen af 1282*, meaning 'deal confirmed in a handshake', in which the king committed to honouring various ancient (as it was claimed) rights and privileges of the country's leading families in return for their loyalty, a Magna Carta-type treaty of the north. The barons were back and the Crown was weak. The king at the time was Erik Klipping, who suffered the indignity of being killed in 1286 while sleeping in his bed, probably by a group of his own men; it was said that he suffered 56 stab wounds.

It was now established convention that new kings were obliged to accept a written pact with 'the people' to be anointed. 'The people' were of course the barons, and the *håndfæstninger* regulated the shifting relative rights and duties of kings and nobles. These pacts were sometimes heeded and sometimes ignored, in later years at least twice being used as the legal base to depose unwanted kings.

If the assassins had wanted to prevent Erik's son, also Erik, known as Menved, from being king, they failed. He was twelve years old and held the throne until 1319. During his time Denmark was in almost constant war with Norway and Sweden, until peace was agreed in 1310. To the south, Menved worked by diplomatic and military means to regain Danish holdings in German and Baltic territories, with some success. His problem, as usual, was finance. His father had started a policy of living off loans from German princes, against security in land. That continued under Menved and under his successor and brother, Christoffer, accumulating to catastrophic results. 'When Christoffer's rule came to an end and the prince without land retired to an estate on Lolland', says Kai Hørby, 'it turned out that all of Denmark was pawned to the dukes of Holstein.' Had the Danish kings been successful in their imperial policy, they might have managed their debt. But they were not, and were unable to reclaim their lands from their financial backers. They in turn wanted their money back, and back they got it, by, as unlikely it may sound today, selling the deeds to Danish lands to the Swedish Crown. Skåne shifted to Sweden. That did not last and Skåne was only later to become permanently Swedish, but for a while Swedish territory was, as the Swedes saw it, complete. Magnus Eriksson, already King of Sweden and Norway, declared himself to be also King of Skåne and hence to be the carrier of 'three crowns', since when *Tre Kronor* has been the Swedish national symbol, as on the national shield and in the name of the royal palace in Stockholm. (But 'three crowns' would also be the symbol of the later Danish-dominated Kalmar Union of all three kingdoms and be used as such by Danish kings long after that union had ended as a way of sticking their tongue out to the Swedes. Christian IV, Danish king from 1588, called the mightiest ship in his navy *Tre Kroner*.)

The Danish kingdom disintegrated and for a while simply did not exist. From 1332 to 1340 there was not even a nominal king on the throne. The Holsteiners were in control until their leading man, Count Gerhard, was killed on 1 April 1340 in his bedroom, having said his evening prayers, by a Danish knight, Niels Ebbesen. This brought a Dane back on the throne, yet another Valdemar. He married the daughter of yet another German count and got some Danish lands back as part of her inheritance. He was later called Atterdag, meaning 'new day' or 'revival', and was, like his earlier namesake, to restore the Danish Crown.

That restoration came about in part by shrewd propaganda: Valdemar elevated himself to mythical proportions by completing a pilgrimage to Jerusalem on horseback and having himself made a Knight of the Holy Sepulchre. And by pragmatic manoeuvres of various kinds. He sold off useless Danish possessions in the east Baltics to the Teutonic Order, so as to buy more useful territories elsewhere.* He let Sweden hold on to Skåne for a while. He rented

---

* The Teutonic Order was a religious fraternity that turned itself into an organised force of state management, under the guise of extending and protecting the Christian dominion. It 'was founded in 1198 in the Holy Land as a hospital order to aid pilgrims. The knights lived in accord with the three monastic vows of chastity, poverty and obedience. The order acquired property through donations from the

out Danish troops as mercenaries in Europe's Hundred Years War. In 1360 he issued a charter known as *Landefreden*, 'Peace in the Land' – effectively a constitution framed as pact between Crown and people (which is to say barons) in a mutual commitment to uphold the peace. And eventually by warfare. He turned on Sweden, which was in internal disarray, and in 1360 and 1361 took and plundered Skåne and Gotland, slaughtering thousands of Gotlanders and extracting a ransom in silver and gold for not flattening Visby, then a German city. His intention was to conquer all of Sweden, but in that he failed. The Hansa, who saw their northern trade threatened, turned against him, in a first war in 1362, which ended in a draw, and a second war in 1368, which ended with the destruction of Copenhagen and defeat for Valdemar. In the ensuing treaty, Denmark was coerced into formalising the League's trading privileges and surrendering most of the tax revenue from Skåne to the Germans for a period of fifteen years (but managed to hold on to the possession). Valdemar had also wanted to get a settlement to the south in Schleswig, but that had not been achieved when he died in 1375, leaving the troublesome border to the south still troublesome.

Harald Hardrade and his heirs gave Norway peace at home for almost a century, until the death of Sigurd Crusader in 1130. Or at least absence of outright civil war. The barons who were on the receiving end of Harald's tyranny hardly had an easy time of it. Harald's son Olav, who had been with his father at Stamford Bridge, went home and ruled in an orderly manner. His grandson, Magnus, said to have been 'the last of the Viking kings', died raiding in Ireland in 1103. In the great-grandson generation, Sigurd, Øystein and another Olav, sons of Magnus by different mistresses, all became kings in 1103. Olav died in 1115, aged seventeen. Øystein took care of

European nobility, especially in the German Empire and in Italy. Akko, or Acre, the last stronghold in the Holy Land, fell to Islam in the year 1291. The leaders moved the order first to Venice, and then in 1309 to Marienburg in Prussia. Under Grand Master Hermann von Salza (1209–39) the Prussian-Baltic tribes were subjugated and converted. A new state grew up out of new castles, cities and villages, administered by some 700 members of the order. In the sixteenth century, Grand Master Albrecht secularised the land as a feudal duchy of the Polish Crown. Though they reorganised the order, their properties dwindled. In 1809 Emperor Napoleon disbanded the order in Germany.' (German Historical Museum, Berlin.)

the kingdom, enabling Sigurd to be away on Crusade for four years, whereupon he, Sigurd, ruled for nineteen years, for the last seven years on his own.

But when Sigurd died, pretenders cast civility aside and went for each other with full force, unleashing the century of civil war. At the young archbishopric in Nidaros, a monk, Theodoricus, was writing the country's history, but would not take his narrative beyond Sigurd's death because 'it would be unworthy to convey to later generations the memory of all the crimes, murders, false oaths, killings among friends, desecration of holy places, sacrilege, rape and abduction and other ill deeds – too many to list here – that then came to pass'. There was personal ambition and greed for power at stake, of course, but it was also a battle over resources. Norway, we must be reminded again, was a poor country. The age of foreign plunder was over, and kings and barons had to live off what the home economy could yield. That was not much. Those who needed capital had to gain control of what little there was and squeeze the people to the last drop.

By twists and turns, out of the civil wars came, eventually, a stronger kingship. Shared kingship was abolished in law, if for a long time not in practice, and the principle of hereditary kingship established, if not always heeded. Kings were to be crowned, normally by the archbishop. The Crown–Church alliance was in the making as the embryo of a new centralised system of power. None of this was plain sailing, but constitutional arrangements were being put in place that could take effect once the fighting had run its course.

This is where Sverre comes into the story to bring slaughter to the barons. Not pretty, but a turning point: the start of the end of the century of civil war. His successor, Håkon, the illegitimate son of an unknown mother, lasted two years but has the achievement to his name of ending the strife with the Church, an indispensable step towards what was to be a firmer kingship.

Enter now the mighty Håkon Håkonsson and after him the blessed Magnus Lawmender. These two, father and son, are the only two kings in all of Norway's history to have exercised royal rule in any real sense. Their predecessors were warlords, their followers, until the collapse of the kingdom, bereft of resources.

Håkonsson's case was weak. He was thirteen years old and the illegitimate son of an illegitimate son of Sverre.* But power relations in an exhausted country were in his favour and the Church gave in to realpolitik. By the time he was sixteen he had taken charge, by 1225 he had crushed another revolt and by 1240 the final one, when the leader and his remaining troops eventually took refuge in a monastery, which the king's men set ablaze so as to fell the last of the rebels when they tried to escape. 'Don't cut my face,' said the chief on surrendering, 'that's not done to chiefs in these parts.' Håkon had spent the first half of his reign bringing the civil wars to an end and now had twenty years ahead of him to make kingship work. 'The realm', says Knut Helle, 'was approaching the first real state organisation in its history.'

Håkonsson was ambitious on a grand scale. He wanted not only to be king, but a *European* king. The bastard who had no right to the throne was determined to show off a reign equal to any. He was a builder, raising an imposing royal compound in Bergen. He built a navy, the largest in Scandinavia. He wanted recognition, which is to say by the pope, which is to say being crowned with papal blessing. He got it, but not until 1247. He had to persuade the pope to disregard Church teaching that only legitimate sons could be kings, which he did with the help of a colossal bribe and a promise to Crusade (which he had no intention of honouring). When he was crowned it was by a papal emissary, one Cardinal William of Sabina, in a ceremony of magnificence never before seen in the kingdom. Håkon got the dignity he craved but had to pay for it. William issued decrees confirming in writing the Church's autonomy in the appointment of bishops and priests and in jurisdiction.

Håkon wanted his court to be known as one of culture. That was to be based on literature. In the north this was limited to the writing of Sagas: Håkon's son had his father's Saga written up in the normal propagandistic fashion. For literary splendour Håkon turned to French and English chivalric poetry, which he had translated into his Norse

---

* Even as an infant, when his mother upheld his right to the throne on behalf of Sverre's line, he was hunted by opposing contenders. Legend has it that, aged one or two, he was carried by two skiers over a mountain range between Gudbrandsdalen and Østerdalen in mid-Norway, a distance of 65 km, thence to be brought to safety in Nidaros. In memory thereof is now held the annual *Birkebeinere* ski run, in which thousands of skiers repeat the mountain crossing. Sverre's men were known as *birkebeinere*, 'birch legs', for their use of birch-bark protective leggings.

language. That worked, sort of. As we have seen previously, the poems were translated but not in their full poetic vivacity. Lost in translation were joy, emotion, pleasure and passionate love. The Norwegians were given only flattened versions of the richer originals. They lacked the grounding that might have enabled them to appreciate the sophistication that was possible in the civilisations they looked to for inspiration.

During Håkon's time all the components of modern kingship we have seen above came into being. Paradoxically, the crowning of an illegitimate heir led on to the enshrinement of the principle that kingship would follow the legitimate line. In 1260, a new law of Crown inheritance was issued, and in a brand-new way. It was explicitly 'given' by the king on the 'advice' of his council.

In foreign policy, Håkon took his ambition west to consolidate a North Atlantic empire embracing Iceland, Greenland, the Faroes, Shetlands, Orkneys, Hebrides and Man. This gave him and Magnus much prestige in Europe, and some tax revenue, but it was a make-believe empire, too scattered to be held together and Norway too poor to do so. Håkon died in the Orkneys during an expedition to protect his holdings. The empire, if it ever had been a reality, disintegrated.

Magnus, king from 1257 to 1280, first jointly with his father, is the most revered monarch in Norwegian tradition, the maker of good and fair law (but, says Kåre Lunden, an obsessive pedantic and bore who worried himself to an early death). Under him, two national and comprehensive codes of law were issued, the Landlaw (1274) and the City Law (1276). These were in one way similar to Valdemar's code in Denmark of more than a century earlier, in theory absorbing existing law from below, but in reality making new law from above. But they were also different. They were explicitly national; gone was the notion of law being regional. They were big and expansive, reflecting the idea that the Crown had authority in almost all aspects of life and business. The Landlaw is enormous in span and detail, consisting of ten books with 225 chapters, divided into innumerable and mostly lengthy paragraphs and sub-paragraphs. An impressive feat, and not in vain. The laws were reasonably effective and in large measure implemented. Forty years after the end of anarchy, people's livelihoods had better regulation and more security than ever before.

The kingdom remained, or so it seemed, in good order under two more kings, Erik from 1280 to 1299 and another Håkon from 1299, known as the 5th. He, however, had no son, only two daughters. With

no immediate heir, the Crown passed to a grandson. He happened to
be Swedish, the son of Håkon's oldest daughter and a Swedish duke,
and is known as Magnus Eriksson, the one who would later hold 'three
crowns'. He was three years old.

It happened at the same time in Sweden that the king there, Birger,
had been exiled to Denmark and his only son killed. That made
Magnus heir there as well – he was Birger's nephew – and he was
declared King of Sweden a month after he had been made King of
Norway. His regents, until he came of age, were to be his Swedish
grandmother and Norwegian mother.

For Norway, this was the first step to being reduced to a union-
kingdom. There was to be one more Norwegian king, Håkon VI, from
1355, but when he died the country fell into union again, now with
Denmark, and had come to the end of the line as an independent
kingdom. Soon, 'Norway as a political entity ceased to exist, other
than as a historical concept.'* (When Norway next had its own king,
in 1905, he took the name Haakon VII.)

Sweden entered the high Middle Ages in chaos (of course). The run
of ineffective kings showed no sign of ending. Sverker the Old, also
called Clubfoot, came to the throne in 1130 by killing a competing
pretender, but ended by being killed himself, on Christmas Day 1156,
on his way to church, by a servant. He was followed by Erik the
Saint, who lasted four years and who was to become the patron saint
of Sweden. He too was murdered, again at church, being stabbed and
beheaded, aged forty. He became known as a good king, a builder of
churches and a Crusader on Finland. He was a devout Christian of
strong personal piety. Legend after his death would have him a maker
of miracles. It was said that a spring with healing waters appeared in
the ground where his cut-off head had fallen. His bones are preserved
in a reliquary in Uppsala Cathedral, built on the site of his martyrdom.

---

* A union, as the term is used here, consists of two or more kingdoms under a joint
king. These kingdoms are constitutionally autonomous. When Magnus Eriksson
was King of Norway and of Sweden he was at the head of two separate kingdoms.
Likewise, when Norway later fell into union with Denmark, there was still (for a
while) the Kingdom of Norway. In 1814, Norway broke free from Denmark and
re-emerged as a kingdom of its own, but again in a union, now with Sweden.

(The original shrine was melted down in the sixteenth century by King Johan III to help pay off a war ransom.)

Erik's killer, Magnus II, lasted only a year, being killed in war, and so it went on with continuing mayhem until this line came to an end with Erik the Lisp and Lame, who died in 1250.

That Erik was not much of a king, although he lasted sixteen years (and was still only thirty-four when he died). Among the many things he did not achieve was to produce an heir, that failure being by far the best service he did to the kingdom. The modernisation of kingship had started with a council of advisors instituted to assist the king, the head of which carried the title of *Jarl*, earl. When Erik died, the *Jarl* was one Birger. A man of unhesitant and forceful action, he stepped into the vacuum at Erik's death and took charge. He had his son, Valdemar, elected king and stayed in post as his son's *Jarl*, and de facto ruler. What one cannot take with violence, he is said to have said – and this was 300 years before the eminent Machiavelli in Florence made himself famous for the same teaching – 'one must take with lies, trickery and deceit'. He died in 1266 and managed, in his sixteen years in power, to bring a revolution down upon the emerging Kingdom of Sweden, the revolution of fully fledged kingship.

The core of his revolution was to eliminate the local barons and shift power to the centre. He forged alliances with the Church and with German merchants. From the Church he got dignity, from the Germans credit. The barons resented being sidelined; they mobilised and engaged Birger in battle, but were outsmarted when Birger pretended to sue for peace. He wanted to be their friend, he said, brought them together to celebrate with him, and used the feast to execute, with sword and axe, then and there, a generation of barons. He confiscated their property and was free from baronial trouble during his reign.

It was not to last. The barons would be back, and for the rest of the Middle Ages Swedish political history was a running battle between Crown and aristocracy. It might have seemed that Birger had settled that power struggle to the benefit of the Crown, but not so. The strong Swedish state was in the making, but not without an interregnum of about 200 years during which power mostly, but not always, rested on the side of the nobility.

Birger used his period of peace to institute tax, legal and administrative reforms. He built royal fortifications around the country which became managerial and tax-extracting centres in the regions, under the management of royal officials. He created national law, removing local lawmaking powers (although the codification of national law, as had been done in Norway by Magnus Lawmender, was not completed until around 1350). He created a robust tax system capable of raising serious resources of governance, and built up an army under central command. He founded cities, including Stockholm (in 1252 it is said), and expanded the territory of Sweden, securing a land corridor through a Danish-held area on the Kattegat to the west and annexing parts of Finland to the east. He was not early in administrative reform, but did it in a big way. This was, says Dick Harrison, 'a watershed in Swedish history', adding that probably no single man has influenced that history as strongly as did Birger *Jarl*.

Valdemar outlived his father, holding on to the throne until 1275, when he was forced out by his brother, another Magnus, after a sex scandal involving a Danish sister-in-law. That was so grave a sin that he had to travel to Rome to seek papal forgiveness. Magnus had himself crowned king, locked up his brother on his return, and ruled until 1290. Royal power earlier on had had a weaker base in Sweden than in Denmark and Norway, but that was now reversed. The strong State, which was to be a characteristic of Swedish political order, and still is, was emerging, if not yet firmly in place.

It was not to be without setbacks, first in the royal succession. When Magnus's son, called Birger after his grandfather, was put on the throne aged four, kingly brothers plunged the country back into another thirty years of civil war. Birger was finally forced into exile, to Denmark in 1318. He managed to have his brothers killed (starved to death in a dungeon, it was said), but not to prevent his own son and heir from being executed by decapitation. That cleared the way for Magnus Eriksson, whom we have already met, to be elected, another child-king.

Underlying the royal turbulence was the old struggle with the barons. After Birger *Jarl*'s dramatic centralisation of power, the next generation, the sons of those he had killed, mobilised about twenty-five years later, as would their sons again in the next generation. It went like this (using a broad brush): after 1290, civil war; from 1319, order again and the Crown building itself up in strength; from 1350, back into chaos for the rest of the century.

Magnus, King of both Sweden and Norway, came of age and made himself more Swedish than Norwegian as king, eventually leaving Norway to his son Håkon. On Magnus's anointment in 1319, a group of bishops and barons had issued upon him a document, known as the *Frihetsbrevet*, the 'Charter of Liberties', much like the Danish *Håndfæstningen af 1282*, in which they laid down the conditions and limitations on which he had been made king. It was not of much consequence at the time, but when state power withered after the calamity of the Big Death, the barons were able to assert their 'ancient rights' and refuse an oppressive, as they saw it, king their obedience. A faction of Swedish barons declared him deposed and tried to take the Norwegian Håkon to be king. Others in Sweden, however, found another candidate, Albrekt of Mecklenburg, and put him on the throne in 1363 – 'the lowest esteemed and most despised of all Swedish monarchs in all times'. Magnus raised an army but was beaten, imprisoned and humiliated, and his kingship in Sweden was over. Håkon, his son, had to buy him free in 1371, after seven years, with a ransom bigger than a year's Crown revenue, and Magnus was reduced to managing a slice of his previous union as his son's junior partner. Albrekt held the Swedish Crown, unhappily for himself and others, until 1389.

In foreign policy, as Denmark had gone south and Norway west, Sweden went east. The enduring legacy was the annexation of Finland, starting with the deal with Novgorod in 1323 to divide the Finnish lands in two. There were to be various unions in Scandinavia, but this was something else. There was no Finnish kingdom. Sweden subsumed the territory of Finland into the *rike*, a state of affairs that was to last until 1809.

The eastern campaign eventually extended to Novgorod itself. It was a war of conquest, but also a religious war. The east was falling under the Orthodox Church. Sweden was encouraged by Rome to Crusade, and at home kings were spurred on by the domestic Church and by religious zealots. One such was the Holy Birgitta, a Swedish aristocrat turned religious mystic who claimed, and was believed, in a state of trance to be receiving messages directly from Christ and the Virgin Mary, who established an aristocratic monastic order, who was commanded by Christ to 'go to Rome and be there until you can meet the Emperor and Pope', who so did in 1350, who stayed in Rome and exercised much influence in the Church, assisting in the pope's return to Rome from his exile in Avignon, who died there in 1373, the year after having completed a pilgrimage to the Holy Land, and who was canonised in 1391. While still in Sweden she had stirred Magnus to

Crusade east, which he did. But later, from Rome, she turned against him and encouraged rebellion for having deserted his kingly mission, for not being true to the faith, and for, she suggested, 'probably' being homosexual.

The deal with Novgorod to divide Finland was not intended to last. By the 1340s the Crown was at the height of its power. Magnus issued an ultimatum to the Russians to convert to the Roman Church, then marched east and laid siege to Novgorod. Sweden was extending its reach and ready to annex more territory. But he had to give up and scurry home – not because he was defeated but because the Big Death struck. Swedish imperial ambition was given up. For now. It was to return with a vengeance 300 years on.

The Great Transformation – a summary

The long 1200s saw Scandinavia's first Great Transformation, with much force and on many fronts at the same time. Its branches – economic, social, religious, political – intertwined and were each other's enablers.

It was, first and foremost, an economic upturn. There were three components: better agriculture, better fisheries, better trade. It was because improvements on these fronts coincided that they added up to a big leap.

The economic revolution gave birth to a new class system. At the bottom of the stratification was created a class of subjugated peasants, at the top one of wealthy landowners. Between these extremes, out of the nexus of increasing trade and rising cities, yet another new class started to emerge, that of city burghers. And all the while, a fourth 'class' carved out social and political space for itself: the men of the Church, in command of norms, land, revenue, organisation and skills. From these changes was born a different society, no longer composed of barons, freemen and slaves but of nobles, churchmen, burghers and farmers-peasants-proletarians-serfs.

It was, secondly, a political transformation that gave the Scandinavians their first experience of State rule, made possible by the initial changes in the economy and class structure. Not State rule as we might think of it today, but still a taste of things to come.

The political transformation had two main components: an

organised Church and the invention of State institutions, such as hereditary kingship, written law and embryonic national assemblies, governments and civil services.

On the back of this double transformation, the Scandinavians were to move forward and upward over the next centuries. Not in a linear fashion: there were to be ups and downs and many setbacks. And not in an agreeable way. The small-folks would be powerless and live in misery and repression, the larger history around them violent and ugly.

One reason for the continued turbulence and setbacks was a remaining flaw in the transformation. There were State institutions but finance was lacking. The Church was rich, the landowners were rich, but the Crowns poor. Finance was to be torture for kings with ambitions.

4

Big Death, Slow Resurrection

Everything in ruin, progress shattered, prosperity ended, statehood crushed. There had been previous plagues, but not like this one. Plague would recur until the eighteenth century, but not again with this force. Even the worst of wars, even the Thirty Years War that left Europe in ruin, did not come near to the same magnitude of destruction. The devastation was immediate. On Gotland, at Källunge, stands a house of God whose building stopped as death swept over the island and is today a working church, still incomplete.

Vision of the Black Death

How it happened

The plague arrived in Europe in 1347, having originated in East Asia four or five years earlier, and spread west and north to ravage all of the continent. We know it today as the Black Death, but at the time, all over Europe, it was the 'Big Death'. It came to Norway in mid-1349, carried by English ships to Bergen, probably independently to Oslo, possibly to other ports. It struck Denmark at about the same time, by both land and sea, and moved across Sweden the next year. By 1351 this outbreak was over, but the damage was compounded by plague returning in several waves during the rest of the century and beyond. In 1654, one in four of the population of Copenhagen perished in yet another wave of plague, and as late as 1711, in the last major epidemic, a third of the population.

The plague is a contagious bacterial disease against which there was no known protection at the time. The contagion spread mainly by infected rats that were bitten by lice that then bit people. In this form, bubonic, it was ugly. Boils and sores broke out on the body, hands and feet went black, the infected would be in desperate pain, eight out of ten dead in two or three days. It also spread from person to person through touch or coughing. This way, pneumonic, death might come faster, sometimes with no visible symptoms, people just falling down dead. It was an indiscriminate disease, sweeping away high and low and people in towns and countryside alike. Children were vulnerable, city dwellers vulnerable. Priests, who cared for parishioners, were much exposed. In Norway, the Archbishop of Nidaros died, as did at least three bishops. In Sweden, King Erik Magnusson (rival king to his father) and his wife Beatrix were both struck down. It spread quickly along routes of human movement, following the instinct to flee, whereby people carried the disease with them. From the cities, where the disease arrived, people would flee 'home' to where they had family and kin.

In Norway, a population of 460,000 or thereabouts was decimated by possibly as much as 60 to 65 per cent. The number of active farms in 1500 was still less than half the figure ahead of 1350. In Denmark and Sweden, it is thought that around half the people perished, the Swedish population falling to half a million. The Danish population had trebled to around 1.5 million between 1100 to 1300 (including the

Danish lands in southern Sweden); by 1400 it was reduced to about 700,000, a century later to around 600,000. It was to be roughly 300 years before the populations were back to what they had been by 1350.

What it meant

National economies were halved. The value of land deflated. State rule disintegrated as revenue from both rent and tax dried up. In Norway, says Ole Jørgen Benedictow, 'the state apparatus collapsed immediately after the first wave'. Church finances crashed, parishes gave up. In Trondheim there had been fourteen working churches; eighty years after the Big Death only five remained. The Church that had been a State within the State was never again to matter as it had done.

Land was concentrated in fewer hands, creating a yet smaller class of super-barons. Villages disappeared; across Danish landscapes today, medieval churches that once served communities stand alone in empty areas. There was a shift back from cereal cultivation to less productive cattle husbandry. Trade withered. Urban populations shrank. No new towns of any significance emerged between 1350 and 1500. 'Not until the second half of the fifteenth century can one detect [in Norway] the first tentative signs of new growth in agricultural settlements. And not until well into the sixteenth century are there clear signs of growth in settlement and population across the country as a whole.' Grain harvest and cattle-holding did not recover to the levels of 1300 until the mid-1600s.

There were further changes in mindsets and ways of thinking. There was a need to find an explanation. Near to hand was God's wrath. In late 1349, King Magnus Eriksson issued a decree to warn of the danger: 'For the sins of man, God is punishing the world with a great scourge and sudden death.' People were instructed to intensify their worship and their demonstration of faith. Many did. If God was punishing them for their sinful lives, their response must be to improve their ways in His image. Cults flourished, of the Virgin Mary, of St Olav, of the Holy Birgitta. There was an increase in self-flagellation and other forms of extreme worship.

Someone had to shoulder the blame. All over Europe, the Jews were a prime target – in Dresden the Count of Meissen ordered the city's Jews to be executed (by being burned). It was being said that the plague had its origin in Jerusalem, meaning the Jewish world, and hence in infidelity to the Christian faith. It was blamed on sorcerers, witches and practitioners of occult arts. In Visby, the city council ordered nine poison-mixers to burn at the stake. They were said to have confessed to various misdeeds, including the poisoning of wells across Gotland and Sweden. A new brutality was born, evolving into ever-harsher persecution of outcasts from the true path of believership.

The people's struggle for survival: aristocracy

Times were not all bad for those who survived, at least for some of them. Land became abundant, hence cheap, hence shifting upward in ownership. Those already the richest in land were the big winners; others were winners on a smaller scale. Fewer tenants were available to work the land and landowners could extract less rent. Survivors were able to hold on to good land, let poorer land lie fallow and pay less for what they had.

One might imagine that living conditions then improved in the farming population, and so they may well have for fortunate tenants, but probably not generally. During the previous period of population growth there had been increasing pressure on land; as a result it was overworked and marginal land put under plough. In Denmark, land had become so heavily exploited that agricultural failure was a crisis waiting to happen. Climate change added to the pressure. The Great Transformation had been aided by mild summers and short winters. Now temperatures were falling and land yield shrank. It became known as 'the Little Ice Age'. In Norway glaciers expanded, making previously arable land unworkable. There might be more land per farm, but there was less to be had from it. Output value fell since there were fewer consumers in demand of produce.

Landlords had to bend to the law of supply and demand and lower rents, but Crown and Church did not similarly renounce their demands on tax and tithe. In theory, the Crown was not supposed – except in periods of emergency, notably war – to tax the people directly but to live off its regular incomes from rent, fines and the like; but now it used the crisis to make taxation more regular. The Church compensated for the loss of tithe income by reviving older fees that had previously been subsumed into the tithe, sometimes inventing new ones, and squeezing 'voluntary' gifts and land donations out of populations tormented by the apocalypse. Peasants knew that if they had anything left over, the vultures would come for it.

Mindsets were different from what we are used to. What the German sociologist Max Weber later called 'the spirit of capitalism' had not yet descended on the Scandinavians, or anyone else. The peasant was in it for subsistence. Profit had no part in his mental landscape, nor the idea, ingrained in us today, that each generation should do better than the previous one; in those days you honoured you parents by following in their footsteps and doing as they had done. You needed enough produce to feed your family, to set aside seed grain for next year, to pay your rent and tax, and perhaps hold a reserve in case of misfortune. More than that did not do you much good. There is no point in cooking more porridge than anyone can eat. You and neighbours might exchange some goods, but you lived in an economy without money and there was nothing against which to sell surplus produce. You were not connected to networks of trade. Your connections were to landlord, Crown and Church, who all fleeced you for what they could. If the peasant satisfied them and also took care of his own, his economy was doing for him what he needed from it. Life became easier, less burdensome, less exposed to want and hunger, less precarious, but not affluent.

In fact, nothing much happened for the small-folks in their standard of living until the nineteenth century, when peasantry faded out. Until then, peasant farmers remained the backbone of the economy and continued to live from one generation to the next as they had done. To be sure, there were good times and bad. People lived better in good years and might go hungry when crops failed, but the ups and downs were between living passably and living desperately, never living well. The bottom line was stability: survival but not much more. Nowhere is that stability clearer to see than in the lives of women. Their chores remained as they had been: the milking of cows, the separating of milk, the churning of butter, the brewing of beer, the rest of the domestic womanly chores, the bearing of children.

*

It has been usual to describe the upper echelon of Viking society as an aristocracy. Certainly there were 'leading' men and families, some of them up there with kings, sometimes as allies and sometimes as competitors, some of them gave themselves titles. The intransigent barons in mid-Norway who gave Harald Hardrade trouble called themselves Earls of Lade. But an established aristocracy it hardly was. There was no clarity as to who belonged to it, and little continuity.

If an aristocracy is made up of an upper class with legally protected privileges, that was to come to Scandinavia with the Great Transformation. The Church made itself aristocratic. It owned land, had revenue from rent and tithe, was above the State's law, was exempt from tax to the Crown, and its men carried titles and lived well. Since churchmen were not (supposed to be) married, it was not a hereditary aristocracy, but nevertheless an upper class of protected privilege.

The 'civilian' aristocracy floated to the top of the new structure of class inequality. Land was concentrated into fewer hands. The men of the landowning class were co-opted into Crown service as knights and commanders. That was an attractive deal: not only were you spared from taxation and had your wealth left untouched, you were admitted into the exclusive élite of the social hierarchy. You had privileges that could be passed on down the family line. You belonged to a cast of warrior landowners. You could give yourself a title and your family a coat of arms. You could indulge in a life of heraldry and romantic militarism. In Sweden, the high nobility was to dominate to such a degree as to collapse kingship itself into an aristocratic republic. 'There is', observe Harrison and Eriksson, 'a direct line from the aristocratic knights of the 1200s to the aristocratic officer class of the 1800s.'

And in Norway? Different, as usual. Here the economic conditions that uphold an aristocratic stratum were absent. Such aristocratic landholdings as there had been were mostly lost in the aftermath of the Big Death. From 1380, there was no separate Norwegian monarchy to maintain a court nobility. By the end of the Middle Ages the Norwegian aristocracy, such as it had been, had died out.

The states' struggle with each other: union

On 17 June 1397, a Danish–Norwegian–Swedish congress, meeting in the town of Kalmar in Sweden, agreed a treaty of union for the three kingdoms and oversaw the crowning of Erik of Pomerania, the son of a German duke, as a three-country king. But he was king in name only; the boss was Margrete, his aunt (known to history as Queen Margrete I, although technically never queen in her own right), who had adopted him for the purpose and stayed in charge until she died in 1412. She has been revered in Scandinavian history, as much as the kings of the Kalmar Union have been reviled.

The Big Death collapsed the Norwegian and Swedish kingdoms into failed states. For Magnus Eriksson in Sweden, it fell apart after the fiasco in Russia. In Norway the Crown just went broke. The situation became dire. In 1370, Margrete was in Oslo, alone at Akershus Fort while her husband, Håkon, was in Sweden trying to raise money. She wrote to let him know that she was running out of food and was having to let her servants go because she could not feed them. She begged him to arrange credit with a merchant in the city, and with a German trader for provisions from the next ship due.

Things were better in Denmark. Valdemar Atterdag had been not unsuccessful in restoring the Crown. Strength in Denmark and weakness in Norway and Sweden were to offer Margrete, Valdemar's daughter, a base from which to forge, with extraordinary skills in statecraft, a united Scandinavia to be ruled by herself and her heirs.

The States that had been coming into being in the previous century were supposed to have freed kings from the tyranny of the barons, but after the Big Death they were back. The most dramatic case was that of the Swedish Bo Jonsson (c.1338–86). He was able and ruthless, fanatically dedicated to acquiring more and more property, amassed with all possible means, including cheating, intimidation and murder, none of which he denied. His wife had inherited property of her own. She was pregnant and dying. In a calculated misdeed, he had her belly cut open. She died but the child was born in time to become the legal owner of her property, securing it for Bo when the child too died. Bo became Sweden's richest man. The king, as usual short of funds, was forced to borrow from Bo, who secured for himself control of Crown domains. He became governor of Swedish Finland and other royal fiefs. When he died he owned or controlled nearly half of Sweden.

The winners abroad were assorted Germans. The Holsteiners held Schleswig, which Valdemar had been unable to incorporate into his Danish realm. Skåne was Danish, but on the condition that tax revenues went to the German creditors. The Hansa manipulated the Scandinavians against each other and fortified their trading privileges. Danish kings had to turn to German princes for finance, which they obtained by again mortgaging counties. That was good business for the Germans, who obtained not only a secure placement of capital but also, at a time when Church teaching was against the payment of interest, a disguised return on their loans in the form of a share of the Crown's revenue from the mortgaged counties. But it was expensive for the king and the country. The king got one-off payments of cash but lost his tax base and had to squeeze all the more out of the populace in his remaining domains.

When Valdemar died in 1375, Margrete came into her own. Aged twenty-two, she hurried back to Denmark and started the machinations that would make her lord of all Scandinavia. She was the arch-Scandinavian, the daughter of one king, Danish, the wife of another one, Norwegian, the daughter-in-law of a third one, Swedish, and related to German clans in Pomerania. She was born in Denmark and raised partly in Sweden. At the age of ten she was married to the Norwegian king; two or three years later she moved to Oslo and was pregnant at seventeen (which was when she wrote to her husband about running out of food). She was a devout and obedient young woman, loyal to her station as consort, who, however, soon proved to be of steely will and ruthless determination. Her husband was king, she was his young queen; she just got up and left.

Here we have three kingdoms that for 500 years had striven to find a way towards nationhood, that in the process had been relentlessly warring against each other, and that now at a stroke were to be subsumed within each other in peaceful collaboration, in an unlikely deal that came into being, says the Danish historian Troels Dahlerup, 'almost miraculously'. Perhaps in Margerte's mind the divisions within Scandinavia were artificial. We may assume she thought the kingdoms were in dire straits, disorganised, at each others' throats, more or less under foreign – German – domination. We may asssume she took the view that the kingdoms should be aligned, that the way to secure that was through a union, and that she was the agent to bring that about, with herself at the helm. Some woman, some vision! And not only that: she saw it realised.

Scandinavian royal families had now become so entangled with each other, and with German families, through generations of intermarriage that rafts of princes had claims all over the place. These were constellations of confusion that Margrete was able to play on. It may also have helped that the Church was more or less out of the game, disempowered by the Big Death. Margrete flattered it with generosity and devotion to the Holy Birgitta and her memory. Of the troubles she had to deal with, the Church was not one.

As kingship was disintegrating around her, she had the ultimate asset: a son. Valdemar had died without a direct male heir; two sons had both died before him. She outmanoeuvred an older sister who also had a son and got her own son crowned king, at age four, which is to say she got herself made regent. Five years later, in 1380, her husband Håkon died in Norway aged forty. He had been a feeble king. One of Norway's most eminent historians, Halvdan Koht (whom we will meet later on at a time of destiny), said of Håkon that there was 'something strangely pale about the man and his doings and that he seemed to have little force of life in him'. Margrete got her son crowned King of Norway as well; he was Oluf in Denmark, Olav in Norway and she could rule in his name. (In the restored Norwegian kingdom after 1905, the second king was Olav V.)

Once her reign was thus established, Oluf died in 1387, aged sixteen. Her own position was now formalised, effectively as queen but in name 'gracious lady and husband and regent of the kingdoms'.

In Denmark, she solved the Skåne problem. The Germans' claim on Crown revenue ran out in 1385, and she got them to accept that loss by leaving their trading privileges intact. She settled the Schleswig problem by leaving Schleswig to the Holsteiners, but on the understanding that it was Danish land which they had in fief from the Danish Crown, the compromise at the core of 'the Schelswig-Holstein question' that made Schleswig and Holstein at one and the same time German and Danish lands. In Sweden, the barons, or most of them, were in revolt against King Albrekt, who was greedily clawing back for the Crown as much as possible of Bo Jonsson's and other barons' property and was hated by aristocrats and small-folks alike for his retinue of German officials and their heavy-handed methods of taxation and confiscation. They saw Margrete as their best bet and begged her to help. War followed. Albrekt was dispatched back to Meckelenburg. Sweden was in Margrete's hands (although Stockholm, a more or less German city of the Hanseatic League, only after years of holding out). All three kingdoms were united under a single sovereign.* As a sign of her statecraft, in Sweden she secured for the Crown the financial deal with the barons that Albrekt had sought in vain and won loyalty for the very dispositions that had been his demise. At the congress in Kalmar it was all formalised when her adopted son was anointed king in all three countries, aged sixteen.

Kings of the Kalmar Union, with years of reign

Erik of Pomerania
King of Denmark, 1396–1439
King of Norway, 1389–1442
King of Sweden, 1396–1439

Christoffer of Bavaria
King of Denmark, 1440–48
King of Norway, 1442–48
King of Sweden, 1441–48

Christian I
King of Denmark, 1448–81
King of Norway, 1450–81
King of Sweden, 1457–64 (nominally)

Hans
King of Denmark, 1482–1513
King of Norway, 1483–1513
King of Sweden, 1497–1501 (nominally)

Christian II
King of Denmark, 1513–23
King of Norway, 1513–23
King of Sweden, 1520–21

* The machinations were intricate, to put it mildly: 'King Albrekt was released in return for his promise to pay 60,000 silver marks within three years. Stockholm was placed in pawn with the Hansa which saw this as a guarantee of peaceful conditions that would lead to the renewal of their privileges. If King Albrekt did not pay the release money in time, he was to return to prison or hand over Stockholm to Margrete. In the following years the queen seems to have supported the activity of the privateers in order to make it difficult for the Hansa to hold on to Stockholm and in 1398 the city was finally handed over to her.' (Jens Olesen, *The Cambridge History of Scandinavia*, Vol. 1, p. 724.)

The Union was ambitious. It was intended to secure peace between the three kingdoms in a defence pact against foreign enemies; an attack on one would be considered an attack on them all – a mini NATO before its time. It was intended to be an economic union, in that citizens in any of the kingdoms should have the right to do business in any of the others – a mini European Union ahead of its time. It was intended to stand up against the power of the Germans. But it was not a success. It held together for as long as Margrete ruled but started to fall apart the moment she was gone. 'Norway was not much of a problem in the union, as seen from the vantage of the Crown', say Steinar Imsen and Jørn Sandnes. 'The country was distant, poor and sparsely populated, the aristocracy weak, the tradition loyalty.' But Sweden was not about to make itself junior partner under the Danish Crown.

HOW DID THEY TRAVEL?

In 1413, the year after she died, Margrete's remains were brought to Roskilde Cathedral, where they still rest in a magnificent sarcophagus. It was a grand ceremony presided over by the Archbishop of Lund in the presence of fifteen more bishops and many other dignitaries from all three countries. How did they get there?

The Kalmar Union came into being at a congress of at least 100 dignitaries from the three countries. While the Union existed, there were constant council meetings and congresses of various kinds, both national and international. Just the year after Kalmar, there was another congress in Copenhagen with at least eighty-eight delegates. Margrete and her follower kings, and their queens, travelled across their realms continuously, and also through Europe. Nobles met, nationally and internationally, for aristocratic assemblies, as did bishops and churchmen for Church meetings. These are big lands of long distances, high mountains and vast forests, much of the territory sparsely populated or not at all. Roads were poor or non-existent. Grandees, who were not young, had to travel in winter no less than in summer. When royals travelled, they did so with retinues. What were the logistics of getting around?

When Margrete hurried back to Denmark when her father died in 1375, she travelled by ship. This was in November, at the very end of the sailing season, and would have been a rough passage for mother and little son. When King Erik journeyed north from Denmark to Oslo in

Norway in the winter of 1405, he went overland. An intended continuation to Bergen had to be given up as not practically possible. When
in 1423 he went on pilgrimage to the Holy Land, the journey from
Venice was by ship, in humble disguise to deceive potential pirates, but
the return from Ragusa (now Dubrovnik) was overland, on horseback
one would imagine. When he and Philippa were married in 1406, the
bride's equipment included a carriage with seats in red leather and eight
saddles, no doubt for ceremonial use. On 20 November 1449, King Karl
of Sweden was crowned King of Norway in Nidaros (although only
in name). Feast done, he set off back home to Stockholm. The winter
journey took two weeks.

Early roads were a local responsibility. They took the form of carriage
wheel tracks that were kept open by farm and peasant carriages. As trade
and transport increased, more sturdy carriages came into use, with wider
wheelbases. More robust roads were needed than could be maintained
locally, and the State gradually became involved in road-building.

The best road in medieval Scandinavia was probably the old *Hærvej*
from Jylland to Germany, along which now flowed a lively Danish–
German trade, in livestock from the north, from the south processed
goods brought north by mule and carriage. Ferries operated across the
sounds between Denmark's islands. In winter, where there was snow,
travel could be by horse and sleigh, often easier than in summer. In the
sixteenth century, under Frederik II, 'royal roads' were built in parts of
Denmark, good roads first open only to the king and his officials, later
for public use. This was the beginning of a network of engineered public
roads, to be realised across the lands in the next centuries.

On 27 February 1461, a new bishop was elected in Roskilde. Shortly
after, a delegation set off for Rome with notification of the election and
for the pope's ratification. They arrived in late May or early June and
on 13 June obtained the papal blessing. Visits to Rome from Scandinavia
were standard, even if the journey one-way would take about three
months. In 1474, Christian I and his retinue travelled from Denmark to
Rome and back, leaving in January, working their way through Germany
in February, arriving in Milan in mid-March and in Rome by Easter,
setting off from Rome again on 27 April to be back in Copenhagen by
August.

Travel by land was predominantly on horseback; there were hardly any
continuous roads capable of accommodating carriages over any distance.
An able rider on a good horse and in easy terrain might manage 50 km a

day, exceptionally more. The road distance from Oslo to Kalmar today is upward of 600 km, which at the time would have taken no less than ten days, probably longer. As late as the mid-1600s, on comparatively good Swedish roads a horse and carriage with an easy load might manage a speed of 2 to 3 km per hour.

Those who travelled needed accommodation, which they would have to find from willing providers. There was much conflict and insecurity, with embezzlement and trouble with payments. From the thirteenth century in Denmark, inns began to be established under royal regulation and privilege. Margrete decreed that there should be inns along main routes at a day's journey distance, 40 km, and gradually a network of 'royal inns' came into being (the origin of today's proliferation of much-appreciated country inns across the country). A similar regulation was issued in Sweden in 1649, but implemented hesitantly.

Communications improved slowly. The first highway of carriage pro-portions in Norway was 40 km long, from the mining town of Kongsberg to the nearby port of Bragernes (now Drammen), which was opened in 1634 and extended to Christiania in 1665. Postal services came into operation during the seventeenth century on a few main routes, started to operate on a few main connections from 1647, and more broadly a century later. In the Sweden-Norway union of 1814, a dispatch from Stockholm to Oslo would take six to eight days. A rail connection opened in 1871, reducing travel time to about twenty hours.

Erik did not have Margrete's feeling for politics as the art of the possible and for exercising strength through cautious compromise and the placating of potential enemies. When he no longer had her guid-ance he became arrogant and took to fighting left, right and centre, reverting to the old Scandinavian folly of overreaching, the mistake it had been Margrete's genius to avoid. It came to war again with the Holsteiners over Schleswig. Elsewhere, he brought in German officials to harass local populations, in Sweden both German and Danish ones. The result was too much conflict, too much humiliation, too much deceit, too much warfare, too much taxation – basically he could not handle it and things fell apart. In both Sweden and Denmark he was up against powerful aristocracies and city burghers who did not appreciate their privileges and businesses being eroded. He fought the Hansa in ways that impeded trade. In Sweden, the mining industry was advancing in importance and needed to get its ore shipped to markets in Europe. It ended in bloody and violent revolt that spread across Sweden and into Norway. In 1439 Erik took refuge in Gotland, where he received, not as he hoped a plea to return, but notification from both the Swedish and Danish *råd* that he was deposed. (He hung on in Gotland for another ten years, providing for himself as a pirate within his own kingdom, until returning to Pomerania in 1449.) The Union had a new king, Chistoffer of Bavaria, from 1440 until he died in 1448. He called himself 'arch-king' in the European tradition for rulers over several domains.

The Union survived on paper, but not in reality. It depended on a strong kingship, but Danish and Swedish aristocracies had so advanced in power as to hold kings in constant check. Christoffer died childless and Sweden and Denmark each went their own way. The big idea had been for the Scandinavian countries to stand together against the Germans, but the German threat was fading. The Hansa cities were losing their autonomy and their ability to uphold trading monopolies. The Swedes, or most of them, had never liked the Union and saw no benefit in it. Soon mighty barons had no need for a king at all, certainly not a foreign king. Christian I was King of Denmark and Norway from 1448 and 1450 respectively, but was for long just disregarded in Sweden, although nominally king there as well from 1457. Finally, in 1471, he arrived in Stockholm with fleet and army to claim his Swedish kingdom but suffered a humiliating defeat, his force disintegrating, many drowning in chaotic retreat, he himself wounded by a bullet to the mouth at the cost of a row of teeth. That was it for the first Christian in Sweden – a repetition of the venture was out of the question for lack of finance. His son and successor, Hans, invaded again and was nominally king from 1497 to 1501, only to be deposed as soon as the Swedish aristocrats were able to set aside their differences; he had failed to reward those who had worked for his case and humiliated those who had not. He was King of Denmark and Norway until 1513, when he exited history by falling off his horse trying to ford a river in flood and died a few days later.

Sweden was effectively a republic; State affairs were in the hands of the *riksråd* and *riksföreståndare*, presidents, literally 'chairmen of the realm' (although the first of them, Karl Knutsson, who was weak in power and could therefore be allowed elevation in title, was called king, for a year even King of Norway). Against that provocation, the next Christian of Denmark, the second, decided to restore the union monarchy yet again. He had served his apprenticeship in the art of kingship as resident dictator in Norway from 1506 to 1513. There he took to governing by murder and terror, throwing bishops in jail and crushing what remained of Norwegian institutions. A first attempt in Sweden failed, but the Danes escaped with a cluster of hostages, among them a young man called Gustav Vasa, soon to make his mark. A second attempt, with the help of mercenaries from Germany, France and Scotland (the latter said to have been particularly vicious), succeeded militarily.

On Sunday, 4 November 1520, Christian is crowned King of Sweden. The feast goes on for three days in the palace at Stockholm, with lavish food and drink, the cream of ecclesiastical and aristocratic élites in attendance, under a promise of amnesty. Then, on Wednesday, the palace gates are shut and the assembled Swedish grandees locked up. The feast becomes a court and Christian its judge. The charges are treason, heresy and infringements of Church rights. Executions follow in Stockholm's central square: bishops first, two of them, nobles by order of eminence. This is the Bloodbath of Stockholm. When it is over, eighty-two men at least have lost their heads, and more are killed later in further purges. The Crown had taken revenge on an aristocracy

The Stockholm Bloodbath, 1520

that had humiliated its constitutional supremacy. Military success, however, becomes political failure. The Union was finished. The reasons for the bloodshed, if there was any rationale at all, have been lost in the fog of history. The blame lies full square on Christian II personally.

The Kalmar Union, in principle designed for peace and security, had in reality been an orgy of fraternal warfare. It was a shame. The Union had been a worthy ideal. Margrete's project, we must think, if possibly in a generous interpretation, was not only about power but also inspired by an idea for Scandinavia: that the peoples of the north should stand together and collaborate. That kind of thinking had been needed for centuries. The Viking kingdoms might have amounted to something had they not constantly fought each other. There had been earlier visions of union, if perhaps not idealistic ones – those of Knud the Great in Denmark and Harald Hardrade in Norway. No doubt Magnus Eriksson, while King of Sweden, Norway and Skåne, and priding himself the bearer of 'three crowns', had seen himself on the horizon as Scandinavian emperor.

But this most serious attempt in Scandinavian history to make real the idea failed. The idea itself, however, survived. It returned in the guise of 'Scandinavianism' in the nineteenth century, in what was to be another case of failed idealism, and again in the twentieth century in various designs for political and economic unions, then with less ambition but finally some success.

MIGHTY WOMEN

Being a woman, Margrete could not be queen, but her gender did not prevent her from being accepted as ruler. Among the small-folks women were workers and counted for little. At the top they could matter, usually as pawns in dynastically arranged marriages, but also in their own right. It was not extraordinary in the mindset of the time that women could be in charge.

Another forceful woman we have met is the Holy Birgitta. She created a following through which she exercised religious and political influence in all of Scandinavia and in European Christendom. She was a vindictive schemer, but strong and influential.

When Magnus Eriksson restored the Norwegian Crown to Håkon in 1355, he held on to various Norwegian fiefs for himself. He had other troubles on his mind but needed to prevent those fiefs from slipping from his grip, for which purpose he installed his queen and wife, Blanka, as governor over his local tax base within the kingdom that nominally belonged to his son.

During a lengthy absence on pilgrimage to Jerusalem in 1423–25, King Erik installed Queen Philippa as regent of the three union kingdoms. She dealt with the Hansa to neutralise, for a while, their enmity against Denmark, in part by negotiating treaties. Later, she served as her husband's de facto regent in Sweden, where she did much to placate discontent in both Church and aristocracy about having to contribute tax to finance Denmark's wars on its southern borders. During a Danish war with the Hansa, in the king's absence, Philippa took command of the defence of Copenhagen, breaking the Germans' blockade and forcing their retreat.

Dorothea was married to King Christoffer of Denmark at the age of fifteen. On his death three years later, she was made regent for the interim until a new king could be elected, and then stayed on as queen by marrying that new king, Christian I. She was now eighteen and queen for the second time. She was an active schemer on behalf of her husband in restoring to him the Crown of Sweden and was instrumental in that happening in 1457, in Sweden generally being reviled as manipulative and mean.

When Christian II's mistress, Dyveke, died in 1517, her mother, Sigbrit, stayed on at the court and became Christian's closest advisor, in charge of customs, finance and more. She was a Dutch tradeswoman who had drifted to Bergen, where she ran an inn and raised her beautiful daughter. It was there that Christian met them and took them into his entourage. Sigbrit was a coarse, vulgar and obese woman, but intelligent and capable, able to make Christian dependent on her so that when he did not have her at his side he slid into doubt and inaction. She was said to be a witch and was blamed for having incited the Bloodbath in Stockholm. When Christian was deposed and driven into exile in Holland Sigbrit went with him, but she was unable to hold on to power and was cast aside. She may have died there in a prison.

Kristina Gyllenstierna was the wife of Sten Sture, Sweden's *riks-föreståndare* (regent) at the time of Christian II's assault on Sweden. Sten was killed in January 1520. Kristina emerged as the leader of the Swedish resistance against the Danes and was in command of the city of Stockholm, which held out until September, when she capitulated in return for a promise of amnesty – the promise that was betrayed in the Bloodbath of Stockholm. Kristina was imprisoned first in Stockholm and then in Copenhagen, whence she was released in 1524, and returned to Sweden, where she schemed with one of her sons and the Danes for the overthrow of the Swedish king, Gustav Vasa. She was imprisoned again but struck a deal with Gustav to marry a cousin of his and cease political activity. She died in 1559.

Fru (Lady) Inger of Østeråt is known under that name from the play by Henrik Ibsen in which she is a crude symbol of Norwegian national pride. Østeråt was an estate of at least 200 properties in the territory of the previous Earls of Lade in mid-Norway, and Inger the richest landowner in what remained of the aristocracy. Five of her daughters married Danish nobles. She worked actively against the Archbishop of Nidaros, near her domains, for the promotion of the Reformation and schemed in favour of aristocratic revolts in Sweden. She died in 1555 in a shipwreck off the coast of western Norway.

5

Reformation

The Church was rich, the Crowns were poor. But power was shifting, from Church to Crown. As the Kalmar Union was laid to rest, the events that would result in the Reformation were unfolding in Europe. It was inevitable that ambitious kings would lay their hands on what they could of Church funds and claw away at their autonomies.

How it happened

People were bewildered. Had their lives been perverted by sin? They turned to cults. Churchmen reached for the Purgatory, which now rose in importance in their teaching. We are all sinners and in danger. But, also, sin can be absolved in a process of purification at the end of which the gates of Heaven open up. From this belief it was a short step for the Church to make itself the custodian of absolution. There was a tradition of doing good, or seeking mercy, by assisting the Church financially. It drifted into the selling of indulgences and soon the Church was hooked, addict-like, on easy money from the trade in forgiveness. 'People knew', says the historian Norman Davies, 'that Christendom was sick; they knew that the ideal of the Gospel of Love was far removed from the prevailing reality.' Their Church was inserting itself between worshippers and God and creating distance where there should be nearness. 'If we should try to sum up Late Middle-Age Church life in its manifold forms in a single word, it would have to be in a demand for *reform*.'

The old conflict between 'high' and 'low' resurfaced with force in the bewilderment following the Big Death and was stimulated further by the Church exploiting people's fears to prop itself up. Renaissance scholarship saw a revival of more open-minded biblical studies. Universities proliferated as factories of ideas, then as now subversive ideas. When Constantinople fell to the Ottomans in 1453, scholars took refuge in the west, bringing with them their grounding in classical studies and

Greek philosophy. Theologians went back to the Greek and Hebrew versions of the scriptures and translated them anew, freed from the official Church version. The understanding of knowledge was changing, from conformity with accepted dogma to building on observation and evidence. The understanding of humanity was changing, from collectivism towards individualism, a new humanism in the making. Literacy was spreading, having previously been monopolised by a tiny élite. The art of printing democratised the written word. Popular languages gained in respect and acceptance. Reforming theologians liberated the Bible from Latin and made it available in the local languages.

The reform movement was exactly that, a demand for reform *within* the Church to restore its lost purity. But the centre in Rome dug in and let itself sink ever deeper into corruption. Reform turned to revolution.

The push for reform had been gathering strength for a century and a half by the time Martin Luther nailed his ninety-five theses to the church door in Wittenberg in 1517. Europe was in turmoil, established orders were threatened from within by peasant revolts and quasi-civil wars, and from without by Ottoman expansions westward. Economies were being monetised, but in the absence of monetary control prices were rising and standards of living deteriorating. People were squeezed by tax-hungry kings and princes. After the Big Death religiosity surged but confidence in the Church plunged. In Oxford, John Wycliffe (1330–84) questioned the legitimacy of the papacy itself, attacked monasticism, thought that priests should live in poverty, and oversaw a translation of the Bible into English. In Bohemia, Jan Hus (1372–1415) preached (mainly in the Bethlehem Chapel, which still stands in the centre of Prague) against the established Church in much the same way, adding attacks on the selling of indulgences. His followers became known as Hussites and much of the Church in the Czech lands worked in compliance with his theology, making itself the first Reformation Church. He was summoned by Rome to the Council of Konstanz, where, upon arrival, in breach of a promise of safe conduct – only a promise to a heretic, after all – he was arrested, put on trial, condemned and burned at the stake, his ashes scattered in the Rhine.

Martin Luther was not an innovative theological thinker but he was a brave, energetic and gifted campaigner – although a nasty specimen of humanity, with 'little patience with the gentle humanists of the day, inordinately rude and bad-tempered, his language often unrepeatable', a burner of books, viciously anti-Semitic. By his time, reform tendencies were taking hold in the Church, fired by widespread social unrest in the German lands – the Great Peasants' Revolt of 1524–25 ended in the slaughter of at least 100,000 rebels – and extremes of Church corruption. The sale of indulgences had taken on industrial proportions, working through a network of agents who sold forgiveness to anyone who would pay, even for those already dead, and coercing believers into buying absolution on the threat of damnation.

Luther's campaign against the Church was not specifically about indulgences but more generally directed at its theology, its claim to both religious and secular power, to being the custodian of salvation, to papal supremacy, and at the whole edifice of hierarchy and symbolism of a power-Church, becoming ever more radical as it unfolded until the pope himself was the Antichrist. The core of reform theology was, and had been, the vision of a humble Church understood as the community of believers in which the churchmen's task was to preach the gospel and deliver the sacraments, and that alone. But, theological argument notwithstanding, it was the racket of indulgences that provided the reformers with the cause that enabled them to give their movement momentum. Luther had visited Rome in 1509 and been shaken by the 'perfection of depravity' he had seen in the papacy. Secular order, he concluded, was to be in the hands of secular authorities, who governed on God's behalf and should be obeyed.

There were other eminent reform theologians and organisers at the time, but Luther was the great campaigner. His weapon was the written word, his instrument the printing press and his strategy simplicity. He translated the Bible into simple German, finishing the translation of the New Testament in eleven weeks in 1521 while hiding out in Warburg Castle under the protection of a friendly prince, having been condemned an outlaw by the Church. He wrote faith manuals, catechisms, a large one for the clergy and a small one for the people (still in use in the Scandinavian Lutheran Churches, as I remember from my own childhood), and a plethora of other sharp, popular and provocative writings and hymns on all manner of faith and Church matters. His medium was the pamphlet, brief, provocative, to the point, cheap, in folksy language. He collaborated closely with printer-publishers and artist-designers and produced works that were as exciting to the eye as to the mind. He exploited, like no one else at the time, the potential in the new technology of printing, and spoke directly to a widening reading public. He rose from lowly prelate to famous celebrity and was without comparison the bestselling author in the German world. His campaign against the established Church was the world's first organised media campaign.

The Reformation spread through Europe. There was a radical version in Switzerland, inspired by Jean Calvin, where Geneva officially became a Reformation city, at one and the same time a centre of reformist repression and a refuge for reform adherents in Catholic Europe. In France there were followers of both Luther and Calvin (himself French), the latter known as Huguenots. Protestants were persecuted in ways that descended into civil wars of religion, and many fled to England, the Netherlands, Prussia and elsewhere, including English and Dutch colonies. There was the Royal Reformation in England in which Henry VIII broke with the papal Church on the question of the annulment of his marriage to Catherine of Aragon in the quest for a male heir. Where the Reformation took hold, Church property shifted into Crown hands. Catholics were persecuted just as reformers were in Catholic Europe.

Lutheranism came with great gifts to high and low alike. It appealed to princes, confirming the legitimacy of their rule and strengthening their authority vis-à-vis the emperor. It appealed to bishops who were also territorial princes; they would be able to marry and keep their wealth in the family by inheritance. It appealed to clergy, not least by freeing them from the hypocrisy of celibacy. It appealed to ordinary folk by bringing God's nearness into their lives. It was in the German lands that the indulgences racket had been at its most energetic, and it was no wonder that people who had seen their Church betters embezzle out of them what little they had were minded to put their faith in a more modest Church. Catholicism hung on in the south, as currently in Bavaria, but most of Germany was soon Lutheran, from 1525 officially the state religion in Prussia and then over the next decade or so in a raft of other German principalities.*

* Reform Churches are sometime said to be 'evangelical', sometimes 'Protestant'. In theology, 'evangelical' refers to the core Reformation principle that salvation is by the grace of God alone. The term was used in that sense by Luther and other early reform theologians and has retained this meaning. The Lutheran Churches in Scandinavia are 'evangelical'. In recent times, the term has become more commonly used for various non-Catholic revival movements. The term 'Protestant' derives from a letter of protestation issued by a group of Lutheran German princes in 1529 against the imperial reconfirmation of Luther's teachings as heretical. Protestantism,

*

Scandinavia followed the German lead. Reform ideas took hold among clergy and in the population, strongly so in Denmark, more hesitantly in Norway and Sweden. Kings recognised in which direction the winds were blowing and co-opted Lutheranism, much encouraged by the prospect of taking over Church wealth.

Christian II of Denmark, the instinctive dictator, had a vision of absolute monarchy and wanted a subservient Church without involvement in secular affairs. His successor, Frederik I, king from 1523, had on his coronation committed to defending the Church and its privileges, but was already disposed in favour of the reform movement and easily reneged on his oath. A Danish translation of the New Testament was issued in 1524, so that, in a Preface, 'no one needs be deceived by priests and monks', and many of Luther's works were circulating in Danish translation early on. (A Danish-language version of Luther's complete Bible was issued in 1550, as Christian III's Bible, in a print run of 3,000, at a price per copy equivalent to that of a good cow.) New bishops during Frederik's reign were loyal to the Crown. He appointed four, who paid the fee for their bishoprics that was due to Rome to him instead.

On Frederik's death, however, in 1533, it turned out that matters were not resolved. Conflict over the succession disintegrated into a messy civil war – Catholics against Lutherans, burghers against aristocrats, aristocratic factions against each other, farmers against aristocrats and burghers, Lübeckers stirring up trouble. The heir in line eventually marched an army of mercenaries on Copenhagen and laid siege to the city, during which people were reduced to eating birds and rats and many died of hunger, forcing the remaining rebels to surrender and pronouncing himself king as Christian III. Intransigent bishops were arrested (three of them), a Lutheran Church order was imposed, bishoprics were abolished and the Church was put under the management of seven 'superintendents' appointed by the king (some of them former bishops, all of them soon to reclaim that title). The veneration of saints, fasting days, priest celibacy and other Catholic forms and

---

then, is historically Lutheran and does not include non-Lutheran reform Churches, such as Anglican Churches, but has with time come to be used as an umbrella term for all non-Catholic Christian Churches and movements that have emerged in the aftermath of the sixteenth-century Reformation.

The Danish New Testament translation of 1524 –
'So that no one needs be deceived by priests and monks.'

symbols were abolished, as was the post of archbishop. Church
services were to be conducted in Danish. Most priests continued in
post. Monks and nuns were allowed to carry on their monastic lives

but new monasteries were not introduced, and the old ones gradually ceased and their property shifted to the Crown as they discontinued. Christian was crowned in a Lutheran ceremony and the University of Copenhagen reopened as a Lutheran institution (it had ceased to function during the civil war). A Lutheran Church Order was issued in 1537, formalising the reformed State Church. Bishops and priests would swear allegiance to the king. Church and monastic property was nationalised, leaving in the Crown's hands three times as much land as before the Reformation. The tithe continued to be claimed, but now, much of it, for the Crown. Christian's campaign had been mega-expensive; the taking-over of Church property and income enabled him to balance the books. (Technically, the Reformation happened in two stages. By 1533, the Church was national and independent of Rome, but only in 1536 was it Lutheran. In Sweden, as well, the Catholic Church was first nationalised, then gradually reformed.)

When the dust settled, following events unfolding over less than twenty years, the Church was of a new kind, brought down to earth, reformed, modest, Lutheran. It had been a controlled revolution, with radical Reformation prevented. The Church was handed over not to 'the people' but to the Crown.

In Norway there was hardly an indigenous reform movement of note, but also, says the historian Øystein Rian, 'the intellectual Catholic resistance could not but be weak in a country without a university or notable monasteries or centres of learning'. Lutheranism was imposed as the official religion by decree from Copenhagen in what was now a Danish–Norwegian Church. Troublesome bishops went into exile, compliant ones continued in post, as did most priests. Monastic orders were dissolved or just discontinued.

In Sweden, the formal Reformation was conducted under Gustav Vasa, in the main for the purpose of confiscating Church property and income, doubling Crown revenue. In slow order, after 1523, tentative Counter-Reformation tendencies were defeated and Protestant priests appointed, including an Archbishop of Uppsala installed without papal consent (who was the first churchman to marry and preach in Swedish), celibacy was abolished, the New Testament issued in Swedish, the supremacy of the Crown over the Church enshrined, monasteries were supressed, Canon Law was abolished and the complete Bible issued in Swedish. A new Church Ordinance was introduced in 1571, to be reconfirmed in 1593 in pure Reformation format, whereupon Lutheranism was formally the Swedish state religion. Uppsala University was refounded in 1595, having been closed ahead of the Reformation. The last monastery, of the Birgitta Order, was closed, also in 1595.

What happened to the remaining Catholics? In one sense, nothing. In many congregations the old practices continued for a good while. But there was also fear of both Catholic resurgence and radical Reformation. From 1569 in Denmark, immigrants and refugees were in some cases refused settlement for not being of reliable faith, according to written regulations called *Fremmedartikler*, 'Alien Articles'. A new ordinance of 1604 blocked students from Jesuit colleges from school and Church posts. Catholics were deprived of the right of inheritance in 1613 and subjected to being expelled from the land, and practising Catholics from abroad were forbidden entry. In Sweden in 1550, 'false teachers' were banned from entry into the country, in 1578 Jesuits expelled. The Reformation also turned on other minorities, notably Gipsies, in Scandinavia long known as *tatere*. In Denmark again, shortly after 1536 they were in principle expelled and, if remaining in the land, outlawed and to be shunned, including from Church burials.

In Norway the Reformation was at first more formal than real. As seen from Copenhagen, it was enough that there was no official Church opposition; what people out there in the parishes really believed and how they worshipped did not bother anyone. Latin was abolished as the Church language but what came instead was not Norwegian but Danish, so that the old distance between Church and people persisted. Lutheran priests, often Danish, were mistrusted. It was to be perhaps another 200 years before it could be said that the Reformation was a theological reality.

What it meant

The Reformation was a theological movement with political consequences. The immediate effect was to split the Western Church in two main parts (with further divisions within each part). The Catholic Church reacted with the Counter-Reformation, reconfirming its theology, strengthening its top-down hierarchy and revitalising its organisation of propaganda. The Society of Jesus – Jesuits – was strengthened to operate with military discipline for the purpose of conversion and reconversion, but also education. The Inquisition was ramped up as the Church's organisation for the rooting out of heresy. An Index of prohibited works was drawn up containing some of the finest works of philosophy and science of the age, deviant publications to be hunted down, confiscated and burned.

But at the same time the Catholic Church adapted and changed, much as the original reformers had envisaged. Even in Catholic domains such as Spain and France, the Crowns rose in supremacy to, in a sense, nationalise their Churches. Careful reforms, such as ending the sale of indulgences, made the Church less forbidding. The Jesuits promoted education, attracting young men from European aristocracies. Jesuit colleges sprang up across the Catholic world as centres of excellence, embracing also students from Protestant Europe. This paradoxical two-sided Counter-Reformation was successful, the big prize being to keep Poland within the Church of Rome, and also pulling parts of Germany back in. For a while it looked as if the Counter-Reformation might prevail in Sweden as well – which, however, in time was instead to become the leading Reformation power in Europe.

Catholic Europe was, counter-intuitively given its repressiveness, the heartland of the European Renaissance. The Church commissioned art, architecture and music, and encouraged education and scholarly study. From Catholic Spain, liberated from the Moors, and Portugal came the great 'discoveries' of America and Asia that created a new understanding of the world and its peoples. Scientists and philosophers sought to harmonise Church teachings and fresh insights into the universe and laws of nature.

The political fallouts from the Reformation were mainly unanticipated, and catastrophic. An early consequence was war. Catholic and Protestant rulers and factions fought each other: the Swiss cantons in 1531, in the German lands the emperor and Protestant princes in 1547. In France there was civil war from 1562 to 1598, as in the Netherlands at the end of the century and into the next. England collapsed into civil war between Puritan parliamentarians and Anglican monarchists. Even in Denmark the religious division dragged the country into civil war. In Germany the parties found a path to live-and-let-live settlements in the second half of the century, but it did not last. The seventeenth century was to be the bloodiest in European history so far, in a combination of conventional and religious wars. 'Swedes were at war with Danes and Norwegians, the English and the Scots with the Dutch, Catholic

French and Habsburgers at each others' throats in Madrid.' The Thirty Years War brought Europe to ruin.

A further consequence was State absolutism. In the old regime, in which the Church had been a state within the State, the State was restrained by the Church's counter-power. With the Reformation and Counter-Reformation, that balance of power came to an end. In Lutheran countries such as Sweden and Denmark, the State turned impoverished Churches into instruments in its own service. As previously, the Church brought the State authority, but was no longer able to claim wealth and privilege in return. Kings were still kings by the grace of God, but that grace was not in the gift of the Church to award or withhold. The Church ceded power to the State, wealth to the State, income to the State. The State stood uncontested at the top of the pyramid of power and kings were on the path to absolutism.

With more authority and property for the State came more responsibility. Education and poor relief had been mainly a Church role. When the State nationalised the Church and took over its income and property, it also saddled itself with what had been Church duties. Those duties were not yet onerous – poor relief, for example was a matter of controlling the scourge of beggary – but they were new State duties nevertheless.

In both Sweden and Denmark, the triumph of Lutheranism was also the triumph of the absolute monarchy and its version of religious dictatorship. But even so, the Reformation did come with some new freedoms for common folk. Medieval people had lived in an environment of fear: the fear of ignorance and of nature, insecurity, plagues, hunger and more. The Church had exploited people's anxieties and added to them. It made them fear Hell and damnation, it made them afraid of the Church itself as the giver or taker of salvation. It made itself feared with its overwhelming power and distance, with its rich and mysterious symbolism, with priests' final authority over right and wrong in all matters of life, with the worship of relics and saints, with speaking to people in a language and in forms they could not understand. It expropriated God and removed His spirit from their experience and understanding. The reformed Lutheran Churches were different. They relinquished some of the power the followers had reason to fear. There was less distance and less mysterious symbolism. They spoke to their followers in their own language, and enabled them to feel free from both ignorance and error. They had told the believers that the Church was fallible and that it was for them to find their way to redemption. This did not translate into liberty in any modern sense. The power the Church surrendered did not flow down to the people but sideways to the mightier State. But it freed people from the old Church's totalitarianism and opened up a space for them which they, in time, could fill with free Church movements under their own management.

In Scandinavia, the Reformation was to exercise a lasting influence on mindsets and habits to create distinctly Lutheran cultures. The new Church was soon established with heavy authority and mono-poly in the exercise of religious practice. They were State Churches, carrying with them the authority of the Crown, and were in each of the Scandinavian countries the only Church, without competition from deviant understandings of Christianity or faith. They were universal; everyone belonged to *the Church*. Attendance was legally mandatory and socially expected. In the predominantly rural populations, vicars were *ex officio* local leaders with remits much beyond Church matters.

With the spreading of schooling, the Lutheran influence would also work through education. There would be One School, as there was One Church. Schooling was religious, religion a core and obligatory subject, not as religious studies but in the form of teaching Lutheran Christianity. Prayers and hymns were a part of the daily routine of school life (still so when I was a schoolboy). The vicar would be the school overseer.

The Scandinavian mentality leans to the honest, the down-to-earth, the modest, the practical, the obedient, the serious, the dedicated, the hard-working, the equal, the frugal. You are not supposed to stand out or promote yourself; community and collectivism are valued. It expresses itself in 'we'-terms rather than 'I'-terms. It is dour, heavy, duty-laden and short on fun. It is not the brilliant that is celebrated but the steady. We Scandinavians are preachers: we preach to ourselves and each other, we preach to others, we preach to the world. We are missionary peoples, both in the narrow sense of Christian mission and in the broader sense of wanting to teach others and make the world better. We feel responsibility to do good and think of ourselves as able. If it weren't alien to the culture itself, we might think of ourselves as chosen peoples. This culture has many nuances and mixed and complicated origins and facets, but there is in it an undeniable streak of Lutheran stricture.

It is a functional culture, conducive to order, efficiency and trust. In the end the people who live under its influence are probably lucky. It is not an attractive culture: conformist, puritanical, socially repressive, moralistic. It is distinct. The Scandinavians are of their own kind and stand out as different in the European cultural landscape, in near-Continental Denmark perhaps less so than in the more remote Sweden and Norway.

Addendum

The Cities

A city is a place where people live and work in close proximity to one another, in sufficient numbers to maintain a complex range of specialised activities, usually with some more or less grand architecture. Cities emerged in Scandinavia as part of the post-Viking-Age Great Transformation. Their numbers say something about the differences between the three countries. By one count, up to 1350, about 100 cities had emerged in Denmark, forty in Sweden and sixteen in Norway. Even in Denmark, the most urbanised of the countries, they were small: a second-order city like Århus had no more than 3,000–4,000 people. The largest Norwegian city was Bergen, which during the Middle Ages grew to a population of between 5,000 and 10,000; Oslo and Trondheim, next in size, had fewer than 3,000 inhabitants. Around 1300, Oslo was made up of sixty to seventy buildings, only occasionally with two floors. Stone was expensive and reserved for a fort and a few churches. The early cities did not look very urban: buildings were like farmhouses and city families kept themselves with livestock.

One way for a city to emerge was for a king to make it his site. Taxes flowed to where the king held court, funding building works which attracted workmen, artisans and trade, which again attracted services. Another way was for the Church to turn a site into a centre by making it a bishopric or archbishopric and raising a prominent church or cathedral, with a monastery or monasteries and lesser churches attached. These two ways would go hand in hand. When a king wanted to make a site a centre of defence or trade, he would build or endow churches and monasteries. Indeed, if he wanted his site to be a city of any significance he would have to have the collaboration of the Church. Any city would need to be propped up by Church activity.

But what explains the emergence of cities does not explain their growth. That was accounted for by trade. In Norway, Trondheim was the site of the archbishopric and of the country's one cathedral, but never became a dominant city. Nor did Lund in Skåne or Roskilde in Denmark, nor Uppsala in Sweden, all (arch)bishoprics. The first Norwegian royal city was Oslo, which did not grow to eminence. The cities that became the dominant ones were Copenhagen, Stockholm and Bergen. Trade was getting to be big business and was regulated to select cities. That brought with it the growth and complexity in other businesses and crafts that make for city life: builders, shoemakers, tailors, weavers, goldsmiths, bakers, barbers, wine sellers, prostitutes.

Medieval city life was regulated in detail, including the shape of buildings, the width of the streets and so on. You could not, in principle, settle in a city without having a legal craft or trade, although drifters and vagrants would come and go. Trades were clustered together, gradually evolving into guilds, gradually making themselves organisations of masters and apprentices with religious and social functions as well. Administration was in the hands of Crown officials and city councils. Eligibility for offices of authority was limited to 'leading men', including churchmen but excluding humble traders, craftsmen and the like who were not property-owners. Business and property were subject to fees and tolls to the Crown. City councils were combined governing bodies and courts of justice. The Church was present as an additional authority with its own organisation. This all came under separate city laws with separate penal provisions: loose women were whipped, thieves burn-marked or had ears cut off, robbers hanged in the central square. Each city had its own hangman.

The beginning of Copenhagen was the building of a fort in 1176. To strengthen the defence of the territory, forts were built at sites along the coast, including at this little settlement strategically across from Skåne. That fort has by twists and turns become today's Christiansborg Palace, now part national assembly, part government premises, part royal state rooms.

The city thrived on the upturn in trade. It sits on the shore of the Sound through which transport goes in and out of the Baltic Sea, the ideal spot from where that transport could be controlled. It became a royal possession during the reign of King Valdemar Atterdag, who expropriated the site from the bishopric of Roskilde, and the royal capital when, during the Kalmar Union, it was the centre from where, for a while, all of Scandinavia was governed. In the long period from then until 1814, it was the capital of united Denmark and Norway. By

1600 it had a population of 20,000; by 1800 100,000. (London was then Europe's largest city with a population of a million.)

If it was its strategic position that made the city, that position was also its danger. It was embroiled in fractious relations with the Hansa and was sacked by their forces in 1368, during the Second Hanseatic War. In the turmoil of the Reformation it was a stronghold of Catholicism and under siege during 1535–36 until surrendering to Christian III. During the Swedish Wars of 1657–60 it was under siege again, and on the brink of being flattened to the ground. It has been ravaged by fires repeatedly: catastrophically in 1728, when half of the city went up in smoke, including the university and university library, and again in 1795, when Christiansborg Palace was devastated.

During the Napoleonic Wars, when Denmark sided with France, the city was sacked to near-destruction by the British, first in 1801 (when Horatio Nelson, of later Trafalgar fame, made his name by disobeying orders to withdraw and instead persisted in destroying most of the Danish fleet), and again in 1807, when they used phosphorus fire artillery to set much of the city ablaze, laying waste to the university a second time. The city as it stands today is the result of reconstructions following repeated destructions, which gives it its feeling of being relatively young.

Until late in the 1800s it was contained within defensive ramparts, with traffic going in and out through four gates. The population was growing rapidly, squeezed ever tighter within the walls. The beautiful Copenhagen we know today was, only 150 years ago, outside the small centre of royal elegance, a squalid slum. An epidemic of cholera in 1853 killed 4,700 people in the course of a few summer months. The city gates were torn down in 1857 and within twenty years most of the ramparts were gone. The population nearly trebled in size during the nineteenth century.

Copenhagen has been and is the country's political, financial and cultural capital, with no competing second city. The university was established in 1479, the East India Company in 1616, the Stock Exchange in 1625, the Royal Theatre in 1748. During the nineteenth century it became the undisputed cultural capital of Scandinavia. The city flourished during the early part of the twentieth century, much thanks to Denmark's neutrality in the First World War, and came out of the occupation in the Second World War relatively unscathed. Subsequently, monumental building works have added modernity to an otherwise charming but modest city. A gracious road and rail bridge across the Sound now connects the Copenhagen area with Skåne in Sweden, creating a Danish–Swedish region – recreating, one might say, the ancient union across the Sound from which Scandinavia originally emerged.

Copenhagen is different in spirit from both Stockholm and Oslo, a spirit arising from its nearness to the Continent. It is a liberal city, broad-minded and laid-back, charming, not grand, like Denmark itself, *hyggelig*. Swedes and Norwegians have traditionally looked to Denmark, and Copenhagen in particular, for a taste of European sophistication.

There had to be a city where Stockholm evolved. It sits at the estuary of Lake Mälaren, into which flow Sweden's rivers from the north and west, on which came much of the country's goods for foreign trade. Those goods had to make their way out to sea, which is to say by way of the Stockholm estuary. Beyond Stockholm are the Bay of Bothnia and the Baltic Sea. Stockholm island is where lake meets sea, connected by way of rapids to the north and south of the island. Those rapids are there in today's Stockholm, the southern one tamed by a lock, the northern one running free. During the Viking Age, the lake and sea levels were even and small ships could be manoeuvred in and out of the lake. Later, the water level in the lake rose and the bigger transport ships could not get through. Goods now had to be brought to Stockholm island over the lake from the west, unloaded and carried across, and then reloaded on to seagoing ships on the eastern side, in reverse for imports. Its location made it a centre of trade and transport.

Stockholm was never the country's religious centre. That was Uppsala, which also became Sweden's premier university city. A university college was established in Stockholm in 1878, acquiring autonomous university status only in 1960.

Stockholm island is today the Old Town, one of Europe's finest city heritages. The layout is as it was under Birger's and his followers' blessing. The two main streets, Västerlånggatan and Österlånggatan, run along what was the early city wall, just back from the shore, and meet at Järntorget, 'Iron Square'. From early on it had a strong German presence, concentrated in what became a German quarter. There is still today a German Street – *Tyska brinken* – and a German church, first raised by the German guild in the fourteenth century.

The city advanced with Sweden's growing strength and was by the sixteenth century the capital of an emerging European power. It outgrew the island and spilled over into broader lands, the northern parts evolving into today's business and middle-class districts, Norrmalm and Östermalm, and the southern part, Södermalm, into the industrial and working-class areas, now thoroughly gentrified.

It is a beautiful city, largely owing to the omnipresence of water flowing through and around it, feeding into an archipelago of perhaps 20,000 islands and islets that trickle into the Bay of Bothnia. But it is also a hard city, having been on the receiving end of much heavy twentieth-century modernisation, without the humane softness of Copenhagen.

The original city, on the island, fell into decline and was by the middle of the nineteenth century in danger of being erased in the interest of slum clearance. Plans were drawn up to tear down all of it except the royal palace and churches and replace it with modern quarters of straight streets and solid buildings. Luckily, this assault failed, for reasons of cost. Only in the twentieth century was there an emerging appreciation of its heritage and the possibility of modernisation with preservation. Old Town residents organised to protect their habitat. A plan of 1942 to erase sections to make way for a government office complex met with massive resistance that succeeded in having the plans significantly modified – resistance much inspired by Vera Siöcrona, author and journalist and one of the many formidable women who have a way of cropping up in the telling of the Scandinavian story. The action resulted in the formation of an Old Town Resident's Association, which has continued to defend the town's dignity. Vera herself is commemorated in a ballad, *Vera i Vintappargränd*, by the troubadour Evert Taube. (She lived in Door 2, Vintner's Passage.)

The early Norwegian kings preferred the safety of the west country, hence Bergen. The east was coveted by both Danes and Swedes, and exposed. However, it was also for that reason that Harald Hardrade in 1048 founded the city that was to be Oslo, to establish a foothold in the vulnerable fringe of his kingdom.

Bergen has flourished on trade. It is still today a trading town, dominated by shipping, shipbuilding and more recently the North Sea petroleum business. It is a city rich in the traditions that come with trade, with prominent guilds and associations and an upper crust of leading wealthy families; a proud and conservative city. The burghers outdid Oslo in founding the country's first theatre, in 1850, under the name The Norwegian Theatre (now *Den Nationale Scene*), where the young Henrik Ibsen spent six unhappy years as artistic director. Its first institution of higher education was The Norwegian School of Economics (in Norwegian Handelshøyskole, 'school of trade'), founded in 1936. When a university was established in 1946 it was welcomed with less than warm enthusiasm by the local bourgeoisie, in the knowledge that it would bring in competing élites. The *Handelshøyskole* was preserved as an institution of its own, while the old élite long kept its distance from the new university. (I know, I worked there in the 1970s.)

Bergen rose to prominence in the thirteenth century under Håkon Håkonsson and Magnus Lawmender. A palace and fort were built of which remains *Håkons Hall*, still containing the city's prime state rooms. By the end of the 1300s the kingdom's political centre had moved to Oslo, and then Bergen, although the country's largest city until the mid-1800s, was all about trade, gradually taken over from the Germans by the emerging native merchant class, the city's destiny shifting uneasily between prosperity and recession. It is the only city in the country that has the feel of genuine historical legacy, save for the cathedral in Trondheim and the fort in Oslo.

The Crown moved to Oslo under King Håkon V, but kingly power was then in decline and could not do much for that city. When the next Håkon died in 1380, the kings would be Danish and Oslo a provincial administrative town.

In the 1290s, Håkon V started to build Akershus Fort to strengthen the city's defence, a fort that is today Oslo's pride of historical heritage, with towers and ramparts that overlook the narrow fjord that forms the seaway into and out of the city. It has over the years served sometimes as royal residence, sometimes as military headquarters, sometimes as state prison, including during the German occupation in the Second World War. It today houses museums, some military quarters and the government's most honoured state rooms.

The city did not prosper. When, in late 1536, the Danish king sent a governor north, he found Akershus Fort in ruins and the town itself home to perhaps 1,000 people, its churches in decay. During the long Danish period it had little function and even lost its name. Consisting still mainly of wooden buildings, it was destroyed by fire in 1624 and was rebuilt on a different location under the name of Christiania. Even though Norway broke free from Denmark in 1814, the old name of Oslo was not restored until 1925.

From 1814, when Norway was again a kingdom, Oslo became the national capital, and started to give itself the look with major construction works: the Royal Palace, Parliament, University, National Bank, National Theatre, buildings that still define the city centre, none of them of architectural note. Industry evolved from the nineteenth century, shipbuilding in particular, and the city divided into the middle-class west and working-class east. During the 1930s a monumental City Hall in modern Brutalist style was raised facing the harbour and fjord as a grand project of the city's social democratic administration, guarded in front by a line of Social Realist sculptures, all men of manual labour – in the humble opinion of this author, in concept, architecture and artistic integrity, far and away the city's most successful masterpiece.

By the dawn of the twenty-first century, Norway had come into wealth flowing from petroleum exploitation, resulting in a building boom in the capital. Where industry had filled the space between city and fjord, gentrification and modernist architecture have crowded in. The result is a peculiar city. It has little history, no old town. It is now transforming itself with a very rapid inflow of modern building works, some successful, such as an Opera House that shimmers out on the waters from the fjord, but the totality is unsettling. As a city, through little fault of its own, its spirit is parvenu and nouveau riche.

Part Three

The Age of Perpetual War

On Midsummer's eve 1523, Gustav Vasa rode into Stockholm, his now liberated city, and up to Birger *Jarl*'s old castle. He was twenty-seven years old and had just been elected king (on 6 June, today Sweden's National Day). The country was emerging from quasi-republican rule and continuous rebellions and revolts. His father had been among those killed in the Bloodbath of Stockholm.

Five years earlier, Gustav had been taken hostage by the Danes, along with five other young Swedish nobles, and imprisoned in Copenhagen. It took him a year to escape. He did not hurry home but returned slowly via Lübeck a year later, not as a dashing young nationalist, more an anonymous loner. He joined the battle for Swedish autonomy hesitantly and was at first unable to attract much of a following, at one point giving up and making his way to exile in Norway.* But barons in Dalarna, the Swedish dales, saw in the feeble man a leader and made him their chief. The fighting went their way. A great monarch was in the making.

Christian II returned to Denmark to continue his reign there, presenting himself as a reformer and moderniser. It was no good; he was another king who was not up to handling the art of governing, being in all matters both reckless and irresolute. After two years he was deposed in Denmark as well. He fled into exile in the Netherlands for the next nine years, returned to reclaim his kingdom, failed, spent twenty-seven years imprisoned (in genteel circumstances), died aged seventy-seven and was laid to rest in a royal funeral.

---

* Legend has it that he fled skiing through Dalarna, from Mora to Sälen. There he was persuaded to turn back and join – eventually lead – the rebellion against the Danes. In memory of these events, the annual *Vasaloppet* has been held since 1922, as, it is claimed, the world's largest skiing competition by number of participants, with a run of 90 km (but in the direction of Sälen to Mora).

6

Two New Kingdoms

Around 1500, the herring abandoned Danish waters to move north up the Swedish and Norwegian coasts and relocate deep into the North Sea. That was an evil omen for the Scandinavians and the Germans alike, and for their uneasy partnership. Not only did they lose the most important resource that had underpinned their symbiosis, that same resource fell into the hands of competitors. The Scandinavians did not have the capacity to follow the herring out to sea but others did, the Dutch and the English. They could fish what was out of the Scandinavians' reach from robust ships and barrel the herring at sea. They had a new supply of salt from Spanish and French marshes, more plentiful than the German mined salt.

The Dutch and English advance came as the Hansa were in decline. With better ships they could trade directly into the Baltic Sea with heavy goods such as grain, iron, copper, timber and tar, and carry those goods away by sea around Denmark. The Hansa had operated by ship in the Baltics but mainly transported their goods to market overland and on rivers. They had dug a canal from Lübeck to Hamburg in the 1390s to improve their route, but this unloading and reloading, combined with limited barge capacity, was now outdone by better shipping. The Germans were getting a taste of their own medicine and found themselves up against superior capital and technology. The Scandinavians took over the business that slipped from the German grip. The Hansa had prospered on monopolies. The traders from the Low Countries were aggressively competitive. 'Capitalism', says the Danish historian Alex Wittendorff, 'was starting to emerge in north-western Europe.' Scandinavia took on a new persona, without the Hansa, with Denmark and Sweden reinvented.

Exit Norway

Christian II was thrown out of Denmark by his uncle, Frederik I,
who marched on Copenhagen with a mercenary army. He had himself
elected King of Norway as well, following the procedures, agreeing
a *håndfæstning* with the Norwegian *rigsråd* and promising to respect
Norway's autonomy – an empty promise, promptly ignored. In theory,
there was a Norwegian kingdom. In theory, there was an autonomous Church. In theory, there was an aristocracy. But there was no
substance. The population was a fourth or a third of Denmark's. In
the élite there were no stable factions or coalitions, no one agreeing
about anything. The *rigsråd* could never be convened with much of a
quorum, sometimes because the distances were forbidding, sometimes
because sundry grandees stayed away. A few years later, a teacher
and clergyman in Bergen, Absalon Pederssøn Beyer, one of the few
Norwegians of the time with a university education, was writing a
history of his country. There was a time when Norway had stood tall
among kingdoms, he said, but soon 'she was done for and had no
power left'.

CHRISTIAN II's LAST FLING

Mass murderer. Incompetent. Deposed in Sweden. Deposed in Denmark.
Still, he thought he had the right to be king. When he left his exile
in the Netherlands to return to Denmark to reclaim the Crown he
sailed first for Norway. He had help from the emperor, Charles V, his
brother-in-law, in exchange for a promise to defend the Catholic faith
(which he probably did not believe in, dithering in faith as in all else).
He aimed to mobilise additional strength in Norway and advance on
Denmark in force. But it collapsed into farce. Half of the fleet was
lost to a storm with about 1,000 men dead; some of it was scattered
along the Norwegian coast. Christian made it to Oslo with the rump,
convened a depleted *rigsråd* and had himself re-anointed king. The
grandees wrote a letter to Frederik telling him that he was deposed,
but backed off from signing it. Christian proceeded to fight his way
south, but whatever battle he engaged in he lost. Rather than allowing

him to sail south to Copenhagen, a fleet from there came north to escort him back home and into his twenty-seven years of captivity. Frederik fleeced the Norwegian traitors with fines and left them to their misery.

Frederik dies in 1533. Three years of civil war follow. Another Christian, the third, takes Copenhagen and is king from 1536. He dictates the *håndfæstning* he in principle negotiates with the *rigsråd*. In one paragraph, the Kingdom of Norway is eliminated with a stroke of the Danish pen and no one in Norway consulted. The reason, it is stated, is that Norway is now so deprived of power and fortune that the Norwegians are unable to maintain a lord and king of their own. From now on, and 'for all time', Norway is to be known as a province of Denmark. And so it becomes (if not 'for all time'). There is one state, Denmark. Officials are Danish, or loyal to the Danish Crown, the official language is Danish, government in Norway local government.

For almost the next three centuries, what being ruled from Denmark meant most tangibly for the Norwegians was to be taxed and taxed again. 'It is our understanding', wrote the Danish governor in Norway in 1676, 'that it is Your Majesty's blessed will that we take what is needed where we can find it.' The tax collectors were the Crown's local officials, who add to the burden through self-serving corruption. The history of Norway in the Danish period was written in a constant flow of petitions to the king over abuses by local officials. Common folk thought of the king as their father-protector whose officials were betraying his goodwill. The petitions were not ineffective and were sometimes heeded, but the abuse never ceased.

The elimination of Norway was illegal. Christian was King of Denmark, but Norway was its own kingdom of which Christian had not been made king. To change constitutional arrangements in Norway legally he would have had to be King of Norway and act in consort with the Norwegian *rigsråd*. The Danish *rigsråd* certainly had no authority to ratify the elimination of a foreign Crown. But there was no power to resist. The rationale given, that the Norwegians were so impoverished that they were unable to maintain their own kingship, was a statement of fact that historians have accepted to be true.

Did it matter? Constitutionally it did. Norway had been a kingdom, albeit under a king in Copenhagen. But there was not much change in reality. Since Margrete's time, Norway had been unified with Denmark. For the fisherman on the northern coast or the farmer and peasant in Gudbrandsdalen, it was not much of an issue where the king resided. It was to matter more that kings were strong than that they were foreign.

Still, the meaning of 'Norway' was ambivalent. The land was poor, distant, large and rugged, the climate hard and communications difficult. It could not in practice be governed like any other Danish province, and was left much to itself. Christian had eliminated the kingdom, but when in control chose to be magnanimous. The Danish wish was for things to stay quiet, and this was best achieved by not provoking Norwegian pride. He did not have to but he let himself be anointed King of Norway (sending his son as his representative to receive the non-existing Crown in his name) and presented his rule as being based on Norwegian law and a continuation of Margrete's union of two kingdoms. Norwegian sense of self survived to some degree and lived on during the rest of the Danish period. The kingdom was constitutionally Denmark but culturally, in some respects, Denmark-Norway. When modern nationalism started to take hold in the eighteenth century, there was a lingering ideological basis for a resurrected Norwegian kingdom.

WHAT'S IN A NAME?

The Danish state of which Norway was a province from 1536 to 1814 is sometimes called 'Denmark-Norway'. There is some truth in that. The illusion of Norway as a kingdom of its own side by side with Denmark survived to some degree, and did occasionally surface in official business. But not much in reality. These were not two kingdoms in union but a single kingdom. The state was Denmark, and Norway a mere part of that state. There was no equality, neither formally nor in fact. Nor does the double-barrelled identity have historical legitimacy. The realm of the king in Copenhagen included Denmark proper, Norway, the duchies of Schleswig and Holstein, the islands of the Faroes, Iceland and Greenland, and various possessions in Sweden. The Denmark-Norway label is a retrospective *politesse* to avoid giving offence to Norwegian pride.

Renaissance

The heavens were shifting. The Church taught that the universe was God's creation, ordered and finished, with our world as the centre and sun, planets and stars circulating around us. But when open-minded men looked out into the universe, men like Copernicus (Mikołaj Kopernik, the Polish minister of finance and astronomer) and the Italian Galileo Galilei (who was able to look into the universe with a workable telescope and confirm Copernicus's theories), they saw more complexity than was accounted for in the established truth.

The earth was shifting. Columbus reached the Americas in 1492. Six years later, Vasco da Gama sailed from Portugal around Africa to India, and from 1519 to 1522 a Spanish expedition was the first to circumnavigate the globe.

So we enter a landscape of incomprehension. How to understand a chaotic universe, and that the Bible does not tell us of Heaven and earth as they really are? How to understand that there is a world of wealth out there of which yesterday we had no inkling – and peoples, races and places for the understanding of which Christian teaching held no guidance? How to understand that trade as ordered in royal mandates is outcompeted by crude competition? Or for that matter, in the north, that the herring, the silver of the sea, the bedrock of our wealth, abandoned us and brought its blessings to others? How to understand?

We are in 'the Renaissance'. The world was presenting itself to the onlooker in a way that elicited variously excitement, fear or curiosity. Those who sought new answers looked back to what they thought of as a golden age of learning before the decay of the Middle Ages. What the Renaissance signified, basically, was a shifting paradigm in ideas, beliefs, mindsets and world views. It was not an easy struggle and much of what followed was ugly, such as extremes of superstition and the burning of witches, but still the human spirit was lifted out of the Church-sanctified 'psychological environment of fear that inhibited bold and independent thought'. The Renaissance has been regarded as 'humanitarian'.

THE DANGEROUS WITCHES

People knew of demons. The Church knew of heretics. Those possessed by demons were shunned, or worse. Heretics were burned at the stake. A rattled Church became obsessed with the Devil. Innocent VIII, pope from 1484, made it official. 'It has lately come to our ears', he said, 'that people of both sexes have abandoned themselves to devils.' They cast spells, killed infants, destroyed harvests, blasphemed the faith. They, most of them women, were known to ride through the night on rams and goats for 'Sabbaths' with the Devil or his agents, which might include sexual orgies, and return by day with evil powers. 'At the instigation of the Enemy of Mankind, they perpetrate the filthiest excesses to the deadly peril of their souls.' The signal had been given. Witch-hunting spread through Europe over the next 300 years, at the cost of 50,000 lives.

Including to Scandinavia. A punitive law on witchcraft was adopted in Sweden in 1608, with death-penalty provisions. In the next half-century there were relatively few trials, with restrained use of the death penalty, until a short period of endemic hysteria from 1668 to 1676 when there were a large number of trials and about 300 executions, sometimes by burning, sometimes by beheading. To bring this wave of violence to an end, a state commission on witchcraft ordered services of thanksgiving to be held in all churches with the pronouncement that the country was now cleansed of witches. Trials continued sporadically. The last execution was in Stockholm in 1704, of one Anna Eriksdotter, by beheading. She had been in service at a vicar's and was accused of having thrown a spell on him when dismissed. The last trial was in 1757, of twelve women interrogated under torture, all of whom were acquitted.

In 1617, on the centenary of Luther's posting of his ninety-five theses and in commemoration thereof, Christian IV of Denmark issued three decrees, one against luxuries at weddings, one against sexual frivolity and one against black magic. That codified witchcraft as a crime. The punishment was death in cases of proven devil-work, or confiscation of property. Following the king's decree, the number of witch trials increased rapidly during the next half-century. The last witch was executed by being burned in 1693.

In Norway, 860 witch trials are known to have taken place between

1550 and 1760, most of them during the 1600s, perhaps half resulting in executions. In 1623, in a town in the south-east, a woman by the name of Anne Holter was burned as a witch. She had killed her husband with an axe and pleaded that she had been possessed by the Devil. She implicated three other women. One confessed, boasting that she had ridden to a nightly encounter on a black calf, feasting with the evil ones. She too was burned. The two others denied involvement. One was interrogated under torture and exposed to the water test of being thrown into a river with her hands tied. She floated 'like a witch' and was burned. The third may have gone free. In 1670, in a mid-country village, a couple, Lisbeth and Ole Nypan, were both convicted, she burned, he beheaded. She had been known as a healer and it was said that she had cast spells to cause harm. He, in quarrels, had threatened opponents with his wife's powers. The couple were interrogated for four months in what was possibly the last trial resulting in executions. There had been uncommonly many witch trials in the north, among the Sami, who had long been suspected of practising black magic. The last trial was held in 1730, in Øyer in Gudbrandsdalen (which happens to be my parish). It took place in the vicarage, in the building which is still in use and in the room which today hosts parish meetings and cultural events. The trial is described beautifully by the Lillehammer novelist Magnhild Bruheim in *Trolldomskraft* ('Witchcraft'). A thirteen-year-old girl, Siri Jørgensdotter, is in service on a farm. She is a simple child who likes telling tales to give herself some standing among the other servants. One of her stories is that her grandmother had taken her one night to feast with the Devil. She is believed: the grandmother, newly deceased, had a bad reputation as a woman with 'powers'. The trial is conducted by the vicar. He understands that Siri has no other ability in an interrogation than to satisfy the interrogator. The village wants revenge on an outcast family, but the vicar guides the trial gently towards acquittal, and in such a way that service is found elsewhere for Siri. A life is spared and goes on.

The Renaissance was breathtaking in its inventiveness: religious reform, scientific discovery, the spread of education in schools and universities outside the Church. It saw the birth of literature in the hands of the Italians Dante Alighieri (whose *Divine Comedy* narrates the poet's pilgrimage through Purgatory, Hell and Paradise) and

Giovanni Boccaccio (in whose *Decameron* young Florentine fugitives from the plague pass their time with feasting and sex, or at least talk thereof). It came with leaps forward in philosophy, such as in the humanist Christianity of Erasmus of Rotterdam, the political theory of the Italian Niccolò Machiavelli and the rationalism of the Frenchman René Descartes. And equally in art and architecture: Titian (the genius of the near-pornographic nude, and much else, who died of the plague), Leonardo (the smartest but also kindest and most generous artist who ever lived), Brunelleschi (the visionary architect and engineer of the cupola of Florence's cathedral), Caravaggio (brutalist in art and life, the inventor of modern naturalism, generally on the run from the law), Michelangelo (the ultimate genius who carved human spirit out of marble with such speed that onlookers did not believe their eyes).

Thus the Renaissance has been seen as a good thing, a period of blossoming. And so it was. But new mindsets also enabled terrible outcomes: kingly dictatorship, wars and more wars, colonialism, slavery, exploitation, events and developments in which common folk, men and women, were worthless and expendable.

As always, there were economic forces at play. Increasing trade, importantly, assisted, just as importantly, by the wealth and competition that is contained in the magic of money. Money had come to an end in Europe with the fall of the Roman Empire. It started to return as of the eighth century, gradually creating (again) monetised economies. The increasing use of money worked as both cause and effect. As trade grew, it needed the assistance of money; as money became more plentiful, trade was made easier.

Money comes with two problems: how to make it and how to manage it. These problems were not solved at the time – perhaps they have still not been solved? It proved difficult for money to retain its value, hence inflation, hence higher prices and lower standards of living. The monetisation of economic life helped the wheels turn but did not come with much benefit to the small-folks. They became dependent on buying things, which kept nudging up in price. The pressure of inflated cost of living would burden ordinary people constantly through the next centuries.

Banking was well established in Europe in the Middle Ages, with organised networks capable of regular giro transfers in operation from at least the early 1300s. Merchant banking arose out of trading profits in major Italian cities, the Medici Bank of Florence being the best known. The Medici family had grown rich from trade and established themselves with a bank in 1397, which was to operate for about a century. Wealth they had; the purpose of the bank was to bring them power. That was successful: the Medicis made themselves superior in Florence and influential elsewhere in Italy and throughout Europe. A century later, the dominant European banking enterprise was that of Jakob Fugger of Augsburg. He was not in it for power, only for money and ever more of it, and was able to operate as financial impresario to popes, emperors and princes.

Kings with money, and the ability to make money, were gaining in standing and power. They hoarded money to buy themselves glory. They built and decorated forts and palaces and made themselves patrons of the arts. They extended their administrative services. They created professional armies recruited from their own populations. In the process they refined the oldest form of taxation, the dragooning of young men into military service. War was taking on new proportions and required more, better and loyal troops. Gunpowder was coming into use to bring enhanced firepower to battlefields on land and sea, again requiring more disciplined troops. Kings became 'Renaissance kings'.

However, although ambitious kings had money to spend, they never had enough – except the Spanish and Portuguese ones who, for a while, had too much silver and gold from the new worlds and fell victim of the curse of excessive wealth. Luckily for normal kings, others had means, the burghers and bankers. They in turn were eager to lend to kings and princes because they could be confident they would be paid back. Kings borrowed more than they were able to pay back in money, but being kings they had other resources. It was attractive for the bankers to be repaid in other ways than with money, since they were not able to charge outright interest. Maximilian I and his grandson Charles V, Holy Roman Emperors, both relied on loans from super-banker Fugger. Loans were repaid in part in silver- and copper-mining concessions, which is where the greedy Jakob was able to make himself seriously rich.

The evolution towards stronger, eventually absolutist, kingship was assisted by a duality of theories (if that is not too grand a term). The understanding of economics, later to be called 'mercantilism', was that economic activity should serve the State and for that purpose be regulated in detail in royal certificates, concessions and monopolies.

The thinking was that the national wealth was measured in the wealth of the Crown and that the State was as strong as it had bullion in its coffers, literally kilos of silver and barrels of gold.

In the rise of cities and their class of burghers, society itself was taking on a different shape. An understanding had been emerging to accommodate a changing reality. Society was a conglomerate of 'estates': clergy, nobility, burghers, commoners. Estates had functions: the clergy to teach, the aristocracy to defend, the burghers to trade, the commoners to work. This was God's order, and it was a duty for everyone to obey their station. There would then be harmony. Kings and princes were above the fray and it was their job to protect and maintain God's order. When kings needed the acquiescence of 'the people' it was the estates they called on, in what became formalised assemblies of estates.

Mercantilism helped kings to amass money and justified the subjugation of economic activity to their purposes. The theory of estates helped to vindicate the claim on obedience from the top down. Together, these theories lifted up kings to supremacy over all others and pushed the mass of ordinary people deeper into powerlessness. Whoever you were, your privilege or deprivation was just. State and economy, it was one and the same. King and country, it was one and the same.

The Scandinavian Renaissance

From around 1400, paper came into general use. Earlier, writing was preserved on parchment, which was expensive and hence reserved for exceptional matters, such as Bibles and State treaties. With the availability of paper, although still expensive and in Scandinavia an import, more things could be written down: contracts, court rulings, formal and private correspondence. Landowners could receive written reports from stewards on business across their estates. With more writing came better accounting and archives.

The breakthrough for printing on paper came in the mid-1400s, with Johannes Gutenberg in Mainz in Germany and his use of movable metal type. He famously printed the Bible, but also, being a businessman after all, absolution certificates for the Church (before going bankrupt). Book-printing spread north with German and Dutch printers. The first known book produced in Scandinavia, one of liturgy, was issued in Odense in Denmark in 1482, the first one in Sweden a year later. A printing business was established in Copenhagen around 1490, producing religious texts, grammars, almanacs and legal material. The first books in the Danish and Swedish languages appeared in 1495, the Swedish one a religious tract about how to resist temptation. Oslo (then known as Christiania) did not get its first book printer until 1643, the first publication being an almanac for the next year (given as the year 5612 after the Creation) of forty-four pages.

These were mostly illiterate societies. Those able to read and write made up a small minority – even by the 1600s no more than five in 100 among common men. But literacy was nevertheless spreading. After the Reformation, cathedral schools were secularised and broadened their recruitment, now being called 'Latin schools'. With urbanisation and economic diversification followed an increasing demand for education and the establishment of city and other non-Church schools. A school might consist of a teacher who took pupils, perhaps to be taught in his home, or an established institution with separate school premises, paid for by pupils or collectively by guilds or associations. Lower schools were known as 'trivial', meaning teaching only the basics, while upper schools were 'gymnasiums'. The first institution of higher learning in any sense was a Franciscan monastery school that offered studies up to college degree level, in Lund from the 1430s. In the competition to establish the first chartered university Sweden finely beat Denmark, the University of Uppsala being established in 1477, two years ahead of Copenhagen. All through the 1500s there was a steady rise in the number of students abroad. In Norway there was no university until the very end of the Danish period, the Royal Frederik University, now the University of Oslo, founded in 1811.

The spreading of literacy and the technology of book-printing spilled over into the use of indigenous languages for writing and reading. Printing was business, and there would be no market for printed material unless it was in a language ordinary people could read. In the Lutheran lands the reformed Church put the people's language to use. Luther created not only a reformed theology but also a reformed German language. In Scandinavia, Danish and Swedish became written languages, essentially the languages still in use. In Norway the language of State, Church and writing was Danish; not until the nineteenth century, and with much difficulty, did Norwegian become a written language.

TYGE BRAHE

Out of the intellectual wasteland of Denmark emerged an eminent astronomer (and astrologer and alchemist) by the name of Tyge (Tycho) Brahe to help carry forward the scientific revolution in Europe. He was a student of law at the University of Copenhagen from age twelve. During a solar eclipse in 1560 he was overcome with curiosity about the composition of the universe. After ten years of study at European universities he returned home, disillusioned with the state of astronomy and determined to improve on the science with the help of systematic and careful observation.

On a November night in 1572, he detected a star that moved across the sky in a way impossible according to prevailing understandings of the universe. The earth was thought to sit in the middle, with stars and planets arranged around it in fixed 'spheres'. But Tyge's star had come and gone and been confined to no sphere. Copernicus's findings had been published in 1543 (in the year of his death) but attracted neither favour nor much interest, its fearful editor inserting a Preface which reduced the author's proofs to mere hypotheses. Now, however, the young Dane had produced an observed fact that should not have been possible. The times were ready for just that discovery. Tyge was world-famous. Science was on its way to where Galileo, Bacon and Newton would later take it. His influence would finally work through Johannes Kepler, the elderly Tyge's young assistant, and his laws for the movement of the planets.

Tyge had been given resources for his scientific work by the Danish king the likes of which no Scandinavian scientist has ever seen again – land, income, buildings, equipment – but was mean to those below him and arrogant to those above, and finally forced to leave the country. He obtained the patronage of Emperor Rudolf II (whom we will meet later as the mad collector) and settled in Prague, with Kepler his last assistant. He, Kepler, took over Tyge's observation protocols and turned these and other findings into the advancements that would clear the way for Galileo and his followers, one of which was to establish that the planets move not in circles but in ellipses. Tyge himself was never able to follow his own observations to their logical conclusion but settled for a 'compromise' in which the earth was still the centre of the universe, the sun circulating around it and the other planets around the sun again.

Around 1400, King Erik issued Danish coins for commercial use, and later kings continued the business. The ambition was to create currency. However, currency depends on trust, which proved elusive. Danish coins of the age never won confidence. Even the Crown did not much trust its own coinage, insisting that fees at the Skåne market be paid in Lübeck silver and tolls for passage through the Sound in English currency. Nevertheless, in a world of monetised business a king who wants to be taken seriously needs to have his own money. He cannot be seen to be dependent on others, and must anyway be able to make money when he needs it. Christian II minted 'war coins' to finance his campaign against Sweden, which he forced on farmers in payment for provisions. They were of miserable quality and soon useless. When Christian was deposed, his successor refused the coins and demanded taxes be paid in silver, withdrawing Christian's coins at their metal value, leaving the farmers with the loss.

You can make coins if you have precious metals. Viking kings had to go raiding for capital since they had no source of silver or gold at home. Kings were now increasingly able to lay their hands on at least silver and copper. They would trade, tax still being paid in part in goods, and earn money by exporting some of the goods they extracted. They would siphon off silver from other trade in tolls and fees. After the Reformation they were big landowners with serious revenue from rent and the nationalisation of the tithe, and could for a while add to their coffers by confiscating Church treasures. They would, when they could, extract taxes in money or precious metals in other forms. Copper was mined in Sweden on a commercial scale from the late 1200s, in Norway from the early 1500s, silver in Sweden from the 1400s and in Norway from the early 1600s. These were royal concessions, securing supplies to the Crowns. The mines were poor and the work deadly, carried out a lot of the time by forced convict labour. 'At the silver mines', says the Swedish historian Alf Åberg, 'was written the darkest social chapters of our early industrial history.' Coinage for commercial use was minted in Sweden from 1534, known as *daler*, from the German *Thaler* – 'dollars' – principally to facilitate international trade. Like Danish coins, they long suffered steady loss in value for international usage.

The first Scandinavian bank was in Sweden, known as *Stockholm Banco*, established in 1657 by a Dutch immigrant by the name of

Johan Wittmacher Palmstruch as a semi-State enterprise to raise capital for the Crown.

This bank was the first in Europe to issue paper money. That is explained partly by the ingenuity of banker Palmstruch, who had the imagination to see that cumbersome copper could be replaced by easy-to-use paper, and partly by inflationary pressures whereby copper coinage was losing value so that ever more coins were required in transactions. The demand on the bank by depositors who needed money was running ahead of what the bank could manage. As a solution Palmstruch issued credit notes, in different denominations, all signed by him personally, by which he could satisfy, for a while, depositors' need for money without having to hand over copper cash. The credit notes became popular because of their simplicity and the bank issued ever more of them. Soon there was too much paper in circulation and the notes lost value. Depositors started to prefer cash to paper and wanted their real money back, more than the bank had in reserve. In 1668 it collapsed and had to be bailed out by the *Riksdag* (Parliament). Its remaining activities were transferred to a new state bank, the forerunner of today's *Sveriges Riksbank* (housed in a fortress-like building in Stockholm's Old Town which is still there). Palmstruch was sentenced to death for reckless management of State funds, but pardoned from execution. The new bank was held under the authority of the *Riksdag* to protect it from interference by kings. Not until 1904 was the National Bank's monopoly on issuing paper money operational.

The first Danish bank, known as *Kurantbanken*, was established in 1736, again with a certificate to issue paper money. It was nationalised in 1773 and later subsumed into the Danish National Bank. Norway got a central bank only after having broken free from Danish overrule, established in 1816.

The Scandinavians had been used to having a say in governance at *thing*. Now participation by 'the people' was reshaped into meetings of estates. Representation on the national level had emerged from the thirteenth century with meetings of nobles, in Denmark known as *Danehof* (Dane-courts) and in Sweden and Norway as *herredager* (assemblies of lords). That metamorphosed into the *rigsråd/riksråd* which we have met previously. These were the councils that enforced on kings the *håndfæstninger* that regulated their authority.

The first meetings of estates more broadly were convened in Sweden and Denmark from the early to mid-fifteenth century, no doubt for kings to counter the influence of the more narrowly constituted *rigsråd*. The understanding in Europe was mostly a division of society into three estates: clergy, nobles and burghers, reflected for example in the composition of the French *États généraux*, first convened in 1302. In Scandinavia, certainly in Sweden, if in Denmark only locally, the understanding became more 'democratically' of four estates: churchmen, nobles, burghers and a fourth estate of propertied farmers.

By the early 1500s, under Gustav Vasa's hand, the Swedish estates were firmly institutionalised under the name of *Riksdag*, giving Sweden one of the longest continuities of 'popular' representation in Europe. No similar continuity prevailed in Denmark, where meetings of estates did not coalesce into regularised assemblies and 'popular' representation soon ceased altogether. Norway, although no longer a kingdom, did continue for a while to convene meetings of estates, such as for the anointment of (Danish) kings, the last one in 1661, events of merely symbolic meaning.

What passed the Scandinavian Renaissance by was the splendour of high art. 'It is difficult to identify a Danish culture. In most areas, Denmark is part of a common North German cultural area.' Sweden was a 'culturally poor land'. Literature, in its artistic meaning (once the vitality of Icelandic literature was gone), did not emerge until the end of the period we are now observing.

There was, however, a living tradition of music, reaching back to Viking Age poetry and recital. The ballad was a popular form of song with themes of aristocratic chivalry, love, hate, the supernatural, adventure and legend, sometimes in accompaniment to traditional ring-dance, 'danced to all over Scandinavia in medieval times'. Small-folks could take refuge in song and oral poetry to give expression to what otherwise could not be said. A first collection of folk songs, 100 of them, was printed in Denmark in 1591, meeting an eager demand, and was reissued repeatedly over the next century. There was enough interest in music to attract wandering foreign musicians, at least to Denmark. The Reformation brought the singing of hymns into Scandinavian popular culture, many of Luther's hymns still being in use today.

If there was music, song and dance, when and where? On festive occasions, no doubt, and at church. Wandering musicians found audiences in town squares and inns. Would the audience join in? Perhaps; hard liquor, beloved by today's Scandinavians as a lubricant to overcome inhibition and known, then as now, as *brændevin/ brennevin/brändvin* (fire wine) was just coming into use. Grandees engaged musicians to entertain guests and show off their status. Would men accompany work in fields or forests with song, and women while churning butter? Neighbours come together for song and dance? Perhaps. Still in my parents' generation, when farm maidens were tending cattle at summer mountain pasture, young men of the village would drift up on a Saturday evening, one with a fiddle, one with an accordion, for all to meet at a dance floor on a hillside which had been there as long as anyone could remember.* The tradition of singing as a companion to daily life persists. The Scandinavian area is vividly musical, with today, for example, in Sweden in particular, an unusually extensive participation in choir-singing at all levels of proficiency.

Sweden and Denmark reinvented

Gustav Vasa owed his kingship to the Hansa. Literally: he was in massive debt to them, having relied on their mercenary forces to suppress remaining rebellions. He needed to get out of that dependency. The

---

* The dance floor in question was on Hulderhaugen, 'Hulder Hill', at Holmsetra in the village of Tretten. Its remains were still there in my childhood, but no longer in use (but later a stage was erected nearby for summer feasts with professional bands). A *hulder* is a mythological fairy-tale figure, a beautiful but dangerous temptress of the forest whom gullible men do not recognise until they see her cow's tail and it is too late. Holmsetra is a cluster of farmlets, *setre*, where cattle were held over the summer to feed off natural pastures, tended by farm women, often young unmarried daughters in their late teens or early twenties. The *seter* economy has its origins in the Middle Ages and is still in operation to some degree, although many a *seter* has been converted to a holiday home. In its heyday it served not only the farms but also the young as a place to meet. My parents met when my mother and her younger sister were tending their *seter* and my father, then a student, was the dairy inspector, who would go from *seter* to *seter* and stay a day and night or two at each. He came from poor circumstances but was a man on the rise. She brought *odel* farm standing to the match. Perfect. You would be forgiven for thinking that the purpose of the *seter* economy was to create a marriage market.

Church had property and income. He took it. Simple as that – never mind that he had sworn on his coronation to protect the Church's privileges. The Reformation in Sweden was first about power and money and only secondly about theology, a matter Gustav took no interest in. It was nothing to him to 'have beautiful, ancient, ecclesiastical parchment manuscripts torn up and used as covers for his bailiffs' account books'. The Church confiscation was quick and brutal. To secure aristocratic loyalty, he returned some land to families who had been coerced into gifting it to the Church.

He had finance and could get on with restoring the slumbering, strong State. The last of the rebel leaders ended with his head on a stake in Kalmar town and his family 'completely extinguished'. Gustav turned to political and administrative reform, now realising the State that Birger *Jarl* had started to construct nearly 300 years earlier. He built forts and castles, installed officials to streamline tax collection, created a central bureaucracy, introduced fiscal accounting, minted coins, imposed conscription to create a national army and built himself a navy, soon the strongest in the Baltic area. He himself had no hereditary claim to be king, yet it was he who imposed hereditary kingship from then on, having his son Erik anointed 'our next king'. He set in motion a systematic colonisation of northern areas to populate the territory and broaden the tax base. He got the *Riksdag* to sanction his takeover of the Church.

He died aged sixty-four, after a rule of thirty-seven years. He had been a tyrant, but a tyrant of his time, effective, a successful builder of the State, giving Sweden independence, importing absolutism (although the absolute monarchy was not formalised until 1693, and even then with the limitations that the *Riksdag* survived). He was a brilliant speaker, a user of the people's coarse and simple language, a cheat and a liar, and a propagandistic author of myth about himself. He was personally the biggest landowner in the country and made himself the richest Swedish king ever.

He stands in history as the king who made the Swedish *rike* and is up there with Birger *Jarl* in shaping the nation's destiny. He at first did not appear to be a natural leader, but was to deliver leadership of consequence. He was a spinner of myth about himself to such a degree that his true persona remains unknown. He was vain, greedy, brutal, bad-tempered, vengeful, as violent as was necessary. But effective, a hard-working and hands-on administrator, a willing wielder of power.

Gustav Vasa, King of Sweden 1523–60

In Denmark, Christian III took kingship in a coup. Like Gustav in Sweden he was to preside over a new State, but was, unlike Gustav, a sincere convert to a simple Lutheran faith and an active theological reformer, which explains why the Reformation was completed earlier in Denmark than in Sweden. He confiscated Church property and brought 60 per cent of land under Crown ownership, trebling its financial base. He stripped the churches of silver and melted down the treasures for the minting of coins. He had his son, the two-year-old Frederik, 'elected' successor. The judicial right to resist an unworthy king, standard in previous *håndfæstninger*, was struck out of his own. He built up an orderly central and local administration, including a ministry of finance with (rudimentary) fiscal accounting, and strengthened the army and navy. He worked for legal and judicial reform, aiming for a national code of law, which, however, was not realised until after his time, in 1683. (In this endeavour he had the old existing law, the Code of Jylland, translated to German, so that he could read it himself. He was born in Schleswig and German remained his language.) Initially he had a great deal of internal opposition to deal with, some of it of Catholic sentiment, some of it supported by Emperor Charles V, who did not recognise him as lawful king until ten years into his reign. He bought that recognition by allowing Dutch traders freedom from tolls in Danish waters. Like Gustav in Sweden, he returned some Church land to previous owners in the aristocracy. He confirmed landowner serf-like authority over tenants. He abolished the Kingdom of Norway.

So then, two Renaissance kings in two restored kingdoms. A new age was commencing. Christian died in 1559, to be succeeded by his son Frederik II. In Sweden, Gustav died in 1560, to be succeeded by his son Erik XIV (an utterly fictitious number, based on the counting of early mythological kings). The fathers had managed to keep peace with each other; they were brothers-in-law. Not so the sons, although they were cousins.

Frederik was eager for war, kept the company of officers and fantasised about restoring the Scandinavian Union and Denmark to the status of a big power, with himself leading his fighting forces. He was not a bright man, poorly educated, near-incapable of coherent writing and spelling, but, not a good thing for a man of limited ability, physically strong and domineering. When prevented from leading his troops against the Swedes he took comfort in hunting, boozing, whoring and Bible-reading. 'If life at court was not enough for the king's tastes', says the Norwegian historian Rolf Fladby, 'there were always drinking companions outside of the palace, and also young ladies who did not deny him his pleasure.' A life of heavy eating and drinking caught up with him to contribute to his early death, of stomach cancer probably, still overeating, finally vomiting up his own faeces.

Erik wanted to break the Danish hold on the trading routes to the west. The Seven Years War between Sweden and Denmark followed (not to be confused with the later Seven Years War of 1756–63 between Britain, France and others). It was a war of extreme barbarity, a naval war at sea and the first total war on land, kept going by, in addition to Frederik's war thirst and poor political judgement, Erik's descent into madness. He, Erik, thought highly of himself and proposed marriage to Elizabeth of England, pursuing her for several years (Frederik also wooed her), and also to Mary, Queen of Scots, Renata of Lorraine, Anna of Saxony and Christine of Hesse – only eventually to marry his mistress, Karin Månsdotter, a servant to a court musician's wife. In the midst of the war, in a fit of insanity, he had five nobles murdered on trumped-up charges of treason, at least one by his own hand, and then had his own old tutor killed for trying to calm him. Norway was dragged in, not by the Norwegians' doing, Christiania and other cities were sacked and Nidaros Cathedral was desecrated into a stable for Swedish cavalry. The war did no good, ending in a draw in which neither side made gains in territory or much else. But it did a great deal of bad. 'This war saw the birth of national hatred in Scandinavia.'

Frederik was lucky not to have fared worse. Denmark lost no territory, but the war had shown that Sweden was now a force that Denmark could not dominate. Erik had inherited a 'Livonian' war with Russia in which he gained control of territory on both sides of the Bay of Finland (the bay that reaches into today's St Petersburg). When he tried to use his control of the bay to block others out of the eastern trade he made enemies first of Poland, then the Hansa, then Denmark. He was deposed in 1569, on grounds of insanity, and the Danish war was brought to an end the year after. The Russian war continued until 1583, with defeat for Russia, and Sweden laying the foundation of its east Baltic empire, which would be the basis for its superpower standing in Europe – 'for the next 150 years a constant misery for our people', according to Alf Åberg.

7

Imperialism

Stronger and richer Crowns, their dedication to warfare – these two tendencies were to be costly in the extreme to both populations and national economies. For two centuries Sweden was almost constantly at war, and Denmark for much of the time, most of it war against Sweden. It was the people out there on the land who had to pay up. They had to provide the manpower: soldiers to fight, others to man guard posts, labourers to build defences and fortifications and offer transport. They had to sustain the armies. They had to deliver the provisions, which Crowns and armies had the power to take. The level of extraction from a poor population was extreme, in periods, says the Danish historian Leon Jespersen, 'exceeding the production that society was capable of'. Where there were young men, there was conscription. Where there was food and produce, it had to be surrendered. Where there was trade or production, there were tolls and fees. Where there was harvest, it had to be given up. Where there was land, there was rent. Where there was sin, there were fines. Where there were local officials, there was corruption. From around 1650 to 1700 the tax burden on the Danish farming population increased fourfold.

Land and people

The Danish economy fared badly. It was all agricultural, with no other resource than land, almost all of it in Crown and aristocratic ownership. The aristocracy was tiny, too rich for its own good, and reactionary, unable to invest and innovate, dedicated to the old, with no mindset of progress. The Crown ploughed its surplus into palace splendour and its war machine. Very little was reinvested and very little went back to the small-folks to encourage effort. 'For most of the people, the 1600s were a cold century of poverty. Beggars thronged the highways, prostitutes, lone mothers in flight from home, former soldiers, cripples and the chronically ill who fell by the wayside in the struggle for survival.' The early 1700s were no better, with failed harvests, export failure, deadly epidemics of foot-and-mouth and other cattle diseases. Population growth reversed into decline.

Norway in some ways did better. More land came under cultivation with a rising number of landholdings. Mining started to take off, mainly of copper. Some of the herring that had deserted the south Scandinavian shores made their way to Norwegian waters, stimulating, for a while, a boom in the export of fish products. An increasing demand for timber in England, Holland and elsewhere in Europe gave a boost to another export, and at home an industry of sawmills (much helped by the great London fire of 1666).

But it did not trickle down. The Norwegians suffered from their country being ruled from Denmark for the good of Denmark. The more Danish kings were at war, the harder the extraction. They looked north for provisions, increasingly timber and ore, and for manpower. Those not taken away into the navy were conscripted to home militias to be on the ready with men and equipment for war, usually with Sweden, when the command came from Copenhagen. Trade, grain in import and timber and copper in export, was regulated for the benefit of Denmark and Danish business.

The Swedish economy benefited from territorial expansion and rich natural resources. The taking over of previously Danish possessions in Swedish territory was an agricultural bonanza and opened up easier western trade. The appropriation of Baltic areas made it the dominant power in the north. The export of iron advanced in quality, from raw ore to processed bar iron. Copper and silver were in high demand. The mining industry was to fund much of the Swedish Crown's never-ending warfare.

Sweden entered the warring period better managed and economically stronger than Denmark, and had the advantage of fighting its wars mostly in foreign lands. Denmark was a country divided against itself, under inept political leadership, with a shabby aristocracy, suffering continuously from wars ravaging its own territory. While the Danish and Norwegian populations stagnated or declined, the Swedish population continued to grow in spite of the hardship of warfare.

*

The aristocracies that had come out winners in the upheavals after the Big Death continued to do well. They had land, wealth and privilege. They were masters over powerless tenants.

But they may not have been able to see through their splendour that the times were against them. The old aristocracies were too small to provide officials and officers for bigger States. Stronger kingships were in need of trained professionals, leaving the old aristocracies short in the delivery of recruits with the necessary competence. New blood was needed. In Denmark that came from foreign, mainly German, imports, ennobled for military or administrative service, and in Sweden from recruits from lower echelons whom monarchs lifted to noble position. By around 1700, two-thirds of the Swedish nobility had been elevated during the previous century. The aristocracies were not the same, gradually less dominated by old families.

While eroding from inside, the aristocracies were simultaneously squeezed by the rising class of burghers, who challenged the land-owners in wealth and edged their way into royal partnership, much by virtue of lending money to kings in need and receiving positions and landed estates in return. A new élite class was on the rise, with nearness to Crown and king, sidelining the old nobles. In the Swedish *Riksdag*, the burghers were on an equal footing with an aristocracy that sank to being only one of four estates. In Denmark, the aristocracy woke up from its slumber to find itself politically irrelevant.

The 1500s onward became a period of migrations. There was out-migration from Sweden, both east to the shorelands in Finland, feeding into what is still a substantial Swedish-speaking minority, and south to areas in the Baltics, giving rise to a Swedish population in present-day Estonia, stimulated by the migrants being exempt from military conscription. A further outmigration was to Holland, and to some degree England, then growing trading powers, especially from resource-poor south-western Norway, men to find maritime work, women in domestic service.

In-migration, in lesser numbers but of economic importance, was increasingly from the Netherlands, but also elsewhere: adventurers and entrepreneurs attracted by the growing States, growing cities and early mining and industry, many of whom were invited for their industrial, military and administrative competence. Trading cities were multinational. Bergen in the 1500s had more foreign than native burghers: Danes, Dutch, German, English and Scots.

A different flow was from Finland west through virgin lands in northern Sweden and into Norway. This migration, of *skogsfinnar* ('forest Finns'), was encouraged in Sweden for the settlement of northern areas. Its migrants were to create lasting communities. A region in eastern Norway is known as *Finnskogen*, where local people still speak Norwegian in a dialect with a hard Finnish edge to it.

Domestic migration was from countryside to cities. By the mid- to late seventeenth century, urban dwellers made up about 15 per cent of the population in Denmark, 10 per cent in Sweden and 5 per cent in Norway.

A second movement, in Sweden and Norway, was to the far north. Here the Sami lived in uneasy cohabitation with other Norwegians and Swedes who clustered along the coasts, in Norway living mainly off cod fisheries and maritime hunting, in Sweden off salmon-fishing in the Bay of Bothnia and trade, such as in furs, some of it with the Sami. As these Norwegian and Swedish migrations intensified, their businesses were to compete with the Sami for territory: farming, fisheries, mining. From about the mid-1500s the inland Sami took up reindeer-herding, which in the northern semi-tundra requires vast areas of land. Here originated what was to be a lasting conflict over land and waterways. The in-migrants brought with them an institution unknown at least to the nomadic Sami: personal ownership of land. The old notion of communal land, here as in other indigenous populations across the globe, proved to offer little protection against the turning of land into property, with the backing of the State, its laws and its Church. This conflict was to turn cultural and take the form of subjugation not only of Sami economic interests but also of their language, conventions and traditions. The northern lands were *terra missionis* into which the Norwegian and Swedish Churches reached with evangelisation, partly liberating, partly repressive. Not until the second half of the twentieth century was this conflict addressed in any serious way by the majority populations. Once that happened, however, impressive action was to follow towards reconciliation in attitudes, cultural recognition and material conditions.

Kings, and two queens, on parade

Denmark and Sweden were emerging as militaristic states. At the top, an officer class was in the making. Lower down, conscription, or the threat thereof, became a constant presence in the lives of ordinary folk. This was most strongly felt in Sweden, where the aristocracy was militarily progressive and the militarisation of the state thorough and determined.

Military might was being professionalised, although with limitations. In Norway, in the absence of aristocracy, there was no other basis of military force than by militias of conscripted men. In Denmark and Sweden, it remained an obligation on the nobility to serve the Crown militarily. It was obvious that the nobles themselves would be officers. It was then for them to recruit the foot soldiers. While navies were Crown forces, armies were more often made up of divisions under aristocratic command. Prominent families served the Crown as military commanders of forces of their own. National armies were, in part, mercenary forces drawn from the home populations. In the field these forces operated by their own logic, certainly in plunder, a war business in which Swedish grandees excelled. Conscription in this form also enabled the recruitment of foreign soldiers. A friendly duke might go into the service of a foreign king and bring his militia with him. In the Thirty Years War, Swedish armies fighting in Germany were recruited in some considerable measure in Germany itself.

This military organisation came with a built-in bellicose logic. A standing army waiting for service was an expensive luxury. The men had to be equipped, fed and paid. But an army in action was self-sustaining. It lived off the land where it roamed and was paid from plunder. With luck it would be a profit-making machine, bringing surplus back to officers, commanders and eventually the Crown. The prominent families, whose sons led their divisions under the king's banner, made themselves rich from warfare. Their foot soldiers fell massively to injury and disease, but that did not matter; it was the order of things. There were always more young men back home to be conscripted.

The system of warmongering militarism was to find its most dramatic manifestation in the Thirty Years War, when soldier bands, including Scandinavian ones, roamed back and forth across Europe in the interest of generating profit for masters and kings. So pervasive was this that it was to delay the ending of the war when armies refused to demobilise until they had their full satisfaction of loot. The last Swedish forces did not depart from the Continent for home until six years after the peace had been signed.

Sweden was to excel in that particular war, coming out of it as the dominant power in northern Europe, and noble families with treasures hitherto unimagined. There was no similar success for Denmark. Sweden had economic strength to rely on, mining on top of agriculture. Denmark was hesitant in militarism, its aristocracy content with its agricultural wealth and otherwise gutless, giving ambitious kings only half-hearted backing.

Absolutism was another European import and another costly legacy of Renaissance thinking. It was the way European kings came to rule, the French ones leading the way, thought by educated élites to be the sophisticated form of government. The theory, or ideology if you will, was that kings had absolute power from two sources: from the people, who out of good sense had surrendered sovereignty to kings, and from God, for the purpose of order in his earthly realm. Young aristocrats from the north observed modern monarchy on display in France and elsewhere and brought ideas with them to be implemented at home. Absolutism in Denmark was formalised in 1665 in a *Kongelov* (law of kingship) according to which the estates transferred absolute power to the king, so that he could grant security to his subjects and they 'could build and live in peace and security without fear of strife betwixt themselves'.

The Crown was supreme. Old élites were reduced from partners to servants. The small-folks were reduced to royal property. Absolutism lasted until the end of the eighteenth century, when the French Revolution, the Napoleonic Wars and the last great Scandinavian wars were to bring it to its final and overdue end. Until then, kings followed kings in a more or less orderly hereditary pattern, with two Swedish queens inserting themselves, bringing their peoples little joy and much unhappiness. Historians call it absolutism. In today's political language we might rather say 'dictatorship'.

The Danish kings of the period were alternately Christian and Frederik, up to Christian VII who departed in 1808, nine of them in all as of Christian III. The Swedish ones lasted for shorter periods, there being fifteen of them from Gustav Vasa on up to Gustav IV, who departed in 1809.

Kings and queens of the age of absolutism

Years	Denmark and Norway	Sweden
1500		
	Frederik I, 1523–33	Gustav Vasa, 1523–60
	Christian III, 1536–59	
1550		
	Frederik II, 1559–88	Erik XIV, 1560–68
		Johan III, 1568–92
	Christian IV, 1588–1648	Sigismund, 1592–99
1600		Karl IX, 1604 (1599)–11
		Gustav Adolf, 1611–32
		Kristina, 1632–54
1650	Frederik III, 1648–70	Karl X, 1654–60
		Karl XI, 1660–97
	Christian V, 1670–99	
1700	Frederik IV, 1699–1730	Karl XII, 1697–1718
		Ulrika Eleonora, 1718–20
		Fredrik I, 1720–51
	Christian VI, 1730–46	
	Frederik V, 1746–66	
1750		Adolf Fredrik, 1751–71
	Christian VII, 1766–1808	
		Gustav III, 1771– 92
		Gustav IV, 1792–1809
1800		

We need to know these kings and queens. They owned their peoples and countries, who were at the mercy of their whims, abilities and madnesses. It is because of the powers they commanded and who they were that the age of war unfolded as it did. Gustav Vasa and Christian III were builders of State capacity and holders of peace, who, in rough ways it is true, brought progress to their countries. That is high praise seen against what was to follow under most of their successors.

Christian IV was a big king: big in body, big in appetites, big in ambition, big in action. Denmark was a formidable power, and Christian its most formidable majesty. He was king at eleven, crowned at nineteen, and reigned for fifty-nine years, the longest of any Scandinavian king. He married twice; his first wife, a German princess, died young and anonymous. Of seven children, three lived beyond childhood. His second wife, Kirsten Munk, of a noble Danish family, who was only 'consort' and not called 'queen', gave him thirteen children by the time she was thirty-one of whom eight lived, only eventually to lock him out of her bedchamber and then be banished from the court when she tried to hoodwink the king into believing that her child by her lover was his. She was carried off in a fish cart, it was said, by two mismatched nags, in orchestrated humiliation. His love for Kirsten was strong and genuine, so that when she betrayed him it drove him to the madness of hatred. He did not marry again but held a subsequent official mistress who bore him two more children.

He wanted not only his kingship to be strong but also his court to be cultural. His tool was music. The king himself loved music, using it for pleasure and comfort, even taking musicians with him on expeditions to sea. He had orchestras with musicians from many parts of Europe and brought leading composers from England and elsewhere to Copenhagen. He had a small ensemble in his winter palace, where he had devised a trapdoor contraption whereby the orchestra played in the cellar for the music to rise to his room, musicians unseen, and had other arrangements of invisible music in other palaces. It was a way of impressing visitors with his ingenuity. But, we might ask, what of the music that emanated from frozen musicians playing frozen instruments and that travelled up by way of tubes, tracts and a hole in a floor? Music, yes, impressive, yes, but deprived of life and spirit.

Christian IV, King of Denmark 1588–1648

We may remember a previous monarch, Håkon Håkonsson in Norway, who had wanted to make his court brilliant with the help of imported European culture, but who may not have been aware that he failed in that ambition because he and those around him lacked the capacity to appreciate the spirit of the literature they consumed. We are 400 years on, and in Denmark, but still in a European periphery more peripheral than its ambitious king would have liked to think. He knew what the best music was, and who were the best musicians, but was he aware that he mistreated musicians and music so that what filled his rooms must have been painful to the discerning listener? It was difficult to be not just king but a *European* king. He was a man of cultural pretension; if you observed carefully you would see that his fingernails were dirty and his tastes crude.

Life at the court of this most glamorous of kings was, behind the façade, less than it made itself appear to be. There was music, but it was perverted. Men and women, by the age of thirty, were worn down in body and soul, the men by accident and injury, the women by constant pregnancy and childbirth, and all through excessive drinking and eating. They had elegant clothing of the best materials, but it tended to be filthy and of poor fit. Teeth rotted, and even the best of false teeth were painful and useless. Breath and body stank – Christian chewed cinnamon to conceal the bad taste. Failing eyesight could not be corrected. Sex was promiscuous and uninhibited, with husbands and wives cheating on each other and children neglected and abused, growing up to be dysfunctional adults, as was the case with many future monarchs. Servants were harassed and underpaid, if paid at all, stealing from their masters as they could. Christian's mother, Queen Sophie, is said to have hoarded enough silver and gold to make her Europe's second-richest person, behind Duke Maximilian of Bavaria and ahead of her son. She could have saved his kingship from paralysing financial distress but, being as mean an old cow as any could be, refused and hid her treasure away out of fear that the king might come for it, only extending a miserly loan which she later coerced the son into repaying although she had no use for the money. When the cost of engaging in the Thirty Years War threatened to absorb his dwindling reserves, and more, he was forced to beg for a subsidy from his brother-in-law, James I of England.

The young Christian was an immensely attractive man: energetic, sociable, learned, fun-loving, hospitable, cultured, a lover of women, courageous, hard-drinking, a good dancer – and rich to boot. Not handsome – ugly, some said, and fat – not kind, but attractive. Also moody, domineering, bullying, vulgar – but always on a grand scale. On a state visit to England in 1606, he gave the English, themselves no prudes, certainly not his host James (and his wife Anne, Christian's sister), a masterclass in hard drinking such as to make the most elaborate palace ceremonies disintegrate in drunkenness. He had a dark side in religious matters, insisting on Church obedience and conniving in the purging of deviant voices within Church and university teaching, promoting the craze of witch-hunting. His failure as a warrior king was God's punishment for the immorality of the underlings. He turned on his people and imposed on them decrees on church attendance and fasting and against fornication, loose living and the enjoyment of luxuries. He was a libertine who left a heritage of pietism that was to weigh on Danish society over the next century.

He added magnificent buildings to Copenhagen that still beautify the city, such as the Round Tower, still there, that has an inside ramp up which a horse and carriage could drive to the top, built churches, palaces and forts, lavished money on art, founded cities, strengthened the navy. Even at age sixty-seven, he led a naval battle against Sweden in which he was wounded and lost the sight of his right eye but brushed his injury aside and rose to encourage his men on to further fighting. He wanted colonies and founded the Danish East India Company. He spent much time in Norway and is revered there. He founded the mining towns of Kongsberg (silver) and Røros (copper), and for a while mined enough iron to supply the Danish army with the new technology of cannons and cannon balls during the Thirty Years War. When Oslo burned to the ground in 1624, he was there and decided that the city should be rebuilt and renamed after himself, on an ordered grid of streets, still in use, known as *Kvadraturet*. But he could not stay the course. The Thirty Years War broke him, financially but also in spirit. An accident when he and his horse fell through a rotten bridge probably left him with lasting brain damage, the effects of which he took to hiding with ever heavier drinking.

No wonder he has fascinated later historians. But his kingship was a failure. An early success was an expedition to the north as far as the Kola Peninsula, in which he secured northern Norway, also eyed by Sweden and Russia, for the kingdom (but not all of the Kola Peninsula as he had wanted). It involved eight ships and several hundred crew and followers and took three months there and back, from May to June 1599. The young king was personally in command, incognito as 'general captain'. It was a rough voyage amid much hard weather, involving confrontation with English and Dutch trading and fishing vessels to establish territorial authority – also a sailors' adventure in which the king was his men's mate in danger, courage, merriment and, as usual, heavy drinking. It took a war, the Kalmar War of 1611, to get the matter finally settled, but northern Norway was secured against Swedish ambitions.

Another success, to some degree, was in colonial ventures and trade in Asia, and the follow-through to Africa and the West Indies. Christian got it going and Denmark was to be a not insignificant colonial power, and a profiteer from the slave trade between Africa and the Americas.

But most of his ventures went bad. He was not an able administrator: a control freak, unable to delegate, obsessed with detail. An attempt to get a silk textile industry going in Copenhagen was an expensive fiasco. Three expeditions to Greenland to rediscover the old Norse settlements failed. An expedition to 'discover' the North-East Passage around Russia failed. So did a subsequent expedition to North America in search of the North-West Passage, most of the crew succumbing to hunger and scurvy in what is now Hudson Bay.* The wars with Sweden were failures. Denmark's adventures into the Thirty Years War, in which Sweden excelled, were failures. The Crown he inherited was rich but fell into financial ruin – the king even had to pawn the royal crown to pay off debt. (It was bought back from a merchant in Hamburg in time for the next king's coronation.) Armies and navies absorbed two-thirds of Crown outlays. By 1650, Crown debt was ten times annual Crown revenue. He had lived the life of a king on a grand scale, but he died disillusioned and unhappy, ill, worn down, friendless. It was to take only ten years under his son and successor for Denmark to be brought to the edge of extinction by Swedish aggression.

* Both these expeditions were in the charge of a Norwegian naval commander called Jens Munk, who as a young man had trained in Portuguese and Dutch colonial service. He was of a noble family that had lost its standing in disgrace and was obsessed with restoring the family's honour, which explains his willingness to take on these and other extreme assignments. While most of the crew succumbed in Hudson Bay, he and two companions made their way back to Copenhagen, where he was first received with honour by Christian, only to fall into disgrace again in a dispute with the king, for all his efforts thus failing to rescue the family's good name. The adventures are captured by the prolific Danish author Torkild Hansen in his *The Way to Hudson Bay: The Life and Times of Jens Munk*.

CORFITZ AND LEONORA

Christian IV's sons-in-law were his close advisors and officials. The mightiest was Corfitz Ulfeldt, married to Christian's favourite daughter, Leonora Christina. Corfitz was unrestrained in corruption and used his position as chancellor to amass a huge personal fortune. He served an ailing king by stealing from him.

During the transition after Christian's death, Leonora made the mistake of spiting the new queen, Sophie Amalie, a vain woman of vengeful instinct. Corfitz was too arrogant of power for the new king's liking. He was dispatched to Holland on a diplomatic mission. While he was away, his many enemies laid bare his criminality. He returned to Copenhagen, but when prosecution threatened the couple escaped back to Holland, where Corfitz had taken the precaution of securing much of his money, and from there on to Sweden, where he bribed his way into royal service and urged war against Denmark. That came to pass, catastrophically for Denmark. Corfitz returned to Denmark as a Swedish negotiator. In the peace, he had his Danish properties and titles restored and received other 'compensations for damage suffered'. But that was not enough. He continued in Swedish service, where he was rewarded handsomely but not handsomely enough for his own taste. When Sweden went to war against Denmark yet again he was accused of betrayal in Sweden and brought to court on a charge of treason, but escaped back to Denmark disguised as a priest. There he and Leonora were softened up by a year in a dungeon, whereupon he swore loyalty to Denmark's king. The next year he was abroad again, and made contact with a German prince who he suggested should claim the Danish Crown, which would be available after a pending conspiracy. In Copenhagen he was sentenced to death for treason, *in absentia*. He vanished into Germany, probably to die the next year.

Leonora, for her part, had gone to England to claim repayment from Charles II of a loan, but was kidnapped and returned to Copenhagen, to face Sophie's revenge and spend twenty-two years in the royal palace's feared Blue Tower, finally being released after the queen died. She turned to authorship, exceptional for a woman then, writing a reflection on her time in prison and leaving an unfinished book on women heroes, with characters from the Old Testament, as a feminist tract, the first in Scandinavian writing. In the Introduction she argued that the source of true human nobility is wisdom, which does not distinguish man from woman, and that the soul does not recognise gender and does not change depending on exterior forms.

It is perhaps only to be expected, given Christian's stature and Denmark's decline, that the next kings were smaller men. Frederik III brought war disaster on the country, as we will see later on, but still became a national hero for defending Copenhagen against Swedish assaults, to death if necessary, he boasted. Christian V, a simple man who had the wisdom to recognise his own very considerable shortcomings and in spite of himself became a reformer, gave Denmark its first national code of law. He left a 'will' to his successors with guidance in the statecraft of absolutism, in which he beseeched them in all their actions to make no distinction between king and kingdom, since the kingdom belongs to the king as his property. Frederik IV was uneducated, ignorant and incompetent, pedantic but also perfectly happy to disregard State affairs even at war; a bigamist who married two mistresses while his queen was still alive, the second of whom he had abducted from her home aged nineteen and married a second time the day after the queen's funeral. Christian VI, in reaction to his father's immorality, made himself a religious fanatic, burdened those around him with unending hypochondria, rooted pleasure from the court and banned peasant festivals in the country and theatres, card games and other entertainments in towns. Frederik V, in reaction to his parents' pietism, was an alcoholic hedonist 'with neither will nor ability for political leadership' whose pleasures included orgies of sexual violence. But he freed the country from religious darkness and his reign was a liberal period in arts and science. Christian VII was king for forty-two years but his life was a tragedy, marred by disabling mental illness that expressed itself in various ways including sexual promiscuity, with back-street prostitutes among others. He was king in name only. Governing churned on in the hands of various stand-ins, from 1784 his son as prince regent. Earlier, his physician, Johann Struensee, a radical reformer, had won his confidence (and that of his neglected queen; he was her lover and probably the father of her daughter Louise Augusta) and for a short time made himself de facto regent, a period described by historians as a 'dictatorship'.

It did not end well: Struensee was deposed and beheaded, his body partitioned and his head put on a stake; the queen was divorced off and expelled from the country, leaving her two children behind, to die at age twenty-three.

Denmark was finding its feet as a modest kingdom, far removed from the great power of Christian IV's inheritance and ambition. Seen from above, from the vantage point of kings whose game was glory, that was all loss. But seen from below, from the lives of ordinary people, it was, in the end, all gain. The great kingdom had been a terrible place for people to exist under the burdens of crushing taxation, feudal suppression, conscription, wars, foreign occupations, hunger and epidemics. The modest kingdom would, with time, in what from a historical perspective was a miracle, become a home of happiness.

In Sweden there were royals of stature and intrigue. Erik was followed by Johan, the second of Gustav Vasa's sons to be king. He boasted that he had liberated Sweden from his tyrant brother, who, mad it will be remembered, had held him in prison and whom he in turn had imprisoned and (probably) killed. He ended one war with Russia and started a second one. When he died, his son Sigismund was already King of Poland-Lithuania, through his Polish mother. On his father's death in 1592, Sigismund inherited the Swedish Crown as well. He was Catholic and remained in Poland while King of Sweden, appointing his uncle regent. That uncle, later Karl IX, organised a rebellion. Sigismund invaded his own kingdom but was defeated and deposed. His remaining supporters in Sweden were persecuted until a cluster of them were executed in another bloodbath, if a minor one, in the city of Linköping: five traitor nobles beheaded. That ended the threat of Catholicism in Sweden.

Karl was regent from 1599 and king from 1604, the third Gustav Vasa son to be king. His reign was one of uninterrupted warfare against Poland, Russia and Denmark. The Sweden he handed over to his son, Gustav Adolf (Gustavus Adolphus), was a big Protestant power with dominions east and south. We can praise Karl as the son of a great father and the father of a great son.

Gustav was an eminent administrator. He modernised Sweden economically, in State finance and governance and in military matters, the army as well as the navy. He had the assistance of a brilliant chancellor, Axel Oxenstierna, whose abilities he had the wisdom to appreciate. It was to be a problem for absolutist kings that they did not have men around them to keep their use of power under some control and that their rule went off the rails. Gustav managed, by force of personality and the assistance of Oxenstierna, who had the respect of his co-aristocrats, to neutralise the traditional power struggle between Crown and aristocracy and mobilise the aristocracy for his policies, even getting them to accept taxation. He was a master orator and forceful persuader. He gave Sweden the administrative State and military organisation that enabled a small and peripheral country to be a big European power.

He was a great military manager and strategist, in weaponry, coordination and supply – the founder of modern war, it was said – and, to boot, a masterful general in the field, rated by Napoleon as one of the greatest of all time. Warfare had been mostly a pretty haphazard matter, more often than not in the hands of kings seeking glory but with a poor understanding of the complexities of military tactics. Gustav understood that success in the field must be secured on the basis of domestic economic strength and meticulous planning. That was precisely the understanding his contemporary in Denmark, Christian IV, lacked, hence Sweden's rise and Denmark's decline in the European wars in which they both engaged.

He was king at sixteen, took charge at seventeen and ruled until 1632, when he died aged thirty-eight. He inherited wars in three directions – against Russia, Denmark and Poland – all of which he brought to an end, only to engage in a fourth one, the Thirty Years War, out of which Sweden emerged as Europe's pre-eminent Protestant power and with much territorial gain. He died in the middle of that war, in the Battle of Lützen. That was a blow to Swedish pride. The hero king, whose ambition it was to be European emperor, should not have been cut down. Swedish historians later tried to salvage his honour by inventing a fog that engulfed the battlefield, creating chaos, explaining that the king did not know friend from foe, got separated from his own men and rode into the hands of the enemy to suffer multiple gunshots and stabbings. In truth, even the supreme general had run out of luck. He should not have been there in front of his troops. His eyesight was poor, he had grown fat and, although only in his thirties, was worn down by injury and illness.

His partnership with Axel Oxenstierna was a rare case of intimate collaboration, even friendship, between a master and a commander who were both strong personalities. Gustav was underage when he became king and Oxenstierna became his chancellor from the outset, aged twenty-eight. He was the aristocracy's man and his and the king's partnership was the embodiment of the Crown–nobility alliance which was at the heart of Sweden's success as a militaristic state. He was a workaholic, measured and calculating, cool under pressure, an administrator at home and a military manager abroad (who even recognised that he himself was not a battlefield leader).

At Gustav's unexpected death, Oxenstierna stepped into the void and took charge of the regency of Gustav's daughter, Kristina, who was six years old. He assumed the role of educating the girl who was to be queen. She soon proved to be strong-willed and came to resent his patronising tutelage, but he probably taught her well. The relations between queen and chancellor were never cordial, but he continued to work at her side until her abdication, which he resented, loyal to the queen as he had been to her father. He died two months later, aged seventy-one, having held the top office of state for forty-three years. He had been the most eminent of *consiglieres* to Scandinavian power monarchs.

Kristina was queen at eighteen, crowned at twenty-four, abdicated at twenty-eight, died in Rome in 1689, aged sixty-two, and is buried in the crypt of St Peter's Cathedral. She was intelligent, eager to learn, and well educated in philosophy, history and politics, as well as classical and contemporary languages. She was indifferent to womanly grace and manners, never beautiful, and gradually grew corpulent. She grew up without emotional attachments (her father dead, her mother mad), was educated as a royal male, dressed like a man, held the official title of king and lived extravagantly. But bear in mind her predicament: as a young woman she was charged with governing an upstart European superpower at war, in a man's world.

She was queen in a big way, a hard-working administrator who at the same time pursued passionate interests in the arts, music, theatre, philosophy and learning. It was too much; she exhausted herself and probably soon into her reign started to think of abdication. By the time she did, she had three achievements to her name.

The first was the end of the Thirty Years War. That war had been destructive for Europe and it is likely that Kristina, as head of one of the dominant powers, contributed to ending it earlier than might otherwise have been, when there was nothing more in it for Sweden.

Her second achievement, that of the 'greatest of royal culture-vultures' – so the historian Hugh Trevor-Roper calls her – was the plunder of Prague, late in 1648, while peace was being negotiated in Westphalia. The war was practically over and the late attack on Prague served no military purpose. The aim was Prague Castle and various churches and libraries and the treasures they contained. Kristina's orders were to loot, and, as she saw herself to be a scholar, to loot in particular libraries. Prague Castle contained the treasures of 'that melancholy hermit, the greatest of collectors', Rudolf II. He had been Holy Roman Emperor from 1576 to 1612, and had been amassing – hoarding – everything from high art to lowly curios. The Swedes made away down the Elbe with barges of paintings, sculptures and manuscripts, for both royal and private benefit. Much was lost in transportation, but 570 of Rudolf's pictures and much other loot eventually arrived in Stockholm. During Kristina's time, Stockholm rose from cultural poverty to, following Trevor-Roper again, 'one of the artistic capitals of Europe. It was a capital stocked entirely with loot. Swedish noblemen copied their queen: de la Gardies, Wrangels, Brahe, Skytte, Oxenstierna, Königsmarck filled their grotesque palaces with their share.' A good deal of the royal collection was later lost, some of it taken back to Europe by Kristina when she abdicated, some of it to later fires, but much still remains in Swedish museums and galleries.

THE SILVER BIBLE

The finest manuscript of Gothic writing, and one of the world's most valuable classical manuscripts, is in the possession of the University Library in Uppsala. It contains the four Gospels of the New Testament. The translation was done around the year 370 somewhere in today's Hungary or Romania. It was completed under the supervision of a Bishop Ulfilas, and may have included the invention of a Gothic alphabet for the purpose, later transcribed into the manuscript now preserved around the year 500 for Theodoric, the Gothic King of Italy, at his court in Ravenna. It is written on purple vellum, with the first letter of each verse designed in silver, hence the name, Silver Bible or *Codex Argenteus*.

With the fall of the Gothic kingdom in Italy the Bible disappeared, to emerge again in the sixteenth century in a German monastery on the Rhine. Rudolf II 'persuaded' the monastery to lend him the manuscript, which thus ended up in his collection in Prague. From there it was removed to Stockholm in Kristina's plunder and deposited in her library. In the year of her abdication it made its way to the Netherlands, where it was probably sold. Six years later it was bought back to Sweden by Count Gabriel de la Gardie.

There is mythology attached to this Bible. A legend of Swedish nationalism has it that the Goths were a people of Swedish origin, and also that the Gothic alphabet was derived from Norse runic writing. (It was in fact of Greek derivation.) In this story, the Silver Bible had been 'returned' to its rightful home. Others have seen it as a sheer product of plunder, and have from time to time argued for its return to Prague. I myself played a minor role in that controversy. With colleagues in Prague, for a while in the early 1990s, I tried to find a historical justification for its restitution, mobilising for the purpose the best competence in Oxford, including Robert Evans, Regius Professor of History. No such argument could be concocted, however: the Swedes may have stolen the manuscript but it still had no rightful home in Prague.

There was nevertheless a lingering anxiety in Sweden. In 1990, Václav Havel, President of liberated Czechoslovakia from 1989, was due in Sweden on a state visit. It had been suggested in the press that he might raise the question of restitution of cultural artefacts, including the Bible. The Swedish Ministry of Foreign Affairs undertook a pre-emptive legal study, resulting in a memorandum of four pages (of which I have a copy). The lawyers concluded that as there was at the time no provision in international law against plunder, Sweden had 'committed no breach of law in taking back home Czech cultural treasures'.

Her third achievement, to which the plunder of Prague contributed, was to turn her court into a European centre of art and learning. She was a relentless and greedy collector of things – art, books, manuscripts, scientific instruments – all of which she stole, bought or commissioned in great quantities. But also of people – scholars, philosophers, poets, dramatists, composers, musicians, singers, dancers – pulling them in from all over Europe. And those she could not get to Stockholm, she corresponded with, as their equal. She was a European superstar.

One of her prize items of collection was the French philosopher René Descartes, whom she attracted to Stockholm with the prospect of establishing a scientific academy. He arrived in late 1649, with 2,000 books and an assignment to instruct the queen in philosophy in, so the story goes, icy-cold 5 a.m. tutorials. She didn't like him, nor he her, and nothing much came of it. Tragically, the great man caught pneumonia and died in February the next year.* Historians have blamed Kristina for his early death.

Among the learned men she brought to Stockholm were also theologians, Catholics and Jesuit. With them she debated faith and doctrine, and set herself on a path of conversion to Catholicism. That was another impetus towards abdication. She was the queen of the protectorate of European Protestantism and could obviously not be Catholic.

What should have been a fourth achievement, to produce an heir, did not come to pass. I will give no explanation, she said, but I'm not made for marriage. Her most intimate friend was a woman, Ebba Sparre, a lady-in-waiting, with whom she shared a bed. But she would later in life engage in heterosexual love, certainly with Cardinal Decio Azzolino, who was assigned by the pope to assist her when she settled in Rome and who became 'the love of her life'.

The succession therefore had to be secured in another way. She chose her cousin, Karl Gustav, who had done service in the plunder of Prague and who had at first wanted to marry her and share the throne. That settled, she was ready to edge herself out from under her Protestant Crown. Better, finally, to seek out European culture in its southern homelands than go through the hassle of bringing it north to Stockholm. She was not a popular queen. People were uneasy about her persona. She was expensive, her extravagance all but emptying state coffers. She negotiated a deal with the *Riksdag* to enable her to

* Descartes had lived the life of a travelling philosopher. He served, from age twenty-two, as a mercenary soldier in the two first years of the Thirty Years War, on both the Protestant and Catholic sides, before establishing himself as a European cosmopolitan scholar of independent means, much of the time in Amsterdam, where he could publish with some freedom, eventually being lured to Stockholm at age fifty-two and to an early death. A Catholic in a Protestant land, he received a modest burial. Sixteen years later his remains were returned to France to rest in a tomb in the Church of Saint-Germain-des-Prés in Paris. He is remembered in Stockholm with a plaque in Adolf Fredrik's Church.

go on living on a queenly scale – and off she went. She had taken care to send ahead a good portion of the royal art collection, treating it as her private property, some of which she would sell off to support a continuing high life.

She was welcomed with open arms, the most famous woman, probably the most famous person, in Europe. She gave up the chilly north in preference for the warmer south. She turned her back on Protestantism and returned to the universal Church. As a guest, she sprinkled Catholic gold dust on eager hosts.

She was on her way to Rome but it took her more than a year to get there, via Hamburg, Antwerp, Brussels, Innsbruck and Bologna: she was hosted by the rich, nearly bankrupting their generosity, accumulating debt, receiving princes and royals by day, feasting by night. Her arrival in Rome was celebrated by the pope and others with festivities, operas and fireworks. She settled in borrowed palazzos, socialised intellectually with the great and the good, established an academy of music, theatre and literature and started meddling in Church politics.

The next year she left for France, where she schemed with Louis XIV to become Queen of Naples, whereby she would be independent of money from Sweden, and caused scandal by executing an Italian noble who had joined her service, on a charge of betrayal, something she claimed the right to do as a queen managing her own court. The Naples business came to nothing; she was back in Rome three years later, settled in another palazzo and busied herself with assembling the finest art collection in Rome, outside of the Vatican, reverting 'to her old methods: she pillaged the Farnese Palace [today the French Embassy], which its owner had kindly but imprudently put at her disposal'.

She returned to Sweden twice, at one point claiming the right to retake the Crown, later also recommending herself as Queen of Poland. That too came to nothing and from 1668 she was back in Rome for good, creating for herself yet again a glittering life of art, music, literature and theatre. She wrote an autobiography, which was never finished, and essays (mostly superficial, says the historian Nils Erik Villstrand) on great men – Alexander, Cyrus, Julius Caesar – and on art and music. And so it went on. One cannot but say, what a life! But also, in the end, how pathetic. What she might have envisaged when she abdicated we cannot know, but it turned out that the option for a had-been queen was no more than the life of a woman famous for being infamous, an 'It girl' of her time, if in style. We may be reminded of the old Norse who thought that the best you can hope for to remain of a life is a good name and reputation. Did she achieve that? Reputation, certainly, but hardly a good name.

What she did leave was a gigantic collection of art and manuscripts. This was over the following years sold off by her estate to settle debts and dispersed in all directions. Much of her library ended up in the Vatican, much of the art in aristocratic France, from there to be sold on to mainly British collectors after the French Revolution.

Now followed in succession three more Karls: the X, who lasted six years, was at war constantly, and tried (almost successfully) to crush the life out of Denmark in the 1657–60 wars, which we will follow more closely below; the XI, who fought another, unsuccessful, war with Denmark, and whom history has been unable to settle on as able or inept; and the XII, the hero king who destroyed everything in front of him. During these reigns the Swedish Empire first rose to the summit of glory and then fell into nothingness.

HEDVIG ELEONORA

She was queen to her husband, Karl X, the mother of Karl XI and the grandmother of Karl XII. She was never queen in her own right but was at times the ruling monarch of Sweden, at others a meddler *extraordinaire*.

Of German family, from Schleswig, she was married to Karl X at eighteen, by the machinations of Kristina as she passed through Schleswig on her way to Rome after her abdication. She was already engaged to a German prince, who was however fobbed off with her less beautiful sister.

They were married in late 1654. Karl immediately set off for war in Poland. Hedvig stayed on to give birth to a child, the future Karl XI. Birth done, she joined her husband in Poland and officiated at the plunder of Warsaw, to much praise. Karl moved the war on to Denmark, where Hedvig again joined him and lived in style in a Danish palace while her husband's forces were physically destroying the country.

When Karl X died in 1660, she was appointed regent during the minority of her son and managed State affairs in an uneasy partnership with the *Riksdag*. That son took charge in 1672 as reigning monarch until his death in 1697, during which time he ruled on the constant advice of his mother. She outlived him and was again regent during the minority of her grandson, this time for only half a year until the fifteen-year-old king took charge. That grandson, Karl XII, was out of the country waging war for much of his reign, during which time Hedvig again exercised much influence at home, although not formally as regent. She died in November 1715, a month before Karl XII returned home to Sweden.

During her fifty years as wife, mother, grandmother and matriarch she managed Swedish court life with splendour and ostentation. She had the summer palace of Drottningholm built, in the style (but not size) of Versailles, outside Stockholm, including the Palace Theatre which is still in use today for summer opera performances in its original format and with the original stage machinery.

Karl XII was a spectacular failure, by mindset, inclination and psychological constitution unable not to wage war. He had the power of absolutism but, unlike Gustav Adolf, no Oxenstierna-like tutor and manager to guide and control him. He lost everything.

He became worshipped as the righteous warrior king who upheld Swedish honour against the evil forces of Russia. On the centenary of his death, Esaias Tegnér, effectively poet laureate, wrote a eulogy in praise of 'the young hero' who fought 'golden-haired' against 'grey-haired and cowardly statesmen' with 'so just a heart in his Swedish chest' that he could not yield but only fall. This worship persisted through the nationalism of the nineteenth century until it was deflated by the dramatist August Strindberg; in his play *Karl XII* (1901) he portrayed a mad king who, again, could not yield, and thereby brought the nation to ruin.

He was a single-minded fanatic. He never married, probably abstained from sex, was probably a repressed homosexual, indeed repressed in all emotion, was possessed by rigid religiosity, was indifferent to danger and pain, brave and dashing – but impractical in judgement. He was king from age fifteen, not only in name but in fact, and was at war from the age of eighteen. In less than ten years he had lost the Swedish Empire. That was in a final defeat to Peter the Great of Russia, at Poltava in present-day Ukraine. Karl fled south into Turkey with a small entourage for Ottoman protection, where he was to spend the next five years in more or less confinement. In 1714 the Ottomans agreed to release him on a promise that he would leave. He did, making his way through Europe to Stralsund, the last Swedish possession on the Continent, in fifteen days, and from there back across to Sweden just ahead of his forces surrendering Stralsund as well. More stuff of heroic legend. Free, he was back to waging war again until the end.

On 11 December 1718, in his final campaign, at the city of Halden in Norway, in the freezing winter, he was hit by a single bullet to the head, in through the left temple and out through the right, and fell down stone-dead, aged thirty-six. Who shot him is not known. It was perhaps an accident. It could have been an enemy soldier, but if so we would most likely know who the hero was. The money of this author is on it being one of his own. Karl had inflicted years of large-scale misery on his people, and it might well be that a soldier finally had enough and saw his opportunity to bring down the king who could not yield.

When he died, his sister, Ulrika Eleonora, became the second Queen of Sweden. After two years she was ousted by her husband and was for the rest of her life his unhappy consort. The men did not like her and she herself was unable to do battle. She had married her husband for love, he her for power. In loyalty to a treacherous husband, she abdicated and he was king. For this he rewarded her with lifelong infidelity, even going so far as to humiliate her by taking an official mistress.

Fredrik I held the Crown for thirty-one years, but had neither the ability nor the interest to make much use of it. There was betterment for the country, except for yet another defeat to Russia in yet another war, but he had little to do with any of it, being probably the most incompetent of all Swedish kings, unable to engage in anything but hunting and womanising.

Much the same followed in the next twenty years under Adolf Fredrik, a German prince who had been forced on Sweden by Catherine the Great of Russia in a 1743 peace treaty, whose abilities did not stretch to more than figurehead proportions and who died in 1771 in a gluttonous orgy of overeating.

*

Gustav III was a different kind of king altogether. He ascended to the throne in 1771 and in the next year orchestrated a military coup to restore the absolutism that had been swept aside at the end of the Great Northern War. He had his personal guard lock up the government in the palace, convened the *Riksdag*, presented it with a revised ordinance of government and dismissed the delegates with a promise that they would be convened again in six years (a promise he kept). That inaugurated a complicated reign that set aside parliamentary rule but cultivated social and cultural progress, which flourished under his patronage. He saw his rule as a case of enlightened despotism, not without justification. His repression was directed mainly against the aristocracy, which he regarded as reckless and corrupt, again not without justification. He gained popularity by improving the economy and public finance (including with the help of a state lottery). A liberal despot, he with one hand extended religious freedom and with the other curtailed freedom of the press and of expression, silencing criticism of himself, of constitutional matters, of foreign policy. He was a man of conflicting instincts, an admirer of the French Enlightenment but also an active supporter of the monarchy in France against the Revolution while at the same time backing the colonists in America in their revolution of liberty. He was obsessed with the old hatred of Denmark, dreamed of conquering Norway, and took Sweden into yet another war with Russia. He established a Swedish colony in the Caribbean and profited, personally, from the transatlantic slave trade. (He owned 10 per cent of the shares in the Swedish West India Company but had the right to 25 per cent of its dividends.) He instituted property rights for illegitimate children and unwed mothers. He abolished torture and capital punishment for certain crimes, and would have taken these reforms further had he not been held back by a reconvened *Riksdag*. He was a dandy, effeminate, whispered about as being homosexual – surrounding himself with 'beautiful young boys', says the Swedish historian Elisabeth Mansén – accumulated enemies from many directions, in particular the aristocracy, was without friends and trusted no one. His enemies finally engineered a conspiracy of assassination, which was carried out during a masked ball in the Royal Opera House (an institution of his own making) at midnight on 29 March 1792 (later commemorated in the opera *Un ballo in maschera* by Giuseppe Verdi).

If hated by the aristocracy, Gustav was loved by 'the people'. He created the Royal Theatre, Royal Opera and Royal Ballet, as well as the

Swedish Academy (today in charge of the Nobel Prize in Literature). He tried, but failed, to bring the sale of alcohol under a State monopoly, not a reform in the spirit of the times. That spirit was libertarian, as expressed most vividly in the songs of Carl Michael Bellman, the most beloved of Swedish poets, whose themes were taverns, women, wine and song, and who praised the king as 'the best in the North' in a cringingly servile poem entitled 'Gustaf's skål', meaning 'toast', making even his praise of the king a drinking matter.

Gustav's reach for power was the last gasp of Swedish absolutism. He was succeeded by his son, Gustav IV, whose stubborn and ill-fated reign resulted in the loss of Finland to Russia, his own overthrow in a military coup, and a new constitution which reinstituted separation of powers between king and *Riksdag*. The unfortunate Gustav – 'a tragic being who was never able to reconcile himself to reality', says Alf Åberg – was escorted out of the country to Germany, divorced by his wife, and died twenty-eight years later in St Gallen in Switzerland where he had been living in a small hotel under the name of Colonel Gustafsson. We are now deep into the machinations following the French Revolution and the Napoleonic Wars, a story we will resume in Part IV. Suffice to say that Sweden was finally free of empire and finding its footing, like Denmark, as a modest kingdom.

CARL MICHAEL BELLMAN

The poem-songs of Carl Michael Bellman (1740–95) were and remain an immensely treasured body of Swedish literature. They were written and composed in the 1770s and 1780s, in the socially liberal atmosphere of Gustav III's reign, and celebrate the libertarianism of their time. They are light-hearted and elegant, with baroque frivolity, melodious, humorous, raunchy, life-affirming, fun-loving, but also with wisdom in observations on love, friendship, fidelity, mortality and more. Many are known by heart by most Swedes and are routinely sung around meal tables and other gatherings in this most music-loving of peoples. They continue to be interpreted and recorded by generation after generation of Swedish troubadours.

Bellman's own story was as bohemian as those of his characters. He came from a family of modest means and from early on settled into a life of borrowing and debt, at least once escaping the country (for Norway) to avoid the debtors' prison. He did not have much success as a student, nor later in the trivial business of working for a living. His life was the tavern and the associated circus of cards, gambling and prostitution. He was himself a performer who relished the entertaining of friends, playing the cittern to accompany his songs. Work, when unavoidable, was a way of being able to socialise, sing and drink. For all his serenading of the low life, he had protectors in high places who would help him into little jobs that didn't demand much work and enabled him to pursue what they and he considered living, the king himself securing him a symbolic position with, of all things, the national lottery. He was an early inventor of Scandinavian literature.

He called his songs *epistler*, 'story-glimpses', and in them he followed a few main characters: the clockmaker Fredman, the nymph Ulla Winblad, brother Movitz, former soldier and alcoholic, father Berg, virtuoso musician, and the bailiff Blomberg. They are at the tavern table, in the gutter outside, in Ulla's embrace, or alone and in painful regret over too much drink. He also wrote poetry and entertaining plays, but it was in his songs that he was original and creative.

With the assassination of Gustav in 1792, the curtain fell on libertarian Stockholm and Bellman's time was up. As it was in other ways. He was deep into alcoholism, suffered from tuberculosis, was finally unable to avoid debtors' prison, died penniless and was buried in an anonymous grave.

Their wars

Scandinavian warfare under royal absolutism starts with the Russo-Swedish wars of the 1550s and goes on until 1814 in the Nordic outreaches of the Napoleonic Wars. This was not the beginning of war in the north, nor was it the end. But it was a period of exceptionally frequent, vicious and aggressive conflict, mainly Swedish aggression. When it was over Scandinavia had taken the shape it has today, the shape, we can imagine, the wise Margrete had wanted to secure in a union of collaboration. What a shame that it took more than two and a half centuries of destructive fighting for the Scandinavians to start to see what should have been obvious all along: that they are, perforce, family, a small family.

Wars were now of a new kind, more constant, bigger, longer-lasting and fought in large measure by armies and navies of conscripted soldiers and sailors, if still also with foreign mercenary forces. That innovation – conscription on a big scale – came as a catastrophic intrusion into the lives of the small-folks. Young men were sucked out of local populations and, once taken, were practically done for, to die in battle or of disease, vanish by deserting, or return home physically or mentally crippled for life. As wars raged on, more were conscripted, and more again and more again. Populations were depleted of young men, of the work they would have done, of the families they would have formed. The destruction came to Norway courtesy of the friendly Danish kings who looked north for young Norwegians to man their navies, during the seventeenth century an estimated 60,000 men out of an already small population. Sweden used Finland for recruitment on an even bigger scale. The conscription and its deadly consequences was of such proportions as to destroy local communities, stall population growth and cause famine. 'An estimated half a million Swedish and Finnish men perished in military service between 1620 and 1719,' eventually a third of all grown Swedish men, leaving Sweden a 'land of soldier-widows'. In the Swedish campaigns of the Thirty Years War, 60 per cent of the soldiers, 70,000 of them in all, were wounded or taken prisoner. Soldiers could not expect to survive more than a couple of years, succumbing to illness and epidemics more than to battlefield injuries. The billeting of friendly troops and the plunder by foreign ones spread disease and brought food shortages to civilian populations. When there was not outright war, there was preparation for the next one. 'The disasters which afflicted Denmark during the 1650s led to a drop in population of 15 to 20 per cent.' Kings desperate for glory physically consumed their own economies and their most productive workforce.

WARS IN THE PERIOD OF ABSOLUTISM

Scandinavian wars:
Seven Years War, 1563–70 (Sweden, Denmark)
Kalmar War, 1611–13 (Sweden, Denmark)
Torstensson War, 1643–45 (Sweden, Denmark)
Dano-Swedish Wars, 1657–60 (Sweden, Denmark)
War of Skåne, 1675–79 (Sweden, Denmark)

Theatre War, 1788–89 (Sweden, Denmark)
Dano-Swedish Wars, 1808–14 (Sweden, Denmark)
Campaign against Norway, 1814 (Sweden, Norway)

Russian Wars:
Russo-Swedish War, 1554–57 (Sweden, Russia)
Livonian War, 1558–83 (Sweden, Russia, Denmark, others)
Russo-Swedish War, 1590–95 (Sweden, Russia)
Ingrian War, 1610–17 (Sweden, Russia)
Russo-Swedish War, 1655–58 (Sweden, Russia)
Great Northern War, 1700–21 (Sweden, Russia, Denmark, others)
Hats' Russian War, 1741–43 (Sweden, Russia)
Gustav III's Russian War, 1788–90 (Sweden, Russia)
Finnish War, 1808–09 (Sweden, Russia, Denmark, others)

European Wars:
War against Sigismund, 1598–99 (Sweden, Poland)
The Four Polish Wars, 1600–29 (Sweden, Poland)
Thirty Years' War, 1618–48 (European powers, Sweden, Denmark)
First War on Bremen, 1654 (Sweden, Bremen)
Polish-Swedish War, 1655–60 (Sweden, Poland)
War of Devolution, 1667–68 (Swedish participation)
Second War on Bremen, 1666 (Sweden, Bremen)
Franco-Dutch War, 1675–78 (Swedish, Danish participation)
Nine Years' War, 1688–97 (Swedish participation)
War of Spanish Succession, 1701–14 (Danish participation)
Rákóczi's War of Independence, 1703–11 (Danish participation)
Pomeranian War, 1757–62 (Sweden, Prussia)
Napoleonic Wars, 1800–15 (Swedish, Danish participation)

English Wars:
Second Anglo-Dutch War, 1665–67 (Danish participation)
Third Anglo-Dutch War, 1672–74 (Danish participation)
Wars against Britain, 1801–14 (Sweden, Denmark, Britain, others)

Wars beyond Europe:
Danish-Algerian War, 1770–72 (Denmark, Algiers)
Action of 16 May 1797 (Denmark, Ottoman Tripolitania)
First Barbary War, 1801–02 (Swedish participation)

Some of the wars were eccentric. The Hats' War against Russia was inspired by a Swedish chauvinistic faction, know as Hats – the competing moderate faction being known as Caps – dedicated, helplessly, to regaining Swedish losses from the Great Northern War, spurred on by France to stir up trouble for Russia. It was too late. Sweden was no longer a big power and had to pay for its aggression by ceding border territories in Finland to Russia – another war in which thousands of soldiers and sailors died in hunger and disease. The Theatre War between Sweden and Denmark is so called because it was more show than reality. It was provoked by Denmark and fought mainly with Norwegian troops. Probably less than ten men fell in battle but at least 3,000 were lost to hunger and disease. The war ended when both sides just went home. The Danish war on Algeria was to protect Danish trade in the Mediterranean from piracy. When Denmark refused to yield to extortion, three Danish ships were hijacked and their crew sold into slavery. A Danish counter-attack failed in an outbreak of typhoid among the crew. Denmark had to pay for peace and buy the freedom of the crew who had been enslaved. The assault on Tripolitania was again about trade and tribute. The Danes blockaded the harbour of Tripoli and negotiated a treaty in which they obtained a lower rate of tribute, but again had to buy the freedom of Danish hostages. The Barbary War was a mainly American war against four north African Ottoman provinces, again about trade, piracy and tribute. Sweden was pulled into it by already being at more or less war with Tripolitania. America was seen to come out of the war victorious, in a display of naval strength, but still had to pay out $60,000 in ransom for captured prisoners. Only with a second Barbary War in 1815 was America able to bring to an end the payment of tribute in its Mediterranean trade.

However, for the most part it was deadly serious. In the Scandinavian wars, Sweden and Denmark started as equals but Sweden gradually prevailed. Denmark had been the stronger power, Sweden the challenger; the sands were shifting. There were many reasons for these wars, including chauvinism, mutual hatred and stupidity on the part of kings with more ambition than sense, but a pervasive issue was the Baltics and the control over territory, trade and tolls. Denmark held the Sound and had the power to tax the trade that had to pass through it. This was essential for Danish kings. It raised big revenues that were direct Crown possessions and which pre-absolutism kings could use without having to seek *Rigsråd* permission. It was also valued for holding Sweden back and in humiliation. For Sweden it was a burden which impeded trade to the west. In the eastern Baltics Sweden gained territorial control and with it a big trade in grain, and was increasingly able to extract tolls on other trade on Baltic ports and in and out of Russia. Control depended on naval force, in which the balance of power gradually shifted to Sweden's advantage.

The main outcome of the wars in Scandinavia, in addition to constant misery for ordinary Swedes, Danes and Norwegians, was a string of territorial annexations by Sweden from Denmark. The Seven Years War had ended in a truce. In the Kalmar War, Denmark was still strong and proud – we are in the early reign of Christian IV – and invaded on three fronts. It might have been Christian's ambition to subdue Sweden and restore the Kalmar Union under Danish supremacy. In that he failed, but he did secure the territories in northern Norway. Sweden in principle obtained the right to free passage without toll through the Sound, a commitment Denmark was soon able to renege on. In the northern fronts of the Thirty Years War, Jämtland and Härjedalen in the borderlands with Norway, the island of Gotland in the Baltic Sea and the German principalities of Bremen and Verden all passed from Denmark to Sweden. In the wars of 1657–60, in a decisive geopolitical shift, Danish possessions in southern Sweden – Skåne and the coastal lands up to present-day Norway – passed to Sweden. For two years, from 1658 to 1660, Sweden occupied the central Norwegian territory of Trøndelag, cutting Norway in two. In the War of Skåne Denmark aimed to recapture its old territories in southern Sweden, but failed. Finally, in the Napoleonic Wars a century on, Norway was lost for Denmark into a union with Sweden.

In the Russian and European wars, Sweden gained territories to the east and south, establishing itself as a formidable empire and a big power in Europe. In the Livonian War it captured present-day Estonia and was in control of the Bay of Finland, and by the end of the Ingrian War of further territories around the Bay of Finland, cutting Russia off from direct access to the Baltic Sea. In the various Polish wars – necessitated by Polish regents continuing to claim their right to the Swedish Crown – Sweden won territories in northern Europe, culminating in further gains during the Thirty Years War. These gains were, however, short-lived, and all reversed in the Great Northern War. By 1710 Russia had taken back Sweden's possessions in the eastern

Baltics, including the territory on which Peter the Great was building his new capital city (a project of forced labour in which he used masses of Swedish prisoners of war). In 1713 Russia invaded and held all of Finland, and in the summers of 1719 and 1720 launched waves of attack on Sweden itself, ravaging Sweden's eastern coasts but failing to take Stockholm. Russia came under pressure from other powers, England and Prussia, to bring the war to an end. Sweden had avoided invasion, but the peace of 1721 was total defeat for the country that twenty years earlier had been a European superpower.

'The suffering caused by the Thirty Years War was beyond all reckoning.' Thus writes Veronica Wedgwood in the Foreword to the second edition of her *The Thirty Years War*, first published in 1938. And further: 'The dismal course of this war still seems to me to be an object lesson in the dangers and disasters which can arise when men of narrow hearts and little minds are in high places.'

It was not a single war but a conflagration of many wars of many kinds that swept back and forth across the German lands and beyond over three decades: wars of conquest, wars of territory, civil wars of uprisings and revolts. Religious war too, as we know, but less so than has often been thought. Protestant Sweden did not team up with Catholic France for religious reasons, Catholic France did not wage war on Catholic Spain because of theological disputes, nor Protestant Sweden against Protestant Denmark. Had it been a matter of religion, said Gustav Adolf, I would have made war on the pope. The Catholic commander Wallenstein 'placed ability above confession and promoted several Protestants to senior positions'. All of Europe was involved, with outreaches to India, Indonesia and Taiwan in the east, the Congo in the south and the Caribbean and Brazil in the west. It was the first world war.

It was ignited on 23 May 1618 when a group of Czech nobles defenestrated two Habsburg governors out of a high window in the Hradčany Castle in Prague. They landed in a dungheap and survived, although much humiliated. The Czechs were protesting against Archduke Ferdinand of Austria's assumption of the Bohemian Crown, as well as the Catholic regime's intolerance of Protestant churches. When they moved to depose Ferdinand as King of Bohemia and instal a Calvinist in his place war followed, soon spreading out over much of Europe. On one side was an Evangelical Union, north German; on the other side a Catholic League, south German. The Bohemian army was crushed in the Battle of the White Mountain and the Bohemian nobility wiped out, bringing to an end Protestant independence in the Czech lands. Here, on the Catholic side, fought the formidable Albrecht von Wallenstein (Valdštejna), a Bohemian noble who had grown up Protestant but converted and entered the service of the Habsburgs as a commander-mercenary, to rise in the course of the war to become one of the richest men in the empire.

The Catholic forces, under the leadership of the ruthless (needless to say) Count Tilly, eventually also Wallenstein, moved north through Germany in pursuit of Protestant armies. 'The unprovisioned armies began to live off the land like so many hordes of locusts.' (Wallenstein was assassinated in 1634 on the order of Ferdinand, when it was suspected that he was thinking of switching to the Protestant side for reasons of profit.) That brought the Habsburg-Catholic threat to the north and spread fear in Denmark and Sweden that both their Baltic domains and their Lutheran regimes were in danger. Christian IV of Denmark mobilised and entered the war in 1625. He was badly prepared, did not get the support from other Protestants he had counted on, and was thrashed. Soon the Catholics had overrun much of northern Germany and moved well into Denmark to occupying Jylland. Christian could only capitulate, but orchestrated enough of an alliance with Sweden to put sufficient fear into the Catholics for them to offer him a generous peace, in which he had his lost possessions returned. After four years of disastrous warfare it was over for Denmark as a power on the European stage. (Even so, back at home Christian threatened not to ratify the peace and blackmailed his own aristocracy, in the *Rigsråd*, for ten barrels of gold in compensation for what the war, which he had forced through against their will, had cost him, in part to enable him to repay his debt to the queen dowager, his own mother.)

The Swedish alliance was never made to last, and it was now Sweden's turn to enter the war, in 1630, as the champion of the north European Protestant cause, having just finished a string of wars against Poland. This was Gustav Adolf's war, a different matter from Christian's amateurism. Gustav had more strength, more allies, better planning. The Catholic forces were pushed back south. Gustav fell, as we have seen, but the Protestant cause prevailed in northern Germany, extracting a generous peace out of an ailing and exhausted emperor.

But we are still only in 1635, and the terrible war had thirteen more years to run. Sweden's adventure looked impressive but was a mistake. Oxenstierna had warned Gustav that he was overreaching and making Sweden a bigger power than it had capacity to sustain. He was right: it took only half a century for the empire to fall like a house of cards.

It was now for France to take the lead and maintain the fight against the Habsburgs, declaring war on Catholic Spain, with the support of Protestant Sweden. That coalition ravaged the south as ruthlessly as imperial forces had previously done the north.

From around 1644, negotiations started to bring the horrors to an end, resulting in the Treaty of Westphalia in 1648. The big war was over (but the Franco-Spanish war dragged on until 1659). Religious strife in Germany was laid to rest in a live-and-let-live settlement. In territorial matters the treaty gave something to most of the contestants, including quite a bit of German land to Sweden: Bremen-Verden, Western Pomerania, Stralsund, Stettin.

So there was some logic to the madness, and we can with hindsight describe the progress of the wars as moves back and forth on a chess board. But for the peoples of Europe at the time it had a different look: armies coming and going, sometimes of one side, sometimes of the other, sometimes of unknown side; sometimes murderous militias, sometimes mercenary bands out to enrich themselves, switching sides as economic gain beckoned, soldiers nourished by too little food and too much drink. They all went back and forth in waves of disease, death, destruction, plunder and rape, with soldiers helping themselves to crops, food, tools, clothing, bed linen, cattle and horses, breaking up furniture for firewood, torturing people to reveal the hiding places of their valuables. In the chaos, civility broke down: servants robbed masters, neighbours settled scores. Corpses on battlefields were robbed by fellow soldiers or local civilians. 'There was an explosion of the rodent population during 1636 that lasted several years and exacerbated the food shortage. Wolves roamed south-western Bavaria during 1638, returning in the early 1640s, while packs of wild pigs destroyed crops. Other animals disappeared as they became alternative sources of food.'

When it was over much of Germany was in ruin, with economic collapse and population loss. It was uneven, some areas faring better than others (or less badly), some starting to recover during the war, but by the end at least a third of the German population had been extinguished, mostly lost to disease and hunger. Towns and villages were abandoned, others bulged with refugees. Once-prosperous families fell into destitution. Municipal governments were depleted of funds, in part from having suffered waves of extortion during the years of fighting, in part from rampant inflation. Peasants were driven off the land, production collapsed, produce confiscated, transport obstructed, trade prevented. The production of books in Germany did not again reach the level it had attained in 1618 for another 150 years. It was warfare like nothing ever before it. 'The most awful of atrocities', says the historian Martyn Rady, 'took place on 20 May 1631, when an imperial army stormed the independent Lutheran stronghold of Magdeburg in Saxony. Death by fire and slaughter accounted for possibly as many as thirty thousand people. Imperial troops drove small children into the fires like sheep. The victorious commander, von Pappenheim, drily noted: All of our soldiers became rich.'

Central to the war was plunder – not only of land for provisions as armies ravaged through, but also, and on a grand scale, of art, manuscripts and treasures. Renaissance princes had made themselves voracious collectors. With the war, a functioning art market collapsed and the champions of cultural refinement made themselves 'art gangsters', filling their palaces with loot from less fortunate potentates. Hugh Trevor-Roper and Peter Wilson write: 'Wherever the Swedish armies went, they seized and sent back to Stockholm the artistic spoils of Europe: Russian icons from Riga and Pskov, altarpieces from Stargard and Braunsberg, pictures by Matthias Kräger from Würzburg, altarpieces by Grünewald from Mainz (which were lost at sea on their way to Sweden), libraries from Würzburg, Bremen, and the looted Jesuit and Capuchin churches of Olmütz.' When Gustav Adolf captured Munich in 1632, he let his generals sack the galleries of Maximilian I for 'the greatest collection in Germany after that of the emperor. The contents of monastic libraries in Mainz were dispatched to Sweden within weeks of the electorate's capture. Others were deliberately sought out later by Swedish generals eager to win favour by sending them to Kristina. Libraries were also depleted by sale as universities, schools and monasteries compensated for falling incomes by selling valuable works.' In Prague, 'Königsmarck let his troops loose for three days. They murdered two hundred inhabitants and plundered the vast treasures of Bohemia's aristocracy and clergy.' Sweden had now been waging war to the east and south for nearly a century. In the process it had become a political power. It was also by war and theft that it became a cultural power.

Meanwhile, in the shadow of bigger events on the Continent, the two Protestant kingdoms in the north, Sweden and Denmark, once united against the Catholic threat, took the opportunity to wage another war against each other, from 1643 to 1645: a Swedish war against Denmark and its now old and exhausted King Christian, the Torstensson War, so called after the Swedish general Lennart Torstensson. The reason for the war was simple: Sweden was strong and Denmark weak.

Torstensson attacked from the south and within a month Jylland was under foreign occupation for the second time during the Thirty Years War. Other Swedish forces attacked from the north and overran Danish Skåne. A united Swedish–Dutch fleet destroyed the Danish navy. France intervened to negotiate peace, handing territorial victories to Sweden and piling humiliation on Denmark.

It took only nine years from the Treaty of Westphalia, which was supposed to have brought peace to Europe, for Sweden to bear down on Denmark again. The combatants were Karl X of Sweden and Frederik III of Denmark. Sweden was a big power. A big power had to have a big army. A big army needed to be at war, since there was no other way of sustaining it. 'The question, therefore, was not whether there would be war, but where.' In the end it was in Denmark, in Karl's last three years. It is worth following this war in some detail, both to see how Scandinavian neighbours dealt with each other and to grasp the meaning of war itself in those deranged times.

Karl was already at war with Russia and Poland (who were also at war with each other) over Swedish possessions in the Baltics. It was from the Continent, the south, into Denmark's soft underbelly, that he attacked in 1657 (as Denmark had been twice occupied during the Thirty Years Was, the last time in 1643 when Karl had participated under the tutelage of General Torstensson.) The Danes knew he was coming, and there was, as often happens in the run-up to war, stupid enthusiasm for combat, in this case on the part of the incompetent Frederik and a feeble aristocracy that wanted the glories of battle but not to pay for them. Technically, it was Denmark that declared war, but it was Sweden's game. When it was over the best that can be said for Denmark is that the kingdom had survived – but at colossal cost: not only in terms of territory but also, says Lars Christensen, historian of these wars, 'the loss of 25–30 per cent of the population, the destruction of productive capacity, notably in agriculture, social and economic breakdown, the loss of international respect, the formalisation of absolutism'.

Karl X had wanted to marry his cousin Kristina, but she left him to his own devices as king. Perhaps it was psychological damage from wounded pride that made him obsessed with conquest. He wished to conquer Poland, where he did much damage but failed. He wished to conquer Prussia, failing again. So he went for Denmark, with a fanatical determination to erase the brother-kingdom from the European map.

Seventeenth-century war horror – 'with a fanatical determination to erase the brother-kingdom from the European map'

Frederik had been handed a weak Crown on the death of his father, Christian IV, and was further disadvantaged in that he was neither wanted nor trusted by the Danish nobles. But his problem was not just that his position was weak: he was unable to understand the elementary facts of power, both domestically and in relation to Sweden. He was delusional; there is no kinder way of saying it.

Having declared war, Denmark failed to prepare. Taxes were levied but not paid. Soldiers and sailors were conscripted but did not turn up. Those who did were often vagrants, ill suited and ill disciplined. The Crown had to resort to borrowing money from underlings who had any to spare and pressing convicts into slave labour in Copenhagen's navy base in a desperate rush to make ships seaworthy. Mainly because of an absence of unity between Crown and aristocracy, Denmark wasn't enough of a war-state to mobilise available resource for its own defence.

Meanwhile, Karl had been marching an army of about 10,000 men (and at least as many camp followers: hawkers, families, laundry women, cooks, prostitutes, cobblers and other craftsfolks) through Poland and north Germany, pillaging, extorting, raping, abducting girls as sex slaves, burning as they went, imposing 'arson taxes' (payments on the threat of arson), consuming what they needed and desired, carrying off livestock, provisions and valuables – all standard warfare at the time. It was another campaign of art plunder, from Warsaw in 1655, Cracow in 1657 and eventually from Denmark and its noble estates when the war moved there. This plundering went some way to restoring art splendour to Stockholm, after Kristina had taken with her much of the treasure from earlier raids when she left the country.

They were a ragtag band of conscripts, mercenaries and bandits, Swedes, Finns, Poles, Germans, Scots, French, all in it for the takings. Within a month they stood in Jylland. The Danes were made to feed and provide the armies that overran them, bled dry by their tormentors who confiscated what they found of valuables. They had their young men dragooned into enemy service. They had enemy soldiers billeted with them, homes and fields destroyed, livestock slaughtered, with violence and repression all around and starvation and epidemics afterwards.

Other fronts were opened in southern Sweden and along the Swedish–Norwegian border, with not much benefit militarily but with the usual devastating consequences for soldiers and local populations alike. At one point, a Swedish army considered retaking the county of Halland in southern Sweden from Danish occupation but decided against it because the land had already been so depleted that a new occupying army could not sustain itself from it.

The Danes initially held on to the fortification of Frederiksodde in mid-Jylland and concentrated their forces there, numbering about 3,000 by October. For the resident population that meant provisioning: bread, beer, beef, pork, oats for horses, barrels in which to hold it all, transport with which to carry it, timber for firewood and building works, shoes and clothing, young men conscripted. Soldiers were billeted in farms and villages, plundering their hosts and buying and selling horses and cattle from and to each other. And that was only the Danes in their own land.

The Swedes held the rest of Jylland, concentrating ever more forces. On 23 October their commander laid on a splendid dinner for his senior officers and their wives (who, as was the custom, accompanied their men in the field), with the best food and tables laid with silver, all looted goods. It was a pre-celebration: the waiting was over. The next morning Frederiksodde was taken after two hours of feeble, unprepared Danish resistance. Two thousand Danish prisoners were taken, with a thousand dead.

The conquest of Jylland had been fast and easy. The Danes were thrown out of their only foothold in the largest part of their own country and the war moved in the direction of Copenhagen. Frederik's plan, mad as it was, had been to use a war with Sweden to restore Denmark to glory. It had taken only three months for that project to collapse to such a degree that Sweden and others, including Cromwell in England, had started discussing how to partition Denmark and Norway once the kingdom was crushed. The Swedish king was rewarding loyal servants with estates in Danish lands he had yet to take over.

It was urgent for him to get on with the job. Jylland had been stripped bare and provisions were running out for his army. Denmark had been negotiating alliances with Germans and others who had reason to fear Sweden and might soon be able to mobilise help. We are in January 1658. The winter turned exceptionally hard and the waters between Jylland and Fyn, the nearest island, froze over. King Karl decided to march his army across the ice, which he did on the last day of the month (minus two squadrons of cavalry that fell through the ice), arriving the next day in the city of Odense. The Danish defence fell apart again and another slice of Denmark was in Swedish hands. Over the next few days, all of Fyn was ravished by plunder: farms, villages, towns, estates, churches, vicarages – down to common people's clothing. These were not uniformed armies, and good clothing and footwear was valuable in the cold winter, as were sheets, duvets, even ovens. Those who resisted were tortured into obedience or cut down dead, farms and towns burned. As often in war, civilians survived by selling their possessions, at poor value. Rape was standard and many a young Danish woman was left with the child of a Swedish father, often with little sympathy from her own folk. Women were known to rub their faces and breasts with tar and soot to make themselves unattractive. Churches were plundered of windows, doors and locks, or just torn down. Forests were cut, game decimated. Towns had to take in and care for wounded Swedish soldiers and pay for the burial of the dead. Even city archives were carried off. Paper deeds had value in that the silk bands that held their seals could be sold. For generations, stories would be handed down of the Swedish terror. Only when the plunder was so great that it threatened Fyn's ability to provide for the Swedish army was it brought to an end. The soldiers had collected their pay.

Karl pushed on and six days after overruning Fyn crossed the next sound, on perhaps the last day the ice might hold on the broad Storebælt: 3,000 men over 13 km of frozen sea. The 'Crossing of the Belt' was to stand in later nationalistic Swedish historiography as a deed of royal heroism, and so it was. The king was there, leading from the front. No one knew it to be safe, the Danes had not thought it possible. The Swedes arrived on the next island, Lolland, where again the defences crumbled. The plundering hordes washed over it, but Lolland got off with less than total carnage since Karl was in a hurry to cross the remaining two sounds and reach Copenhagen. On 9 February 1658 the Swedes were in Sjælland. All of Denmark was occupied except for Copenhagen, which was under siege.

Negotiations had now started. There was pressure from Holland, England and others to end the war. Karl could dictate the terms. The Peace of Roskilde was signed on 26 February. Denmark surrendered the Skåne lands, the county of Bohuslän, the island of Bornholm and the central Norwegian province of Trøndelag. The loss to Denmark was monumental, in Skåne the richest third of the kingdom and the eastern shore of the Sound. Frederik had to commit Denmark to not entering into treaties to Sweden's disadvantage. Sweden was in control of the Baltic coasts and all of its southern territories. The kings met to seal the peace with a feast. Frederik had been as humiliated as a king could be but it was still his obligation to receive his tormentor with all possible royal civility. For three days, from 3 to 5 March, Karl and a large retinue were treated to lavish generosity of food and drink, all extracted from a country already unable to feed itself.

The two kings had promised each other 'peace forever' but it did not even last the year. The Swedish troops did not leave. Sweden was still at war with Germany and Poland and Karl needed his army. It was

better positioned in Denmark and it was better economically to have it
live off enemy land than at home. Basically, for all that Karl had been
given in the peace, it was not enough. It tormented his troubled soul
that Denmark still existed. Victory was insufficient. What he wanted
was the destruction of Denmark as a kingdom and its subjugation
as a Swedish province. He drew up plans for the administration of
Denmark and Norway as parts of the Kingdom of Sweden, in preparation for which Copenhagen was to be razed to the ground.

He resolved to finish the job and gathered the cream of his troops in
Kiel in northern Germany. On 6 August he sailed a flotilla north to join
other troops already in Denmark, reigniting the war he had already
won with more satisfaction that any warrior-king could rightly expect.
This time there was no detour via Jylland and the difficult sounds;
he went directly to Sjælland and laid siege to Copenhagen again. He
could have taken the city, in which case it would have been over for
Denmark. But he didn't; things did not go as he had planned, he
hesitated. Copenhagen did not show any sign of surrendering. Frederik
was able to mobilise a reasonable defence of the city with officers
and troops that had abandoned the rest of the country, stood firm
and promised to defend it to the end. In Norway, the Swedes tried
but failed to invade in the south and were chased out of Trøndelag in
mid-country. Dutch and German help was on the way. The Dutch had
never liked Danish authority over the Sound, and did not now want it
replaced by Swedish control. They sent north a fleet which was able to
break the Swedish sea blockade of Copenhagen. The Germans knew
that they would be the next target for Karl, and sent troops up Jylland.

The year 1659 was one of utter horror in Denmark, as if there
had not already been horror enough. Much of the country was under
Swedish occupation. The German troops in Jylland brought epidemics with them that swept over the land, resulting in mass death. The
harvest failed. The ravaging by occupying forces continued. Refugees
streamed to towns and cities for survival. In November a Danish fleet
reinvaded its own country, routing some of the Swedish forces, 'men
and horses in heaps on the battlefield, the dead and wounded plundered by soldiers and civilians alike'. The tide had turned; it was now
for Swedish captives to see their wives mass-raped before their eyes.
For the population it was more of the same, with liberation armies
showing no restraint in plundering the liberated peoples. The winter
became 'the winter of hunger'. Parishes reported a tenfold increase in

funerals. Foreign powers were again working for peace, but the war rolled on. All of Denmark lay in ruin.

On 13 February 1660 King Karl died, aged thirty-seven. He had fallen into a fever some days before, and mistreatment by his doctors secured the outcome. Allies on both sides had been pushing for a settled peace. Denmark was exhausted, Sweden demoralised. The Treaty of Copenhagen of 27 May 1660 was a reiteration of the Peace of Roskilde, with a few amendments. The province of Trøndelag reverted to Norway and the island of Bornholm to Denmark. Sweden held on to the Skåne lands, enshrining the borders between Sweden, Denmark and Norway that still apply today. This time, the evacuation of Swedish troops from Denmark proceeded without too much delay. (Denmark, with control of the western shore of the Sound, continued to toll the Baltic traffic until 1857, when it came to an end under American pressure, against hefty one-off compensations from other nations to ease, for a while, the stress of liquidity on the Danish treasury.)

The Treaty of Copenhagen did Sweden little harm and Denmark some good. Sweden was still a big power in Europe. Denmark had survived as a kingdom. In spite of massive losses in territory and economic capacity – the country destroyed, the State in debt – King Frederik turned the outcome into a fairy tale of success, spun around his personal heroism in the defence of Copenhagen. That the people had suffered during the wars was their own fault, they had too much power and he not enough. The aristocracy was morally bankrupt, having failed in its duty to protect the kingdom. He convened the estates, had the *håndfæstning* with the old *Rigsråd* struck down, had the assembly of estates abolish itself, erased the old constitution, and gave himself the authority to dictate the new *Kongelov*. The kingship that had brought the Danish kingdom within a whisker of being swallowed up by Sweden rewarded itself with elevation to absolutism.

That absolute kingship set about preparing for revenge. The priority was State finances, with continued heavy taxation ahead of any reconstruction of the destroyed land. 'Surprisingly, 15 years on Denmark was ready for another war with Sweden, better prepared than in 1657. Whether the Danes as well were prepared is another matter – but then they were not asked.'

MAKING SKÅNE SWEDISH

It was a big deal for Sweden to acquire Skåne and its neighbouring lands, but not easy. The lands had been Danish for 800 years, governed from Copenhagen, the aristocracy was Danish, the Church Danish, the population Danish, the language Danish. Making it Swedish took time, and another war, that of 1675–79.

The first problem was aristocratic. Skåne was now in Swedish possession but with aristocratic land still in Danish hands. This problem was solved in a deal between victor and vanquished whereby major Danish holdings were surrendered to the Swedish Crown, to be handed out in reward to Swedish grandees in gratitude for war service, while the Danish grandees were compensated with Crown land in Denmark. Other lesser barons switched their allegiance and made themselves Swedish, under a promise of various privileges. Some sold out and left.

A second problem was to make Skåne Swedish in economic terms. This was dealt with by extending Swedish infrastructure into the new province. Young men were distracted from resistance by being drafted into military service and civil work projects, notably road construction to connect north with the rest of Sweden. Also, trade and business were redirected northward by the introduction of heavy tolls on exports to break traditional trading bonds with Denmark.

A third problem was cultural. The University of Lund was established in 1666, to prevent young men in search of learning from going to Copenhagen and to take in hand the training of future opinion formers, clergy and administrators. The Church was made Swedish in the hands of Swedish vicars.

And a final problem was to crush resistance. The people, many of them, were not happy to be Swedish and saw it as oppression. More or less organised armed resistance by sniper bands, sometimes disguising semi-criminal activity, spread across the territory guerrilla-fashion. The Swedish Crown struck back with brute force. Militias of opportunists were recruited to hunt down resisters. The penalty was torture and/or death by decapitation or worse, including for failure to swear allegiance. Deadly reprisals were meted out to communities suspected of harbouring or otherwise assisting traitors. The resistance was fought down but it took time, not being brought to an end until after Denmark's war of revenge fifteen years later. The Danish king proclaimed that war to be one of liberation, but his troops behaved as occupiers and any remaining loyalty to Denmark fizzled out. By now, Swedification was doing its work. The last remains of Danish rule were removed and Swedish law and taxation were made to apply, as in any other part of the country. The city of Karlskrona was founded on the south coast of Blekinge in 1680 and would become Sweden's main naval base.

In 1700 Russia, with the support of Denmark and Poland, launched an attack on Sweden, thinking it vulnerable under its young king, Karl XII, starting the Great Northern War. Karl's hero reputation stems from initial successes in these wars, first against Denmark, then against Russia, then against Poland. These were indeed remarkable victories, in enemy territories, often against superior forces, the stuff of legend.

But against Russia Karl made the ultimate mistake of marching on Moscow. His army, 35,000 men strong, set off east from Poland in the summer of 1708, heading, it seemed, for more victory. But the march turned into hunger and disease and was abandoned in the Russian forests. The ambition to take Moscow was Karl's downfall, as it would later be the downfall of Napoleon and later again of Hitler. Rather than east to Moscow, the army was forced south to Ukraine, in midwinter, the winter of 'the great frost'. They laboured through thick forests with no roads, without food, pursued by Russian partisans, leaving a trail of men and horses frozen to death. They regrouped at Poltava, having shed at least 10,000 men. There, in the early summer of 1709, the Russians bore down on them with twice their force, annihilating the Swedish army; 16,000 officers and soldiers surrendered into captivity, plus about 5,000 non-combatants. Karl fled into Ottoman protection.

In his absence, the war moved back north. The Danes decided this was a good time to attack Sweden yet again to retake lost territory. The decision was made by Frederik IV, the bigamist king. While his world was on fire he left for a year on holiday, mainly in Venice, where he made himself popular with generous extravagance. Back in Denmark, in November 1709 he launched an attacked on Skåne and started what would be eleven more years of war – Denmark's final and futile attempt at revenge over the hated Swedish enemy. It was another disaster for Denmark. In Copenhagen the king neglected the war he had started and devoted himself to balls, feasts and a string of mistresses. In Norway, a population on its knees had had enough and revolt spread. When this war finally ground to a halt it was because all three countries were economically and politically depleted. Denmark's only scrap of success was an evacuation of troops back home from their final holdout in a town on the Skåne coast – but at the cost of putting down 5,000 horses to prevent them from falling into enemy hands. 'It was a total breakdown', says the Norwegian historian Knut Mykland. 'In many areas, there were hardly any young men left.'

Sweden was now disintegrating in wars from all directions, with Poland and Denmark to the south and west, with Russia to the east, Russia taking Finland and threatening Sweden proper. The country was destroyed after twenty years of futile warfare, a generation of young men wasted on the battlefields. The architect of that destruction, Karl XII, was back in Sweden and fought on. He mobilised yet again and marched on Norway to attack Denmark in the back, first in 1716, with little success, then in 1717, failing again, and finally yet again in 1718. He reached the town of Halden in south-eastern Norway and

Karl XII, carried back on a stretcher through the snow, after the 1718 assassination – 'No event in Scandinavian history should be celebrated with more jubilation than the bringing-down of Karl XII'

laid siege to the fort of Frederiksten while a second army marched into mid-Norway.

Karl fell to an assassin's bullet, as we have seen, and it was nearly over. But not before the second army further north tried to retreat home over the Norwegian mountains in the dead of winter. Of 5,000-plus men, 2,300 died on the march, 1,400 later and 450 were demobilised as invalids. Horses in the hundreds, probably thousands, were left frozen to death.

But then it was over – not only this war, not only this kingship, but the business of perpetual warfare itself. It had done no good at all, not to kings, not to countries, not to populations. Sweden, says the Swedish historian Kurt Samuelsson, was liberated from the burden of big-power ambition. Scandinavia stood at the dawn of the second Great Transformation in its history. The first one was the economic upturn of the thirteenth century which had enabled the building of kingdoms. This one came out of collapse, collapse in the experiment of building big kingdoms. The Scandinavians were forced to try another way, the avenue of peace.

8

A Taste of Colonialism

In 1638 – we are in the middle of Europe's Thirty Years War – a small wooden fort was erected in what is today Wilmington in the American state of Delaware, called Fort Kristina, after the Swedish queen. This was the beginning of a colony that became known as New Sweden, the only Scandinavian attempt to establish a foothold in North America, after the attempt by the Greenlanders 600 years earlier.

It was triggered by a letter from one Peter Minuit of Amsterdam, dated 15 June 1636, and brought to Sweden by a colleague of his, Peter Spiring, for the attention of Axel Oxenstierna. Spiring and other Dutch colonial adventurers had for some time been encouraging the Swedes to take an interest in North America and now thought the time had come. Peter Minuit had been the governor of the Dutch colony of New Netherland from 1626 to 1631 and is credited with having purchased the island of Manhattan from the Lenape Nation (for the equivalent of perhaps $1,000 in today's money), but was dismissed from Dutch colonial service for alleged corruption and had returned to Holland. In the letter, he offered his services to the Swedish Crown – 'it seems to me that the Crown of Sweden ought not forbear to make also its name known in foreign lands' – suggested the location of a colony, and spelled out in detail what an expedition to North America would require in shipping, equipment and crew.

The Swedes took the bait. Two ships set off from Gothenburg in late 1637, in the charge of Peter Minuit and with a combined Swedish and Dutch crew, and arrived on the Delaware after a crossing of three months. Minuit signed a treaty with the local native Americans to start the settlement. The colony gradually expanded to about 200 square km, containing various scattered settlements, living off agriculture, hunting and trade. Relations with the native Americans were peaceful and when the colony failed it was not, contrary to the attempt of the Greenlanders, because of conflict with the locals. The settlers eventually numbered about 600 people – Swedes, Finns, Dutch,

Germans and others. Many stayed on when the colony was dissolved, maintaining a Swedish cultural presence for some time. Theirs was the first Lutheran community in North America, served by pastors from Sweden. A church, Holy Trinity in present-day Wilmington, was dedicated in 1699, and stands today as the oldest stone church in the United States. Two more Swedish churches were added, in 1677 and 1703. Lutheran services in Swedish continued until 1791, when the last Swedish pastor left and an Anglican was assigned to the congregation. (When, on 7 November 2020, Joseph R. Biden claimed victory in that year's presidential election, he did so at a venue on the Christina River in Wilmington.)

The colony was under the management of the New Sweden Company, which over seventeen years sent out twelve expeditions with provisions and settlers and brought back cargos of tobacco and furs. If the colony got on peacefully with its native American neighbours, the same was not true for the more powerful Dutch colonists. Their governor, Peter Stuyvesant, forced the surrender of New Sweden in 1655. New Netherland was in turn ceded to Britain twelve years later. The Dutch had called their trading post in lower Manhattan New Amsterdam, which became New York when taken over by the British.

To Asia

From the great discoveries had followed, with speed, the European colonial scramble. In both Denmark and Sweden, the Crowns saw themselves as big powers and tried to carve out a share for themselves in Asia, Africa and the Americas.

While it lasted, colonialism was a multinational and global business. Captains on Scandinavian ships might be Dutch and their crews made up of many nationals in addition to Scandinavians. Gothenburg grew as a trading city, with half the population Dutch. The settlers in the colonies were an equally mixed group. A majority of the early settlers in the Danish West Indies were Dutch and Dutch was the prevailing language. Swedes were a minority among the Europeans in the Swedish colony of St Barthélemy. Among the plantation and slave-owners on Denmark's Caribbean isles were a few dozen Brits. Trade in and out of the colonies was by ships under various flags. Goods travelled the world with ease, textiles from India both for the European market and on to Africa for the procurement of slaves, tea and porcelain from China bound not only for Europe but also for the colonies in the Americas. Ivory from Africa was brought to Europe via two Atlantic crossings. 'The ship, *Fly*,' writes the historian James Walvin, 'traded for slaves with a cargo that included brandy, Virginian tobacco, a range of Indian textiles, brass kettles and pans, pewter basins, firearms from France and Denmark, iron bars from Sweden, linen from Ireland, knives, swivel guns, beads and earthenware.'

Christian IV set up the Danish East India Company in 1616 and two years later sent an expedition of five ships under Dutch commanders and with Dutch and Danish crew, bound for Ceylon with the intention of establishing a trading station there. The voyage took 535 days, cost the lives of a number of sailors, and failed to get a foothold in Ceylon. They continued north to India and in a treaty with a local prince took possession of the small town of Tranquebar, where they erected a fort before returning to Denmark with a modest cargo of pepper and textiles.

From Tranquebar the Danes engaged in trade, with many ups and downs, across Asia, west to Africa and Arabia and east to China. More trading offices were set up, the easternmost station in Canton. A second possession was secured in India, Serampore in Bengal. We might perhaps, generously, call them colonies. There were settlers, there were garrisons, there were parsons (the first to bring Lutheran missions to India and the pioneers of aggressive Scandinavian missionary outreach, still going strong). But it was on a modest scale. In 1790, Tranquebar had a population of about 3,500, of whom fewer than 200 were Danes and other Europeans. In Serampore there were fewer than forty Danes in a population of 10,000. They never amounted to much and were absorbed into the British East India Company in 1845.

The Danish Asia trade was of various kinds, some of it 'official' in the hands of the East India Company and its successors and some in the hands of private companies, some of it bringing goods back to Denmark and other ports in Europe, some of it inter-Asian trade. The most important goods going back to Denmark were cotton textiles (from India) and tea and ceramics (from China), as well as spices from various Asian sources. Although Denmark had colonies in India and only a modest rented station in Canton, the China trade was more than equivalent in volume and value to the India trade. Some of the inter-Asia trade was to serve Asian plantation economies, such as on the French island of Mauritius, then known as 'Isle de France', and included slave transportations. As in the Caribbean, the Asia trade was cosmopolitan, with Danes, Swedes, Dutch, English and others intertwined, sometimes in collaboration, sometimes competition.

At times, the Asia trade was of significant value to both Danish merchant houses and the Crown, in particular in the last decades of the eighteenth century when wars in Europe and the Americas offered profiteering opportunities for neutral Danes to trade where others were excluded and as intermediaries between enemies who could not trade with each other. Whether, all things considered, it was a profitable trade is questionable, given that the meaning of 'profit' is ambiguous in a trade based partly on royal monopolies; but, until it petered out in the eighteenth century, it undoubtedly did bring quantities of goods to Copenhagen for further trade into European markets and for use in the purchase of slaves in Africa, and put a great deal of money into circulation in the Danish economy.

Sweden entered into the Asia trade late, but did well. The Swedish East India Company was set up in 1731. It traded mainly in China (a pathetic attempt to set up a mini-colony in southern India came to nothing) and followed Denmark in setting up a station in Canton. It was based in Gothenburg, did much to develop that city as a trading centre, was competently run, suffered less loss of shipping and cargo than was standard, and was the foundation of wealthy trading families. The organisation was ingenious: iron (plentiful in Sweden and in high demand in Europe) went to Spain in exchange for silver (plentiful there from the Spanish America trade), silver (in high demand in China) to Macau and Canton for tea, silks and ceramics (all in high demand in Europe). 'The Swedish East India Company', says David Abulafia, 'had been, until the start of the nineteenth century, a remarkable success story.'

To the Americas

In 1784, Sweden, during the reign of Gustav III, returned to the Americas and established a presence for slave-trading in the West Indies by buying the tiny island of St Barthélemy from France, in return for French trading privileges in Gothenburg. The island was made into a transit hub for Caribbean trade – it was unsuitable for agriculture – which for a while was successful. An extensive trade in slaves from Africa was promoted by the Swedish Crown, luring slavers to the island by charging them no toll but taking revenue in fees on slaves sold on to elsewhere in the Caribbean.

The Swedish West India Company, which had been established to manage the island colony, was chartered for participation in the transatlantic slave trade. Swedish shipping probably had some direct engagement in the trade, but it is not known to what extent. There was also an indirect participation through the leasing of permits to non-Swedish ships for the benefit of sailing under neutral Swedish colours. The exact volume of the slave trade through St Barthélemy is not known but was considerable, in particular when Sweden delayed banning the Atlantic slave trade until 1813 while Denmark had banned it in 1803. From then on the island was in decline. After many failed attempts, Sweden was able to sell it back to France in 1878. Its capital city is still called Gustavia.

Sweden, curiously, formally had possession of the island of Guadeloupe for a year from 1813 to 1814. The island, now a French *département d'outre-mer*, had been taken by Britain from France in 1810, and was offered to Sweden in return for joining the alliance against Napoleon. But before Sweden could engage with its new possession, it was handed back to France in the Treaty of Paris of 1814.*

Danish colonialism in the Americas was of different proportions. Trade in the Caribbean had started in the 1640s. A West India Company was chartered in Copenhagen in 1671, sending out an expedition to take possession of the island of St Thomas. A fort was raised, Fort Christian, and around it a town emerged, Charlotte Amelia, named after Christian V's queen. With time, this was to become an important Caribbean transit port for the slave trade and the second-largest city

---

* But Sweden did receive a compensation of 24 million francs, some of which went into a 'Guadeloupe Fund' to partly pay an annual annuity for the benefit of the Swedish crown prince, Karl Johan, and his heirs. He was French – we will meet him later – and the Guadeloupe Fund payments were to compensate him for the losses he had incurred when turning traitor on France. The last payments from the fund were made in 1983.

in the Danish realm, with as many as 2,000 ships arriving annually in the early 1800s. In 1718 Denmark took another island, St John, and in 1733 bought a third one, St Croix, from France, merging the three islands into a Crown colony. The population peaked in the 1830s, at around 43,000. The slave population had reached 35,000 by about 1800.

The plan was to grow sugar cane, for which purpose the islands were soon fully cultivated. The benefit to Denmark was limited. As most of the planters were foreign, not much capital flowed to investments in the home economy. What came out of it was mainly raw sugar, which was to form the basis of a still-important refinery industry, a lasting influence in Denmark itself of its slave-based plantation venture.

Sugar production depended on slaves. The West India Company was reorganised into a West India and Guinea Company for integrated slave trade and plantation agriculture. It was itself not successful in trade and at times turned to renting out its monopoly to private shipping entrepreneurs from Denmark and other countries. One such, typical of the cosmopolitan capitalists of the time, was a certain Jørgen Thormøhlen, a profiteer of German origin who settled in Bergen in Norway and married into the wealthiest local family. He was a man of energy and industry who rose to become the most eminent of the new class of industrialists and traders. He became the country's biggest ship-owner on the back of the fish trade from northern Norway and various other ventures. When the West India opportunity presented itself, he took to it as he would any other business. That was at first profitable, but it led him to over-invest on a scale that contributed to a collapse of all his enterprises except a soap factory. When Frederik IV visited Bergen in 1704, his admiral's diary mentions in passing 'a man called Thormøhlen'.

The colony prospered on trade, sugar and slavery, yielding considerable revenue to the Danish Crown, but gradually declined in the nineteenth century under heavy Dutch, British and American competition. The Danish slave trade from Africa was abolished in 1803, but inter-Caribbean slave-trading continued. Slavery itself was abolished in 1848, fourteen years after emancipation in the British West Indies, and then only by the unilateral action of the local governor, to stem a slave revolt, and not by any decision from Denmark. (The governor was in a later inquiry criticised for not having put the revolt down.) The plantation economy went on for a while with freed slaves as labourers, but was soon not competitive when the price of cane sugar declined under the competition of East Indian (not slave-grown) sugar and European beet cultivation. Denmark offered the colony to America for the first time in 1867. Various deals stranded on domestic opposition in one or the other country, but in 1917 the sale went through for $25 million (plus recognition from the US of Danish sovereignty over all of Greenland), and the colony became the United States Virgin Islands.

A central personality in the Danish colonial economy was the landowner and statesman Ernst von Schimmelmann (1747–1831), finance minister, foreign minister and the country's richest man. He personified the inherent contradictions of the moral depravity and economic profitability of the slave-based plantation economy. Politically he was a moderniser and reformer, but as a plantation-owner also an investor in the slave trade. He had four plantations in the Danish West Indies and was, with about 1,000 slaves, the country's biggest slave-owner, and at home the proprietor of the most important sugar refinery in northern Europe. He was an advocate for the abolition of the slave trade, although continuing to invest in it. On slavery itself, his liberalism was limited to improved living conditions.

Slave emancipation was enabled, in the Scandinavian as in other Caribbean colonies, by compensation being paid to former slave-owners for the surrender of their human property. (In all, in various countries, more than a million enslaved people were freed, mainly in the Americas, by compensated emancipation.) In Sweden's St Barthélemy, which was not a plantation colony, this was relatively easy. The slaves, who numbered approximately 600, were in local ownership and some modest compensations were paid out. In Denmark's case, the number of slaves and slave-owners was larger and the slaves in part in Danish ownership. This was the same pattern as in Britain, where a very significant part of the population were involved in slave-ownership, some on a large scale but also many on a small scale, such as 50 per cent ownership of a single slave. By the Slavery Abolition Act 1833 the British State paid out £20 million, the equivalent of 40 per cent of the annual State budget, to former slave-owners. The Danish Parliament in 1853 decided to award slave-owners compensation to the order of fifty West Indian dollars per freed slave, generally paid in government bonds. The owners wanted more than they got, arguing, with much passion and invoking the law, ancient rights, justice, civility, equity and property, that the compensation was only half the market value of the slaves. Even so, some, such as the Schimmelmann family, would have done well from what they were able to extract from a failing economy. The freed slaves had less joy from the settlement. There was no compensation for them and real emancipation was still years off.

To Africa

It was Sweden that opened the Scandinavian trade in Africa, in the 1640s, but half-heartedly and soon to be crowded out by competitors, including from Denmark. They in turn struck a deal with the King of Accra to establish a trading post and built Fort Christiansborg there (still today, with many modifications, now as Osu Castle, in use for various governmental purposes) and other posts and forts along the coast. Thus Denmark entered the immensely profitable Atlantic triangular trade, bringing commodities from Europe and Asia to purchase slaves on the African Gold Coast, shipping them to their own and other colonies in the Americas, and returning home with commodities such as sugar.

The Africa-to-America nexus of slave trade and slavery is the vilest business devised in all of humanity's infinite inventiveness. From 1500 to the late nineteenth century, 12.5 million Africans were shipped out of their homelands by Portuguese, British, French, Spanish, Dutch, American and Danish traders (in order of the numbers shipped). At the other end, 10.7 million were disembarked. The Atlantic 'middle passage' is an immense hidden African graveyard. Young men, women and children, the best specimens, were extracted from their communities, leaving them and their economies in ruin, in a legacy that is part of persistent underdevelopment in parts of Africa up to our times. From when they were taken they were in bondage, some in (temporary) work at the European trading stations, some just in captivity waiting for shipment. Sexual abuse was rampant. A mixed-race population was created of children born into social limbo, tied to the trade, some working as low-level slave managers and labourers, some prospering. On the ships the slaves were packed as tightly as was physically possible, in chains, left to urinate and defecate where they lay, with perhaps a daily outing on deck for fresh air, being after all valuable commodities. Food and water was a problem and in some cases ran out. Early crossings might take months, later on less time – to the nearest destinations in Brazil eventually a few weeks. Disease was unavoidable, the dead being thrown overboard as so much waste. On the receiving end, the slaves were unloaded and distributed by sale into plantation work for the rest of their lives, chained and beaten as necessary, killed as necessary. The pattern of sexual abuse at the African stations was replicated during the passage and at destination plantations, mixed-race children mostly remaining in bondage. A by-product was to bring Black slavery to Europe. It became a fashionable accessory in stately homes to have Black servants, mainly boys and young men (a small 'immigrant' population soon absorbed into the host populations). The utter depravity of it all was made possible by racial prejudices which deprived Black Africans of the dignity of even being recognised as human beings. Slave forts had chapels for Sunday service. There was no contradiction in the European mind between sincere religiosity and the slave business.

The Danish Africa trade was initially for gold and ivory, but soon turned to human commodities. From the 1660s to 1806, 111,000 African slaves were shipped from the Gold Coast on Danish ships, in a mainly State-organised trade; 91,000 survived the passage (as compared to 3.2 and 2.7 million respectively on British ships). There were at least twenty-five voyages in and after 1803, when the Danish slave trade was legally abolished. An unknown number of additional slaves passed through Danish stations to non-Danish traders. The worry for the Danish Crown and Danish traders during most of the century and a half of their dealing in human chattel was that the volume of trade was too small and that profit which could have been made was forfeited.

The decision in Denmark to abolish the Atlantic slave trade was made in 1792, effective 1803. (Denmark had banned slave transportation in Asia fifty years earlier.) Slavery itself was not abolished, or intended to be abolished. In the years before the ending of the Atlantic trade the shipment of slaves increased significantly, in particular of female slaves, deliberately and with the help of State subsidies to plantation owners, with the aim of establishing a self-sustaining slave population in the Danish West Indies and continuing the slave-based plantation economy.

With the end of the slave trade, the Danish trading stations in Africa were soon obsolete. For a while they continued to provide slaves to other traders, but that failed. Attempts to engage in the Africa trade proper, in particular in palm oil, were not successful, nor was the idea of establishing plantation colonies on the African side. It was the slave trade and that alone that had enabled the Danish presence in Africa. In 1845 the Danish trading stations, five forts and various territorial possessions, were sold to Britain for £10,000. The Danish Africa adventure was over.

So what?

It's a strange little story, this, sad and pitiful. In the hands of the English, the Dutch, the French, the Portuguese and the Spaniards, European colonialism was big business, the making of worldwide empires that endured into the twentieth century, shaping domestic economies, in Britain fuelling the early Industrial Revolution. The Scandinavians wanted to be included in that game. But as their imperialism in northern Europe was shattered in the Great Northern War, so also their attempts at more distant colonialism turned into stories of some success and decisive failure. While the legacy of colonialism and slavery looms large in certain contemporary cultures, such as in Britain, it is in Denmark and elsewhere in Scandinavia mostly forgotten. The eighteenth century was a Swedish and Danish schooling in realism. As with their warfare, they had grasped at more than they could hold. They had wanted to be big, but were learning the hard way that they were not. The colonial experience was part of that lesson.

Part Four

Into the Modern World

No event in Scandinavian history should be celebrated with more jubilation than the bringing-down of Karl XII. The whole rotten edifice of dictatorship and grandeur was finally killed off. We are finished with kingdom-building and on the threshold of nation-building, 'a new kind of society', says the Danish historian Ole Feldbæk – in an understatement. We might rather say 'invention of society'. Until now, the top, the few, had decided, while those lower down would grin and bear it. From now on, social conditions would progress through exchanges between high and low. The eighteenth century: new ideas. The nineteenth century: innovations. The twentieth century: democracy.

9

The Invention of Society

In 1755, the Danish government issued an appeal to 'all honest and patriotic men' to submit to it 'such insights as might serve to maintain the country's prosperity, reduce expenditures, increase incomes and the provision of people's necessities'. It was a success. Proposals flowed in, and were published in eight volumes in a periodical called *Danmarks og Norges oeconomiske Magazin*.

There was a government that was interested in the people and thought those people might have experiences that could be useful. That government had the service of officials who saw themselves as servants not only of king but of country. In the populace there was engagement, and what people contributed came out of a running debate around social, economic and cultural matters. A magazine was to hand in which to publish the material. Ideas were starting to circulate in a lively, if not very broad, public space: ideas of reason, happiness, tolerance and equal dignity.

Enlightenment

New men, and not a few women, proposed to run with reason and shine its light – French philosophers called themselves *les Lumières* – into the debris of darkness left behind from the Renaissance. They wanted to bring together the entire body of human knowledge, *les encyclopédistes* in France, Germany and elsewhere becoming ever more ambitious in compiling universal encyclopaedias and dictionaries. They looked for order and wanted tolerance. They wanted liberty. They wanted the freedom to explore and debate. They wanted education, by which they meant schooling for the many as distinct from religious teaching for the few. The Enlightenment.

We know of it as philosophical creativity in the hands of the great British, French and German thinkers. In England, John Locke proposed, in his *Essay Concerning Human Understanding* (1689) that all knowledge comes from experience, which is to say not from religious teaching. In two *Treatises on Government* (also 1689), he advocated the principles of government by consent and the separation of powers, ideas that would be articulated with yet more clarity and spread more forcefully by the French Baron de Montesquieu in *De l'esprit des lois* (1748). In France, Voltaire (1694–1778) – philosopher, poet, historian – spent a life of writing, in an oeuvre that fills 100 volumes, in rage against Church dogmatism and for tolerance. Rousseau (1712–78) was a prophet of unencumbered liberty. His *Du contract social* (1762) starts with the revolutionary dictum that 'man is born free'. But he turned on the Enlightenment to make its achievements impediments to true liberty, which he, romantically, thought realised, including for the education of children, in natural lives free from the decadence of civilisation. In Germany, Emanuel Kant elaborated theories, in the impenetrable style of German philosophy, of moral rationalism. In Scotland, Adam Smith, in his *Wealth of Nations* (1776), took on the legacy of protectionist mercantilism in economic life to advocate the merits of liberal, if morally restrained, enterprise. The term 'middle class' entered learned language. In Scotland, the philosopher-historian Adam Ferguson, in an essay of 1767, coined the notion of 'civil society'.

It gave birth to literature in a modern understanding. In France, Molière (1622–73) invented the staged comedy. In England, Daniel Defoe produced the world's first popular novel in *Robinson Crusoe* (1719), and in *Gulliver's Travels* (1726) Jonathan Swift made the giant and the Lilliputians learn to tolerate each other in spite of their differences. Poetry blossomed as a literary form suitable to the quest for order. In Germany, Johann Wolfgang von Goethe (1749–1832) lifted Enlightenment into Romanticism.

Women found a platform from which to express themselves publicly. Mary Astell (1666–1731), later called the first English feminist, wrote, with religious inspiration, and anonymously, for women's right to education on a par with men. In France, Olympe de Gouges (1748–93, who died under the guillotine in the reign of terror), was a playwright and pamphleteer who wrote on a range of social issues, from slavery via divorce to children's rights, and followed the ideals of the Revolution into her *Déclaration des droits de la femme et de la citoyenne* ('Declaration of the Rights of Woman and the Female

Citizen,' 1791). In England, in the same spirit, Mary Wollstonecraft published *A Vindication of the Rights of Men* (1790) and *A Vindication of the Rights of Woman* (1792). Women of the Enlightenment were inspired, if that is the right word, by the general hostility of their male contemporaries. A forceful poem entitled 'In Defence of Women' (1761) by the Swede Hedvig Charlotta Nordenflycht was a riposte to Rousseau and his patronising learning on the subordinate capacities of women. Feminist tracts were well received and respected, much read and influential in their time.

There was musical inventiveness as never before, by the great Germans: Bach, Mozart, Beethoven and others (building on the inspiration of the Danish–German organist and composer Dietrich Buxtehude; the young Johann Sebastian Bach walked across Germany to Lübeck to be the master's pupil). Opera was reinvented as narrative musical drama, pioneered by the German Christoph Willibald Gluck (1714–87, from 1748 to 1749 court composer in Copenhagen). Music was to the Enlightenment as art had been to the Renaissance.

In science, Isaac Newton (1642–1727) explained the laws of nature, and he and Gottfried Leibniz in Germany discovered new laws of mathematics. In Sweden the botanist Carl von Linné (Linnaeus, 1707–78) created an orderly system for classifying plants and species. In moral philosophy, a young Jeremy Bentham (1748–1832), in England, proposed, with lasting influence, a 'utilitarian' measure of right and wrong: the greatest happiness of the greatest number, thereby making the human condition the measure of all things.

The Scandinavian Enlightenment

To Scandinavia came, from 1720 and on, peace. Remarkably, *peace* – it had long not been known. Not total peace. There were to be more Swedish wars with Russia and Prussia – more Swedish humiliation – and some involvement in other people's wars on the Continent. But Scandinavia itself would not be at war for the rest of the century. That enabled the Scandinavians to start taking care of their own affairs and make themselves receptive to new ideas.

DRAWING A BORDER

In the peace after the Great Northern War, Denmark and Sweden agreed to collaborate to draw up the precise border between Norway and Sweden, Europe's longest land border. A binational commission was established in 1734, and the practical work commenced in 1738. It was cumbersome and time-consuming, involving inspection of the entire border – 'walking the border' – and much fieldwork from both sides over many years, including hearings with local populations to establish historical understandings of border demarcations. The most difficult issues were in the Sami areas in the north, where local nomadic populations had no concept of a border and where Denmark and Sweden had long held overlapping claims.

By 1751, a treaty was ready and agreed, establishing the border that still applies. In an addendum, the right of the Sami to migrate freely across the border was formally enshrined. It took another fifteen years to complete the work with border markings and a final set of maps.

The border that was established in 1751 was 2,228 km long. Finland was then part of Sweden and the Norwegian–Swedish border stretched to within a whisker of the Arctic Sea. Finland was lost to Sweden in 1809. Further border treaties of 1810 and 1826 established the borders between Norway, Finland and Russia, reducing the Norwegian–Swedish border to 1,630 km. It is marked with cairns, now about 800 in all, of specified shape and size. By agreement between the two countries, the border is subject to joint inspection and maintenance every twenty-five years.

From peace followed economic betterment in modernising economies, pushing city capitalists to the fore and liberating farming families from subjugation. Economic life started to free itself from the grip of an all-commanding State. There was early social mobility. Administrative and military élites were opening up to some degree. Ambitious men from outside the aristocracy could be educated and climb the ladder. New avenues of investment opened up for the rich. In the growing cities there were labouring jobs for men and service jobs for women, and business opportunities by which new families could rise to position and wealth. Manufacturing, mining and city life lifted, if that is not too grand a word, farming boys and girls into paid employment.

During the long periods of incessant war, the Crowns had sunk into massive debt. Some of this was cleared by the sale of Crown land. The buyers were the burghers who had money to spend. Some of the property was maintained in large estates under new ownership, some of it chopped up and sold on further in smaller holdings. On the coming of absolutism in Denmark in 1660, half of all land was in Crown ownership. Thirty years later half of that had been sold off, starting a process of multiplying many times over the number of landowners. Mining concessions (in Sweden and Norway) went up for sale, landing with the burghers again, who had the capital for expensive operations.

Economic modernisation was dramatically visible in Norway, the most backward of the economies. The population was small, by the mid-1700s not yet 700,000. And poor: agricultural output was less than was necessary for sustenance and livelihoods depended on imported grain. But there were improvements to increase productivity. The right to lifetime tenancy had been (more or less) normalised during the 1600s. From around 1700 priority rights for tenants to the purchase of tenancies were laid out for sale. During the 1700s, the class of small-scale owner-farmers grew from a minority to becoming the majority of farming households. The potato was introduced around 1750 (first hesitantly, but given a boost by the discovery that it could be made into alcohol, the Scandinavians' *aquavit*, cheaper than that distilled from grain). The trade in fish continued, now a combination of dried and salted cod and herring, most of the produce originating in the north to be traded through Bergen, but increasingly also Trondheim and other coastal towns, in the hands of merchant houses with improved competence and organisation. With the upturn in demand for timber in Europe, Norway experienced a bonanza. Sawmills on both farm and industrial scales cropped up along the coast in the thousands. The immediate result was deforestation in easily accessible areas. That triggered State regulations, while forestry moved to inland areas where it required more capital, again to the benefit of the capitalist class. By 1730, the export of timber over Christiania was in the order of a million planks a year, twenty years later 2 million. In the trade with England, the Norwegians benefited from regulations which required export goods to be carried on domestic ships. At the beginning of the eighteenth century Norway's merchant marine counted about 500 ships, by the end of the century three times as many, twice the size of the Danish fleet. Mining prospered as a semi-royal, semi-capitalist enterprise. The most important sites were the silver mines at Kongsberg – the country's biggest industrial enterprise, with a workforce upward of 4,000 by around 1760 – and the copper mines at Røros, in both cases fuelled by easy access to firewood from surrounding forests. The first glass mill started production around 1740, others following in short order, producing bottles, window panes and drinking and decorative glass. The Hadeland glass mill, opened in 1765, still today producing quality glassware. Whaling emerged as an industry with the technology of hunting at sea from ships. Regular expeditions went out from Bergen to the edge of the Arctic ice at springtime, for seasons of two to three months, for blubber, oil, skins and meat.

THE END OF PEASANTRY

My great-grandfather was a tenant farmer. He was born in 1855 and died in 1942, aged eighty-seven. From 1879 to 1924 he and his wife, also born in 1855, held a tenancy in the village of Fron in Gudbrandsdalen. They were called Johannes and Gjertrud and went by the family name of the tenancy, Stebergløkken. You would know from the name – løkken, meaning 'the yard' – that it was a smallholding. Other tenancy names might be bekken ('the creek'), haugen ('the hill') or hågån ('the field').

He held a piece of land to work, which, with the houses on it, was the property of his landlord on the Steberg farm. He paid a rent and had some duty-work. The farm would have had six or eight cows and yielded a sparse livelihood for a family.

Tenancy conditions had been improving over the preceding century. Johannes had more security than previous tenants, as well as the security of being able to pass on the holding down the family. He could invest with confidence and get more out of it. Living conditions were not bad, as is seen in the age they reached and the number of children they raised. He had some cash earnings from delivering milk to the local dairy and livestock to the abattoir. He was able to scrape out a surplus for himself from his farming and over the years build up a modest amount of savings.

They had nine children. Those children and their children in turn could ride the coat-tails of better conditions in farming and new opportunities in industrial labour, an emerging public sector and emigration. Four sons emigrated to America, three to farm and one becoming a banker and mayor in Petersburg in Alaska. A fifth son became a tenant under the local vicarage, a sixth a laboratory technician. The final son took over Stebergløkken from his parents. Two daughters married out, one of them being Karen, my grandmother.

Shortly before handing on the farm, Johannes and Gjertrud bought a strip of adjacent land on which they built a house and a small barn and food storage unit, and where they lived out their lives. This was land owned by Steig, the mighty farm that Snorri mentioned near the site of Olav's encounter with Dale-Gudbrand. It had not been in use for some time, and not much money would have been exchanged for it, but it is still remarkable that on retirement this humble *husmann* was able to make himself a proprietor. Not only that, the son who took over Steberglokken did not continue as a tenant but was able to buy the farm and become an owner of farming property. Subsequently, additional land was acquired elsewhere in the village. The farm is still in operation and is now a good family business.

My grandmother married Anton Ringen, of a neighbouring holding, also Steig land, and the two of them took another small tenancy where they started a family. Anton was establishing himself as a livestock trader, and the day-to-day farming would have been my grandmother's responsibility. Between 1909 and 1915 they had five children. In 1918 Anton died, leaving Karen to raise the five children on her own with the tenancy as their livelihood. The oldest son became the manager of the dairy in a neighbouring village, the next son a teacher at the regional agricultural college, my father a senior civil servant in the national government, the daughter married into a substantial *odel* farm, and the youngest son became a local government official.

Having raised her children, Karen gave up her tenancy, moved back in with her parents and cared for them in their old age. She took over their homestead and lived out her life there, to die in 1967, aged eighty-three. She worked it with a cow and a calf, a pig or two or a couple of sheep, some hens and a patch of potatoes. She had a bit of cash income from surplus produce – milk and cream – and eventually a small pension; a means-tested State old-age pension had been introduced in 1938.

When I was growing up in the 1960s, my parents, my brothers and I would spend a week or so in the summer at my grandmother's. My mother would lend a hand with domestic chores and my father, now the Director General of the National Agricultural Research Council, would help with the harvesting of hay. There was one cultivated field, with thick sturdy grass, and some patches of natural fields with thin and delicate grass. It would be cut by scythe, hung to dry on fence-like *hesjer*, and when dry carried into the small barn, for which purpose a back harness of wood and leather ropes was used, the same kind of rope Ottar had traded in the Viking Age.

Stebergløkken farm, 1911

Johannes and Gjertrud at eighty

So there was progress – but it was not pretty. More farmers owned their land, but population growth also gave rise to a growing rural proletariat of tenants, known as *husmenn* ('house men'), some with only a slice of land to work for themselves, many of whom paid rent in kind in the form of duty-work for landlords. In the fish trade, new merchant houses used their monopoly in credit to shift profits to themselves, leaving people in costal communities behind in poverty. It was to be two more centuries for prosperity to trickle down to the lower reaches of the social ladder.

Deforestation followed not only from the trade in timber but also from mining. Concessions came with rights in surrounding forests and obligations for local populations to cut and transport timber, produce charcoal and maintain roads. Even today, the high-elevation areas around Røros are barren of forest. There was work to be had, but pay and prices were dictated by the company and honoured, if at all, with much irregularity. The mine work itself was high-risk in the extreme in injury and death.* The country had its first taste of industrial unrest, in which, generally, companies, State and Church conspired against workers. Shipping was high-profit and high-risk, even more so in times of active European wars. Whaling was on the way to becoming an industry of shame.

In Denmark, with its rich agricultural economy, reform came in the shape of land restructuring, and in a big way. The feudal character of the country had been remarkably stable for hundreds of years, with ownership (of non-Crown land) in the hands of a small number of large landowners. That structure now crashed. Population growth could not be accommodated except by increasing productivity; new land to add to the arable territory had all but run out. There was rising demand for foodstuffs from Europe and money to be made. The way to increase productivity, so thought the modern men who ran the State, was to make life better for those who worked the land.

By a combination of landowner initiative and State legislation – an Agricultural Commission of 1786 is a milestone in Denmark's social history – Denmark was de-feudalised. Not completely: the landowners had power and not all were enlightened, so the outcome was a compromise. One class of tenants obtained hereditary rights to their holdings, but not property and freedom from rent. Another class were able to buy their holdings outright, some with the help of cheap State credit. Within a generation, half of the tenants had become freeholders. The duty of work for landowners was retained until 1799, but many were able to buy themselves free. To different degrees in different parts of the country and over time, tenant-serfs had been tied to their estates without freedom of movement except by landowner permission,

* The eighteenth–nineteenth-century Røros community is portrayed in a series of novels by Johan Falkberget. His father was a miner, as had been several generations of his family, and Johan was at work in the mines from age seven. He was born in 1879, learned to read and write within the family and had his first story published in 1902, eventually producing about fifty novels and rafts of other writings. He grew up in a cultured and religious home and considered himself a Christian socialist. He chronicled the lives and destinies of working folk in and around the mines, culminating in four epic novels centred on the character of An-Magritt, a woman who carved out a living as a mine provisioner and who came to stand as a symbol of human, and female, strength in a brutal world.

known in Danish as *stavnsbånd*. That was now abolished outright. Landowners were still big, but no longer judicial masters. Denmark had become a land of free farmers.

Well and good for the 60,000 farm families. Not so good for the 90,000 families of the proletariat who did not have access to land ownership. The State had listened to barons and farmers, but no one listened to the underclass – Enlightenment had not yet shone that far. Some of them became small-scale tenants again, under the new freeholders, while others remained day labourers. The social distance between landowner and farmer may have been reduced, but the gulf from the top and middle to the bottom widened.

Danish and Norwegian shipping prospered, Norwegian shipping much from Norway's exports of fish and timber, Danish shipping more in the service of other trades. It was a business of war profiteering. During the many colonial wars, the American War of Independence as of 1778 and the French Revolutionary Wars from 1793, when warring powers disrupted each other's trade, Danish ships had the protection of neutrality. They did transport service, but also rented out their neutrality for blockade-running by foreign ships flying Danish banners. A sideline was money-laundering, as we would now call it, on behalf of British officials of the East Asia Company who needed to move corruption profits made in India back home around British regulations. The British profiteers lent capital to foreign shipping which they could reclaim in London from the foreigners' sale of cargos, then as now with the helping hand of discreet financial service houses. For a while, after France, Spain and Holland entered the American War of Independence (1775–83) against Britain, Danish companies had a monopoly in this particular market and could dictate their terms. Copenhagen prospered and became a significant European trading centre.

In Sweden, by around 1750 half of all agricultural land was in farmer ownership, up from a quarter a generation earlier, in a process, says Kurt Samuelsson, of 'farmer liberation'. The incorporation of Skåne had come as a massive uplift. Around the mid-1700s, the blessed herring returned to Sweden's west coast, as plentiful as they had once been on the Baltic shores. Young men could for a while make sufficient money to buy enough land to be owners and have a livelihood. This time there was a spin-off in the manufacturing of oil, exported as a raw material for the production of soap and for other uses, such as in lighting; the streets of Paris were 'lit by oil from Bohuslän'. But also, as in Denmark and Norway, the size of the rural proletariat increased, in 'growing masses of desperate property-less work-seekers'. This population surplus would in the next century feed into, on the one hand, rapid industrialisation and, on the other hand, a million-strong emigration to North America.

A by-product of militaristic absolutism was a bureaucratic State in the hands of a class of assertive officials of now considerable size. Into that class flowed new men, better educated, inspired by Enlightenment thinking. This officialdom, once the grip of royal dictatorship was eased, could take an interest in matters that had not previously been State affairs and start to fill society from above with new institutions of public administration.

One such matter was population. It was becoming understood that people were labour, that a growing population was a sign of progress, that mortality was a waste, that healthy workers and soldiers were better than worn-down ones, and that country and economy depended on population.

In the response to the Danish government's appeal in 1755 for ideas and insights, there were heavy representations on population matters. For about a century, parishes had been obliged to record births and deaths and vicars could follow the ups and downs of the populations under their charge. Now these data started to be brought together centrally for statistical purposes. Sweden's first census, the first in (post-Rome) Europe, was in 1749, followed in Denmark and Norway twenty years later. A Collegium Medicum was established in Copenhagen in 1740 as an advisory authority on public health. The first hospitals in a modern sense opened in Uppsala in 1717, Stockholm in 1752 and Copenhagen in 1756.

Following from the new awareness of the importance of population came the understanding that if people were to better their conditions and be productive, they needed competence and skills. Elementary education had been a Church matter; it was now becoming a public responsibility. Confirmation was made obligatory in Denmark and Norway in 1736. That required of the young that they could read – but it turned out that they could not. The Crown responded with an audacious undertaking. Elementary schooling was to be universal and free. A law to that effect was issued in 1739. Too rashly, it turned out. The localities refused. They could not afford the cost and parents wanted their children at home for work. The State had to back down and revoke the law the next year. Even so, schooling did spread, if slowly. It was basic, primarily reading; writing and arithmetic were introduced more slowly as an add-on to be paid for by ambitious parents. Even at the beginning of the next century, only about half of the young, if that, were literate. In rural Norway, itinerant teachers offered schooling for up to a week a month for eight months over five or six years, with quite a few boys attending, if not many girls. In Sweden it went even more slowly. There was much debate – John Locke's *Some Thoughts Concerning Education* was translated into Swedish in 1709 – but less action. At the beginning of the nineteenth century, only 10–15 per cent of Stockholm's children were in schooling.

While the bureaucratic State started to fill society with institutions from above, citizens themselves did the same from below – enlightened citizens, of course, of the better classes. Trade and industry created wealthy families. The newly rich made themselves landowners, set themselves up in baronial ostentation, built palatial residences in Copenhagen and Stockholm. Another new class of learned men and women was on the rise: poets, authors, intellectuals, professors – eager for the generosity of the men of money. They were the drivers of such novelties as we met above: a running public debate and magazines in which to publish news, opinions and research. Denmark's richest man, Ernst von Schimmelmann, the profiteer of slave-trading and plantation ownership, created in his Copenhagen palace and country estate a cultural milieu in which he surrounded himself with bright men and lavished patronage on poets and scientists. In the meeting ground of wealth and learning, in saloons, in clubs, in coffee houses, in debating societies, in universities and academies, ideas were cultivated and taken forward into action. Carl von Linné led a group of academics to establish an Academy of Sciences in Stockholm in 1739, the institution that a few years later managed the first population census. A Royal Academy of Sciences was set up in Denmark in 1742, and in 1769 a Royal Society of Agricultural Sciences. New monarchs, Frederik V in Denmark and Gustav III in Sweden, pitched in as patrons of arts and education. A Royal Academy of Arts opened in Copenhagen in 1754. In Stockholm Gustav III created theatres, operas, ballets, museums and academies.

Regular newspapers, at least weeklies, were issued in Copenhagen from around 1720, *Berlingske Tidende*, still today a major paper, from 1749. The first daily in Stockholm, *Dagligt Allehanda*, appeared in 1763, and the same year also the first paper, a weekly, in Christiania, *Norske Intelligenz-Seddeler*, consisting of four pages, two for adverts. Journals and magazines proliferated. A Royal Society for the Improvement of Nordic History and Language was established in Copenhagen in 1745, distributing historical material through its *Danske Magazin*. Professor Jens Sneedorff lectured on constitutional modernisation and edited an influential journal on related matters, *Den patriotiske Tilskuer* ('The Patriotic Observer'). Scandinavia's first publishing house, Gyldendal in Denmark, still the country's leading publisher, was started in 1770. Censorship was lifted, relaxed in Denmark, in Sweden abolished by law in 1766.

Among the many clubs that blossomed in Copenhagen was The Norwegian Society, established in 1774. Young Norwegian men who wanted to study, or were in search of government service or bohemian pleasures as poets and authors, gravitated to Copenhagen. There they congregated for each other's company over meals and drink, for debate. They formalised their togetherness in a society and celebrated it and themselves in irreverent song and poetry. Inevitably, they gravitated to origins, to identity, to the genuine fatherland. They were expats who had been forced out and from their exile romanticised the home country, part of an awakening of Norwegian national sentiment.

Out of these and other influences, intellectual life blossomed. Olof von Dahlin (1708–63) was a pioneering Swedish author, playwright and historian, a bringer of Enlightenment ideas to the north and a moderniser of the Swedish language. Through his *Then Svänska Argus*, inspired by *The Spectator* in Britain, he lobbied for educational reform and the teaching of utilitarian skills. Hedvig Charlotta Nordenflycht, whom we have already met, was Sweden's first modern poet. Both enjoyed royal patronage. We have also met the poet Carl Michael Bellman, again a grateful, if careless, recipient of royal beneficence. After the death of Christian VI, theatrical and musical life resumed in Copenhagen. Frederik V bequeathed to the city a new theatre which would eventually become today's Royal Theatre. In Stockholm, Gustav III himself wrote plays and operas which were performed to (obviously) great acclaim. International influences were pulled in. Adam Smith's *Wealth of Nations* appeared in Danish translation in 1779, and in part in Swedish translation in 1800. The American

Declaration of Independence was published in full in a Danish journal three months after being issued in America.* In Stockholm, Anders Bachmanson Nordencrantz, a highly esteemed author, popularised the ideas of Montesquieu, Rousseau and others to advocate in politics the division of power and in society the abolishment of both aristocracy and censorship. Anders Chydenius, a Finnish theologian and economist, in his *Den Nationnale Winsten* ('The National Wealth', 1765) developed modern theories of economic liberty ahead of Adam Smith (including the 'invisible hand' logic and terminology), and exercised much influence both in his writings and as a member of the Swedish *Riksdag*. He was a driving force behind the Freedom of Press Act of 1766.

The universities (although small, Uppsala circa 1750 had 1,000 students, Lund 700) played their part. They had mainly been schools for the teaching of clergy; now they branched out, including administration for the training of officials. A professorship in 'rhetoric and state science' had already been established at the University of Uppsala in 1622 (the world's oldest chair in political science). In 1741 a professorship in *oeconomia publica* followed, and in 1761 a professorship in constitutional law. In Uppsala again, Carl von Linné created the modern system of taxonomy, and the astronomer Anders Celsius (1701–44) the temperature scale that carries his name. Ludvig Holberg wrote a history of Europe (1711), a general history of Denmark and Norway (1729) and a history of the Jewish people, 'from the beginning of time' (1742). In Stockholm, the *Riksdag* commissioned von Dahlin to write the history of Sweden, published in several volumes from 1747. Travel came into fashion. Roads were being built – easily in Denmark, feasibly in Sweden, then as now an art of extreme difficulty in Norway. Linné undertook travels through all parts of the country, collecting plants and other specimens and observing nature and life, compiling careful records. Travel diaries became much in demand, spreading as they did knowledge of lands and peoples.

---

* The version in Danish had two 'improvements' on the original. The blame that was directed against King George III was redirected to the British government, George III being Christian VII's brother-in-law. The 'inalienable' rights (to life, liberty and the pursuits of happiness) became 'un-purchasable', in Danish *'ubetalige'* rather than *'ubetagelige'*, but that was a typographical error.

The great intellect of the age was that same Ludvig Holberg (1684–1754), academic, author, historian, philosopher, theatre manager and more. He was born in Bergen and educated in Copenhagen, Norwegian of birth, Danish in life. After travelling and studying widely in Europe, he was, from 1717, Professor of, in turn, Metaphysics, Latin and Geography at the University of Copenhagen. During the 1720s he wrote twenty-six comedies in the style of Molière, performed to packed houses in his own theatre, which were warmly sympathetic to

Ludvig Holberg – 'The great intellect of the age, 1684–1754'

the plight of the little man and woman, scornful of the snobbery of their betters. Many of them continue to be performed to much delight in today's Scandinavian theatres, in particular *Erasmus Montanus*, the story of the country boy Rasmus Berg who learns some Latin in a city school and returns to his village with a Latinised name to show off his great knowledge, and *Jeppe på Bierget*, which tells the tale of a peasant who drowns his sorrows in drink, wakes up in the baron's bed and thinks he has gone to Heaven, before being thrown back in the mud, to the general merriment of his many tormentors. 'Everyone says that Jeppe drinks, but no one asks *why* Jeppe drinks.' Theatrical life had come to a halt in Copenhagen with the heavy monarchy of Christian VI. Holberg was among the many who welcomed Frederik V on the throne, and with him the revival of the Enlightenment spirit, even if it was inspired by an immoral king. The theatre was back, and with it Holberg's plays. He was now the elder statesman of cultural life, affluent enough to acquire a country estate and with it a baronial title. In his will he left his estate to the Danish Aristocratic Academy at Sorø, the same academy from which Professor Sneedorff would soon be preaching constitutional modernity.

A product of all this energy and inventiveness in romanticism, liberty, debate, poetry, history, travel and observation was a further novelty: that of national sentiment. People started to think of themselves as Danes, Norwegians and Swedes. Towards the end of the eighteenth century, the idea of love of fatherland had become established and fashionable. That was stimulated by efforts to improve, indeed save, the Danish and Swedish languages by men like Holberg and Dahlin. In Kai Hørby's Danish history of the period 1250–1400 there is already a remark tucked away about 'Germanification'. Germans were inserting themselves into the northern lands. They came as traders and immigrants, gradually becoming numerous in the emerging cities. Kings were Pomeranians, Mecklenburgers, Oldenburgers; they brought with them German officials, nobles, clergy and language.

By the 1700s, the native languages were in a bad way, thought by the educated classes to be vulgar, and not much used at all in writing. Administrative, military and business élites were cosmopolitan, with a large contingent of foreigners. Native élites looked to France and Germany for sophistication and took pride in mastery and use of their languages. In the Danish court, Christian IV was the first king to prefer

Danish, but after him court language relapsed back to German.* In Sweden, Gustav III preferred French. When Swedish and Danish were used in writing at all, they were rigid languages riddled with terms and forms of Latin, German and French derivation. Holberg worked through his life on improving the Danish language by re-editing his own works, rooting out foreign imports and inventing simple Danish terms and forms.

New winds blew through religious life. The old division between high and low had not been laid to rest. The Scandinavian Churches were now Lutheran State Churches, but not unified. Beneath the mainstream was a counter-current of pietism which preached a personal and emotional religiosity, based on the individual's own godliness, independent of top-down theology. Churchgoers wanted their religion to be simple and humble. They wanted to worship in congregations under their own management. Women asserted themselves on an equal footing with men.

This was a dilemma for ambivalent Crowns. It was one thing for gentlemen to debate language, society and government, but an entirely different matter if the small-folks wanted control of their worship. In Sweden, the otherwise liberal *Riksdag* of 1726 banned free congregations, as did also Christian VI in Denmark in 1741 (in a decree which also imposed a ban on women taking part in public speaking). He was himself chief pietist in theology, but that did not translate into welcoming free congregations. In Sweden, the ban was followed by some organised resistance and secretive free worship, which again was met with repression, against women activists in particular, several of

---

* In 1772 a book was published in Copenhagen to celebrate a great Danish achievement, but in German, under the title *Beschreibung von Arabien* ('Description from Arabia'). The author was Carsten Niebuhr, a German scientist in Danish service. He led a royal expedition to Arabia that set off in 1761, progressing via Cairo and the Sinai to Yemen, and on to India and Persia, in the course of which five members of the expedition died (including one Peter Forsskål of Finland, who in 1759 had published a Swedish-language pamphlet, *Thoughts on Civil Liberty*, which the Swedish government banned, ending his academic career there), leaving Niebuhr the only survivor to return to Denmark after six years. He brought with him maps and sketches of Oriental lands and cities, and from Persepolis copies of inscriptions which played a part in deciphering cuneiform writing. The story of the expedition is told by Torkild Hansen in his *Arabia Felix*.

whom were sentenced to hard labour in atrocious conditions. A young student, Sven Rosén, confessed to having published uncensored texts and was sentenced to deportation, dying as a preacher in America. In Norway, Hans Nielsen Hauge, an industrial entrepreneur, stimulated a nationwide following of, as they became known, *haugianere*, in an early indication of what was soon to be a vigorous popular movement. In the years 1797–1804 he walked the land, staying at farms and helping with the work by day, in the evenings bringing people together and preaching the gospel in house assemblies, leaving organised groups behind as he travelled. The ban of 1741 was still in place and Hauge was to spend seven years' hard labour in prison, only to be released with body and health broken and die at the age of fifty-three.

EMANUEL SWEDENBORG

Emanuel Swedenborg (1688–1772) was a Swedish religious mystic who became a theological innovator. He grew up in a religious family of pietist leaning and seems to have thought of himself from early on as a person of 'calling' who had 'visions'. His early career was as a scientist and government official in chemistry and mining.

In midlife he experienced a religious crisis in which, in dreams, he was visited by Christ and conversed with angels. He claimed to be Christ's messenger and to communicate with spirits from across the cosmos. He believed that these influences brought him a unique wisdom in religious, moral and philosophical matters and an ability to see into the future. From then on he wrote frenetically, in Latin, on faith and related topics, which he thought had been obscured by a theology insufficiently con-nected with the spiritual, to communicate the truth of which he believed himself to be the conduit, offering reinterpretations of faith, Creation, the Trinity, the nature of love, the afterlife and more.

His theology-philosophy attracted much interest in his time and has continued to do so since. He was and still is considered by some a crank, possibly suffering from mental illness, but also has a large following in New Age religious movements and Swedenborg-inspired congregations in Scandinavia, Britain and America. He was not tolerated in Sweden in his time and lived the last part of his life chiefly in Amsterdam and London, where he published most of his work. His final book, *Vera christiana religio* ('The True Christian Religion'), a synthesis of a life's teaching, was published when he was eighty-three.

He died in London and was buried in the Swedish Church there. He was subsequently accepted in Sweden as an original thinker. In 1908, his remains were removed from London and returned to Sweden, where they were interred in Uppsala Cathedral in a solemn ceremony, near the remains of the scientist von Linné.

It transpired, however, that the skull in those remains was not Swedenborg's. His real skull had been stolen from the grave in London and later sold through an antiques shop in Wales. From there it found its way to auction at Sotheby's in London in 1978, where it was bought by agents of the Royal Academy of Sciences in Stockholm and brought to Uppsala to be united with the rest of Swedenborg's remains in a second solemn ceremony. The former outcast has the distinction of being twice accepted into the embrace of the Swedish Church in two separate ceremonies in its main cathedral.

With the coming of peace, the absolutist grip on political power was relaxed, setting in motion a slow journey towards constitutional monarchy and eventually democracy. It started in Sweden.

No sooner was Karl XII dead than the barons tried to reassert themselves. A secret opposition had been brewing and now set in motion a rapid succession of events. High officials loyal to the old king were deposed, some imprisoned, some executed. The dead king's sister, Ulrika Eleonora, was elevated to queen. The *Riksdag* was convened to adopt a new constitution. The barons tried to get it 'elevated' to a kind of constitutional convention and have practical power vested back into their narrowly constituted *Riksråd*. But it was too late. The *Riksdag* gave the power that was wrested from the demolished Crown back to itself.

Ulrika did not last but was not quite the puppet the barons had thought, and the Swedes have much to thank her for. Before she could be dismissed, she agreed (if reluctantly) with the *Riksdag* to abolish absolutism and restore co-rule between monarch and parliament, and signed the constitution to that effect. That was a big deal. It was early – we are in 1720 – and a great leap forward in constitutional modernisation. It was radical, not far short of a revolution of the kind the French revolutionaries had in mind, but did not manage, seventy years later. The result was a constitutional monarchy in which the counter-power to the Crown sat not with the aristocracy but with a national assembly made up of the four estates. It was the beginning of the short century that Swedish historians have called the Age of Liberty.

The new *Riksdag* was remarkable. It was to meet at least every three years. It was big, with up to about 1,000 nobles, 50 or so churchmen, 100 burghers and 150 farmers. (The *etats généraux* that was convened in Paris in 1789 was made up of 1,200 delegates.) It was cumbersome. The estates met separately at different locations across town. Decisions needed the support of three of the four estates. It was slow. The *Riksdag* that convened in September 1726 sat until August 1727 (the delegates who could afford to stay in Stockholm that long, that is). It was lively. Royal dictatorship was blown away. 'The people' had power, and liked it. They debated, endlessly, and relished it. They dealt with real matters. Manufacturing industry was advancing. State money was put up for its support, to be raised by protective tolls on imported goods. Poverty was on the rise. State money again. One remedy was to build workhouses for (punitive) poor relief.

But for all the progress and liberty, it was not a happy time. Much of both the rural population and the city proletariat lived in dire poverty. Women on average had ten children, one in five of whom would die in their first year. There were repeated periods of failed harvest and famine; 1757, 1771, 1787 and 1799 were all years of hunger. Foreign travellers in Sweden described horrific displays of wretchedness, lack of hygiene and filth. 'Children were pale and emaciated, unwashed, with no change of clothing as long as the rags hung on to the body, shy, retreated and frightened.' Mary Wollstonecraft travelled through Scandinavia in 1795. She was struck by the enormity of the landscape, but equally by the misery of the people. Children were filthy and adults stank. Servants were underpaid and mistreated in comparison to what she was used to in England. Mortality in Stockholm was rampant, even by general city standards of the time. More children were workers than in schooling. A peasant revolt in 1743 was put down with military force and the execution of six of its leaders.

Political progress was set back for a while by Gustav III, who struck down the liberal constitution. It was not unwelcome. Liberty was for the few. There was hope that a stronger Crown could spread blessings more widely. But the time was up for absolutism, and Gustav's failed.

When he was taken away during that masked ball the *Riksdag* was back in business and Sweden, eventually, back on the path of reform.

There was no similar upheaval in Denmark and no constitutional innovation until the nineteenth century. The Crown remained absolutist by law; it just refrained from being strictly absolutist in practical governance. That relaxation was assisted by the incompetence of Frederik V and the madness of Christian VII, whereby governance was protected from royal excess and in the hands of practically minded officials, allowing for a slow on-off opening up of social life.

It was an ambivalent liberalism. Although debate and literature flourished, censorship remained in effect (in the hands of a professor appointed for the purpose by the University of Copenhagen). Even Holberg, the most elevated of authors, was for a while obliged to publish anonymously. The autocratic regent Struensee wanted, in a contradiction, to be a reformer and tried to abolish censorship, but it backfired. Free spirits used their liberty to criticise Struensee himself, which the liberally minded dictator branded an abuse and made punishable. Firebrands in Copenhagen pushed the envelope by ridiculing Crown and Church beyond what was tolerable, resulting in a new royal decree, in 1799, again limiting free expression. A leading bohemian poet, Peter Andreas Heiberg, was sentenced to deportation the following year, leaving behind his wife and children and settling in Paris, where he died friendless, half blind and in poverty.

The big reconfiguration

France and Britain were up against each other for top-dog position in Europe. Through the eighteenth century, power drained, in ups and downs, out of French hands and shifted, first economically and then militarily, to Britain. Sweden and Denmark had 'settled down to an existence of inoffensive obscurity' which, however, did not prevent them from being pulled into the maelstroms. They needed protective alliances against perceived threats. The big powers were balanced against each other and could shift that balance by making alliances with even small players.

France had been fighting relentless colonial wars, at great cost and with little success. True, she engaged against Britain in the American War of Independence, on the winning side, but again at great cost.

Simply, the French State went bankrupt. A blunder by that same State in its attempt to solve its financial crisis brought on the French Revolution. The plan was to convene the estates for their consent to a programme of financial relief, new taxes in other words, in return for measured concessions against reasonable complaints. But it was too little too late. Concessions are a dangerous gamble for a wobbly autocracy; those who are offered crumbs of reform will see that the master is weak and reach for more than he is willing to concede. So it was in this case. The conditions of deprivation in cities and country alike were such that the response from below was inevitable revolt.

The estates had convened in May 1789. In June, the third estate grabbed power and set about issuing a raft of declarations, laws and decrees, including, importantly, the Declaration of the Rights of Man (26 August), and adopting a division-of-power constitution. The first product of the Revolution was to give prominence to a set of ultimate Enlightenment ideas.

France descended into chaos. The king fled Paris in disguise but was caught and brought back in disgrace.* The Republic declared, King Louis XVI and Queen Marie-Antoinette executed, the country sank into ever viler terror.

Throughout, however, there was nevertheless a great deal of continuity. French chauvinistic aggression persisted, in the Revolutionary Wars from 1792 and from 1802 the Napoleonic Wars. In the madness of

---

* The architect of the king's flight was a Swedish marshal, Axel von Fersen. Louis had been playing a double game of pretending to move with the Revolution while secretly opposing it in collaboration with other European monarchs, in a cabal in which Sweden's Gustav III was, says Norman Davies, the 'ringleader', with von Fersen his representative at the French court. The escape was cloak-and-dagger dramatics, von Fersen himself driving the royal carriage to a meeting place outside Paris. The royal family headed north but were discovered at Varennes two days later and brought back to Paris. That was the end for Louis. Von Fersen avoided captivity and returned to Sweden to be given ever higher State positions. However, after the loss of Finland a chauvinistic faction was suspected of conspiring against the restored monarchy. When the anointed crown prince fell off his horse and died at a ceremony in May 1810, rumours started to circulate that he had been killed, with the finger of accusation pointing to von Fersen. In the crown prince's funeral procession on 20 June, von Fersen's carriage was attacked by a mob and the great man clobbered to death, the guard standing by and letting the mob do its work. They continued to batter the corpse long after the man was dead.

revolutionary management the generals took control, in a 'directorate' from 1795, in a three-man 'consulate' from 1799, under a 'first consul for life' from 1802, and finally under an emperor from 1804. That first-consul-cum-emperor was Napoleon. He was the most successful general to emerge from the Revolutionary Wars and set about turning all of Europe into a French empire. In a string of victories over a ten-year period he was near to achieving that ambition but overreached himself, finally to be defeated by a coalition under British leadership at Waterloo in 1815. The second product of the Revolution, then, was twenty-three years of warfare.

In the European wars of the eighteenth century, Denmark's strategy had been, mostly, neutrality, and Sweden's to sign up with France for protection against Russia (and for the benefit of a stream of French hard-cash subsidies). Come the French Revolution and its aftermath, both Danes and Swedes were forced to reconsider. The European landscape was now one of constantly shifting alliances in which Sweden and Denmark were tossed around in search sometimes of advantage and sometimes protection. Danish neutrality was shattered by British aggression, which forced Denmark into aligning with France. Sweden was pulled into active warfare in various campaigns against France. When the dust had settled, Denmark was on the losing side and Sweden with the winners.

In February 1808, Russia marched an army of 24,000 men into Swedish Finland. Russia had taken many of Sweden's possessions in the Baltics in the Great Northern War. Now it was time for the remainder in Finland. The Swedish defence crumbled and by September all of Finland was in Russian hands. The inept king, Gustav IV, blamed the military and shattered any semblance of unity. He wanted to mobilise again for another campaign but there was no will in the country to follow him. Russian troops were in northern Sweden and threatened Stockholm itself from bases in the Åland archipelago (as they had done a century earlier at the end of the Great Northern War). Finland had been an integral part of the Swedish realm since the thirteenth century. It was now incorporated into the Russian Empire as a grand duchy. Sweden was reduced to the geographical contours it has today.

In Stockholm, the king was forced to abdicate and leave the country. The *Riksdag* wrote yet a new constitution, which reaffirmed the

division of power, an independent judiciary and freedom of the press.*
That done, it put the deposed king's uncle on the throne as Karl XIII.

It was not a smart choice: he was sixty years old, incapacitated by
illness, and childless. A crown prince had to be found. The choice fell
on the Danish prince who at the time was military commander-in-chief
in Norway, Christian August. Sweden and Denmark were enemies at
war, but that did not prevent the Swedes from making a Danish prince
their sovereign, even the same one who was leading the Norwegian
theatre of the war against Sweden itself, nor that prince from accepting. In January 1810 he became Crown Prince of Sweden under the
name Karl August.

Again, not a good move. In May he was already dead (having fallen
off his horse, as we have seen). Yet another crown prince and regent
had to be found, and again the choice fell on a Danish prince, the
first one's older brother – a third unsuccessful move. He accepted but
suffered the humiliation of having the offer withdrawn.

On 25 June 1810, one Carl-Otto Mörner, a twenty-nine-year-old
lieutenant in the Swedish army, obtained a meeting with Marshal
Jean-Baptiste Jules Bernadotte in Paris. He had been given a commission to bring a copy of a dispatch from the Swedish government for
Napoleon via the Swedish Embassy in the French capital. The dispatch
itself was on the way, but was important enough for a copy to be
sent separately. Mörner arrived in Paris ahead of the official courier,
leaving the Swedish minister to wait before approaching the emperor.
Mörner had previously done apprentice army service in France and
had contacts which helped him approach the marshal.

Bernadotte was a distant member through marriage of the French
imperial family. He was a brilliant commander, was elevated to the
rank of marshal (one of eighteen) on the proclamation of the empire,
and served with distinction under Napoleon both as a commander and
in various viceregal governorships. But he had an uneasy relationship
with the emperor, who may have been suspicious, or jealous, of his
dashing prowess. At this juncture he might have been, or felt he was,
out of favour.

The meeting was unlikely: between an imposing member of the

---

* Press freedom in Sweden: introduced by law in 1766, curtailed by Gustav III,
reintroduced 1809, curtailed again by Karl Johan, and reintroduced yet again in
new legislation in 1835 and 1845.

French élite and a little man from Sweden without position and representing no one but himself. Mörner offered Bernadotte the Swedish Crown. Bernadotte was interested.

A group of young officers in Sweden didn't like the prospect of a second Danish prince being made their king. They thought the new monarch should be someone with military experience and authority. They entertained the dream of reconquering Finland from Russia. Mörner was one such officer.

In Paris, he acted with speed. The dispatch from Sweden was for Napoleon's consent to the Danish crown prince plan. As it was arriving, Mörner was laying the Kingdom of Sweden before Bernadotte and got another Swede in Paris, a general, to encourage him. He, Bernadotte, sought out Napoleon, who gave his blessing. True, he had by then given his consent to the official plan but was indifferent to the whole business and let the Swedish minister know that he had changed his mind.

Back in Sweden, the government had offered the Danish prince the position. Three days later, Mörner turned up with the Bernadotte plan. The government was enraged and sent the young man home under house arrest. But Bernadotte had now decided not to be refused. He arranged for a delegate to meet the Swedish foreign minister with a promise to solve the Swedish government's dilemma by way of a massive bribe in credit and property. When to that was added Napoleon's consent, the deal was done. The Danish offer was retracted. Bernadotte headed north and arrived in Helsingør on the Danish side of the Sound on 19 October. He was met by the Swedish archbishop, converted to the Lutheran faith, crossed over to Sweden the next day, arrived in Stockholm on 2 November and was adopted by the king. It had taken only four months from the day a solitary Swedish nobody had called on him in Paris. He took the name of Karl Johan. Historians have speculated that his scheme was to be called back to France as emperor or king. If so, it went wrong for him and he was stuck in the cold north.*

---

* For Mörner the kingmaker it did not go well. He had Karl Johan's confidence for a while, but imposed on him by needing to be bailed out of repeated debt incurred by financial imprudence. He ended his career in a lowly command in a Stockholm outpost, where he spent much of his time reminiscing about better days in Paris and promoting his own reputation.

*

For Denmark, as for Sweden, the question was Norway: Denmark to hold on to it, Sweden to take it. Denmark sought the protection of France, and 'Frederik VI remained Napoleon's most faithful ally right to the bitter end.' And therefore an enemy of Britain. Denmark had a strong navy. Britain feared it could be put into French service and decided on a pre-emptive strike. That came as a combined navy and army operation in August 1807 in which Copenhagen was laid under siege from land and bombarded from sea in a campaign of terror against civilian targets, setting much of the city ablaze. The British sailed away with the Danish ships they did not destroy and imposed a blockade which caused widespread distress; in Norway, with its dependence on imported foodstuffs, waves of famine.

Denmark, however weakened, now decided to attack Sweden before Sweden could attack it. A supporting French–Spanish army was moved up to Denmark in the early winter of 1808, under the command of none other than Marshal Bernadotte, the same Bernadotte who two years later would be king-in-waiting in Sweden. The plan failed. Bernadotte's army disintegrated when the Spanish contingent deserted in order to return home and join an uprising against Napoleon. Sweden moved to counter-attack Denmark through Norway. That also failed. Sweden had inadequate forces and unmanageable lines of supply. The Norwegians refused to engage. For more than a year, the armies stood in stalemate against each other along the border. In Norway, military provisioning resulted in civilian famine, which again caused epidemics of dysentery and typhus. In the south-east of the country, mortality during 1808–9 was three to four times the norm, with up to one in ten of the population perishing. Both sides gave it up and went home. This all coincided with the Russian invasion of Finland, also in early 1808, and the Swedish–Russian peace in 1809.

In the messy European theatre, Sweden joined the anti-Napoleon coalition. The plan was to force Denmark to give up Norway, with Russian support in exchange for Swedish assistance to Russia in the expected French invasion. That invasion came in 1812. Napoleon famously failed. In the French retreat back through Europe, war flared up again in Germany. Napoleon suffered more defeat and his remaining men were pursued westward by Russian, Prussian and Swedish forces. Denmark, still allied with Napoleon, declared war on Sweden yet again. Another mistake. The Swedes, from their position in Germany, lured the Danish corps into a trap in Holstein and forced its capitulation: give up or have the whole of your country invaded. This was the last proper battle ever that Swedish armed forces have fought on any military battlefield. The result was the Peace of Kiel of 15 January 1814 between Sweden and Denmark, underwritten by Austria, Britain, Russia and Prussia.

Norway reborn

In that treaty, Denmark surrendered Norway to Sweden.* What the Norwegians themselves wanted was no one's concern. However, it turned out that the Enlightenment had done its work even in the northernmost periphery. The Norwegians wanted a say in their own destiny and thought they should be masters in their own house.

The Danish period had been a brutal reality for the people of Norway, one of oppressive taxation, conscription into army and navy service, wars for others' causes, of a foreign officialdom indifferent to local people. There had been more than a streak of colonial exploitation to it. Norway depended on imported grain. The government in Copenhagen had introduced a grain monopoly for the benefit of Danish producers and traders at high and stable prices and to the detriment of the Norwegians, who had to pay more than market prices for their necessary imports, at times paying the price of famine.

Denmark had been relaxing its absolutist rule and instituted various cultural, social and property reforms, reforms that were also brought to its Norwegian province. The American Revolution and constitution turned lofty principles into practical reality. The French Revolution, through the Declaration of the Rights of Man and its constitution of 1791, set a new political agenda across Europe. In Copenhagen, ideas were debated as never before. In The Norwegian Society young

---

* What was surrendered in the wording to the treaty was 'the Kingdom of Norway', which constitutionally, although with some ambiguity, had not existed since 1536. What was not surrendered was Iceland, the Faroe Isles and Greenland, although these were historically possessions of the Kingdom of Norway. At the last moment the treaty was changed from Norway being handed over as a Swedish possession to it being a kingdom in a union with Sweden. In a secret protocol, Denmark was paid a sizeable cash compensation.

radicals wrote poetry and composed songs in celebration of nation and fatherland. Johan Nordahl Brun, later Bishop of Bergen, composed in 1771 a rousing song of praise, still sung on festive occasions (as I and friends did in our student days), for 'Norway, birth-land of giants, for which we dream of freedom and for chains to be broken'.

In reaction to Danish rule, the Norwegians had been less docile than they have sometimes been described by historians. They had bombarded Copenhagen with a flow of complaints against abusive officialdom. There had been peasant revolts, refusal of taxation and conscription, and desertion from military service. Norwegian identity had not been extinguished and it hurt to have it trampled on.

On 8 June 1786, a man called Kristian Jensen Lofthus, a farmer from the south of Norway, obtained an audience with Crown Prince Frederik in Copenhagen. He came, he said, 'on behalf of the fatherland', and brought a letter of complaint against local officials. He obtained a friendly hearing and was encouraged, he thought, to go home and compile a dossier of documentation for the government. He so did, only to see his activism turn from documentation to organisation. A revolt was in the making. Petitions were compiled with hundreds of signatures. A peasant army was on the march, a sizeable contingent heading towards Copenhagen itself. The authorities reacted in two separate ways. They issued an arrest warrant on Lofthus, hunted him down and put him in chains, crushing the movement. But they also established a commission to review the complaints that had been compiled, which was done methodically and in earnest and resulted in officials being suspended from post and charged with dereliction of duty.

The Lofthus revolt would be followed by the Hauge awakening, another movement of social organisation by the small-folks in a nationwide network of 'societies of friends'. The war years in the early 1800s brought inflation and hardship, culminating in widespread hunger revolts in 1813. The people were rising, or there was threat thereof. Social organisation from below was too dangerous to be permitted, but nevertheless had causes that needed to be understood.

One reason why it had been easy for Denmark to subjugate Norway was that there had been no Norwegian élite able to resist. Now, while there was unrest below, there was also movement above; this did not come from an aristocracy, which was all but absent, nor primarily from a rising class of burghers and capitalists, who were too few. But there was an officialdom that the absolutist State had created throughout the country, from a leadership in Christiania to men in positions of civil, judicial and military authority in regions and counties down to the local level, including bishops and parish priests of the State Church. This officialdom had been sometimes Danish, sometimes foreign, sometimes Norwegian, often alien and hostile to the folk under its charge. But they were the educated men of the country, the ones who were susceptible to Enlightenment influences. The government was taking more care to appoint competent managers. More young Norwegians were in Copenhagen to study and later fill posts at home.

These new men were coming to identify with Norway as a nation. They saw themselves as modern men in a new age. It was they who were able to see beyond the crushing of the Lofthus and Hauge movements to what was stirring underneath. They were making themselves a social class. Norwegian historians have called them an 'estate of officials', *embetsstanden*, a class of mandarins. Within only a generation, says the Norwegian historian Ståle Dyrvik, 'a strong sense of national identity had evolved among the men who framed the articulated public opinion'. Come 1814, it would be men of this class who would write the constitution for an independent Kingdom of Norway. They would remain the country's uncontested upper crust deep into the century, 'in charge of governing power and the architects of public norms'. It was a tiny class, still in the 1830s comprising no more than 2,000 families, but it bred the men and women – the high officials, professors, bishops, parliamentarians, authors, poets – who could guide a population as it was reshaped into a nation.

During the war years from 1807 onward, Norway was left to fend for itself. A 'governmental commission' was appointed, not quite a government but something starting to resemble it. It tried, if with limited success, to get provisioning under control, the difficult matter of grain imports through the British blockade. It led the war from Norway against Sweden, if with much hesitancy. When the Swedish king was deposed in 1809 the Norwegians could have marched into Sweden, but they did not. It has been thought that the Swedes had been in touch with Christian August and offered him the crown prince job, in other words bribed him in a big way. There were forces in Norway, including in the governmental commission, who were favourable to a union with Sweden, and they may have been colluding with the Swedes.

In January 1810, Christian August departed Norway for his elevated position as Swedish crown prince. The Danish king sent more princes north to be governors, finally in 1813 his own crown prince, Christian Frederik. He was twenty-seven years old, smart, well educated, handsome, charming. He knew Norway and important Norwegians well. He was keen for the job. The king wanted him to fortify the bonds with Denmark, but Christian made himself more Norwegian rebel than Danish agent.

The next year, Norway was surrendered to Sweden, but Christian Frederik was still in Christiania and the nearest the Norwegians had to a national leader. He convened a meeting of 'leading men' on 16 and 17 February. It was agreed that Norway would claim independence. Parishes across the country appointed representatives to a constitutional assembly. It convened on 11 April 1814 at Eidsvoll, just north of Christiania, with 112 delegates, thirty-three of whom were from the military and the rest from the regions. It took a month to write the constitution, which was formally adopted on 17 May. Christian Frederik was elected king, unanimously. Norway was its own kingdom.*

But that independence was a doomed enterprise. It found no support from others, obviously not from Sweden, nor from Denmark, nor from any European powers.

Even so, the assembly had produced a constitution (which has survived and is still today, with modifications, the country's basic law). Norway was to be a kingdom with democratic authority in an elected legislature, the *Storting*. Nearly half of adult men had voting rights:

---

* In her constitutional history, Linda Colley says that the constitution was written in 'an elegant neoclassical mansion' outside Oslo. So it was, but 'elegant' is to put a gloss on the event. The mansion was more like a country house and the available meeting room small and cramped. The men sat packed on hard wooden benches without back support. In a painting of the meeting (now in the *Storting*), a window at the back is open, to let fresh air in and stench out. They were accommodated on nearby farms, mostly two or three to a room, and somehow managed to be fed and cared for. In April–May, Norway was still in semi-winter and covered in slush. It was a miracle that the delegates had managed to make their way across a country that hardly had roads. Their coming and going for meetings, many with commutes of an hour or more, would have been battles with mud.

those over the age of twenty-five and with property and tax-paying capacity (conditional on an oath of loyalty to the constitution). It ensured an independent judiciary, property rights and freedom of the press. Lutheranism remained the official state religion, Jesuits and monastic orders were 'not tolerated', and Jews were 'excluded from access to the realm'. There was to be no aristocracy (two remaining earldoms were finally abolished in 1821). May 17 remains Norway's national holiday – its constitution day, its day of independence – and is celebrated each year with great ceremony in every city, town and village. All schools arrange parades in which the children saunter in their Sunday best, wave flags and cheer their liberty.

The constitution was remarkable in its radical enlightenment, considering that the kingship left behind in Denmark was aristocratic and absolutist. The legislature was unicameral, unheard of at the time. Even the American constitution, a model, instituted a Congress divided between a lower and an upper house. The function of upper houses was to give aristocrats, landowners or other élites a bastion of control in government matters. But Norway was a society without an aristocratic or even non-aristocratic landowner élite and therefore without a privileged class that would normally claim upper-house privileges. Denmark and Sweden did not make their legislatures unicameral until 1953 and 1970.

In Sweden, Karl Johan mobilised an army to march into Norway at the end of July. It was hardly a war; there were some skirmishes but in two weeks it was over. A convention was signed on 14 August. Christian Frederik was to convene the *Storting*, abdicate and leave the country. Karl Johan agreed to the Norwegian constitution being maintained, with modifications as necessary to accommodate the fact of union. On 4 November, Norway's *Storting* adopted the revised constitution, conceded to the union and elected the Swedish king to be theirs as well. On the same day, Christian Frederik set foot back in Denmark. Swedish historians have judged Karl Johan to have been generous to the Norwegians – rightly so.

THOSE DANISH PRINCES AND
THOSE CONFUSING NAMES

Christian VII was King of Denmark from 1766 to 1808, but disabled by mental illness. His one son, Frederik, was regent from 1784, and king, as Frederik VI, from 1808.

Christian August (1768–1810) was the son of an earl of Schelswig-Holstein (by the name of Frederik Christian) and a member of the extended Danish royal family. From 1803 he was military commander in Norway, and from 1807 governor. In 1809 he was elected Crown Prince of Sweden, as Karl August, but died the next year.

Frederik Christian (1765–1814) was the older brother of Christian August/Karl August. In 1810 he was invited to become Crown Prince of Sweden, the invitation that was rescinded in favour of Bernadotte. After that he was out of favour in Denmark and spent the remainder of his life without any significant position.

Christian Frederik was Crown Prince of Denmark under Frederik VI. He was the king's nephew, his father being another Prince Frederik. He was governor of Norway from 1813, the next year becoming regent and King of Norway, only later that year to abdicate and return to Denmark, where an unhappy king assigned him a lowly post as regional governor. From 1839 he was King Christian VIII, the last absolutist monarch in Denmark.

The Golden, and Not So Golden, Age

Denmark was free of the burden of Norway. Sweden was free of the burden of Finland. Norway was free from being under colonialism. Again there was peace. Society was opening up. Liberalism, Romanticism and nationalism combined in a pressure cooker of energy, generating economic, cultural and political creativity.

Innovation I: Industry

The Göta Canal stretches 190 km through central Sweden from the Baltic coast in the east to the inland lakes of Vänern and Vättern. It opened in 1832 and was the biggest infrastructural project at the dawn of Sweden's industrial age. It is still in use, now serving mainly the tourist trade.

Most of the country's export produce – iron, copper, timber – originated in the east and north. Transport was by river and lakes into the Bay of Bothnia and the Baltic Sea, around southern Sweden, through the Sound, north around Denmark into the North Sea. In the age of sail, this came with massive costs in time and outlays. Denmark was claiming tolls on transport through the Sound. The idea was to open direct transport overland to the west. There was already a Trollhättan Canal, opened in 1800, between Lake Vänern and the port of Gothenburg which connected the network that was opened by the Göta Canal to the west coast.

It made sense, but that sense had to be seen. The realisation of the project depended on competence, finance and manpower, but ahead of that on vision. It depended on men who had ideas of big things, big projects, big investments – and big profits. A century earlier, people would not have been able to think in these ways. The breakthrough to industrialism, explained the Swedish economic historian Eli Heckscher, was enabled by a breakthrough in people's minds of new ways of thinking.

The Scandinavians had much help from abroad in honing their minds and outlooks, from Britain in particular. There the Industrial Revolution was in full flow and included the building of canals and, subsequently, railways. It was the same old story of developments in the north coming on the back of influences and imports from Europe. In the planning of the Göta Canal, the Swedish government recruited Thomas Telford from Britain as a consultant. He had previously overseen the building of the Caledonian Canal in Scotland. It was to be a constant in the next century that industrial developments were enabled by foreign expertise and capital. It started with canals and was followed by the steam engine, by railways and steamships, by the telegraph, by electrification, by the taming of hydroelectric power. The Scandinavians wanted it all, and would get it, but generally with the help of forerunners and money from Europe.

The canal was dug by hand. It took twenty-plus years to finish, and 60,000 men worked on it for longer or shorter periods. An early product of early industrial entrepreneurship was a class of itinerant construction workers who would move from project to project as work and pay beckoned, digging canals, building railways, drawing power lines, young men, strong, hard-working and hard-living, in rough conditions, expendable in injury and death, using Scandinavia as an open labour market. In Sweden and Norway they became known as *rallare*, a derivation, possibly, of the Swedish word for wheelbarrow. They would be a constant in the industrial uplift through the century. Much romanticism has later been attached to them and their lives, in literature and ballads, but there was not much glamour to it at the time. Living quarters were in basic barracks or tents, health care was little or absent, food crude, supplemented by the energy of hard liquor.

But even digging by hand requires tools: spades, sledgehammers, buckets, means to blast through rock, and more. Canal work, then, creates demand for produce of various kinds from secondary industries. Much is needed in technology: fortification of sides so that they do not fall in, roads along and bridges across, locks to control the waters and lift barges up and down (the Göta Canal is served by fifty-eight locks). In the town of Motala, the canal company set up its own mechanical plant to produce cranes, dredgers and other technical equipment. The company was soon independent and established itself as the country's leading engineering enterprise, moving on to steam engines, locomotives and rail rolling stock, propellers, shipbuilding (delivering the country's first steamship), bridges, tractors and turbines. It is still going strong, with anything from kitchen sinks to the spires of Uppsala Cathedral to its name. Other enterprises, under names still well known today, arose as spin-offs: Bolinder, Kockum, Husqvarna.

Thus from big projects followed more opportunities. A man by the name of Olof Ericsson was a mining manager in the early 1800s who moved on to the Göta Canal project. He was able to get his two sons into engineering apprenticeships from their early teens. One son, John, emigrated to England, where he worked on railway projects, and on to America and into naval engineering and warship design. By the time of the American Civil War, he had designed armoured battleships with rotating turret cannons powered by screw propellers of his own design, which were decisive in giving the North the upper hand in naval strength (and rewarded him with fame and wealth).

The other son, Nils, stayed in Sweden and worked on further canal projects up to 1850, when he moved into railway construction. The *Riksdag* decided that the State would build the main lines west from Stockholm to Gothenburg and south to Malmö. Nils was appointed to lead the projects. These were again huge investments, giving birth to supply industries and railway communities and towns along the routes. The first steam locomotive was produced at Munketells Mechanical in Eskilstuna, a firm established in 1832 in anticipation, after studies by its founder in England, of the future for steam and steel. Nils led the work for ten years until all of the western line was open and died in 1870, having been rewarded with royal elevation into the nobility.

Another Ericsson, Lars Magnus (1846–1926), of another family, was a mine labourer from age twelve, an apprentice in telegraph-equipment work from age twenty, and studied instrument-making abroad, for a while at Siemens in Germany. He returned home in 1876 and set up a mechanical workshop in Stockholm, which he developed into a telephone company, copying Siemens technology and inventing the table-top telephone (on display in an international exposition in Stockholm in 1897 as evidence of Swedish industrial inventiveness). The company flourished and is today the global telecommunications corporation that carries its founder's name.

Decisive in modern mechanical industries is the ball-bearing component which enables machinery to move reliably. Steel ball-bearings capable of supporting heavy and precision machinery came into use in the latter part of the nineteenth century. Breakthrough innovations were made in a textile mill in Gothenburg, on the back of which the SKF corporation (*Svenska Kullagerfabriken*) was established in 1907, soon to become one of the century's most successful industrial ventures. Within five years there were production and distribution offshoots across Europe, into Russia and on to North and South America and Australia. By the 1930s, SKF held a global near-monopoly in high-quality ball-bearings and controlled about 70 per cent of the world market. In 1926 SKF established the Volvo subsidiary for automobile production, hived off as an autonomous corporation in 1935. SKF and Volvo are brands that, perhaps more than any others, have contributed to Sweden's reputation for high-quality industrial manufacturing.

Works like canals and railways require the ability to blast through rock. The available explosives were ineffective and dangerous. Alfred Nobel (1833–96) invented a more effective and less dangerous nitroglycerine-based explosive. He called it dynamite (after the Greek for power). He was the son of a tools, weapons and chemicals entrepreneur who made his fortune in Russia at the time of the Crimean War. Alfred studied privately in France and America, for a while working for John Ericsson, and became an inventor, eventually owning more than 300 patents, winning the one in dynamite in 1867. He became an industrialist in control of a multinational network of companies in chemicals and weaponry.* Nobel was a complicated man, driven by enterprise, a believer in progress, possibly with the conviction that better technology would make war obsolete. His work was in explosives and weaponry, but he was a man of peace, solitary,

---

* One of these was the Swedish Bofors, which he acquired late in life and assigned to armaments production. A century later, Bofors, now a major weapons company – it provided anti-aircraft guns to both sides in the Second World War – was subsumed into the SAAB corporation, which in turn unloaded the heavy weapons division, but not the missile division, to United Defence Industries in America, which was then taken over by BAE Systems in Britain, of which Bofors Weapons is now a subsidiary. Bofors Dynamics remains a unit of SAAB in Sweden. The light NLAW shoulder-carried anti-tank weapon that proved effective in the Ukrainian defence against invading Russian forces in 2022 is a SAAB product, the ones provided to Ukraine being assembled on licence in Britain.

suffering pangs of depression, possibly riven by conscience. When his brother, also an industrialist, died in 1888, obituaries of Alfred were published in error. A newspaper in France, where he lived, described him as 'the merchant of death'. This may have been instrumental in his decision to leave his very considerable fortune to fund the Nobel

Alfred Nobel, champion of Swedish industrialism (1833–96)

Prizes, one in literature and three in science, to be managed by Swedish institutions, and the Peace Prize, to be managed by a committee under the Norwegian *Storting*.

The Göta Canal project created enough enthusiasm for the necessary capital to be raised domestically, mainly from eager trading houses in Stockholm and Gothenburg that hoped the cross-country transport would boost their business. If that early start was simple, further industrialisation would depend on more sophisticated financial services. Projects needed funding to be put together from varied sources both at home and internationally. In 1856, a man by the name of André Oscar Wallenberg (1816–86) settled in Stockholm and established the city's first private bank, known as *Stockholms Enskilda Bank*, now *Skandinaviska Enskilda Banken*. He had been out in the wider world for twenty years, during which time he had studied banking in America, and saw an opportunity in Sweden, a niche for money to be made. He led the bank until his death and made it the country's leading financial powerhouse, especially in the crucial import of capital from abroad. It remained under family control for nearly a century, making the Wallenbergs far and away the dominant financial dynasty in Swedish and Scandinavian capitalism. Their bank sat at the centre of a web of local banks and core industrial enterprises under full or part ownership, in charge of which were lieutenants loyal to the Wallenbergs. It worked closely with the State, including in the issuing of paper money, laying the foundations of the Swedish brand of State-capital collaboration. One brother, Knut, served as foreign minister during the First World War. The Wallenberg family has been to Swedish capitalism as the Medici family was to medieval Florence.

In the end, the canal was not as important as had been hoped. Rail transport soon made canals obsolete and the Sound would be free from tolls. But the project had created new industrial and financial enterprises with the dynamics that are known as the Industrial Revolution. By following offshoots, we can see direct lines from the early industrial ventures 200 years ago to Swedish industry and finance today. During the nineteenth century, the Swedish economy was transformed from an agricultural to an industrial one.

The Swedes were lucky. Their country was rugged, cold and difficult, transport distances long. Taming it was a matter of interventions on a big scale which called for ingenuity in engineering and finance, creating work and jobs for decades. Big personalities rose to callings in manufacturing and banking.

The Danes were less lucky. Their country was small, kind and easy, without mountains of minerals or forests of timber. Their exports were in agricultural goods, compact for transport. Canal-building, elsewhere the early engine of industrialisation, was virtually non-existent. From early in the nineteenth century there were improvements in the network of roads, reducing travel times and easing transport, but the building of roads over short distances in a flat landscape and mild climate does not ask for much. The islands were far apart, putting projects of bridge-building out of reach until deep into the twentieth century.

They were unlucky with their aristocracy, reactionary as ever, with no notion of progress, content to be landowners and disinterested in industry. They were unlucky with their king, Frederik VI, an incompetent administrator, desperately fearful of any change, any letting go of power, anything new. The lively debate of the early Enlightenment was silenced by the return of censorship. Norway had broken free from absolutist Denmark and adopted a democratic constitution. It was admired by liberals in Denmark, but in silence; it had become dangerous to speak openly of constitutional modernisation. The turnaround in mindsets that was conspicuous in Sweden was absent in Denmark, which sank into economic and political sclerosis for much of the century. 'The class mentalities from the age of absolutism lingered in people's minds.'

The peace that brought boom to Sweden came with bust for Denmark and Norway, which were bankrupt and without the capacity to invest in economic innovation. Even in the mid-1830s, public debt in Denmark was ten times annual public revenue. The new Norwegian State had to shoulder its share of Danish war debt and had nothing to spend. It was forced to maintain export tolls on industries already on their knees and to impose extraordinary taxes on a poor population. When Karl Johan was crowned King of Norway in Nidaros Cathedral in 1818, he had to pay for the royal crown and other fineries out of his own pocket. Monetary systems were in disarray and inflation rampant. In 1822, the estate at Eidsvoll – with its ironworks, timber, industry and land – which had been one of the wealthiest in the country and had hosted the constitutional assembly in 1814, collapsed in bankruptcy.

Industrialisation in Denmark, compared to that of Sweden, was delayed by half a century or more. And when it started to unfold it was of a different kind. What in Sweden was industrial industrialisation was in Denmark agricultural industrialisation: textiles, clothing, tobacco, sugar, agricultural machinery, brewing (Carlsberg was established in 1847, Tuborg in 1875). As late as around 1930, 80 per cent of exports were agricultural, 60 per cent pork and butter alone.

The first railway, from Copenhagen to Roskilde, 30 km long, opened in 1847. From the 1850s, Samuel Peto, a British railway entrepreneur, obtained concessions to build railways across Jylland, first east–west, with a connecting steamship route to England, and eventually a north–south line completed in 1869. Trade begot shipping, which begot shipbuilding. The forerunner to shipbuilders Burmeister & Wain was in operation from the 1840s.

Only towards mid-century did the long Norwegian recession start to abate. The first improvements were in the traditional economies of agriculture, fisheries and timber. The transition of the previous century of peasants becoming owners continued, and with it increasing agricultural productivity. The inflow of cod and herring to the Norwegian coasts was plentiful, four-fifths of the catch being for export and by the 1860s constituting a fifth of the county's total export value.

LOFOTEN

The most notable islands on the Norwegian coast make up the Lofoten archipelago, north of the Polar Circle. A string of six or seven major islands and some smaller ones, most mountainous, reach out into the Norwegian Sea from the narrow sliver of land which here constitutes northern Norway like a long, crooked finger. It ends in the island of Røst, which is so low and flat that if you see it from the air you wonder that the sea does not wash over it. Beyond Røst are three rocks, known in Norwegian as *nyker*, that jut straight out of the sea to a great height. The seaward sides are the home of bird colonies, puffins and swallows in the millions, so dense that if you fly around the rocks in a helicopter on a summer day (as I have done), the roar of the motor causes the colony to lift, creating for a moment the optical illusion that it is the side of the rock itself that detaches and evaporates into thin air.

Life on Røst was observed by Italian seafarers who were shipwrecked there in the 1430s. A Venetian named Piero Qverini had left Crete in

1431 with a shipload of wine destined for the Flemish market. Out of the Mediterranean, the ship ran into ferocious weather, lost masts, sail and rudder and was blown helplessly north until it was abandoned. Of sixty-eight men, eleven survived to drift ashore in the north of Norway and be found by fishermen from Røst, who rescued them and nurtured them back to life, with, according to Qverini, much grace and generosity. They were surprised to find the people living comfortably off the sea and some cattle husbandry. They traded fish to Bergen in exchange for grain, textiles and other necessities, maintaining a standard of living better than farming populations in rural areas further south.

The archipelago and the mainland form a natural fish trap which from at least the fifteenth century has been the basis of rich winter cod fisheries. Here, menfolk from along the coast would migrate for the season. They came ten or so to each boat, still in the age of oar and sail, and lived a team to the room in barracks on the islands, usually with a woman hired for cooking and chores. The days would be cold, wet and back-breaking, the nights not much better. The money was good in an abundant season, but much was lost in wild living, and more again flowed to the trade captains down the coast who equipped the boats and took receipt of the catch.

The epic story of these fisheries and of the men who made them is rendered in one of the most dramatic novels of Scandinavian literature, *The Last of the Vikings* (Den siste viking) by Johan Bojer, published in 1921. It is, besides much else, a masterclass in political analysis. A fjord is teeming with fish, the fishermen scramble, a minor civil war breaks out – until the regulator arrives, in a steam-engine frigate and with the authority of naval uniform: linesmen in that part of the fjord, netsmen in the other. 'A thousand men were transformed from animals to human beings again.'

These fisheries are now history. They have become mechanised and even fishermen work in conditions fit for people. The barracks in which the teams lived, miserably, have been gentrified as *rorbuer*, now bases for modern and comfortable adventure tourism.

With the end of the European wars, international trade was liberalised and the seas opened. The Norwegians had experience and grasped new opportunities, internationalising their shipping. Shipyards cropped up, as had sawmills a century earlier, most small and primitive, one or more in every town along the southern coast. By around 1870, Norway was the world's third-biggest shipping nation in tonnage, behind only Britain and America; by 1914 it was still number four, now also behind Germany. Steam replaced sail, towards the turn of the century becoming dominant even in long-haul and Atlantic trades. The old trading town of Bergen took the lead. It had ship-owners with progressive minds who saw earlier than others that the future was in steam.

It was a shabby business. Norwegian-built ships were cheap, of poor quality and second-rate technology. Wreckage was more frequent than in other fleets, sometimes profitable because of insurance back-ups. Norwegian sailors were paid at exceedingly low rates, at half the pay of sailors in the British fleet. In Norwegian mythology, shipping is 'our glory and our might' – but early on the Norwegians were the tramps of the oceans who made money by undercutting others.

Also to be revived, from around mid-century, was whaling, another shoddy business. The harpoon gun with an explosive missile was a Norwegian invention (by Svend Foyn) that came into use in the 1860s, revolutionising whaling first in the North Atlantic, eventually worldwide. It was a business that profiteered during a long century in a theatre of barbaric animal cruelty and the decimation of whale populations across the globe.*

Canal-building took off in the 1850s, a half-century later than in Sweden. Steamships came into regular use in both coastal traffic and on inland lakes. The first railway, from Christiania to Eidsvoll, 65 km long, opened in 1854 (engineered by Robert Stephenson of British railway fame). Steam engines came into use in improved sawmills from the 1860s.

But it was painfully slow. By 1900, Sweden had 12,000 km of railway, Norway 2,000. There were developments in timber- and wood-processing, in machinery, in fish-canning, but of modest proportions. What brought serious industry to Norway was electricity and with it the understanding that waterfalls are worth their weight in gold. In water running down mountainsides Norway is super-rich.

* In 1904, a Norwegian whaling station (with several mostly seasonal settlements) was established on the British island of South Georgia in Antarctica, to be in operation until 1965, from which a total of 175,000 whales were slaughtered, about 10 per cent of the total catch of Antarctic whales. A remnant of the Norwegian activity on the island is a population of reindeer, today about 2,000-strong, the first ones having been brought from Norway in 1911 as a source of fresh meat.

The breakthrough came at the start of the twentieth century. Sam Eyde, an engineer of German training, started to buy up the rights to exploit the force of river falls, of which farmers and other land-owners had no understanding. He teamed up with Professor Kristian Birkeland at the University of Oslo, who had been experimenting with the industrial use of electricity. The brothers Wallenberg in Stockholm had money to invest and brought even more French capital into the bargain. In 1905, an enterprise was established under the name of *Norsk Hydro*, which throughout the new century was to be the lead-ing industrial force in Norway. The original product was fertiliser produced by extracting nitrogen from air with the help of vast amounts of electricity. Later electricity-based production was in metals – zinc, aluminium, magnesium – and was to be essential in the country's industrial modernisation after the Second World War.

By 1909, more than a third of ownership of Norwegian industry was in foreign hands, particularly Swedish, spearheaded by the Wallenbergs, but also French, German, American and others. (For simplicity I will from now on use the modern name of Oslo for Norway's capital city, although it was still Christiania/Kristiania until 1925.)

Innovation II: Culture

Culture was to be brought to the common people through learning. Schools were bestowed on them by those above, who knew better. It was hard going, against much resistance in the localities and farmer conservatism: education was alien and imposed, there was too much of it and too much that was useless, and not enough simple religiosity.

Obligatory schooling was finally introduced in Denmark in 1814, daily in cities, every second day in rural schools, with holidays revolv-ing around agricultural needs for child labour. Schools were local, under the management of local school boards, generally headed by parish vicars. It took time to realise – there was a shortage of teach-ers, local finances were strained, parents resisted – but by the 1830s children were generally in schooling and it was exceptional if the young were not literate, an early achievement in European comparison. Further schooling, still for the very few, was in Latin schools and, for the even fewer, the University of Copenhagen.

A similar law followed in Norway in 1827, introducing obligatory schooling in rural parishes, broadening the curriculum from religion and reading to writing and arithmetic. There was not much enthusiasm, little finance and poor provision. Schools were mostly ambulatory, teachers poorly trained and on low pay, parents resistant. In reality the school year was about four weeks (the law stipulated eight). One in five of town children had no schooling. Commission after commission put proposals to a reluctant *Storting*, which held back: it would cost too much, a small and poor country could not afford to be ambitious.

Sweden lagged. Not until 1840 was there early legislation towards universal elementary schooling, and even then the children of poor families were exempt. Again, schooling was not popular and far from welcome, and was rolled out slowly with little government enforcement behind it.

If children were to be schooled, their teachers needed to be educated. Teacher-training, in State-run 'seminaries', became the first reasonably broadly based further, if not higher, education, and an early engine of upward social mobility. From here, a class of moderately educated men and women spread over the countries. They brought with them a combined ethos of knowledge, modernisation and religion. They were educated in the Lutheran faith and were to work in its service. Many were active in religious awakening and free congregational life, and agents of other forms of popular organisation. Teacher-training attracted women. They were in demand as good teachers and because they were cheap, their pay being half the male wage.

In the latter part of the nineteenth century, education progressed in the standard European pattern. Most children were taken through elementary schooling. More of them had access to further education in secondary schools and emerging agricultural and technical colleges, and eventually also universities. Women won access to university study in Sweden in 1873, in Denmark in 1875 and in Norway in 1882, when a single woman, Cecilie Thorsen, matriculated as one of 248 new students.

Nikolai Frederik Severin Grundtvig (1783–1872), priest, poet and historian, was *the* public intellectual of the Danish national and liberal awakening. He was born into a family tradition of clergy, was a brilliant student, set himself up for a career in academia, entered the priesthood around 1810, and was soon a noted polemicist in literary and religious life. He enjoyed royal patronage and was a beneficiary of the old king's duty-bound, if not enthusiastic, support for cultural enterprise.

Grundtvig was to be the intellectual force behind a uniquely Scandinavian educational innovation in what became known as *folkehøjskoler*, 'folk high schools'. He saw the Denmark of his time as standing at a historical juncture, rising from 1,000 years of cultural battle between 'the German' and 'the Danish', when the time had come for Denmark to embrace its true Danish persona. He reached back to Norse mythology and to Saxo and Snorri, both of whose works he translated into modern Danish, in search of a Nordic spirit. In faith matters he raged against the established Church and its 'rationalism', forcefully so, enough to cost him for a while both his job and the right to publish. He was the leading voice of the 'light' strand in the religious revival, in opposition to a 'dark' strand around which less folksy guardians of the true faith gathered. After ten years in the wilderness, in 1839 he was back in the embrace of the Church and moved to a simple vicarage in Copenhagen, where his services, animated by vivid song and congregational participation, attracted a wide following. He wrote simple and popular verses and psalms, many of which remain in use in Scandinavian churches. He made himself a public lecturer, bringing hundreds together to listen to narratives of Danish history. He was handsome and charismatic, a prophet of his time who attracted followers in all of Scandinavia, people who became known as *grundtvigianere*. When he visited Oslo in 1851, the *Storting* paused its deliberations to enable members to hear him speak. 'He loved God, history, the Danish people and their language, and not a few women, including three wives.'

He brought his ideas on nation, religiosity and community together into a programme of civic education. There could not be, he thought, a democratic culture without a broadly educated population. The way to narrow social divisions was to spread popular learning. He championed a new school, a 'school for life', against the oppressive strictures of Latinate learning, to be grounded in people's lives and experiences, in non-paternalistic dialogue between teacher and pupil, in the Norse heritage and the national languages, without the pressure of exams or even much use of books.

The first *folkehøjskole* was established in 1844 in Schleswig, where the pressure on Denmark from German culture was seen to be intense, the first ones in Norway and Sweden in the 1860s. It became a broad movement: some schools were religious, sometimes of 'light' and sometimes of 'dark' inspiration, others were secular, bringing country and farm sons, and soon daughters, into education beyond the basic. In no time at all a network of schools came into being across the lands, with a combination of private and State funding. Diverse as they were, they added up to a movement of national pride and belief in progress. They remain a feature of educational life today, in colleges outside the formal academic system, with thousands of students attending mostly one-year-long programmes of humanistic non-degree learning for the sake of learning.

The young Adam Oehlenschläger (1779–1850) in Denmark opened the door to a culture that was to embrace the Scandinavian Golden Age of literature, music and art. He brought to the north European, notably German, Romanticism with its themes of passion, love, longing, senti-ment, nature, genius, madness, destiny, tragedy and death. His – and its – breakthrough was in 1803, in a collection called simply *Poems*, in which he criticised the prosaic vulgarity of contemporary life and looked back to a more spiritually rich past. He was a prolific poet and playwright who spoke to the Scandinavians about sublime hope in a time of war and decay. That melody – the national, the Romantic, the natural, the people's memory, the ancient mythologies – was to energise two or three generations of rich minds and imaginations.

For centuries, the Scandinavians had been dependent on imports for high culture: Håkon Håkonsson borrowed, Christian IV bought, Kristina stole. Now suddenly they were partners and contributors. The Europeans had traditions to build on, the Scandinavians next to none. Yet they made themselves equals, self-sufficient in creativity. As always, they absorbed European influences, but now with the capacity to bring contributions of their own back into the European landscape. That breakthrough came out of two influences: first the explosive force of Romanticism and then the uplift from Romanticism to realism. The Scandinavians moved as participants into a cultural domain of which they had previously stood at the outside edge.

NEW NORWEGIAN

Norwegian language became a matter of contested identity from the moment people started to search for national awareness. The written language was Danish – the greatest ever Norwegian dramatist, Henrik Ibsen, wrote in Danish – but Norwegians spoke differently. For the Danes and the Swedes, the task was to save existing languages; for the Norwegians to invent one. The idea was to find that language in the dialects of country folk, where a lost language was though to linger. Ivar Aasen (1813–96) was a self-taught linguist who realised that ambition. In 1848, he published a *Grammar of the People's Language* and in 1850 a dictionary. His approach was radical. He thought dialects were more genuine the more they were archaic, less polished by alien influences. His work is the basis of one of the two versions of the Norwegian language still in use, New Norwegian (sometimes called *landsmål*, 'country language'), now much simplified from Aasen's original but still faithful to its origin in the dialects. The other, conservative, version, *bokmål*, is a derivation of Danish. The 'language question' has been and remains a core dimension of alignment in Norwegian politics.

We are in a new age of musical expression. Composers and performers had audiences to present themselves to, middle-class audiences, paying audiences. They were less dependent on royal and aristocratic beneficence and could work freely. They could make money. Their music was audacious and innovative. Men like Beethoven, Liszt and Paganini were famous in the way rock stars are today.

So was Ole Bull (1810–80), violinist, Romantic, nationalist, Norwegian. He was a composer, inspired as he saw it by folk traditions. Some of his music remains performed, but it was as a violinist that he gained fame. He made big money: at the top of his game he was able to arrange a European tour and come home a millionaire in today's reckoning. He was a virtuoso who had everything going for him: exotic, brilliant, tall, blond, handsome, Nordic, up there with Paganini in fame. He played the best violins money could buy.

He spent lavishly on idealistic projects. One was to establish a theatre in Bergen dedicated to the Norwegian language. It collapsed in bankruptcy. Another was a utopian community in Pennsylvania in America, under the name of Oleana. He was popular in America and put his earnings into the colony, subsidising migrants from the old country. It was a mad enterprise, established in a faraway land in a spirit of Norwegian nationalism against the reality of a home country not even able to feed its own people. The first settlers arrived in 1852, in the early stage of Norwegian emigration. After a year it was falling apart. Bull himself left and soon returned to Norway. He built a fairy-tale villa – he called it Troldhaugen, 'Hill of Trolls' – on an island near Bergen, which is still used today as a venue in the Bergen Festival of Classical Music, and there he died aged seventy, of cancer.

Bull had known the young Edvard Grieg (1843–1907), recognised his abilities and persuaded his parents to send him to Germany to study music seriously. Grieg became one of the European greats, often compared to Smetana and Sibelius. His inspirations were Romanticism, German music and Norwegian traditions.

He spent his adult life moving around Europe and back and forth to Norway, combining performing, as pianist and conductor, and composing. He wrote music for piano, violin, cello and orchestra: a single full-length symphony (which he himself did not like). He set music to the poetry of Heine, Goethe, Hans Christian Andersen, Kipling and others. As a person and an artist he was European, Scandinavian and Norwegian, never, as Bull had been, dogmatically Norwegian.

When Henrik Ibsen decided to produce a theatre version of his narrative poem *Peer Gynt*, he asked Grieg to compose the music. The result was a beautiful fusion of song and orchestral music, perhaps Grieg's best-known and most-loved work (certainly by this author). But it was a theatrical failure, which caused a century of misunderstanding of the play. The story is a realistic criticism of the capitalism of the age, Peer being an international tycoon, swindler and arms dealer. He grew up in the rigidly class-divided Gudbrandsdalen and was not of good enough family to have the upper-class girl he wanted. On her wedding day he abducts her into the mountains where, having destroyed her life, he abandons her and sets off into the world to make money. At the end of the play, the old Peer tries to make sense of his life and finds it to have been vacuous: it is like peeling an onion, there is no core. Grieg turned this story into one of national Romanticism. Perhaps he did not care about the play, just took it as an opportunity to make good music (and for the money, which was good). It was a tremendous success, and has remained so, but it took different music by later composers for the Norwegians to understand the meaning of the play.

The Romantic period produced the first Scandinavians who were to win a lasting presence in the European cultural pantheon: Bertel Thorvaldsen (1770–1844), master sculptor, Hans Christian Andersen (1805–75), master storyteller, and Søren Kierkegaard (1813–55), master philosopher, all Danes.

Thorvaldsen was an orthodox sculptor, not original but clever, whose life was an uninterrupted parade of triumph, as a star student at the Danish Academy of Art and a jobbing artist during forty years in Rome. He obtained commissions from the great and the good across Europe and delivered celebratory works for palaces, city squares and churches from a workshop of up to fifty assistants. He did not return to Denmark until he was nearly sixty, and lived another five years there to enjoy a shower of praise and honours. On 24 March 1844, he was at work on a bust of Martin Luther in his studio, attended a supper in the company of Oehlenschläger, Andersen and others, went to the theatre, died in his seat. His position was such that an illegitimate daughter – he never married – was declared legitimate by royal decree.

An early Romantic endeavour was to rescue the inherited culture that was carried in popular memory by recording folk songs and tales. The brothers Grimm had started collecting German folk tales early in the century. New collections of folk songs were published in Sweden and Denmark around 1815. In Norway, two friends, Peter Christen Asbjørnsen and Jørgen Moe, issued a first collection of *Norwegian Fairy Tales* in 1841 (*Asbjørnsen og Moe* still being beloved by today's children).

While others collected, Andersen created. He was a poet, playwright and more, best remembered for his fairy tales, about 150 of them in all, written and published consecutively over forty years, now to be found in more than a hundred languages across the world. A dominant theme is sentimental identification with outsiders and unfortunates. It is from him that we have the emperor's new clothes, the ugly duckling, the princess and the pea, the ice maiden, the little girl with the matches and other memorable metaphors. He is portrayed as a lovely, loving man, for example in a sculpture in New York's Central Park, where he sits surrounded by adoring children. He was internationally famous in life, and his fame has continued to grow.

His personal life was one of sublime tragedy, as in a Romantic script. He was a man of sincere religiosity which in his mind confined him to sexual celibacy. But not in his soul. He longed for love but solved, perhaps, his dilemma by loving women whose love he could not attain. He loved men as well, out of, he said, the femininity of his nature, in relationships that were for the times conspicuously intimate. His childhood had been violent and abusive. He wrote four autobiographies which later scholars deem to be, to put it tactfully, unreliable. Whether he, in a tortured emotional life, experienced the fulfilment of love, or sexual fulfilment with or without love is unknown.

Kierkegaard modelled himself on Socrates, walking his city and talking to those who would talk to him; but unlike his hero he also wrote – incessantly, frequently at night, often under pseudonyms – many works per year, short and long, some *very* long, in a career of about twenty years (he died aged forty-two). He wrote diaries, infused with ambiguity, for the benefit of posterity, which were later published in thirteen volumes. By the beginning of the twentieth century his works were appearing in German, French and other translations, and by mid-century he was an inescapable reference in philosophy and theology, expropriated as the father of existentialism.

Of a wealthy family, Kierkegaard lived as a gentleman of means, in luxurious accommodation with servants and secretaries. His father was a merchant and investor. Søren lived off his inheritance, paying for the publication of his books himself.

He was witty, good company, proud, self-absorbed, polemical, vain, vindictive. He rejected everything: the rationalism of his age, the value of theoretical knowledge, the writing of philosophy (he made himself a philosophical poet), his fellow Danish philosophers, who only wanted to be like the Germans, official religion and the State Church, which merely offered consolation, not inspiration, and reduced God and Jesus to references. He even questioned the meaning of philosophy. The problem, he thought, was not how to understand but how to make an existence, how to live in God and understand what God wants of one, how to love. Reason does not take the soul far; there must also be emotion, hurt and despair. In mid-life, in short order, his father died, he proposed to a beautiful girl, he broke down in distrust of himself and called off the engagement, by all of which he brought upon himself an anxiety and suffering that he carried for the rest of a life energised by tragedy. He lived and wrote, wrote his life.

There was something very small about that writing life. Copenhagen was provincial Europe. His intellectual community was a handful of pastors, professors and publishers. They went about insulting each other in petty disputes. His books were published in print runs of a few hundred. He was unappreciated by men beneath him who made themselves important. From his mid-thirties he was preoccupied with death, particularly his own, which he thought imminent.

But he wrote on, wanting, he thought, to stop, but on he went. He obsessed about his broken engagement and the lady he loved, and wrote works on marriage. He churned his theology around in discourse after discourse, not quite sermons but deliberations, raging against the official Church for having abandoned the truths of the New Testament. Absorbed by rage, he collapsed in the street and died in slow paralysis in hospital, of causes unknown, exhaustion perhaps. He spent the last of his father's money to pay for the publication of anti-Church pamphlets.

Thus he died a polemicist and an outcast. It was thought that his concern had been with the Church; it was not seen that it had been with life. He left writings that contained a philosophical programme which was not recognised at the time. For all he had written, he had not explained what he wanted to say. It was only later that others unearthed his radical provocation in the exercise of philosophy. The problem is how to be a human being in this world. He had hardly succeeded himself but he never stopped agonising over it. One can only say, what a life, what a *romantic* life!

Norwegian Romanticism was soft. There was the music: Bull and Grieg. They idealised the people's experiences.

There was art. Romantics romanticise nature. Norway is a landscape flush with natural drama. The artists found it and brought it to their canvases. Nature was by tradition dangerous and ugly. Now it was to be an experience of joy and pride. The master was Johan Christian Dahl (1788–1857), born in Bergen, educated in Dresden, a professor at the academy of art there teaching other budding Scandinavian artists. He brought to life big panoramas of high mountains, deep valleys, wild oceans and raging storms, occasionally people as well: a farm perched on a hillside under black mountains and a dark sky, shepherds tending their flocks on patches of grass between the rocks. It was monumental, and was so intended.

There was literature. Henrik Wergeland (1808–45) was the son of the vicar of Eidsvoll, who had been a delegate to the 1814 constitutional assembly. He was a dramatist, historian and editor, but above all a poet of the national. He was a polemicist, active in any debate he could get himself into and dedicated to arousing national awareness in people. He wanted the Norwegians to liberate themselves from cultural dependency on Denmark and political dependency on Sweden. He designated 17 May as a day of national celebration of independence and liberty. His artistic legacy has not in the main survived, but his personality has: he lives on as a trailblazing national hero. He fulfilled the Romantic ideal of dying young.

Bjørnstjerne Bjørnson (1832–1910), who won the Nobel Prize in Literature in 1903, was a poet, dramatist (he wrote at least twenty plays), novelist, journalist, theatre director and all-purpose intellectual, with a commanding presence across Scandinavia and throughout Europe. He was a follower of Wergeland at home, a combatant in the liberation of Slavic peoples and other minorities in Europe, and a front-page liberal presence in French newspapers during the Dreyfus affair.

His huge oeuvre spread over a career of fifty years and spans the arc from Romanticism to realism, from tales of farming life via historical dramas and on to contemporary criticism around capitalist ethics, the practice of press freedom, and public morality. There was no issue of public debate on which he did not have and express strong and loud opinions, not always consistent with each other.

His plays were performed in much of Europe in his time but have not survived, having been overpowered by the later Ibsen, who was more forthright in his realism. He is remembered today for the text of the Norwegian national anthem, 'Yes, We Love This Country', a song every bit as bombastic as its author. *Yes*, defiantly, we love this country, in spite of its hardships. 'For all that fathers have fought and mothers have wept, the Lord has gently provided that we won our right.'

There is something disturbing about this person and his oeuvre: his entitlement to being in the thick of it, his inability to keep silent, his always stepping in and never back. He just tried too hard in all things for most of them to last. He died in Paris in 1910, where he had been brought for medical treatment in the Danish king's private

train and was the guest of the French Republic, in a clinic set up in
the Hotel Wagram. He was desperate to live. There was more to say.
He was in Paris for an impossible miracle cure. His body was returned
to Copenhagen in the Norwegian king's carriage and from there to
Oslo on a ship of the Norwegian navy, to be received by a delegation
headed by the king and prime minister.

Swedish Romanticism went hard. The loss of Finland felt to Swedes like
an amputation of the realm. A new constitution was cobbled together,
opening up an uncertain future. Russia remained a dangerous threat.
Nationalists looked back to Sweden's imperial 'Age of Grandeur'.

Leading men formed a fraternity which they called the 'Gothic
Society'. Its purpose was to cultivate a made-up Gothic spirit of
freedom and manly courage, grounded in a mythology of an ancient
influence in Europe which had its source in the Swedish area.

Erik Gustaf Geijer (1783–1847), poet, philosopher, historian,
composer and educator, was the great intellectual force in Swedish
conservative nationalism (until he 'converted' to champion causes such
as press freedom and voting rights for women). He was Professor of
History at the University of Uppsala and at times the university's rector,
a co-founder of the Gothic Society and the first editor of its journal.

As a historian and philosopher he aimed to build grand theories on
the evolution of civilisations and economic systems, ambitions which
were never fulfilled. As a Swedish historian he was a medievalist and
a chronicler of eminent men and heroic pasts. In the first issue of the
Gothic Society's journal he published a poem, his most famous, 'The
Viking', which rehabilitated the old Norse and drew connecting lines
between past and present. He was in search of Swedish identity and
of that which was genuinely Swedish.

Esaias Tegnér (1782–1846), author, professor of classical Greek,
bishop, loved his fatherland, hated Russia and followed Oehlenschläger
in Romantic poetry. He was another member of the Gothic Society.
He admired great men, Napoleon very much so, welcomed the union
with Norway, held Karl Johan's conciliatory policy towards Russia in
contempt and dreamed of Scandinavianism. His writings were aggressively chauvinistic, frighteningly so to us now, but received with broad
admiration at the time. A poem of 1808, 'Warsong', was a cocktail of
war, Swedish courage and love of freedom. In a further poem, 'Svea'
(1811), he called for Finland to be reconquered and brought back

inside Sweden's borders. In 1818 he gave poetic voice to the celebration of Karl XII as hero king.

In Sweden as elsewhere Romanticism gave way to realism, but not without a fight. In 1845, Richard Dybeck, a scholar of Nordic runic writing, composed the poem that was to become Sweden's national anthem. It speaks, aggressively, to the nation: 'You ancient, you free, you mountainous north... I salute you, most beautiful land on earth... You are enthroned on memories of bygone great days, when the honour of your name flew across the world. I know that you are and remain what you were. *Yes*, I will live and I will die in the North.'*

Henrik Ibsen (1828–1906) remade his persona in midlife. As a young man he had been a hellraiser, later the perfect bourgeois, immaculately dressed in long black jacket and top hat, punctual, a man of habits, aloof. His appearance was against him: he was small, at 157 cm tall (wearing high heels to compensate), with an exceptionally large head in which sat two eerily asymmetrical eyes, hiding himself away behind forests of whiskers and hair. 'Poor great Ibsen,' said Grieg. 'He was not happy, his soul frozen to ice.' When he moved home to Oslo late in life, he would walk through town at a fixed time – people could set their watches by his coming and going – to the café in the Grand Hotel where he would sit at his own table with his customary drink in a glass the café had had engraved with his initials, alone, silent, unapproachable. He even changed his handwriting, making that too pedantic and void of person, his signature being thus: *Henrik R. Ibsen* He was given an honorary doctorate from the University of Uppsala and from then on insisted on being spoken to and about as Dr Ibsen.

He took to writing early, with little formal education behind him. It has remained a mystery from where he gained the insights he put into his dramas, having little life experience to draw on. He had an ability to be helped. Ole Bull plucked him at age twenty-three out of nowhere, took him to his theatre in Bergen and made him a man of the

---

* The Danish national anthem, by Oehlenschläger, is simple: 'There is a lovely land... of noble ladies, fair maidens and brisk swains.' It shows love of one's country, not as for the Norwegians in spite of hardship, or for the Swedes in awe of grandeur, but just because it is lovely. All national anthems are caricatures, these as well, but the similarities and differences between these three reveal cores of truth in the national characters.

stage. After five further years as an instructor in Oslo, he was given a State stipend to study theatre abroad and lived for twenty-seven years in Italy and Germany. When the stipend ran out, Bjørstjerne Bjørnson stepped in with more money. Out there he lived quietly, mostly seeking other Norwegians for company, to which he contributed silence and the reading of out-of-date editions of Norwegian newspapers. In 1891 he moved back to Norway, now famous and wealthy, with honours from Scandinavia and elsewhere, but not the Nobel.

The Ibsens had a single child, Sigurd. He studied in Germany and Italy, had a doctorate in public law, and lived his life in the shadow of his great father. In 1895, the University of Oslo decided to establish a professorship in sociology. Sigurd was the sole candidate. The university was apprehensive and invited him to give a series of lectures for the benefit of the appointment committee. Father Henrik lent them authority by attending in the front row. Having listened for a year, the committee turned him down (and the early professorship in sociology came to nothing). He did become prime minister in Stockholm (where Norway had a delegated prime minister at the court) and played a constructive role in the dissolution of the union in 1905, but being professor of sociology was beyond him.

Ibsen wrote his first play in 1850 and his final one, of twenty-five, in 1899 (a helpless banality called *When We Dead Awaken*). He started romantically with Norwegian history, but broke through to realism with *Brand* in 1866. A vicar is unbending in his demands on himself and others and brings life to ruin. Ibsen's standing rests mainly on his harsh social and psychological criticism. In *Pillars of Society*, a merchant in a small town is a fraud, willing to kill for his reputation, living a lie, but is saved in a sentimental ending. In *A Doll's House*, Nora breaks out of her stifling marriage and leaves home and children – to go where? In *Ghosts*, the next generation cannot escape the sins of the former one and they confront questions of suicide and euthanasia. In *An Enemy of the People*, Dr Stockmann discovers that the waters in the town baths are contaminated but is branded an 'enemy' by the town's 'compact majority'. In *The Wild Duck*, a family's life is grounded in lies and falls apart when the members find they cannot manage the truth. In *Hedda Gabler*, Hedda loves not her husband but his rival, whom she encourages to suicide, giving him a gun. When she discovers that his death was not heroic but a messy affair in a brothel, she shoots herself to escape disgrace. In *The Master Builder*, a young woman desires an older man and wins his confidence but not his love. Knowing that he suffers from fear of heights, she prompts him to climb the scaffolding of his ongoing building, from where he falls and dies, and the woman triumphs that he has now become hers.

Ibsen is said to be performed more than any other playwright in the world, save Shakespeare, of whom he is sometimes said to be an equal. The present author is ambivalent. His works deal with big issues but his characters are often less than sublime.

August Strindberg (1842–1912) was a strange man. Photos show a face with intense eyes, a weak chin and a mousy little mouth adorned with a wispy moustache, which he brushed upward, as he did his hair, pulling it up at the sides to form a halo. So here we have one of the world's greatest dramatists, busy day in and day out getting moustache and hair to defy the law of gravity. Munch painted his portrait, which he framed in a wild border with the ghost of a naked woman, and misspelled the name, leaving out the 'r'. Was that to suggest that there was something sinister about the man, something missing? Strindberg never forgave him.

He was enormously productive, writing plays, poetry, stories, novels, diaries, correspondence, journalism and scientific treatises on chemistry and the origins of language. His collected works run to fifty-four thick volumes, not including the correspondence. He was a painter, an experimental chemist fanatically out to prove 'the professors' wrong, an alchemist. He was preoccupied with spiritualism and the occult, a follower of Swedenborg. He was a militant misogynist, even by the standards of the day. He thought women did not and should not have joy from sexual intercourse and that their pleasure was in anticipation and childbirth. For a man to sleep with a woman was to 'own' her. On his wedding night with his third wife he 'owned' her twice, with little satisfaction for either of them.

He was a serial complainer: people were out to kill or persecute him in other ways (when they sought to get back money he owed), he suffered from a feeling of inferiority (so he said, but he never doubted his own powers), he was ill, his hands falling apart with sores and cuts (but his handwriting stable and elegant). He was the maker of myths about himself, a relentless self-promoter, fixated on being the centre of attention.

The prevailing view in Swedish and international Strindberg research was long of a mad genius whose life raged from crisis to crisis from which he wrenched autobiographical works, brutally exposing his own torment in an unforgiving search for truth. That view owned much to a book with the title *Inferno*, published in 1897, purportedly about his own life over four or five years, living in cheap hotels in Paris and Austria, in the course of which he is pulled down into Hell and escapes again in miraculous survival.

But in 1979 arrived the definitive biography, written by Olof Lagercrantz, grand master of Swedish letters. He found that there never was an inferno crisis. August Strindberg did write about a man called August Strindberg, but the Strindberg written about is different from Strindberg the author. The character did fall into Hell, but the author never lost his faculties. He was a searching and curious genius who used any means available to him, including his own life experiences, to experiment his way to understanding. His life, found Lagercrantz, was intense and troubled, but not irrational.

Strindberg is today remembered as a dramatist, one of the finest. His influence comes from the examples he set in psychological brutalism, the imperative that the dark workings of the soul should be explored and presented in all their horrors, with no holding back. In *The Father* (1887) a wife and husband fight over how to raise their daughter, in a shockingly naked exposé. The wife, with cool determination, manipulates the family doctor into thinking that the husband is mad and provokes the husband to violence, which is then taken as proof of his madness. She is victorious through strength, however much she is in the wrong. The husband is weak and driven to death, however much he is wronged. His best-known play, *Miss Julie* (1888), has the form of a realist tragedy. Julie is of noble family, Jean a servant in the house. They are alone in the kitchen while a dance is under way outside. Julie flirts with Jean in the mistaken belief that she, the woman, can be in control. That might have been the case in *The Father*, but only through deceit. Here, power favours the man. Jean seduces, or rapes, Julie. She has brought it on herself, and death, at Jean's instigation, is the only way out.

Strindberg died as he had lived, in uncompromising strife. Towards the end of his life, when he was back in Stockholm, still venerated (but not with a Nobel), the Swedish literati turned on him and tore asunder his legacy by insisting, as Munch had suggested, that there was something lacking in Sweden's greatest man of the theatre. He was a great dramatist but not a great spirit, dying in the midst of a vicious war of words, loved and despised in equal measure in his homeland.

Knut Hamsun (1859–1952), who won the Nobel Prize in Literature in 1920, was, like Ibsen, poorly educated and determined to write and make a success of himself. He changed the course of literature in Scandinavia and beyond with his use of language. His writing was lyrically beautiful, direct, simple and magical. He wrote in Norwegian but in such a way that his unique mastery of language is equally visible in translation.

He did it in subject matter. He explores the human psyche and the subconscious, following on from Ibsen and Strindberg; not in its entirety – some of his work is plain good storytelling – but his project was to penetrate the labyrinth of subjective existences.

His breakthrough came with the novel *Hunger* (1890), about the introspections of a young man who lives on the edge of existence in Oslo, as told by the man himself, on his mental experience and the workings of irrationalities and demons in his inner life. There are layers upon layers: we witness poverty, hunger, confusion, self-observation, incomprehension, bursts of understanding, articulation. *Mysteries* (1892) is a stream-of-consciousness novel in the mind of a man who goes ashore in a small town and spends his days in his hotel room or wandering in forests in monologue with himself, raging against the greats of his time (including Ibsen), seducing, or trying to, a woman who is engaged and may have left another suitor behind in suicide. He carries a bottle of poison and in the end kills himself.

With these books Hamsun was a literary sensation. Over the next sixty years he wrote and published constantly. Book after book recounts the comings and goings of tramps, vagabonds, charmers and merchants in the remote north of Norway. *Pan* and *Victoria* are delicately beautiful love stories. In 1917 came *The Growth of the Soil*, about a man and wife who clear land and over years of work create a substantial property, a book about the synthesis of man and earth. Another ten or so books followed. As did wealth and fame.

The author of the most generous and lovely prose and storytelling, Hamsun was in his own life a monster. He engaged in public and literary debate, eagerly, aggressively and without restraint in meanness, back-stabbing and offensive language. He was a tyrant to his wives and children. He was generous and willingly helpful – not atypical of bullies – but fundamentally raw. He was a committed reactionary, against modernisation, against industry, against city life, against democracy. He idealised the soil and was himself a model farmer (and in that capacity a self-contradicting pioneer of modern technology). He was pro-German and anti-British and sided with the Germans in the First World War.

He went with German Nazism. In the Second World War he supported the German occupation of his own country and encouraged friendship with the occupiers. He never recanted. On Hitler's death he wrote an obituary in praise of him: 'We his followers bow our heads.'

Edvard Munch (1863–1944) was a kindred spirit of Strindberg. His paintings explore the dark human sentiments of anxiety, fear, jealousy, pity and hatred. The two of them have no doubt done more than any others to create the stereotype of Scandinavian life as dour, gloomy and angst-ridden (later helped by the film-maker Ingmar Bergman, as worthy an heir as any of Strindberg's in laying bare the traumatic workings of the human psyche).

Munch was artistically in a different universe from the Romantics, different both in subject matter and style. Dahl's tableaux depicted nature, with people, to the extent that they were included, as tiny still-life set pieces. Munch showed us people with less background, in a way that looked into their inner lives. An ill girl is reduced to translucence. Frightened women and men stare at the onlooker with wide open eyes through which their torments are revealed. In Dahl, no matter how vast the landscape, every leaf and straw of grass is formed in meticulous detail. In Munch, paint is applied in simple brushwork only to what is essential. In his oeuvre, we see that Romanticism had to pass and realism prevail.

Munch lived much of his formative life in Germany and France. It took him twenty years to win recognition, longer in his home country where he was only accepted when he came back with evidence of his success in Germany. From the turn of the century his position was secure, artistically and financially. He had struggled, and cultivated a mythology around it. He was, perhaps, mentally unstable, at least enough to maintain that he lived on the edge of madness. He did not deal well with women, whom he feared. The war between the sexes is recurrent in his work. A love affair with the bohemian Tulla

Larsen ended in tragedy, or farce, depending on how you see it. She wanted marriage; he, perhaps, promised it but was always evasive. A final encounter involved a gunshot and for him the loss of a fingertip. Munch made much of the betrayal and got out of it three dramatic paintings with much blood, *On the Operating Table* (1903), *The Killer* (1906) and, no less, *Death of Marat* (1907), plus various portraits of Tulla and self-portraits under her influence.

Munch held on to much of his work and left his collection, 5,000 paintings and drawings and 20,000 prints, to the city of Oslo. It built the Munch Museum, which the social democratic administration of the city sited in the eastern working-class area in a beautiful park landscape. It was small and the displays were rotated; if you made a habit of visiting, there was always something new to experience. A new museum was opened in 2021, as part of the richer city's modernistic building boom, in a heavy-set high-rise with the architectural twist of a sideways kink two-thirds up. Compared to the old museum, the new one is imposing. The city is showing off Munch to show off itself.

MUNCH FOR THE STUDENTS

Rolf Stenersen – investor, sportsman, author – compiled a vast collection of works by his friend Munch which he donated to the city of Oslo but continued to manage until he died in 1978. In 1952, Oslo built an accommodation complex for the Winter Olympics, to be used thereafter as student residences and a summer hotel. Stenersen chaired the building committee and lent most of the original Munch works from his collection – paintings, drawings and prints – to be hung in student and common rooms. Pictures started to disappear, at the rate of about one a year. In 1972, an Oslo newspaper arranged a stunt theft of a work then valued at NOK 100,000, uninsured it turned out. The next year, a major work disappeared in a real theft. The university decided to take down the collection and put it in safe museum custody. That was the end of two blissfully naïve decades in which undergraduates at the University of Oslo lived with original Munchs on their walls.

*

Class was not much of a theme in Golden Age art and literature; it was a middle-class affair. But gender was. In *A Doll's House*, Ibsen laid bare the torment for women in the repressive stricture of marriage, and equally of men in their inability to comprehend the institutional brutality of which they were a part. Strindberg wasted much of his energy in rebuffing any notion of women's equal dignity. They were both responding to forceful women who demanded presence and respect. There were many of them. They were influential. Writing was one thing women of ability could do. But not without difficulty: many published anonymously or under male pseudonyms. They were not all radical, but even to insist on being heard was to take a feminist stand. Women writers exercised a decisive influence in lifting Scandinavian creativity out of the limited world of Romanticism and into the universality of realism.

Women had many demands – economic equality, inheritance rights, voting rights – but above all they confronted the institution of marriage. That met with resistance. The Swedish author Victoria Benedictsson (1850–88) lived with a Danish lover, in defiance of her marriage. That lover was Georg Brandes, Scandinavia's leading literary critic and a champion of radical liberalism (the translator of John Stuart Mill's *The Subjection of Women* into Danish). She published under a male name and wrote realistic stories of daily life, informed by her own unhappy experience of bourgeois marriage. In her second book, *Money* (1885), her protagonist, like Ibsen's Nora, breaks away to make for herself a life of self-reliance. But in her next novel, *Mrs Marianne* (1887), the protagonist rejects free love for marriage. Brandes belittled the author, his partner. It was too much: her life ended in suicide and he was forced into exile.

Camilla Collett (1813–95) was the sister of Henrik Wergeland, he being the Romantic, she the realist. She was a diarist and essayist and the author of a single novel, published anonymously, *The District Governor's Daughters* (1854–55). One sister marries for love, unhappily. The other sister takes fright and marries sensibly, also unhappily. Either way, there is no space for women to shape their existence. Marriage is not a start but the end. Camilla won recognition and was awarded an 'author's salary' from the *Storting*, at half the male rate.

Amalie Skram (1846–1905) grew up in a working-class family in Bergen. She was pressured into a socially advantageous marriage at eighteen, and terrified by the shock of sexual expectations. She published around thirty novels, plays and collections, radically critical and pessimistic, dealing with sexuality in a way that was unprecedentedly realistic at the time.

Divorce was initially denied her, out of fear of scandal, and she had her first experience of confinement in a mental asylum. She moved to Copenhagen and married the Danish author Erik Skram, another marriage that failed. Further episodes in mental asylums followed. Her debut novel, *Constance Ring*, was published in 1885 in Oslo at her own expense, having been rejected in Copenhagen as 'excessively realistic'. Two novels drew on her experience of mental illness and the treatment thereof, and laid bare the abuse of power by doctors over patients. They were shocking and scandalous, resulting in the resignation of the medical director of mental care at Copenhagen Hospital, until then a pillar of the Copenhagen establishment.

Fredrika Bremer (1801–65) was of upper-class Stockholm stock. She rebelled early against the narrow expectations on her, rejected marriage and settled into a life of writing, publishing some twenty novels, collections and travelogues, soon under her own name. She wrote of daily and family life, specifically women's experiences, not radically but perceptively. Her works were popular and much read throughout Scandinavia, being translated in her own time into many languages. She used her popularity and upper-class authority to champion economic autonomy, education and voting rights for women, but also general social causes such as orphan care and prison reform.

Sophie von Knorring (1797–1848) and Emilie Flygare-Carlén (1807–92) were, along with Bremer, dominant voices in Swedish realist literature, productive, innovative, much read, much translated. Von Knorring's life was one of genteel poverty. She wrote of unfulfilled love and the impossible dilemma, for women, of love and duty, in which love was the inevitable sacrifice. Flygare-Carlén, of a provincial middle-class family, took to writing in early widowhood as a way of providing for herself and family, remarried upward into Stockholm's literary élite and published under her own name. She was in her time Sweden's most-read and most-translated author. She wrote family dramas of provincial middle-class life with perceptive analyses of women's limited possibilities, which were well received but also harshly criticised for immorality. The three women were rivals, von Knorring being criticised by both Bremer and Flygare-Carlén for moral frivolity.

Thomasine Gyllembourg (1773–1856) wrote novels and plays about

Danish family and daily life. She was married at sixteen, to her private tutor, who neglected her and their family for a literary life, won a divorce in which she sacrificed custody of her son, married again at twenty-eight, was widowed at forty-two, and started to write at fifty-three to provide material for a journal her son had started. She was instrumental in drawing Danish literature out of Romanticism, opening up the intimacy of family life to literary treatment, and giving identity to the lives of women. She was among the most-read Danish authors of her time, although she published anonymously and was only identified as the author of her works posthumously when they were published in a collected edition of twelve volumes.

Mathilde Fibiger (1830–1872) published her first novel at age twenty and was the first explicitly feminist Danish author, her project being straightforwardly 'the emancipation of women'. Two further novels dealt with patriarchy, extramarital love, incest and suicide, in an uncompromising criticism of prevailing gender relations and sexual norms. They met with vicious criticism, of such force that she gave up writing. She later worked as a translator and telegraph operator, with the minor victory of being the only woman employed in that capacity by the State Telegraph. Three years before her early death she published again, a brief and sensitive story about the domestic life of a single working woman.

A new generation of female authors followed Fibiger in explicit feminism. In Sweden, Ellen Key (1849–1926) wrote non-fiction on feminism, sexuality and child-rearing. Anne Charlotte Leffler (1849–92) authored a string of feminist plays, performed to acclaim in Sweden, Germany and Britain. Alfhild Agrell (1849–1923) was likewise a feminist playwright, for a long time successful but later neglected even in her lifetime, who died in lonesome poverty.

The Golden Age wave of women in literature, and the Golden Age itself, culminated with Selma Lagerlöf (1858–1940), who won the Nobel Prize in Literature in 1909, and Sigrid Undset (1882–1949), who also won the Nobel Prize, in 1928. Lagerlöf grew up in provincial Sweden a sickly child, withdrawn and bookish. She never married, and her few friendships were with women. Her father had been moderately affluent but was forced in financial distress to sell the family estate, which Selma later bought back with the Nobel Prize money and there lived out her life. She trained and worked as a schoolteacher until she could support herself from her writing from the age of about thirty-five. She was productive, world-famous and the recipient of all nature of honours, lived quietly and uneventfully, and died peacefully at age eighty-two.

Her debut novel, *The Saga of Gösta Berling* (1891), is a raunchy fantasy about Swedish more or less upper-class rural life that spins around the adventures of priests, poets, charmers and revellers in the style of magic realism. It was an instant success and remains a classic in Swedish literature.

In *Jerusalem* (1901–02), a novel based on real events, a group of people in a remote parish are gripped by religious fervour and moved to sell property and possessions to join an American community in Jerusalem to await Jesus's return and the final judgement, with disastrous results for both the participants and the community they left behind. (The then Jerusalem community has by twists and turns evolved into the city's American Colony Hotel.)

In *The Wondrous Adventures of Nils Holgersson* (1906–07), a boy is shrunk to the size of a thumb and flies on the back of a goose through Sweden's geography and history. The book was commissioned by the National Association of Teachers for schooling purposes and is the most fantastic schoolbook ever devised.

Sigrid Undset grew up an orphan and from age seventeen supported herself as a secretary. At thirty she married the painter Anders Svarstad. He had three children from a previous marriage and they had a further three children together, one a daughter with severe disabilities. The marriage was unhappy; they separated after seven years and later divorced. Sigrid acquired the property of Bjerkebæk in Lillehammer, where she settled with their children. She converted to Catholicism in 1924 and three years later entered the Dominican Order, but not residentially. In 1940, at the German invasion, she fled Norway and made her way to America (across the Soviet Union and the Pacific), from where she worked for the Norwegian national cause for the duration of the war. The two giants of Norwegian literature, then, herself and Knut Hamsun, were on opposite sides and bitter enemies. After the war she returned to Bjerkebæk, where she died in 1949.*

---

* When Aleksandr Solzhenitsyn was deported from the Soviet Union in 1974, the Norwegian government offered him Bjerkebæk as a residence and workplace, which he however found inadequate for his needs. It is today the Sigrid Undset Museum and Cultural Centre.

She took her inspiration from the Norse Saga literature and Norwegian medieval history but had her debut with the novel *Jenny*, a partly autobiographical story of unsuccessful love. Her masterpiece is the trilogy *Kristin Lavransdatter* (1920–22). The story is set in the early 1300s. Kristin is the daughter of a local chief in Gudbrandsdalen and the books follow her from childhood to widowhood and death. She is promised to a suitable husband but falls in love with the dashing Erlend and prevails over her parents. The marriage does not work. Erlend is easy-living and leaves Kristin responsible for the farm and children. She is riven by guilt, irrational female guilt. She joins a monastery and seeks forgiveness by helping local people against the ravages of the Big Death, but herself dies of the plague aged fifty.

The combination of nationalism and Romanticism is a powerful brew, intoxicating. It led dreamers to see a virtuous purity in 'the Nordic' and the Norse peoples as in some way genuine stock in the European menagerie, more direct descendants of past cultures than other peoples of gradually diluted heritage. Although realism would overtake Romanticism, Norse chauvinism was not stamped out. The Goths in pre-medieval Europe were of Norse origin. The Vikings were bearers of Norse prowess. Sweden was a superpower. The tall, blond Scandinavian became a much-cultivated stereotype.

The adoration of the Nordic spread beyond the north. Into the twentieth century, until the Second World War, Germany was, as seen from the north, the cultural metropole. The idea of a shared Germanic-Norse heritage exercised a strong attraction in Germany itself. It is recognisable in the operatic world of Richard Wagner, in which Nordic mythology and German nationalism coalesce with frightening force. Among many eminent Wagner interpreters, two Nordic sopranos, from Norway Kirsten Flagstad (1895–1962) and from Sweden Birgit Nilsson (1918–2005), have represented that mythological world in ways that inspire both awe for artistic brilliance and shivers of fear of Germanic force. Nordic Romanticism carried through, in a perverted form, into German Nazi Fascism and the idea of the pure Arian-Nordic race, in a way that partially explains the attraction of that ideology to many Scandinavians. In 1939, a group of Swedish organisations presented Hitler, on his fiftieth birthday, with a bust of Karl XII, whom Hitler admired as a protector of European civilisation against Russian barbarism.

Aberration I: The Schleswig-Holstein question

Since the Middle Ages, Danish kings had laid claim to the territories that make up the borderlands with Germany, south towards today's Hamburg. While Norway became defined as a province within the kingdom, the duchies were constitutionally autonomous under the Danish Crown. Schleswig was a Danish duchy, Holstein a German one. In Schleswig, therefore, the King of Denmark, as Duke of Schleswig, was under allegiance to himself. But in Holstein he was a German duke under allegiance to the Holy Roman Emperor and subject to German law.

This confused confederation of Denmark, Schleswig and Holstein might have been tenable in the age of royal absolutism, but not in a new age of nationalism. Danes wanted more from the duchies: they wanted them Danish.

When the Holy Roman Empire ceased to exist in 1806, there were movements, including from Napoleon, to incorporate the duchies into the Danish kingdom. The Danish government issued an ambiguous resolution to that effect, which only served to stimulate Schleswig-Holstein chauvinism in Denmark and anti-Danish sentiments in the duchies. When the German Confederation came into being in 1815, Holstein was reconfirmed with the contradiction of being German and in the hands of the King of Denmark.

Germany was moving towards unification. A first attempt was made by the confederate *Reichstag* in Frankfurt in 1848. That failed on Prussian resistance (because the draft constitution did not make Prussia uncontested topdog), but the writing was on the wall. The Germans in Schleswig and Holstein rose in revolt against Danish oppression. The Danish government sent army and naval forces into Schleswig. Prussia mobilised in favour of its German brethren and sent an army to occupy Jylland. Denmark had its first of two Prussian wars.

The Prussians withdrew from Denmark proper and retreated into Schleswig. Sweden and Norway sent supporting troops to Denmark. Britain offered mediation. Denmark and Prussia agreed a truce which was, however, ignored in the duchies, including by the occupying Prussian forces. The German factions in Schleswig and Holstein adopted a democratic constitution for an independent state of Schleswig-Holstein. This was in September 1848. War broke out once more in April 1849. German troops moved back into Jylland again, Britain offered mediation again, there was again a truce.

Under international pressure, Prussia and Denmark agreed a peace in July 1850. But nothing was settled for the duchies. War recommenced, but now without Prussia. The Schleswig-Holsteiners could not on their own withstand the superior Danish force. The fiction of an independent Schleswig-Holstein collapsed.

Britain yet again offered mediation.* In the Treaty of London of 1852 the status quo was restored, under the guarantee of the major European powers. The duchies were reconfirmed as independent entities in a confederation with Denmark under the Danish Crown. (Technically, the deal included a third duchy of Lauenburg as a subduchy within Holstein, but set that aside; there are complications enough already.) However, the renewed confederation required a fix. Frederik VII of Denmark, king from 1848, was childless and it was known that he was unable to father children. As things stood, the line of inheritance to Holstein in the Danish royal family would die out with him. It was therefore necessary to secure the Danish inheritance for whomever would succeed Frederik. This was achieved in the treaty by other potential heirs renouncing their claims – or achieved after a fashion: when matters came to a head again, it was partly because the waters were muddied by competing German claims in the duchies being put back on the table.

It was only to kick the can down the road. What could not be restored was harmony. Denmark had adopted a new constitution, liberal and democratic, which, however, did not apply to the duchies. The King of Denmark was supposed to be in charge democratically in Denmark and autocratically in Schleswig and Holstein.

In an attempt to make the impossible possible, a joint *Rigsråd* was established for Danish duchy affairs to work side by side with the Danish Parliament. But that turned the governing of conflicting domains into a hopeless circus of national and democratic conflicts along confusingly criss-crossing dimensions. The Holsteiners subverted the situation in a string of complaints in Germany against Danish

---

* Initially under the guidance of Lord Palmerston as British foreign minister, later prime minister, who, when asked by Queen Victoria to explain the Schleswig-Holstein question, famously replied that only three people had ever understood it and that one was dead, one had gone mad and he himself had forgotten.

abuses, resulting in various German threats and provocations against Denmark.

Fast-forward to 1863. Denmark was rewriting its constitution. The revisions would incorporate Schleswig into the Kingdom of Denmark and impose a joint law of succession for 'the entire Danish monarchy', including Holstein. That would be contrary to the Treaty of London, at least in the Prussians' understanding, overturning the status quo and, to boot, introducing the possibility, at least in theory, at least as the Prussians chose to see it, of a female successor in Holstein, which would be contrary to German law.

In Copenhagen, the king and his government let go of any grip on reality and decided to take on Prussia in war. After 1850, Danes, including the king, including military leaders, including nationalistic dreamers such as Hans Christian Andersen, had started to cultivate a fairy tale about how their heroism had defeated the Germans. They persuaded themselves to believe that they would have Swedish–Norwegian support, including military support, in a new confrontation, and that Britain would be at their side. As Gudfred a thousand years ago thought he could stand up to Charlemagne, Frederik thought himself equal to Bismarck.

It spun out of control. The Danes decided to go ahead and incorporate Schleswig into the kingdom, knowing that this would be seen as a declaration of war on Prussia, but not understanding that it was the provocation Bismarck wanted. Then, on 15 November, the king died aged fifty-five and total confusion broke out in the Danish leadership. The new king, Christian IX, wanted to pull back from the abyss but his hand was forced. It became clear that Denmark would have support from nowhere. The government in Copenhagen fell. No one was in charge of anything and there was no one to see sense.

Frederik had been a man of the people, never happier than when travelling the country and meeting and conversing with common folk. In return they gave him sincere love, and continued to do so in spite of his visible derangement.

There was something wrong with the man; there was something wrong emotionally and sexually. He was sterile, the result, historians think, of generations of royal inbreeding. An arranged marriage to a cousin failed and ended in divorce. An enforced marriage to a German princess failed and ended in divorce. He had a mistress, Louise Rasmussen, a Copenhagen social climber who probably already had a lover, one Carl Berling, a book printer and publisher and a friend of Frederik's. Once king, Frederik insisted on marrying Louise, who became Baroness Danner and moved into the royal palace with Berling, where the three of them formed a *ménage à trois*. Louise and Carl established themselves as the king's trusted advisors and turned the court into a comedy of intrigue.

There was something wrong intellectually. Frederik was unable to concentrate, unable to follow a line of logic, unable to analyse, prone to fits of fantasy, feeble in decision-making. He had a habit of telling tall tales of heroic deeds about himself, including in military battles, tales he probably believed. He had, he would boast, been on the battlefield in the First Prussian-Danish war and had personally turned back the Prussian assault. Following that first Prussian war, and during the years leading up to the second and disastrous one of 1864, policymaking in Copenhagen was in cloud-cuckoo-land disarray; the country was being sleepwalked into slaughter. The blame needs to be shared broadly in the civilian and military leadership, but a good portion falls on a king who chose not to see what he did not want to see and to believe that a country under his inspired protection could stand up to any superior force.

Bismarck declared that the prevailing treaty had been violated and gave Denmark an ultimatum to reverse its Schleswig decision. The Second Prussian-Danish War was on. It was only a pretext. Bismarck had no interest in any treaty or status quo. His objective was German unification. This was the first of three wars he used to settle the borders. That he did to the north by annexing both Holstein and Schleswig, which were then lost to Denmark. His next wars were in 1866 against Austria (which had assisted him in the war on Denmark) and in 1870–71 against France.

The Danes had failed to prepare. There were no proper plans either for mobilisation or for the execution of war. There was confusion and disagreement in Copenhagen and between political and military leaders. The army was underequipped and under untrained command. Delusion prevailed: the old *Danevirke* would stop any Prussian advance, other powers would support and help Denmark. The Prussians on their side had been planning for months, under the leadership of Marshal Helmuth von Moltke (who would also lead the Prussians to victory over France in 1870–71 and who had his first military education in Denmark, where his father had served as an officer in happier times). The Prussian army marched north and occupied much of Jylland; it was the old story of undefendable Denmark yet again. The Danes dug in at a fortification in mid-Schleswig where on 18 April they were overrun in an epic bloodbath.

A peace conference was convened in London at which the Danes once more mismanaged their affairs. They now had sympathy, certainly from Britain, and could have come away with the northern part of Schleswig, but insisted on their right to all of it. The peace conference collapsed and Prussian forces marched up through Schleswig again. A peace was forced on Denmark in which Holstein and all of Schleswig were lost.

The Danish Crown had once held Denmark itself, the Skåne and western lands in Sweden, the duchies, various other German possessions, Norway, the islands of the Faroes, Iceland and Greenland. In the Thirty Years War, the German possessions were lost. In 1659, Skåne was lost, and in 1814 Norway. Now the duchies were lost. What remained was little Denmark and the islands. In 1920, in the settlement after the First World War, the German–Danish border was pushed south to run through the middle of Schleswig, the border the Danes could have had in 1864 and the one they still have today.

A casualty of the Second Prussian-Danish War, in addition to the loss to Denmark of Schleswig and Holstein, was a romantic package of ideas that had been promoted as 'Scandinavianism'. Communications had been improving, first with steamships coming into regular traffic and even more with railways. That meant more contact and interaction between the peoples of the three countries, and with more interaction came more cooperation. There was scientific collaboration. There was student interaction, in regular all-Scandinavian student meetings and conventions. The cultivation of the national in each country encouraged awareness of the Norse heritage and joint histories. They had enemies, Denmark in Germany, Sweden in Russia. There was a sentiment that these peoples should stand together. They looked back to the time of Margrete and the union she had forged. Liberals in Sweden and Denmark sought inspiration in the Norwegian constitution. Scandinavian unity was a matter of warm enthusiasm in academic and literary circles. King Oscar I of Sweden had fantasised about a 'Greater Scandinavia' under his own hand.

When Prussia attacked Denmark in 1864, the King of Sweden, now

Karl XV, promised the Danes military support but did so behind the backs of both his Swedish and Norwegian governments. They resisted and Denmark was left to itself. There was probably no other way. The war was provoked by madness in Copenhagen and the Danish position against Prussia was hopeless. Scandinavianism was put to the test – and failed. There was, once you scratched the surface, no real force of brotherly solidarity, no enthusiasm except in words, no will for action and sacrifice. It turned out to have been largely a student infatuation in which others took little interest and which had little practical meaning.

Aberration II: Emigration

We now know the numbers. At the beginning of the nineteenth century, the Swedish population was 2.4 million, the Danish and Norwegian ones 926,000 and 884,000 respectively. Sweden was big brother. Over the century the populations grew steadily, to 5.1 million in Sweden and 2.5 and 2.2 million in Denmark and Norway. For centuries, population numbers had fluctuated or increased slowly; now they shot up explosively. This was caused not by more births but by reduced mortality. Children lived longer and adults died less early.

All these new people needed somewhere and somehow to live. They came out of rural populations, most of which stayed rural. There was improvement, if in ups and downs, in agricultural output. There were more autonomous farms and better productivity.

But there was also the pressure of poverty. Many had no option other than a life of smallholding or work as day labourers. The 'life-threatening brutality of class division and poverty in rural Scandinavia was not softened in spite of economic growth'. Population growth produced workers to advance industrialisation by keeping wages low. Living conditions for town and city workers, and in the emerging industries, were raw and exploitative. There was intense awareness of the problem of poverty, and much concern, but less understanding. The governments appointed commissions of study. They were better in observation than in explanation. A Norwegian poverty commission of 1850 saw that even if the country was richer, the 'conditions of the poor had worsened in that the divide between them and the more prosperous had widened', but had no way of solving the problem it had identified. The Scandinavians were to be masters of redistribution, but that had to wait another century. For now there was neither will – the prevailing understanding of property rights was rigid – nor ability – there was not much public money to work with.

For many, the way out of misery was to move. Some moved internally, some to districts with better agricultural prospects, some to towns and cities where there were jobs to be found. Some followed infrastructural works, such as the building of canals and railways, some back and forth across state borders. In Sweden and Norway, people moved north where there was a sparser population and land to be had.

These were the poorest of the migrants. Others moved out in the hope of better lives in lands of more promise, above all North America. These were the less poor, often younger farmers' sons, who could raise the fare. City migrants saved enough to move abroad.

The early emigration was religious. A group of fifty-two people set off from Stavanger in Norway in 1825, in a small sloop called *Restaurationen*, arriving after a crossing of three months, with the addition of a baby born in transit. They were mostly Quakers and it was the desire for religious freedom that drove them. They sold the sloop and tried to settle on Lake Ontario in upstate New York, but their community fell apart and most of them moved on west, into what were to be the main areas of Scandinavian immigration.

In 1846, a Swedish prophet by name Erik Jansson led a group of at least 1,500 followers, many children, across to America to establish a religious colony in Illinois, which they called Bishop Hill. Property was communal, women and men lived separately, children were raised jointly. The commune prospered through discipline and hard work, but was doomed. Two ships had gone down in the passage, with at least 100 passengers. Another hundred died of disease. Jansson turned out to be a tyrant and was shot dead in the colony's second year when he tried to prevent a young woman from leaving. His replacement squandered the colony's money in failed investments. The colonists fell out with each other and moved on. After fifteen years, Bishop Hill was no more.

Mormon missionaries arrived in Denmark from Salt Lake City in 1848, attracting a following among the poor, encouraging thousands to the freedom of their New World Zion. Their arrival proved less free than they may have hoped for. They were in debt to the Church that had paid their passage, many working for years to pay back their dues. One particular Danish migration in a quest for liberty was from Schleswig after the defeat of 1864: a third of the Danish population in the duchy left for America to escape the pressure of Germanification.

The driver of mass emigration, however, was simple: poverty at home and the promise of land over there. American authorities campaigned for migrants across Europe. Shipping companies and entrepreneurs promoted emigration and arranged finance and passage.

From 1850 to 1920, 1.2 million Swedes emigrated to North America and more than half a million Norwegians, the equivalent of about a quarter of the populations. The emigration from Denmark was less, in the order of a tenth of the population.

In America the immigrants dispersed into many activities, some in industrial work and laying the railways, some as longshoremen or sailors on American ships – there was for a long time a sizeable Scandinavian colony in Brooklyn, New York. Some went into business, some doing well. Some became preachers, some socialist and union organisers, with variable success. Many ended in failure, poverty and early death, others gave up and returned home. One of the failures was the young Knut Hamsun. Back in Norway, he published a mean-spirited pamphlet about moral degeneration among the Americans. He never forgave them. When they later did not take to his books as did the Germans and Russians, it was their own fault.

JOE HILL

Joel Emmanuel Hägglund was born in Gävle in northern Sweden in 1879. He grew up in child labour and had little formal education. In 1902, he left for America, where he travelled the country in a rough existence as a labourer. The Industrial Workers of the World, the IWW, was founded in 1905 as a radical labour union organisation. Joel joined as an agitator and organiser. He knew about song and music from his upbringing in Sweden and made himself a songwriter for the union movement. His songs were widely adopted and he himself became well known in the organisation; the best-known one is 'The Preacher and the Slave', in which he coined the phrase 'you'll get pie in the sky when you die'.

In 1914, he was charged with murder during an armed robbery in Salt

Lake City, probably on a trumped-up charge, although he was treated for a gun wound the same evening. He was found guilty, sentenced to death and executed on 19 November 1915.

The trial attracted widespread attention across America and internationally and made Joe Hill a global celebrity. Stories about him proliferated, making him a heroic martyr of the labour movement. He had unionised across the country. He had fought the police, been repeatedly beaten up and thrown in jail and changed his name on the run from the law. He had participated in rebellions in Mexico and recruited American volunteers for the struggle. At the trial in Salt Lake City, he held back on establishing an alibi for himself to protect the honour of a lady over whom he might have been involved in a fight in which his gun wound could have been inflicted. After the sentence was passed he was entitled to choose the mode of execution: 'It will be by shooting, I've been shot before and I can take it.' The day before the execution he cabled the head of the IWW: 'Farewell Bill. Don't waste time mourning. Organise.'

The songwriter is today remembered in a song about himself, now an anthem of radical unionism. 'The Ballad of Joe Hill' was written ten years after his death, with words by Alfred Hayes and music by Earl Robinson. It has been recorded by innumerable artists, from Paul Robeson via Joan Baez to Bruce Springsteen:

> I dreamed I saw Joe Hill last night,
> Alive as you and me.
> Says I, But Joe, you're ten years dead.
> I never died, said he,
> I never died, said he.

But most made their way to the Midwest – Minnesota, Wisconsin, the Dakotas, some to Canada – where they could take land and farm. Early migrants sent letters home, some warning friends not to follow, but most in double praise of opportunity and freedom. They clustered in communities that remained Scandinavian for generations. When our family lived in America in the 1950s, we visited kin who were farming in Montana and the Dakotas, the first visitors from the old country. Third generations were still speaking Norwegian, although with Americanisation. ('The river', in Norwegian *elven*, had become 'river'n', a bridge, *broen* in Norwegian, 'bridge'n'.) The Sunday service was still Lutheran, still in Norwegian.

Mass emigration was a traumatic experience on both sides of the crossing. Many died before even making it to the promised land. Families broke up. Those who left and those who stayed were not likely to see each other again. Many a girlfriend or fiancée or wife, who were supposed to follow, found themselves abandoned, their children left fatherless. It was one thing to take land, quite another to cultivate it. The start was invariably hard, and many lived in huts of planks and mud through the first winters. They came from lands of mountains and forests; the flat, barren prairies were alien to the eye and the soul.

Countries and cultures in the grip of national romanticism bled, in the interest of survival, streams of their own people, their best and most able youth. There was much backlash from above against emigration and campaigning to resist it, but to little effect. It went on as long as economic imperatives dictated.

The emigration experience has been explored in a literature which is among the most powerful in all of the Scandinavian oeuvre. Ole Rølvåg (Rolvaag) was brought from Norway to South Dakota at age twenty by an uncle who had emigrated earlier. Supporting himself as a farmhand, he studied and after ten years graduated from the 'Norwegian' St Olaf College in Minnesota, where he subsequently had a distinguished teaching career. He wrote in Norwegian, describing the early struggles of settlers, his most acclaimed book being *Giants in the Earth* (1923–27) with themes of hardship, loneliness, separation and the carving-out of a meaningful living in a hostile setting. (His son, Karl Rolvaag, was governor of Minnesota in the 1960s on a Democratic-Farmer-Labor Party ticket, and later served as American Ambassador to Iceland.)

A generation later, Vilhelm Moberg, the Swedish author, journalist and radical public intellectual, published a four-volume series of novels under the title *The Emigrants* (1949–59), which stand as the crowning achievement in Scandinavian emigration literature and a monument in Swedish literature generally. They follow a group of kin from leaving rural Sweden at the dawn of mass migration to their new life in Minnesota, driven by a combination of poverty and religious intolerance. The main characters are Karl-Oskar and Kristina, who set off with three small children, leaving behind a fourth child who died from social neglect. The story follows the party through their crossing to New York and into their existential struggle in Minnesota. It chronicles the drama of America seen through immigrant eyes, the California gold rush, the Civil and Indian Wars, and on to Carl-Oskar and Kristina's late life, the final novel being entitled *The Last Letter Home*. The director Jan Troell later compressed the stories into two epic films, *The Emigrants* and *The New Land*, with Max von Sydow and Liv Ullmann in the leading roles.

Innovation III: Popular movements

From the early 1800s, religious awakenings swept across Scandinavia. Lay preachers held house meetings, wandering the lands, inspiring 'groups' and 'societies' where they travelled. As previously, the followers wanted a conservative and direct religiosity under their own management. They did not want the State Church's modern theology, nor its new teaching and psalm books. Some of them allowed uneducated men to be teachers and women to preach. Quakers and Catholics did not acknowledge the authority of the State Church.

It was at first not a matter of organisation in any formal meaning or of political activism, but was nevertheless driven by pressure from below, outside official control. The small-folks had been expected to obey; now they were coming together and making themselves felt. The State reacted to stem the tide. In Denmark, the prohibition of 1741 against free congregations still applied and was put to work again. Meetings were broken up and preachers confined.

But the awakenings flourished. Common people were brought out of slumber and the idea took hold that they could engage and participate. As that mentality gripped people's imaginations, 'causes' presented themselves for which they could put their energies to work. These causes mobilised not only involvement but also disagreement. They gave rise to conflicts and battles and from there to the creativities that are born out of deliberations over the big issues of the day.

The original cause was *faith* itself and the true interpretation thereof. But the awakening was also a broader clash of cultures, between high and low in both religious and social terms, that was to have a constant presence through the century and beyond. Education was spreading. That brought knowledge with it, down the social ladder and into remote areas. People could get together and read the texts. It also brought a new class of officialdom, the teachers. They were not impressive, did not have all that much education themselves and did not always know how to teach. But they were nevertheless bearers of learning, and because of their modest circumstances leaders, if that is not too grand a word, with closeness to the common folk.

The long-term trend was towards toleration. Laws of congregational freedom were passed in Norway in 1845 and in Sweden in 1873. In 1851, the constitutional ban in Norway on Jews entering the realm was removed. Catholics, Methodists and Baptists preached and missioned, Mormons likewise. Most of these movements, except for the Catholics, attracted followers from among the poor and the working class; there was an element of early social–political organisation to it.

From faith and conviction the road was short and direct to the cause of *mission*. Once you are an agent of the true faith, you want to spread it. In the interest of saving others from wilderness or damnation, missionary associations sprang up across the lands. While the religious awakening itself remained local and decentralised, the follow-through to missionary work was quickly organised.

Some looked out into the world and to the idea of sending out emissaries to bring the good word to the heathens. It fell on local associations to raise funds, giving many people an early experience of, and education in, disciplined organisational activity. Women found an arena of out-of-home engagement, making themselves the core of local missionary associations. They knitted and sewed, sold their produce, arranged collections and raised trickles of money.

The first missionary from Norway, Hans Schreuder, was sent out to Zululand in 1843. It would take fourteen years before he could report back on the first convert. The first woman to be sent out, to Madagascar, was Marie Føreid, in 1870, to work primarily in leprosy care, which she did until 1925.

Others looked inward. Their calling was to uphold a true and basic Lutheranism at home and to rescue people from spiritual poverty – as well as other dangers such as revolutionary impulses. While the external movement organised from bottom up, the internal movement was top-down, in the hands of conservative pastors of the official Church, many of whom preached a fiery gospel of Hell and damnation for those who dithered in beliefs and practices. They weighed into the culture wars over faith, church, schooling, family, morality, drink, prostitution, literature – but also engaged in social work. They wanted to preserve education as religious and Lutheran, strictly so. They stood guard against the influence of free thinkers and secularists. In 1907, traditionalists within the Norwegian Church established *Meninghtsfakultetet*, the 'Faculty of the Parishes', a private institution of higher theological study, as an alternative to the University of Oslo. The schism was triggered by the appointment of a liberal theologian to a professorship at the university. The Faculty, still outside the university, today remains the country's main school of priestly education.

A third early, and again related, cause was *temperance*. Drink was of epic proportions. Hard liquor was everywhere and consumed by everyone, morning and eve, by industrial workers as a matter of routine, even by children. Distilling of liquor was free, at least for domestic use. Servants and day labourers might be paid in liquor. Drinking was daily and normal, and getting drunk a respite from misery and poverty. Parishioners slept through the Sunday service in a haze of intoxication. The average consumption of alcohol in the early 1800s was five times that of today.

The temperance movement was successful in attracting followers and from there in organisation and political influence. Legal home distilling ended around the mid-century, bringing the obscene level of alcohol use under some control. There was a close and obvious link to the missionary movements. This nexus was to be the breeding ground of other, later popular movements, especially of the rising working class. Early labour organisation was educational, often of religious inspiration, devoted to improving culture among workers. The removal of the demon drink was an obvious cause for those who wanted to lift the working class to better living and political awareness.

Other forms of associational life followed, giving each other momentum. 'If it was a matter of godly gatherings, a friendly society, a reading circle or a political association, it was most often the same circle of men and women who were in the lead.' Savings banks were in the making in the cities, as business ventures. Initiatives followed in rural districts, there more in the form of cooperative saving societies and ones of mutual insurance among the rising class of propertied farmers, often with local teachers assisting with documentation and accounts. Singers formed associations, and arranged national and cross-national festivals of song. Students gathered nationally or more broadly in feasts of Scandinavian brotherhood. There were shooters' associations which arranged shooting competitions and formed militia-like organisations. Offshoots included movements for physical exercise, eventually organised sports, and for rambling through the countryside and mountains, which came together in associations of 'tourism'. Readers formed reading circles, sometimes women-only, sometimes running early library arrangements. Women formed associations and fought for presence and rights, voting rights in particular, a cause in which they had a good deal of male support and in which they also encountered a good deal of female resistance. Cooperative movements emerged and gained traction. In Norway, those who promoted 'the people's language' formed *mållag*, 'associations of the language', to work both locally and nationally, still today in vigorous operation. Come the twentieth century Scandinavian society was democratised, not only constitutionally but also socially. People enjoyed belonging, community and participation. They worked together, they promoted causes, they defended interests, they knew about agendas, fundraising, meetings, minutes, joint efforts and mass demonstrations.

It went political. The agricultural upturn out of the eighteenth century and the Industrial Revolution of the nineteenth century gave rise to a class of propertied farmers and later a class or classes of impoverished workers. Politics was being democratised, offering 'the people' arenas in which they could come together around class interests. The farmer class won representation in local councils and national parliaments and gradually organised themselves into a force, eventually into parties, in opposition to the traditional establishments of power. The working class of rural poor and industrial labourers started to organise and demand representation. These two movements progressed differently: the farmers were included and could work by parliamentary means; the workers were excluded and were confined to taking their battle to the streets. It became violent.

Worker mobilisation started early, even before there were working classes in any modern sense. Strangely, it was in Norway, the least-industrialised economy, that radical labour organisation first reared its head in a serious way. Europe was in the grip of revolution, with the influence of the February Revolution in France of 1848 spreading across the continent. A young editor of a local newspaper, Marcus Thrane, built himself a political platform with the aim of mobilising the downtrodden to political activism. By 1850 he was at the head of a movement of 30,000 members in a nationwide net of associations. There was the threat of revolution in the air, at least as seen by a fearful establishment. Workers clashed with police and the military. A competing national assembly to the *Storting* was convened in Oslo and petitioned the authorities for workers' rights, backed up by a threat of militant action. The authorities reacted as they had to the Lofthus movement sixty years earlier. Thrane and other leaders were arrested and sentenced to various periods of imprisonment, Thrane to eight years (whereafter he left for America, where he died in 1890).

From the mid-1880s, strike followed strike, most spontaneous and poorly planned. In 1889, Oslo's typographers launched a well-organised strike for better pay, but lost. The employers were able to recruit willing workers from out of town. Later the same year, female match workers, also in Oslo, went on strike for better pay, shorter hours and protection against the health danger posed by the phosphorus they worked with. They won much sympathy, but not much in terms of better conditions. The lesson from both episodes was the need for more rigorous organisation.

The Thrane episode had created lasting fear. The lower classes were numerous and were capable of rising. There were matters that needed to be understood. The *Storting* appointed a Workers Commission, and this time in addition turned to an individual of recognised ability. He, Eilert Sundt, was given an assignment to study the conditions of the common people. This he did in a number of projects over a period of twenty-five years, in an enterprise of sociological ingenuity that has since not been surpassed in scientific inventiveness, neither in Scandinavia nor hardly anywhere else.

Sundt was educated in theology and had no training in anything resembling science, never mind social research. He held no established post and had no scientific community to collaborate with. He was a sociologist, demographer and ethnologist before these were acknowledged disciplines. He was a brilliant methodologist before there was knowledge of social science methodology, mastering for example the art of representative sampling before any theory thereof had been formulated.

He conducted studies of the Gipsy-traveller population, of the urban poor, of mining and fishing communities, of demographic trends, of patterns of mortality, of sexual mores and marriage, of drink and the use of alcohol, of domestic life from household production to cleanliness, of rural architecture and more. He travelled the country tirelessly, speaking to people about their conditions and combining that information with a rich use of statistical analysis.

As he worked on he became ever more ambitious. He perceived rationality even in the living conditions of the poor. That was contrary to educated thinking at the time, which held that the poor were poor because of their ignorance. Sundt found that people did as best they could in their circumstances and that the poor were not to be blamed for the ills of a hard social order. One such matter was population growth and the burden of numbers. The poor were having too many children, it was thought, more than they could provide for. But Sundt saw a different pattern. It was true that birth numbers were high at the time of this controversy, but that was not because poor people were having more children. Parents at the time came from large birth cohorts of a generation earlier whereby total birth numbers increased although individual families behaved as they always had.

As Sundt's research grew in quality, he himself became increasingly controversial. People arranged their lives, he thought, according to *skikker*, conventions and habits that had survived the test of time and experience. It came to a head in the 'great porridge controversy'. P. C. Asbjørnsen, of folk-tale fame, had published a cookbook in which he criticised farming women for ignorance in food management. They had a habit of throwing a fistful of raw flour into the porridge when it was cooked and ready to be served. That, thought Asbjørnsen, was a wasteful superstition and proof of ingrained ignorance. Not so, said Sundt in a withering review; they had good reasons for preparing the porridge in that way, otherwise they would not have persisted in doing it. But he was unable to explain what those good reasons were and lost the debate. His research career was coming to an end and his intransigence over porridge-cooking clinched it. He was forced to take up a vicarage, a good one, at Eidsvoll, but against his will. He had wanted to bring his research together into a synthesis but that evaded him. (He was later proved right in the porridge controversy. It turned out that the fistful of raw flour had the effect of slowing down the digestion of the porridge and keeping hunger at bay longer, thereby enabling longer work shifts between meals. But too late for our hero.)*

In Denmark an inspirational agitator, Louis Pio, of French heritage, founded a socialist party in 1871, the first in Scandinavia. The next year it called a strike in Copenhagen demanding regulated working hours. But it was poorly organised, with no means of support for striking workers. A mass meeting was called to raise money – a provocation too far. The meeting was banned, soldiers were called out and battle ensued, orchestrated with the intention of crushing the nascent movement. Pio was imprisoned and sentenced to six years; he was released after three, his health broken. He gave up and left for America after being bribed to leave, the money having been put up by some of Copenhagen's captains of industry. Strikes continued, mostly local, mostly poorly organised, causing continuous disruption. The employers counter-organised and in 1899 instituted a lockout against 40,000 workers nationwide which lasted for three months.

Socialist parties followed in Norway in 1887 and in Sweden in 1889. Sweden had 80,000 industrial workers in 1870, 300,000 by 1900. As in Norway and Denmark, they rose in revolt. The early demands were for regulated and shorter working days, industrial protection, the end of child labour, and voting rights. The last decades of the century came with waves of strikes, many local, many by women whose conditions were even worse than those of the men. Employers responded with lockouts, blacklisting and police and military crackdowns. A strike across the sawmill industry in northern Sweden in 1879 was crushed by military means. Unionisation progressed and striking continued, culminating in a three-month-long national combined strike and lockout in 1909.

---

* In 1972 I was appointed project director of the Norwegian Level of Living Study, a mega-project initiated by the *Storting* to map living conditions in the Norwegian population, not unlike Sundt's assignment. Whereas he worked on his own for twenty-five years, we were a team of up to twenty researchers over four years, with the best research tools. As a sociologist, I am a pupil of Eilert Sundt. I, with others, consider him to be one of the greatest European sociologists ever, perhaps the greatest. His work is less well known than it should be (although much of it is now available in translation), partly because he operated on the European periphery and in a small language, partly because he was prevented from pulling it together into a final synthesis. However, the body of work he left us contains all the elements of a general sociological theory of the quality that would later be elaborated by the man who *is* considered Europe's most eminent sociologist, the Frenchman Émile Durkheim (1858–1917).

By the end of the century, the dual force of labour organisation that was to define twentieth-century politics, the union branch and the party branch, was established in all three countries. The union branches formed strong central organisations and the party branches would move their main activism from the streets into parliamentary work. The strike weapon had proved productive in advancing labour organisation, but less so as a means to improving conditions for working women and men.

Innovation IV: Constitutions

The political job of the nineteenth century was to create democracy. It unfolded differently in the three countries, with ups and downs, but under a common logic. Around 1815, old, narrow and conservative establishments were in control. With economic and social modernisation, new groupings, classes if you will, presented themselves with strength and demanded influence. A political 'Left' was born to give representation to country farmers and city burghers. They did battle with the establishments of the 'Right' to shift power from élites to 'the people'. As industrial modernisation churned on, another new class, the workers, claimed space to splinter the original Left. Moving into the twentieth century, constitutions were irreversibly, if imperfectly, democratic. The stage was set for a socialist Left to continue the battle against a more broadly based Right.

The Norwegians set about governing themselves, if under union paternalism. The king was Swedish but Norwegian matters were in Norwegian hands. They had a shining constitution but otherwise started from scratch. The government was organised in six ministries, with in all sixty permanent officials. In 1850 there were seven ministries, served by from three or four to thirty officials each. Oslo was a small town with a population of 10,000. It had a single mansion, Paléet, used by the king when in residence, otherwise by his governor, the *stattholder*, and a single hotel worthy of the name, Hôtel du Nord. *Stortinget* was to meet every three years, in rented accommodation in the Cathedral School, using its auditorium for its sessions. The university had 180 students and premises in ten rented rooms, drawing recruits from four schools that offered university-entrance qualifications. A royal palace was realised in 1849, a university complex in 1851. The *Storting*

Kings, and a queen, of the modern age

Years	Denmark	Norway	Sweden
1800		Christian Frederik, 1814	Karl XIII, 1809–18
		Karl II (XIII), 1814–18	Karl Johan, 1818–44
	Frederik VI, 1808–39		
	Christian VIII, 1839–48	Karl Johan, 1818–44	Oscar I, 1844–59
1850	Frederik VII, 1848–63	Oscar I, 1844–59	Karl XV, 1859–72
	Christian IX, 1863–1906	Karl IV (XV), 1859–72	
		Oscar II, 1872–1905	Oscar II, 1872–1907
1900	Frederik VIII, 1906–12	Haakon VII, 1905–57	Gustav V, 1907–50
	Christian X, 1912–47		
1950	Frederik IX, 1947–72	Olav V, 1957–91	Gustav VI, 1950–73
	Margrethe II, 1972–		Karl XVI, 1973–
		Harald V, 1991–	
2000			

moved into a building of its own in 1866. A national hospital began to be built in 1826 (in the entire country there were 150 doctors), the national bank in 1827, a theatre opened in 1837 (after a failed attempt ten years earlier) and the Grand Hotel in 1874. The new State inherited ownership of previous Danish State enterprises: the silver mines in Kongsberg, there also an iron mill, a textile factory and a weapons factory, five glass works, a salt factory and a mill for the production of blue cobalt. These all ran deficits and were, except for the silver mines, which were profitable, sold off during the 1820s.

The Norwegians took pride in their constitution. Some of the Swedes liked it less, including Karl Johan, who regretted his generosity in 1814. It gave the *Storting* too much power and Norway too much autonomy. The king bombarded the *Storting* with proposals to rein in the constitution, proposals which the *Storting*, in a spirit of zealous constitutional conservatism, consistently rejected.

The constitution was the most democratic in Europe but its management less than impressive. There was not much interest in national politics out in the country. Voting participation was low, even among those who had the right. It was convoluted. You had to prove your eligibility, register and swear allegiance to the constitution. It worked in a combination of direct and indirect elections. The men of the educated élite knew how to game the system in a way that enabled them to constitute what would long be the dominant 'party'. But the set-up was still democratic enough to enable 'the people' to elect enough of their own to create a sizeable opposing 'party'. Thus national politics was a tug-of-war between two groups, if fluid and ill-defined, the 'officials' and the 'farmers'. The officials wanted 'modernisation', the farmers were 'patriots'. The farmers' fear was government spending and the follow-through in taxation. The modernisers had the upper hand, but the patriots enough power to temper excesses.

The constitution said nothing about local government; that was a concern of the patriots, whose identities were local. Important matters of public administration and spending were in local hands: schools, poor relief, road maintenance. The farmers pushed for organised and democratic local government. A law was passed in 1837 to institute elected municipal assemblies for the management of local affairs, for example taking charge of schooling, previously the remit of school boards under the *ex officio* chairmanship of parish vicars. Hence the democratic spirit of the constitution followed through to local management as well. The farmers soon learned to make use of their voting power. It mattered: by the 1860s, local spending accounted for 40 per cent of all public spending. Thus, however imperfect the constitutional system in our eyes, it still gave 'the people' some hold on the combined national and local levers of government in a system in which powers from above and below were balanced against each other.

There was much work remaining to be done in democratising the system, but the constitution was sufficiently modern for that to be accomplished within the established framework. The main problems were to establish the supremacy of the elected legislature over the executive and to broaden voting rights. That unfolded pretty easily. From 1871, the *Storting* met annually. The Left wanted to impose a duty on government ministers to attend proceedings in the *Storting* and thus answer to 'the people'. The *Storting* passed a law to that effect. The king vetoed it, the *Storting* passed it again, and again a third time, declaring it to be constitutionally valid. Not so, said the king and his cabinet. The election in 1882 gave the Left a landslide victory. The government refused the order to attend. The *Storting* moved to impeachment. The prime minister was up before a court of seventeen legislators and nine justices, who ruled to dismiss him (and obliged him to pay court costs). He obeyed, as now did the king. The majority leader in the *Storting*, Johan Sverdrup, was prime minister. The division of power between legislature and executive was de facto abolished. The year was 1884. It was illegal. The constitution was crystal clear on the division of power and was not rewritten. But the reality was that from now on there could be no government without *Storting* consent.

The extension of voting rights took more time. Secret ballotting was introduced in 1884. In 1898, voting rights in *Storting* elections were extended to all men from age twenty-five (except recipients of poor relief, an exception that stood until 1919). Women over a certain threshold of income and taxation had voting rights in local elections from 1901 and national elections from 1909, from 1913 on the same terms as men.

In Denmark and Sweden, democratisation came through hard constitutional battles. Denmark did not even have a national assembly, Sweden an outdated one of estates. When Denmark instituted a national assembly and Sweden abolished the assembly of estates for a representative one, they both adopted dual-chamber assemblies with upper chambers in which narrow establishments retained control. The Norwegians in 1814 had the wisdom, or luck, to make their national assembly unicameral, which saved them from many of the troubles the Danes and the Swedes had to fight their way through.

Reaction held firm in Denmark. Frederik VI was king from 1808 to 1839. He had been regent since 1784 but did not rise in stature on his elevation. He was not an impressive man, says the Danish historian Claus Bjørn, 'short of height, weak of stature, with albino-white eyebrows, protruding and watery eyes, a sagging lower lip. He spoke in the manner of military command to disguise a lack of control over his own emotions. Few would ever see him smile. He was poorly educated, wrote a faulty Danish, had a limited spiritual horizon, and was without much interest in art or the aesthetics of life.' He was a sincere and hard-working monarch, without, however, 'abilities of political leadership or military command, utterly devoid of constructive imagination or empathy'. His personal tastes were austere – he lived in a small combined study and bedchamber in the palace (when not with his mistress in her nearby townhouse) – but was zealous in the protection of the symbols of royal power and insistent on their respect. He was a pedantic administrator, easily absorbed by detail, stubborn, disinclined to listen and even more to change his mind once made up.

When, in 1835, 572 professors, priests and officials signed a humble petition, not for freedom of expression but for legal management of censorship, his riposte to the 'unexpected' missive from 'loyal subjects' was that 'We alone are in a position to judge what is for the good of people and State.' In his last years, his influence was mainly 'in resistance against modernisation'.

A reform, of sorts, was introduced in 1835–36, in the curiosity of consultative assemblies of estates, two for Denmark proper and one in each of the duchies. The assemblies were elected by 2 to 3 per cent of the population, had no role beyond an advisory one, and were to learn that king and government paid their advice no heed. Europe was in the grip of revolution, spreading from Paris in 1830; monarchs were thrown off their thrones, constitutions ripped up. In Denmark, the king moved to allow a tiny minority a symbolic say.

Frederik died in 1839 and was followed by Christian VIII, the same Christian Frederik who had been a revolutionary in Norway in 1814. He did not come as a breath of fresh air, being now a man of not much energy and little vision. But a new generation was rising into élite positions in officialdom and business, bringing with them a spirit of liberalism. Through the 1840s, diverse demands started to gel into a concert of opposition against the absolutist order. City burghers wanted liberalism in trade and industry. Rural people wanted equality in property rights and the end of landowner privileges in taxation and military service. Nationalists wanted a more secure incorporation of Schleswig and Holstein into the Danish nation. What united these movements was a vision of a better constitutional order.

Slowly, the economy started to pull itself out of recession. There were improvements in agricultural productivity, followed by increasing exports, followed by some revival of shipping. Savings banks started to turn themselves into investment banks to create a credit market. Trade was liberalised. There were shoots of early industrialisation. People could start to think in terms of development and progress.

When Christian VIII died in 1848, it was clear that absolutism could not survive. The February Revolution in Paris set Europe ablaze. A new constitution would have to be liberal.

The government convened a constitutional assembly, which met in October 1848 and deliberated until a new constitution was agreed and sanctioned on 5 June 1849. Denmark was reshaped into a constitutional monarchy with an elected national assembly, the *Rigsdag*, a Lutheran State Church, an independent judiciary, and enshrined civil freedoms of worship, expression and association. The *Rigsdag* was made up of a lower chamber, the *Folketing*, with 100 members, chosen by an electorate of men over thirty years of age who were economically self-supporting, and an upper chamber, the *Landsting*, with fifty-one members, elected indirectly by a college of electors who were at least forty years of age and chosen by the *Folketing* electorate.

It was a step too far. Denmark was in the midst of its first Prussian war. In Europe, revolution was suppressed and reaction reasserted itself. The Danish establishment clawed back power to the Crown and executive. The rising class of propertied farmers remained unable to shed their complex of inferiority. Aristocratic landowners were ruthlessly reactionary, modelling themselves on the Prussian *Junkers*. They were able, from their bastion in the upper *Landsting* chamber, to engineer a revision of constitutional practices to de-democratise elections, set in stone paralysingly complex procedures of decision-making, and rule autocratically by emergency decrees. The reactionary sclerosis was fortified by the demoralisation of national life following the defeat to Prussia in 1864. The next thirty years were to be a prolonged and chaotic battle in which the Left slowly, oh so slowly, liberated political power. It became nasty. The language was hard, confrontations were sharp, elections rigged. There was fear of civil war. Of public policy there was little, except for massive expenditure on military fortifications around Copenhagen, already out of date even as they were being built. The king persisted in appointing conservative-aristocratic governments, in defiance of public opinion.

Elections in early 1901 were a victory for the Left. The constitution of 1849 was revived and put to work in the spirit in which it had been written. The king, through gritted teeth, appointed a government according to the majority in the *Rigsdag* (although his consent had to wait four months until he returned from his annual spa recreation in Germany). Constitutionally, the significance was an implicit acceptance of parliamentary supremacy, and within the *Rigsdag* the supremacy of the lower *Folketing* chamber, principles that were from then on established practice. This followed through to extended voting rights, equally for women and men from age twenty-five by 1915 (although non-repayment of poor relief was still disqualifying). In 1953, the upper *Landsting* chamber was abolished and the national assembly made unicameral under the name *Folketinget*.

*

If the economic story in Sweden was industrialism, the political story was militarism. Sweden was a militaristic state. The monarchy was militaristic. The aristocracy was militaristic. Industry was militaristic. The abiding concern for the Swedish establishment was *försvarsfrågan*, 'the defence question'. All through the century, the Right pushed for military investment and a standing army. The key issue was infantry-training. It improved gradually but slowly, until a reform in 1901 extended the period of conscription service from ninety to 240 days. It was still not enough. After an election setback for the Right in 1911, a liberal government put a stop to various defence investments and struck fear into the political Right. The king, Gustav V, weighed in personally, publicly and unconstitutionally to demand immediate extension of the army. The liberal government fell. A conservative government pushed through a full year of conscription service. War was looming in Europe, putting aside (for a while) Left–Right political confrontations. Its outbreak in 1914 forged national agreement for neutrality (except for an ultra-Right fringe that called for engagement on Germany's side), and also around the understanding that neutrality had to be protected by a credible military force. The defence question was settled and laid to rest. Swedish militarism survived.

The two stories of industrialism and militarism were intertwined. Early Swedish industry had been iron- and copper-based, ideal for the production of weapons. A Dutch immigrant, Louis de Geer, had come to Sweden in 1627 to exploit the potential and made himself the country's first industrial tycoon. There was a boom in the demand for weaponry in the Thirty Years War. De Geer sold his wares to all sides in the war in which Sweden itself was a combatant. Since then, the Swedish economy has had a heavy component in the weapons industry. In the nineteenth century it became a matter of defence to have good networks of canals and railways and the best possible capacity in industrial production. Military installations were located according to canal access. The routing of railways was decided in part by military concerns. The southern main line ran inland, rather than along the coast, so as to be more easily defended. Mining was becoming big business in the very north, in the mines that even today are the main sources of Swedish iron. That was a business which needed defending. A northern railway line was built, and from 1903 a connection through Norway to the port of Narvik.

Militarism has persisted. Sweden remains a formidable military power and is a significant manufacturer and exporter of weaponry. When, in the Second World War, Germany spared Sweden when it occupied Denmark and Norway, it was, among other reasons, because Sweden would have been able to resist.

The Swedish constitution of 1809 preserved the anachronism of a *Riksdag* of estates: nobility, clergy, burghers and farmers. It took half a century to get it modernised, in an overdue reform in 1866 which abolished representation by estates and established a *Riksdag* of two chambers: an upper chamber elected indirectly in such a way as to secure upper-class control, and a lower chamber elected directly by men of some property and income – about 20 per cent of the adult male population – to secure middle-class dominance. It was a step in the direction of democracy – moderately, we would now say – but at the time considered no less than a revolution. In the old *Riksdag* of estates, the aristocracy had its own bastion of power. In the new one it had no privilege at all. People took to the streets and celebrated with songs and flag-waving. In *Operakällaren* (a splendid restaurant known to many a visitor of today), a reform enthusiast stood on a table to deliver a speech expressing gratitude that 'Stockholm's streets did not need to be coloured in aristocratic blood.'

The new *Riksdag* put voting power in the hands of the farmer class, which constituted itself as the political Left and remained the dominant non-establishment force for the rest of the century. The Right was preoccupied with military reform, and the Left was able to use that preoccupation to negotiate reforms of its own, mainly to ease the agricultural tax burden. Otherwise, the more 'democratic' *Riksdag* was socially conservative and notably unable to deal with the rising force of industrial labour.

The breakthrough for parliamentary supremacy was delayed until 1917. The Left had won the elections to the lower chamber and formed a coalition government of liberals and social democrats, in defiance of the will of the king. As in Norway and Denmark, the principle was not formalised but became the accepted convention. That government, amid the fear of Russian-inspired revolution, pushed through general voting rights, equally for women and men from age twenty-three, in 1918 and 1919 for local and national elections respectively (if still with limitations that excluded about 4 per cent of potential voters, including recipients of long-term poor relief who were not enfranchised until 1945). Not until 1970 was the *Riksdag* made unicameral.

So, to summmarise: elected national assemblies in 1814, 1849 and 1866; parliamentary supremacy in 1884, 1901 and 1917; universal suffrage (almost) in 1913, 1915 and 1919; unicameralism in 1814, 1953 and 1970. In all matters, Norway first, Sweden last.

The union of Sweden and Norway was not made to last. It had been a fix in 1814, dictated by the big powers. The Norwegians, most of them, had not wanted it. The Swedes did not have their hearts in it. It was an anachronism in a world of national sentiment and emerging democracy. Sweden was a society of aristocratic stratification, Norway one of democratic equality.

Norway managed its own affairs, except in foreign relations; that was an issue of pride, but also of practicality. Shipping had grown into a considerable fleet. The Norwegians wanted a consular service of their own to manage their interests abroad. The Swedes refused. Matters came to a head in 1905. The Norwegian *Storting* pressed ahead with a consular law, the king refused to sanction it, the Norwegian government resigned, the king declared himself unable to appoint a new one, the *Storting* chose to interpret it as the king relinquishing his duties in Norway and resolved, on 7 June, that the union had ceased to function. As a face-saving exercise, the Swedes insisted on a referendum in Norway, which returned a massive majority in support of the 7 June decision: 368,208 votes for, 184 against. Women were excluded from the vote, but an unofficial women's referendum was arranged in which the women voted as patriotically as the men. Negotiations followed and in October the Swedish *Riksdag* accepted the outcome. There had been some tension on both sides, even mobilisation and the manning of border forts, but it had become clear to everyone that the union was over and that it was only a matter of finding a way out of it.

According to the constitution, Norway was a monarchy. A Danish price, Carl, was invited to accept the crown. He insisted on a referendum and thus arrived in Oslo as Europe's only elected king, stepping on to Norwegian soil on 25 November 1905 with his two-year-old son on his arm, the future King Olav V. He was the son of a Danish king and a Swedish princess, and was married to a daughter of the King of Great Britain. He took the name of Haakon VII and became the first exclusive King of Norway in 525 years.

11

Wars and Progress

As we move into the twentieth century, we see no prosperity, rather widespread poverty in countries shedding populations in mass emigration. There was no equality, rather brutal class divisions. Cities were not attractive, rather cesspits of slum living. There was no welfare state, rather persistent precariousness and neglect. There was little collaboration between the three countries, rather animosity after the failures of 1864 and 1905. There was no social democracy other than in its early shoots. 'Scandinavia' is an invention of the twentieth century.

To Hell and back

At the outbreak of the First World War, the Scandinavians declared themselves neutral. Neutrals can trade with all sides. Business was good. Danes exported agricultural produce at high prices. Swedes exported iron and armaments. Norwegian fish exports boomed, to both sides. Shipping commanded extraordinary rates, and ship-owners and share speculators, of whom there were many on frenzied stock exchanges, became super-rich overnight. Most of the Norwegian merchant fleet went into Allied service. About half of it was lost: 829 ships, more than any other national fleet, including those of the warring nations. Two thousand sailors perished.

Business proved no protection against shortage. None of the Scandinavian countries was self-sufficient and all depended on imports of foodstuffs, fertiliser, animal fodder, coal, oil, raw materials and machinery. Price inflation was felt from early on, turning to dire want when Germany's uninhibited submarine warfare in the North Sea and Atlantic destroyed supply lines. Smuggling and black market profiteering were rife. It resulted in hunger, people freezing through the winter in their homes, plunder, uprisings. Mounted police were called out against riots in central Stockholm. In Copenhagen, a mob stormed the stock exchange.

Governments responded to the war economy with unprecedented market interventions in order to regulate production and prices and ration access to necessities. To make restrictions stick, their administration was put in the hands of collaborative commissions of government agencies and relevant business organisations, in a new reality of government-managed markets and organisational co-optation in the administration of public policy. The war produced stronger states and new mentalities, says the Norwegian historian Anne-Lise Seip, 'pulling down mental barriers against public interventions'. Post-war economies were roller coasters of boom and bust, making emergency interventions more the rule than the exception, culminating in the combined effects of crisis management after the financial crash of 1929 and the economics of war preparation again from the mid-1930s. Economic liberalism was no more.

A curious case of wartime regulation was in the sale of alcohol. In Norway, it was prohibited altogether in 1915 (except for beer). A law of 1894 had opened for local referenda on the sale of alcohol, and by 1915 it was banned in 485 of 600 municipalities. A national referendum in 1919 made the wartime ban permanent.

It did not work. There was widespread opposition and much illegal home distilling and smuggling. Drunkenness persisted. Norway was forced to import unsellable brandy and wine from France, Spain and Portugal to maintain fish exports. The ban was relaxed from 1922, but sales were restricted to State-controlled monopoly stores. A new referendum in 1926 put an end to prohibition but not the State monopoly.

Sweden avoided prohibition. It was put to a referendum and turned down by 925,000 votes to 889,000. Women voted 60 per cent in favour but men against. Distribution was, as in Norway, put under the control of a state monopoly. Households could apply for a quota (larger for upper-class families, normally none for unmarried men, women, the unemployed or recipients of social assistance) and be issued a ration book. Municipal 'temperance committees' were empowered to refuse irresponsible quotas. Purchases could only be made in your designated outlet and entered into your book and a central register. The hated ration-book system lasted until 1955.

In Denmark, attitudes were, as so often in cultural issues, different. Municipalities could hold local referenda, but few did and there was little restriction in access to alcohol. Even today, alcohol, except for beer, can only be bought in State-monopoly outlets in Norway and Sweden but in Denmark in supermarkets.

The twentieth century had commenced in an atmosphere of progress and optimism. True, there was intense class conflict amid unruly labour relations and political constellations. But things were getting better. There was peace in Europe and confidence that it would last. Communism was but an abstract fad, Fascism not yet known. There was population growth, economic advancement and better standards of living. Industrialisation, mechanisation and urbanisation were progressing. In 1906, Jacob Christian Ellehammer of Denmark was the first European to fly an aeroplane: forty-two metres on his first attempt. In 1911, Roald Amundsen beat Robert Scott to the South Pole and planted the Norwegian flag in an area not seen until then by the human eye. In 1914, on the eve of the European Armageddon, Norway celebrated a century of progress with a proud exhibition of industrial modernity.

THE AGE OF EXPLORATION

Fridtjof Nansen (1861–1930) was a Norwegian scientist and explorer who shot to fame for crossing Greenland on skis in 1888 and almost reaching the North Pole in an expedition in the mid-1890s with the ship *Fram*. He did highly recognised work in oceanography, mainly in the North Atlantic. Ahead of the dissolution of the union with Sweden in 1905, from his position as one of the country's pre-eminent scientists, he gained recognition across political divides as a national leader. In the turbulent years after the First World War, when there were movements on the political Right for a 'strong-government-above-politics' constitution, Nansen was the movement's candidate to take charge, campaigning he neither engaged in nor distanced himself from. He went into Red Cross and League of Nations service as High Commissioner for Refugees, from which posts he undertook work of great consequence for displaced people in Russia and east and central Europe, and for which he received the Nobel Peace Prize in 1922.

Sven Hedin (1865–1952) was a Swedish explorer and geographer, famed throughout Europe for expeditions to the Himalayas and Central

Asia, finding unknown lakes and the sources of great rivers, discovering lost cities and grave sites and mapping the Great Wall of China, all of which he wrote up in colourful and much-read books of manly adventure. He used his fame for political influence in anti-Russian and pro-German campaigning. He was a royalist, militarist and anti-democrat. When political battles over the defence question came to a head in 1911 and the king intervened with an inflammatory speech that triggered the fall of the liberal government, he, the king, had schemed with Hedin and a handful of other aggressive nationalists who spurred him on and wrote his speech for him. He remained pro-German into the Second World War and promoted the view that Hitler's Germany was the victim of others' aggression, notably that of the United States.

Roald Amundsen (1872–1928) was the Norwegian explorer who was the first to take an expedition to the South Pole. Before that, from 1903 to 1906, he had led the first successful expedition by ship through the North-West Passage around Canada. In 1910 he launched an expedition nominally for the North Pole, using Nansen's ship *Fram*. It, however, sailed south. On a stopover at Madeira, he informed his crew that they were heading for the South Pole. It took them two attempts, after near-mutiny by expedition members, for five of them to reach the pole on 14 December. They had set off from base camp on 19 October 1911 with fifty-two dogs and returned on 25 January 1912 with eleven surviving ones.

Not all expeditions were successful. In 1897, the Swedish engineer Salomon Andrée tried to reach the North Pole by hot air balloon. The expedition was amateurish; the balloon crashed into the ice and the crew of three, Andrée included, perished after three months in the frost. (Their remains were found years later.) After the South Pole, Amundsen launched various new ventures in the north, including a three-year expedition from 1918 to traverse the North-East Passage and/or drift in the ice over the North Pole, neither of which was achieved. Attempts in 1923 and 1925 to cross the North Pole by plane failed, but succeeded by airship in 1926. In 1928, the Italian airship *Italia* crashed in the ice on its return from the North Pole. There were survivors, including the designer Umberto Nobile, but seventeen crew and rescuers died. Among them were Amundsen and five others, who disappeared on a flight north to join the rescue, never to be recovered.

The war put an end to confidence and comfort. Living conditions deteriorated and inequalities widened. Businesses and speculators made money, and splashed it about in conspicuous consumption and black-market extravagance. Wage earners were squeezed by inflation and unemployment.

The war's end brought all but relief. The Russian Revolution of 1917 injected assertiveness into revolutionary tendencies across the Continent and into Scandinavia. During the winter of 1918–19 revolutionary councils of workers and soldiers took power in a range of cities and garrisons in Germany, Austria, Hungary and Italy. In Finland, 'reds' and 'whites' fought a bloody civil war. The Spanish Flu of 1918–19 took more lives than had been lost in war and took no pity on neutrals. The wartime economic boom crashed. Businesses collapsed. Small farmers were overwhelmed by debt, many evicted from their properties, many taken over by predatory loan sharks. Banks went bust. Savers lost their deposits. Unemployment increased, to hit one in four workers in the early 1920s. Leftist socialist parties were formed in Sweden and Denmark, while in Norway the revolutionaries took control of the Labour Party itself. The political Right counter-mobilised with Fascist-style anti-politics organisations and vigilante brigades.

The following years were turbulent in the extreme. Economic bust was followed by more bust, culminating in the crash of 1929 and the Big Recession of the early 1930s. Unemployment reached a third of the industrial workforce. Weak governments replaced each other in short order, many lasting a year or less. The Left became more revolutionary in its language while the Right took inspiration from Mussolini's Fascism. Young socialists marched under red banners and called for an end to capitalism by violent means. With Hitler's rise in Germany, hotheads on the Right took to wearing uniforms, sporting swastika armbands and greeting each other with the Nazi salute.*

* A Fascist party was formed in Sweden in 1926, under Italian inspiration, from 1930 known as the Swedish National Socialist Party. Electoral failure in 1932 caused even that minute party to split. A new National Socialist Worker's Party failed again in elections in 1936, winning about half a per cent of the vote. A National Socialist Worker's Party of Denmark was formed in 1930. In the election of 1939 it won short of 2 per cent of the vote, but concentrated on Schleswig, winning three seats in the *Folketing*. In Norway, Vidkun Quisling's Nazi Party in 1933 won about 3 per cent of the vote where it fielded candidates, in the next election in 1936 about 2 per cent, and obtained no representation in the *Storting*.

However, for all the turmoils, which were real and intense, there was an undercurrent of moderation. Class constellations were being crystallised. There had been an uneasy balance of social power in a triangle of the rural farming class, the urban middle class and the urban-rural working class. Moving into the new century, the farming class was in decline, the middle class in ascendancy with a core of increasingly wealthy owners of capital, and the working class growing in numbers as well as in power thanks to better organisation and democratic voting rights. The triangle of power dissolved and the conflict was to stand between the capitalist middle class and the proletarian working class. That made for hard confrontations, but also straight and manageable lines.

Economic growth, if interrupted by setbacks, continued. Most people were better off. Governments, if weak, had more capacity to introduce protective measures against at least some of the fallout from unemployment. Democracy stood firm. The political Left and Right were enemies but nevertheless sought collaboration. Unions and employers did battle but also sought peace. There was conflict but also deal-making, and deal-making was to outlive conflict.

Moderation was latent, waiting to temper conflict. When the Left fought down royal power and was able to institute parliamentary supremacy in Norway in 1884, the new prime minister of a 'people's government', Johan Sverdrup, chose as ministers not firebrands but moderates. When that government was followed by a conservative one in 1889, the new prime minister, Emil Stang, chose not counter-revolutionaries but again moderates. They both signalled that politics was going to be competitive, yes, but within a collaborative culture. The instinct to moderation has persisted. Towards the end of the twentieth and into the twenty-first centuries, extremist rightists grasped for political presence, in a 'Progress Party' in Norway, a 'Danish People's Party' in Denmark and a 'Sweden Democrats' party in Sweden. They were successful in attracting sizeable shares of the vote and in pulling the political culture in their direction, but only by shedding extremism and being subdued by the heavy hand of mainstream moderation.

In Denmark in 1899, the combined strike and lockout that was the country's biggest labour conflict ever, involving half of the unionised workforce, ended in a pioneering deal known as the 'September Compromise'. The employers accepted workers' right to unionisation and union-led negotiations. The unions accepted the employers' right to 'lead and distribute' work, which meant that employment was in their hands. Negotiated agreements were to be binding down the ranks on both sides. Both sides accepted a duty of peace for the duration of agreements, time lags for suspending agreements, and procedures of mediation over disagreements. It represented a framework for peaceful conflict resolution in order, ideally, to make strikes and lockouts unnecessary. That was still too much to hope for and the deal did not prevent future conflicts. But it had established an early ideal of peaceful relations, said to have been 'a labour market constitution for the next 60 years'.

In Sweden, after a wave of strikes and lockouts commencing in 1902, unions and employers struck their first national agreement, taking the Danish September Compromise as their model. From 1906, State-appointed mediators were available to assist in peaceful resolution of conflicts, 'an institution that with time would prove greatly significant for Swedish social order'. In Norway, the right to unionisation and union-based negotiations was agreed in similar circumstances in 1907, again in the first ever nationwide deal. Following a five-month-long combined strike and lockout in 1931, the deal of 1907 was extended to a General Agreement between the union and employer organisations to establish a comprehensive and mutually accepted framework for peaceful conflict resolution. The last big confrontation thus marked, says the Norwegian historian Knut Kjeldstadli, 'the end of fighting and the entry into an atmosphere of collaboration'. A similar General Agreement was struck in Sweden in 1938, following two and a half years of union–employer negotiations, known as the Saltsjöbaden Agreement after the luxury resort in the Stockholm archipelago where it was negotiated. It was on paper an agreement between union and employer organisations, but came to be seen as a messianic pact of peace between capital and labour, a 'historical compromise' according to the sociologist Walter Korpi.

As in labour relations, deal-making in spite of enmity was the spirit of politics. Ahead of elections in Denmark in 1906, the Social Democrats had a programme of proletarian class battle but nevertheless settled for parliamentary collaboration with the Liberals. On the non-socialist side the rhetoric was unity against the socialists, but the Liberals accepted the Social Democratic invitation. The result was 'a durable and effective alliance that, with a few interruption, would last for sixty years to dominate the century's parliamentary development'.

In Sweden in 1917, the Social Democrats joined their enemy the Liberals in a coalition government that would last for three years in order to push through parliamentary supremacy and the universal vote. The spirit of collaboration endured into the period of social democratic dominance. It was thanks to pragmatic deal-making with the Right that the radicals could prevail.

In 1933, formative political deals were struck in both Denmark and Sweden: between Social Democrats and Liberals in Denmark, known as the 'Kanslergade deal' after the prime minister's address, where they negotiated (Mr Stauning's drinks generously lubricating goodwill), and Social Democrats and Agrarians in Sweden, known as the 'big cow trade' (a deal with farmers, after all), in both cases to secure parliamentary majorities for active counter-crisis policies. In 1936, the Norwegian Social Democrats struck a similar deal with their Agrarians to form, as had already happened in Denmark and Sweden, a coalition government.

The hard 1920s turned out to be an interim period. Organised labour marched with red banners and did not hesitate to call members out on strike, but early on turned to forging compromise deals on wages, working conditions and procedures of negotiation. Employers and captains of industry warned of socialism or worse and were not restrained in the use of lockouts and violence against unionised workers, but also colluded with that same enemy in the building of systems of collaboration. It worked. The conservative counter-mobilisation was modest, with anti-strike brigades not turning into armed militias, at least not of any force. Communist parties were formed but were not successful. Tentative Fascist groupings attracted little following. Historians of the period have asked, why not revolution? The question is rhetorical. Revolution, be it of the Right or Left, was never a relevant scenario.

It is Sunday, 7 April 1940. Gudrun Martius is a junior official in the Norwegian Ministry of Foreign Affairs, the first woman to have been admitted into the diplomatic service. She is on weekend duty. Early in the evening, an urgent message arrives from the embassy in Berlin, dictated in code by telephone, by the ambassador himself. As she decodes it she feels 'shaken and shivering'.

The embassy reported that about twenty German troop transport ships had left the port of Stettin and were heading west out of the

Baltic Sea. Gudrun needed colleagues to consult with but no one else was on duty. The top official was inaccessible on holiday. She decided to call the foreign minister himself at home, the forbidding Halvdan Koht.

This is the same Halvdan Koht whom we have met once before, the one who said of King Håkon VI that there was 'something strangely pale over the whole man'. He was an academic historian whose synthesis of Norway's history was framed, in quasi-Marxist terms, as progress driven by peasant and worker pressure from below. He was active in social democratic politics from early on, and became minister of foreign affairs in 1935, a post he held until November 1940 when he was squeezed out of the exile government in London, being replaced by Trygve Lie, later the first Secretary-General of the United Nations. After the war, Koht carried much blame for Norway's lack of war preparations ahead of 1940. He and the Foreign Ministry had been receiving warnings of aggressive German intentions, both directly from Berlin and also via London and Stockholm, warnings which he had not really absorbed and failed to bring properly to the attention of the cabinet collective. When his home municipality on the western outskirts of Oslo, conservative-run, later reluctantly agreed to name a road in his honour, it became 'Professor Kohts vei', deliberately in honour not of the politician but of the historian.

He asked Gudrun where she thought they were heading. For Norway, she answered. Koht retorted that there was not much to do. Either the message was wrong and there was no problem, or it was right and there would be no way of stopping the German fleet. End of conversation.

The Danes had been warned in the same way. Swedish diplomats in Berlin were alerted by German anti-Nazi officials. They alerted Danish diplomats, who warned their principals in Copenhagen, who chose to not believe the warnings.

On 9 April 1940, at 4:15 in the early morning, German divisions crossed the ever undefendable Danish border into Jylland. At 4:20, 800 troops stepped off the battleship *Hansestadt Danzig* in the port of Copenhagen and took up positions in the city. Other centres across the country were taken at the same time. German bombers filled Copenhagen's airspace in a stark warning: give up or see your city in ruin. At about 5:30, the government and king met and decided on surrender. The capitulation has been branded cowardly. But the alternatives were crystal clear: surrender now or unleash a bloodbath and surrender later.

Denmark had gone to lengths to placate Nazi Germany. It had received refugees, including about 4,500 Jews, but quietly. Being accepted was on the condition of refraining from political activity (which many ignored), and was only exceptionally accompanied by a work permit.* The press was under sustained pressure not to offend German thin-skinned sensitivity. In 1935, the Royal Theatre, under pressure from the government, cancelled a planned controversial production, *Umbabumba Revises Its Constitution*, by the dramatist Carl Erik Soya. The government refused a Swedish initiative to consider a defence union, out of fear of provoking Germany, and instead tried to get the other Nordic countries to accept a German-framed pact of non-aggression. It refrained from any provocative rearmament. In April 1939, the government sent the head of the army and the head of the navy to Berlin with its congratulations to Hitler on his fiftieth birthday. Hitler assured them that Germany had no intention of disrespecting Danish neutrality.

The invasion of Norway was planned to coincide with that of Denmark. In the early hours of 9 April, naval and airborne troops were on their way to Oslo and cities and towns along the coast, north to Narvik.

While the invasion of Denmark was flawless, that attack on Norway failed in its objective of securing the capital in the morning of the first day. A German fleet was on its way up the Oslo Fjord destined to take the city. It had to pass Oscarsborg Fort at the narrowest point of the fjord, about a half-hour's sailing from Oslo harbour. The commander was Colonel Birger Eriksen. He was on his own, communications with

---

* The Scandinavian countries, like other democracies, became recipients of refugees from Germany. One was Willy Brandt, then a young Left-socialist, who fled to Norway in 1933, on to Sweden in 1940, returning to Norway at the peace in 1945. The year after, he was back in Germany, where he in 1948 regained his German citizenship, becoming in turn a member of the German Bundestag, Mayor of Berlin and Chancellor of West Germany. From his time in Norway a photo later emerged of him in Norwegian uniform, which was used against him in German election campaigns. Another refugee was the dramatist Bertolt Brecht, who lived quietly in small-town Denmark from 1933 to 1939, and there wrote *Mother Courage and Her Children*, *The Life of Galileo* and *The Good Person of Szechuan*. Ahead of the occupation, he moved on to Sweden and from there to America.

central command not functioning. The approaching ships were without identification and might, as far as Colonel Eriksen was concerned, have been British; it had been thought that the British might launch pre-emptive action on Norway. They had laid out mines along the coast, or threatened to, and encroached on Norwegian waters in the south-west.

By the rules of engagement, the fort was obliged to shoot warning shots to enable approaching vessels to stop, but that was not possible. It was equipped with outdated German Krupp cannons which could not be reloaded in time to fire again if the warning was ignored. At 4:21, Colonel Eriksen gave the order to fire to kill. The lead ship, the *Blücher*, was carrying 2,000 troops. The fort released two rounds of mortar which hit the *Blücher* with perfection and stalled her progress. The rest of the fleet turned back. The *Blücher* keeled over and sank, its oil leaking. About 800 German soldiers died in the burning sea. The wreck is still there at the bottom of the fjord.

The taking of Oslo was delayed until the afternoon, by airborne troops from the airport to the west. The delay enabled the *Storting*, the government and the royal family to escape and saved Norway from the surrender that had been inevitable in Denmark.

All three countries were ill prepared for war. They had made some preparations to survive as neutrals. After the outbreak of war in 1939, they put their economies into wartime administration, drawing on the experiences of the First World War: price and wage control, rent control, rationing of basic necessities. But they were not prepared for fight. Sweden had preserved some military force; Denmark and Norway had next to nothing, only rudimentary army and navy forces, with no air force at all. After the First World War they had scaled down their already inadequate defences. They thought the big powers could not want yet more war. They had managed to stay neutral and believed, because they wanted to believe it, that if it came to tension again their neutrality would be respected. Public finances were strained. There were anti-militaristic lobbies for total disarmament. With Hitler's rise in Germany the security situation in Europe changed, but not until the last couple of years of the 1930s was it accepted that Germany was bent on war again. There was then some attempt to improve military capacity, but too little too late. The Danes were resigned to the impossibility of standing up to German aggression, should it come. The Norwegians fought back against the invasion. This was later celebrated as a campaign of heroism, which it was, but at the cost of the bloodbath that had been avoided in Denmark. It was also doomed. The young men, and some women, who laid their lives on the line were badly armed, badly equipped, badly trained, badly organised, badly led and badly supported.

The Danes governed themselves under the oversight of the occupation force. The normal institutions continued to function for the duration of the war: the *Folketing*, shifting governments, the monarchy, the administration, the judiciary. Elections were held according to the normal schedule in 1943 (but with the Communists barred from participating). The government was constituted as a broad coalition, excluding Nazis and Communists, eventually as a non-political administrative council. The local Nazis sought to ingratiate themselves with the occupiers but the Germans had no time for them. The Communists took the lead in organised resistance.

The collaborative occupation turned ugly. The German command made incessant demands which the Danish authorities were forced to accede to. Ministers and parliamentarians thought to be unfriendly were dismissed. The judiciary was pressured to dispense retribution beyond Danish law. In June 1941, Danish police arrested 300 members of the Communist Party, the *Folketing* legalising the action retrospectively by passing a law against (suspected) Communist activity, enabling further arrests, some to confinement in camps in Germany. Danish defence equipment was confiscated, much of the police force, collaboration notwithstanding, dismissed and sent into imprisonment in Germany, releasing waves of criminality. Danish businesses were pressed into German service.

Official policy initially took the form of active collaboration. Germany looked to be winning the war and Danish manoeuvres were in preparation for Denmark's future in a Europe under German control. At the outbreak of the war, much of the Danish merchant shipping fleet was in Allied territory and went into Allied service, but not under government auspices. America was granted bases in Greenland but not by the government, the Danish commitment being made by the Danish ambassador in Washington who by then had been released from his post and technically had no authority. Not until after the war was the treaty ratified retrospectively by the Danish government. Resistance was to emerge on the home front, but again not under government auspices and not until near the war's end with government blessing. In 1942, the main architect of active collaboration, Eric Scavenius, was, under German pressure, promoted from foreign minister to prime minister. He spoke, possibly with conviction, possibly opportunistically, of a new Europe emerging from the ashes of war and branded resistance at home meaningless, irrational and against the interests of the fatherland.

By the middle of 1943, as the Allies were gaining the upper hand in Europe and Germany was pushed on the defensive, orderly Danish–German collaboration broke down. Home resistance came under a unified command and expressed itself in a steady campaign of sabotage. Actions, small and large, against Danish and German production and transport facilities ran into the thousands. The German occupation authority reacted with counter-terror. The first execution was on 28 August 1943 when a Communist resistance fighter, Paul Sørensen, was shot. In June 1944, the Danish Hvidsten Group blew up a weapons factory known as Riffelsyndikatet, the culmination of a campaign of sabotage. In reprisal, eight members of the group were executed the next day and Danish newspapers forced to carry articles about the executions as a warning against resistance. The people of Copenhagen reacted in a 'people's strike' lasting a week. Public transport ceased to operate, production ground to a halt in many workplaces, strikes spread across the country. A state of emergency was declared, a nighttime curfew imposed, rioters and soldiers clashed in the streets and people were killed.

On orders from Berlin in September 1943, plans were drawn up to confine Danish Jews. However, the German administration was partly demoralised and the plans were leaked.* That enabled the finest act of resistance in the Scandinavian theatre during all of the war. Jews were given early warning and many were able to go underground. By Danish–Swedish collaboration, clandestine small-vessel transport was organised across the Sound. About 7,000 Jews escaped to Sweden, some of them German or east European refugees, with about 700

---

* The information was leaked by the naval attaché in the German legation in Copenhagen, G. F. Duckwitz. He had lost faith in the Nazi cause. In Copenhagen he maintained contact with leading social democratic politicians whom he warned of the impending action. In 1955, he became West Germany's first ambassador to Denmark.

non-Jewish family members. When the Gestapo set their plan in motion they were able to round up only 400, of whom fifty-two died in German camps. In all, about 120 Danish Jews died in the Holocaust.

The occupation was relatively easy for most Danes, for most of the war, until things hardened towards the end. Life went on. Work was good, much of it in German service. Newspapers continued to operate, under mild censorship, as did radio broadcasting. People could listen to the BBC from London. Cinemas and theatres continued to run. Restaurants were open, clubs likewise, and social life was hectic under the tension of war and occupation. Svend Asmussen's quintet played the Copenhagen clubs; he was a brilliant jazz violinist whose career continued into his nineties and the next century. Provisions were relatively plentiful. On the coming of peace, Danes could organise collections of foodstuff and clothing to assist the Norwegians and Dutch, who had suffered harsher conditions under occupation. In 1944, the Danish conservative leader, Christmas Møller, who was in exile in Britain, obtained a declaration from the Allied command that Denmark was recognised as a partner in the Allied camp.

NIELS BOHR (1885–1962)

The most eminent Danish scientist since Tyge Brahe, Bohr was from 1920 head of the Institute of Theoretical Physics at the University of Copenhagen. In 1922 he received the Nobel Prize for pioneering work in nuclear physics. He used his reputation to make the institute a meeting place for physicists from around the world who were working on matters of nuclear energy. During the 1930s, he received and gave sanctuary to scientists fleeing Nazi Germany, helping many of them to work elsewhere in the free world.

In 1941 he was visited in Copenhagen by his German colleague, Werner Heisenberg, who was the head of German research on nuclear weaponry. What they spoke about privately during this visit is not known and is much disputed (and is the subject of the 1998 play *Copenhagen* by the British playwright Michael Frayn). It is possible that Heisenberg wanted, via Bohr, to alert the world to German advances towards an atomic bomb, although Bohr later suggested that if that had been Heisenberg's intention he had not understood it.

In 1943, he was warned that he was on an arrest list and fled to

Sweden, where he helped to clear the way for the evacuation of Danish Jews, and subsequently to Britain, where he was included in nuclear weapons work. He soon moved on to the United States to collaborate on similar research in the Manhattan Project. He was one of many nuclear scientists who were worried about the dangers inherent in nuclear weapons and lobbied for international sharing of the technology, including with the Soviets, something that caused him to be seen with suspicion in at least the British wartime leadership. At the war's end he returned to Copenhagen and to further work as a scientific entrepreneur in Scandinavia and in international collaboration on theoretical and nuclear physics.

The Norwegian authorities fled north out of the capital as the Germans marched in from the west. Neither government nor parliamentarians knew where they were going or what to do. The one man who kept his cool was the conservative leader, Carl Joachim Hambro, also president of the *Storting*. He mobilised a train and managed to keep most members of the *Storting* together. That enabled them to convene later in the day at Elverum and pass a resolution delegating their powers to the government, and then dissolve. The next day the German ambassador presented an ultimatum to the king: surrender and appoint a Quisling government or see the country suffer heavy reprisals. The king put the matter to the government for them to decide, but added that should it decide in favour of the German ultimatum he would be forced to abdicate. That put an end to such temptation as there might have been in those days of demoralisation for a Danish-style solution.

The Germans were in control of coastal Norway and set about occupying the interior. The government, king and crown prince moved steadily north ahead of the occupiers until they reached Tromsø on 1 May. The king was a widower. The crown princess, Märtha, with her three children, including today's King Harald, had been taken to safety in Sweden and was soon evacuated to America. She became a confidante of President Roosevelt and spent much time in his company in the White House and elsewhere. The Norwegian authorities in London and Washington were concerned to improve Norway's reputation as a war ally. Märtha had Roosevelt's ear and was used as an 'agent' with him on behalf of official Norway. On 16 September 1942, the president in a speech recommended that those who wanted to understand the nature of the war and resistance against it should 'look to Norway'. It did Norway's reputation no end of good. Märtha's influence was seen behind it.

There was some hope that a free Norway could survive in the north, but that proved impossible. On 7 June, the British cruiser HMS *Devonshire* carried king, crown prince and government into evacuation in Britain, where the legal Norwegian government remained for the duration of the war. The Germans had been challenged along the Norwegian coast by British, French and Polish forces. It was a shambles. The supporting forces were poorly equipped and untrained for winter warfare – for any warfare. The Germans had air control. Towns along the coast were bombed and burned. A thousand Norwegian lives were lost, both combatants and civilians, homes destroyed, livelihoods shattered. When Germany moved west on the Continent the British and French forces were recalled. The war in Norway was over in two months and the occupation commenced.

SAVING THE GOLD

On 9 April 1940, the Norwegian minister of finance, Oscar Torp, was at work in his office from early morning. The urgent matter was to get the state gold reserve out of town ahead of the occupation. He continued working until he was told that a German patrol was entering the building from the front and then made his way out the back to a waiting car and joined the government evacuation.

The gold was stored in the National Bank in downtown Oslo, forty-nine metric tons in 1,503 crates and thirty-nine barrels. Lorries, twenty-six of them, were requisitioned from removal firms, the last one leaving the bank at 1:30 in the afternoon as occupying forces were entering the city. By evening, all the gold had arrived in Lillehammer, 200 km north, and was stored in the vaults of the local National Bank branch (today the site of the city's most fashionable restaurant).

On 19 April, as German forces were advancing north, the gold was loaded on to six railway carriages which set off north from Lillehammer in the early morning, reaching Åndalsnes on the west coast twenty-four hours later. That city was under German bombardment. On 24 April, 200 crates were transferred to the British cruiser HMS *Galatea* to be brought to safety at Rosyth in Scotland.

The rest of the gold was transported on to nearby Molde, also under German bombardment. British and French forces were now abandoning Norway and the area was falling under German control. Late in the evening of 29 April, HMS *Glasgow* entered the port of Molde in the midst of bombardments, the city in flames. The mission was to evacuate the king, crown prince and government, who, about twenty of them, were hoisted into the *Glasgow* from a small transport vessel. Also loaded on to the *Glasgow* were 756 crates and thirty-nine barrels of gold before she was forced to set to sea shortly after midnight, leaving ten tons of gold behind. About half of the remaining gold was loaded on to a civilian vessel, the *Driva*, which was requisitioned to evacuate officials who could not make it to the *Glasgow* and which set off north in the early hours. The 287 remaining crates were removed from the burning port by lorries to a smaller port up the coast where five fishing vessels were requisitioned by the local mayor. The *Driva*, now damaged, made it to the same port. Here the gold from the *Driva* and the remaining gold on land was loaded on to the fishing boats, which set to sea at daybreak on 1 May, with evacuating officials from the *Driva*.

The *Glasgow* brought king, crown prince and government ministers to Tromsø in the far north, returning to Greenock in Scotland with its load of gold on 4 May. The five fishing boats zig-zagged north through waters of active warfare, making it to Tromsø on 9 May. On 22 May, all the remaining gold was loaded on to HMS *Enterprise*, which arrived in Plymouth a week later. All of the gold that had left Oslo on 9 April, minus 296 coins that had been stolen aboard the *Glasgow*, had been rescued to England.

The second in command of the gold transport was Nordahl Grieg, poet and Communist. In Tromsø, for 17 May, Norway's national day of independence, he wrote a poem which was broadcast by radio in that part of Norway that was still free and which today remains part of the national canon:

We are so few in this country
Each who falls is a brother and friend.

Grieg died on 2 December 1943. He was a war correspondent on board a British bomber that was shot down over Germany.

Officially Norway was from day one, by default, a participant in the Allied war against Nazi Germany, first at home, soon in Europe and beyond. Norwegian troops, eventually numbering some 15,000 men, trained in bases in Britain and Canada and participated in Allied action, usually under British command. The home front collaborated with the British Special Operations Executive, in the north of the country with similar Soviet authorities. Personnel, equipment and intelligence passed back and forth across the North Sea in more than 200 missions in 1941 alone, much via Shetland.

At the outbreak of the war the Norwegian merchant fleet comprised 1,024 ships manned by 35,000 sailors, scattered around the globe. This fleet was nationalised into a single holding company, *Nortraship*, under the government in exile in London and put into Allied service. Half the fleet was lost during the war; 4,000 crew died. The fleet was now modern and of high quality, and sailors were well paid. The British did not want pay inflation in their own fleet and put pressure on *Nortraship* to hold their wages down. In return, some *Nortraship* profits were preserved in a fund for compensation to sailors and their families after the war. A similar fund for sailors had been built up in Denmark, which distributed compensation shortly after the end of the war. In Norway, the fund was bogged down in controversy and bureaucratic mess and disbursements much delayed, continuing into the 1990s, in many cases too late for the surviving sailors themselves.

The Norwegian occupation was from the start different from that of Denmark. Ingar Sletten Kolloen, who is writing a people's history of the war, says that what struck him in his research was that no one, not a single person or family or association or business, was unaffected. Everyone had their lives convulsed.

There were some similarities. There was economic collaboration by both businesses and workers. The occupiers were investors in fortifications, bases, roads, railways, ports and airports. There was collaborative administration and also, of course, resistance – but with differences. Working with and for the occupiers was tolerated in Norway, encouraged in Denmark. Initial administrative collaboration was passive in Norway, active in Denmark. The justices of the Norwegian Supreme Court resigned collectively. Resistance was officially sanctioned from the start. There was to be nothing easy for the Norwegians. About 40,000 were imprisoned during the war,

10,000 in German concentration camps. The first executions were on 10 September 1941, of Viggo Hansteen and Rolf Wickstrøm, both trade union officials, inconspicuously in a shooting range on the outskirts of Oslo. The bodies were buried on the spot and all traces of the event wiped out; not even death notices published.

Life did not go on. Such newspapers as were running were under hard censorship, cinemas likewise. Radios were confiscated (except for members of the Nazi Party) and made an illegal commodity; from 1942 listening to non-authorised broadcasts, such as the BBC, was a capital offence. People lived under periods of curfew; socialising was a risk. Restaurants were for the Germans and their collaborators; others did not fraternise. There were shortages in provisions of all kinds, raw hunger afflicting parts of the population during the latter part of the occupation. Some people prospered but most suffered, mentally and materially.

A big difference was in the role of the local Nazis. The party that before the war had next to no following by 1943 counted 43,000 members. Vidkun Quisling (who has lent his name to the English language in the meaning of arch-traitor) was a military man with an early reputation for brilliance. He made his name in humanitarian work in Russia, Ukraine, the Balkans and Armenia in the 1920s (with Fridtjof Nansen, whose Nobel Peace Prize in 1922 was in recognition of their work). From 1931 to 1933 he served as minister of defence in a centre-right government, from which position he schemed for a dictatorial *coup d'état*. Having failed to mobilise much following, he formed his own party, *Nasjonal Samling* ('National Unity'), with the mad expectation of being called by the country to national leadership. In 1939 he met Hitler and promised collaboration in a coup or occupation. On 9 April, the day of the occupation, he went on national radio and announced himself prime minister of a collaborative government and ordered the country to surrender. It turned out that he did not have German support and his self-proclaimed government came to nothing. By late 1940, the German administration had set up a Norwegian puppet government. From 1942 Quisling was 'minister president', a position he held until the end of the war. He was the most pathetic of traitors, taking responsibility for a regime of terror in which he had no authority. He established his chancellery in the royal palace and set up residence in a splendid villa in Oslo west, Villa Grande, bequeathed to the State by the shipping magnate Wilhelm

*Vidkun Quisling, 1887–1945 – 'lent his name to the
English language in the meaning arch-traitor'*

Wilhelmsen in 1926. He had it fancily decorated and gave it the Old
Norse mythology name of *Gimle*. (The villa today, fittingly, houses the
Norwegian Centre for Holocaust and Minority Studies.) At the war's

end he was arrested, sentenced to death and executed by firing squad under the walls of the old Akershus Fort.

It had been the Germans' mistake to align themselves with Quisling. Had they not, and, as in Denmark, held the local Nazis at arm's length, they might have connected with the willingness that existed among Norwegian politicians for an occupation of cohabitation. The German commander in Norway, *Reichskommissar* Josef Terboven, did not want the assistance of a man he held to be a distraction, but Quisling had protectors in Berlin who were impressed with his ideological zeal.

Nazi collaboration extended into the wider country. The police force was with some success Nazified, sufficiently to do the work of rounding up and deporting much of the small Jewish community, which numbered some 2,100 people in 1940. About 1,200 were able to flee before being captured, 754 lost their lives, twenty-six survived captivity in Germany. Nazi bands collaborated in terror. Infamous was the Rinnan gang in the Trøndelag area, a group of about fifty dedicated Nazis and psychopathic cut-throats. Their method was to infiltrate resistance groups for information and take members in the hundreds into captivity, leading to torture and execution; more than 100 were killed.

What was the impact of home-front resistance? There was much of it, from civil disobedience to armed sabotage. Sportsmen and women withdrew from competitions, churchmen and teachers mounted mass protests, parents stood up against the indoctrination of children, voluntary organisations and unions took their work underground. Activists printed and distributed illegal newspapers. Others spied on German activities, others again set up armed cells. Secret armed 'home forces' were built up, by the end of the war counting some 40,000 men in a reasonably tight organisation. There was retribution from the occupiers, from imprisonment at home or in German camps to torture, murder and execution.

In a dramatic initiative in February 1943, a team of eleven resistance fighters made their way into the Vemork power plant in which heavy water was a by-product, used in German efforts to develop nuclear weapons. They placed explosives in the plant which destroyed a considerable store of heavy water. Production stalled for a while but was resumed after two months. All the fighters survived. In February 1944, partisans placed explosives in a passenger ferry on Lake Tinn near the plant which carried barrels of heavy water, successfully sinking it. Fourteen Norwegian crew and passengers were killed, as were four German soldiers.

The pushback was atrocious. Telavåg was a fishing hamlet on the Norwegian west coast and a resistance transport hub across to Shetland through which men and equipment moved in and out. In April 1942, the Gestapo, having infiltrated the operation, on the night of the 26th ambushed two partisans who were hiding in a loft awaiting orders. It came to a shoot-out and two German officers and one of the partisans were killed. In reprisal, all seventy-two adult men from the hamlet were imprisoned, most sent to the *Sachenhausen* concentration camp in Germany where thirty-one of them died. Women and children were removed to confinement elsewhere in Norway. The village was eradicated – houses, boats, livestock. A number of other Norwegian prisoners who were not from Telavåg were also killed in the reprisal.

Was resistance worth it? Civil disobedience helped to preserve morale and unity, but did not prevent collaboration. Actions of sabotage did disrupt occupation activity and may have contributed to tying down some German forces. Both civil disobedience and armed resistance have formed part of the post-war narrative of peoples that stood tall against injustice. In Denmark, organised resistance from around 1943 was instrumental in getting the country accepted as an Allied partner. But it was all at a terrible cost.

Sweden managed to do what Denmark and Norway had wanted, to stay neutral. It had some defence capacity to lean on; Germany would get what it needed from a neutral Sweden and did not need to occupy it. Taking on Sweden in addition to Denmark and Norway was not doable.

Neutrality came at the price of German threats and pressures. German military action was a looming danger. Sweden was initially dependent on Germany for both exports and imports. The sale of iron ore continued, on which Germany depended, as did the sale of other war-relevant commodities, such as ball-bearings. The accommodation included restrictions on press freedom to repress potentially provocative material. The country's favourite stage comedian was banned from performing for having a way of making fun of Hitler.

Germany was in control of transport routes for Swedish iron ore through Narvik in Norway, and was in need of other transports via Sweden. From July 1940, after the end of fighting in Norway, to the summer of 1943 Sweden allowed German transportation of troops and materiel, including weaponry, to and from occupied Norway. Britain and the Norwegian government in London rightly considered this a breach of neutrality, but it was seen by the Swedish government as unavoidable. Was Swedish policy pro-German? Better to say 'realist', as policy in occupied Denmark in the same period was 'realist'. To Stockholm as to Copenhagen, it initially looked as if Germany would win the war.

The author Astrid Lindgren, of Pippi Longstocking fame, kept a diary from the outbreak of the war in 1939 in which she followed events in detail with perceptive observations and comments. She worked as a mail censor, a snoop reader, she said, (fascinated by the sexual frivolity in the servicemen's letters to wives back home). From early on, life was regulated by rationing, hoarding, blackouts and various restrictions. There was constant fear, both that Germany would attack and also, on Astrid's side more so, that the Russians would come. She held it to be a 'miracle' that Sweden could stay out of a war that engulfed the rest of the globe and had no remorse about the benefits of neutrality. The middle-class Lindgren family could celebrate birthdays, Christmas and other feasts with abundant food and gift-giving. She was well aware of German concentration camps and, from early in the war, the destiny of Jews under Nazi rule.

From 1943, as Germany's position weakened in Europe and Sweden had been able to strengthen its own defences, Sweden, like Denmark, edged towards the Allied side. The German transportations to Norway ceased and trade agreements were signed with Britain and the United States. From about the same time, resistance fighting intensified in the two occupied countries, to which Sweden lent support. Resisters who had to flee, in the thousands, found refuge in Sweden (although some were rejected – during 1941 about one in four Norwegian asylum seekers – and others in Sweden were blocked from moving on to active war service elsewhere). The action of saving Danish Jews succeeded thanks to Swedish participation. Many Norwegian Jews made their way across too. Humanitarian assistance was given to Norway, such as basic and much-appreciated 'Swedish soup' for Norwegian schoolchildren. Both Norwegians and Danes were able to build up quasi-military forces in Sweden, not for fighting during the war but at the ready to return to their homelands at the gradually anticipated German surrender. Under the umbrella of neutrality, the young diplomat Raoul Wallenberg operated a scheme in Budapest to shelter Jews and issue them with protective Swedish papers, which is recognised to have saved thousands of Jewish lives. He himself was kidnapped by the Red Army in 1945 and disappeared into the Soviet Gulag, never to be heard of again. In the spring of 1945 another diplomat, Count Folke Bernadotte, acting on behalf of the Swedish Red Cross, negotiated the release of about 15,000 inmates from German concentration camps, half of them Danes and Norwegians, in a campaign known for the 'white buses' (some of which were rough lorries) in which the inmates were evacuated. The campaign continued through the surrender to evacuate another 10,000 freed inmates. After the war, Bernadotte served as a United Nations peace negotiator in the Middle East, where, in 1948, he was assassinated in Jerusalem by a Zionist paramilitary group.

The war ended, although wrapping it up proved all but easy. In the north of Norway in late 1944, the German occupiers, ahead of the advancing Soviet Red Army, abandoned a territory about the size of Denmark, pushing out a population of 70,000, minus about 20,000 who spent the winter hiding in caves, tunnels and sheds, leaving behind a scorched earth where no town, no farm, no house, no school, no church, no port, no telegraph line, no road was not destroyed.

At the capitulation in May 1945, there were about 350,000 German troops and officials in Norway. They surrendered but had to be disarmed, interned and returned to Germany. There were inadequate means of transport and no organised reception for them amid the total chaos in Germany. It took nearly two years to finish the repatriation. The Germans had held up to 100,000 prisoners of war, mostly Russian, in forced labour in occupied Norway. After the surrender about 85,000 were returned, more or less willingly, to Russia, perhaps half of them vanishing into the Gulag. About 40,000 other non-German non-Russian 'displaced persons' were absorbed into various destinations in Europe during the next two years, a few remaining in Norway. From 1947, Norway participated with a brigade of 4,000 men in the British occupation zone in northern Germany.[*]

The German occupying force in Denmark, about 250,000-strong,

---

[*] It created a storm of indignation back home when it became known that soldiers in the brigade were provisioned with condoms. A petition of protest to the *Storting* gathered 440,000 signatures.

surrendered and could with relative ease be marched back south. Except on the island of Bornholm. The German contingent wanted to surrender to the Western Allies but were refused. The island was occupied by the Red Army, which stayed until April 1946. Bornholm, then, was for nearly a year part of the post-war Soviet-occupied western Europe from which the Soviets subsequently withdrew, as they did from northern Norway. In the last months of the war about 250,000 German refugees had made their way to Denmark, most fleeing ahead of the invading Red Army. At the German surrender they became a Danish responsibility and were gradually, minus thousands who had died, returned to Germany, the last ones in 1949.

About 2,700 German soldiers from the eastern front had made their way to Sweden. By 1946, most of them had been forcibly repatriated to Germany. Not returned to Germany were 167 Balts who had arrived in German uniform and whom the Soviets demanded be handed over. This became a heated issue in Sweden. About 30,000 Baltic refugees had been given sanctuary during the war, most of them from an Estonian population of Swedish descent which had survived for about 650 years (with a surviving dialect of Swedish). The sentiment among most Swedes was that the 167 should be treated likewise, all the more so since many of them would have been forced into German service against their will. The government, however, relented under Soviet pressure and in January 1946 handed over 146 of the Balts to an unknown destiny. (The remaining twenty-one were ill or had died.)

Norwegians and Danes who had sought refuge in Sweden could return to their home countries, including their quasi-military forces which were put into police service and contributed to a relatively orderly transition. Both countries faced the difficult matter of dealing with occupation collaborators. 'Collaboration' was not a clear-cut matter, certainly not in Denmark, where business and work interaction with the occupying force had initially been encouraged by legal Danish authorities. In both countries the settlement required retrospective legislation, normally unconstitutional, and the retrospective introduction of the death penalty. Nevertheless, the processes unfolded mostly in an orderly manner in ways that subsequent review has held, if not in full agreement, to have been reasonably sound and legal. There was some, but not much, unlawful revenge against known collaborators and women branded, in indiscriminate misogyny, 'German whores'.

In Denmark, about 34,000 people were interned by mid-May, of whom more than a half were released within a few days. There were eventually 13,000 convictions, of whom 60 per cent were sentenced to two years or less. There were seventy-eight death sentences, of which forty-six were carried out, all on men, all after a final ruling by the Supreme Court. A parliamentary commission considered governmental collaboration, concluding after eight years with no recommendations for impeachment. One wartime minister, a Social Democrat, was 'tried' by his own party and forced to resign his position in the *Folketing*.

In Norway there were 46,000 convictions for collaboration, 3,300 of them for 'economic treason', resulting in 20,000 prison terms; others were given fines or had property confiscated. Membership of *Nasjonal Samling* after 9 April 1940, then not illegal, was made punishable retrospectively. *NS* members were deprived of civil rights such as the right to vote or hold public office. Thirty Norwegians and fifteen German war criminals were sentenced to death, thirty-seven of whom were executed.

WAR CHILDREN

During and shortly after the Second World War, an estimated 10,000–12,000 children were born in Denmark and Norway to local mothers and German fathers. Many of these children have carried burdens of discrimination, blame and mental ill-health through their lives, in one of the most enduring human after-effects of the war. In the first post-war years, it was standard for 'good' Danes and Norwegians to shun known war children (and also children of known collaborators), and have their own children shun them. War children themselves would live under a weight of shame and conceal their origins.

Danish public archives contain register information of approximately 5,500 cases, until in 1999 they were closed even to the children in question. Since then, war children in search of paternity information have been able to apply for access to relevant register information.

In Norway, the German *Lebensborn* organisation recorded approximately 8,000 children of German fathers during the war. The organisation maintained nine institutions for mothers at birth and the postnatal period in which about 1,000 children were born. A small number of war children were moved to or adopted in Germany during the war or when it ended, but most grew up in Norway, many with single mothers,

others with mothers and stepfathers, others again having been adopted or in foster families, some in orphanages. Women who married German men were in the first post-war years obliged to take German citizenship and were subject to being deported.

After the war, official policy in Norway was initially to have war children adopted out to neutral or distant countries. Many of the children were taken forcibly from their mothers. The policy of out-adoption failed and many of the children caught up in it ended in orphanages or domestic adoption. A Norwegian Association of War Children was formed in 1986, and a similar Danish association ten years later. In 2002, the Norwegian *Storting* issued a formal apology to the war children for the suffering they had been exposed to.

Peace – and union?

After the war a new world was in the making. But not in the form of Scandinavian unity. In finding their footing in Europe and the wider world, the three countries went their different ways.

Sweden took an initiative which might have been a first cornerstone in the building of an all-Scandinavian edifice, proposing a defence union around shared neutrality. Denmark was favourable (if not enthusiastic) – the German threat was no more – but not Norway. The country came out of the war determined to solve its security problem in an Atlantic alliance. That, and soon the Cold War, brought Norway and Denmark under the American umbrella and, from 1949, into the North Atlantic Treaty Organisation, NATO.

During the war, the Swedish defence force had been built up to make the country one of Europe's strongest military powers, by 1950 with the world's fourth-largest air force. By the 1960s, more than half of State research funding was for military purposes and the (secretive) Defence Research Institute was the country's largest research institution by far. Plans were made to strengthen the country's defence with nuclear weapons, finally abandoned only in 1968. The country was confident that it could underwrite the envisaged all-Scandinavian neutrality, but the Norwegians did not share that trust. Was it Swedish capacity or Swedish will that they distrusted? Perhaps both. During the war, all three countries had dealt with Germany, if in different ways, in a combination of collaboration and resistance. There was nevertheless some sentiment, fairly or not, in Denmark and Norway that Sweden had let the side down.

The three countries did, however, find their way to closer economic and cultural collaboration on a broader Nordic basis. Except for Finland, which was under Soviet coercion, all the Nordic states participated in the Marshall Plan from 1948. In 1952 the Nordic area was made a zone of passport-free travel, from 1954 a common labour market with free movement of people (including Iceland and the Faroes from 1966). The Nordic Council was established in 1952 as a body of mainly cultural collaboration, Finland joining in 1955, after the death of Stalin.

In 1968, Denmark proposed a fully fledged Nordic Common Market. A treaty was negotiated but never implemented. Finland was unable to ratify it. But also, it turned out, the others were less than keen. The Scandinavians were edging up to the bigger European unification.

This was to cause them much grief, both in relations between the three countries and in domestic divisions. Denmark had applied for membership of the European Economic Community in 1961, along with Britain, as did Norway, hesitantly. Sweden at the time held membership to be incompatible with neutrality. It came to nothing because of de Gaulle's *non* to Britain. In Norway it brought to the surface deep ruptures in public opinion which survive to this day.

After the failure of the Nordic Common Market, Denmark and Norway again applied for membership of the European Community in 1970, again following Britain. Treaties were negotiated and put to referenda in the two countries after campaigns of intense ferocity, in particular in Norway, where the question divided the country down the middle, destroying friendships and shattering families and neighbourhoods. Norway was first, on 25 September 1972. The country's political, business and union establishments, and most of the press, were solidly on the side of membership. 'The people' were not: 53.5 per cent voted against membership. Then in Denmark, on 2 October, 63.3 per cent voted in favour of membership. Scandinavia was divided again.

In Norway, the Labour government that had negotiated the treaty resigned and was replaced by a centre-right coalition which returned to Brussels for a free-trade agreement. But the question would not go away. The European Community became the European Union and attracted further membership. Norway applied again in 1993, now along with Sweden, Finland and Austria. Treaties were again put to referenda in the four countries. It was carefully arranged for Norway to go last, in the hope that anticipated positive results in the first three countries would shift even the stubborn Norwegians. They did not. Twenty-two years after the first referendum the proposal was voted down again, by 52.2 per cent. Scandinavia was still divided, Norway out in the cold.

That was to some degree alleviated by the creation of a 'European Economic Area' including Norway, Iceland and Lichtenstein (but not Switzerland, which has a separate free-trade agreement with the EU). That has meant, on the one hand, the preservation of the Nordic common labour market, and, on the other hand, virtual membership for Norway of the European Union, with rights and duties in the European single market (with some exceptions for agriculture and fisheries), acceptance of most EU law and directives, participation in most EU programmes, including in the Schengen Area of passport-free travel, and payment of participation fees on the same footing as member states. Not included is any formal say in EU decision-making. This peculiar arrangement has suited the Norwegians well.

Norway's reluctance for union, with both Scandinavia and Europe, is perhaps not surprising. The country had won full independence only in 1905. Its reticence to commitment may have been influenced further by a developing tectonic shift within the Scandinavian family. Norway was starting to find itself rich, filthy rich, from having discovered a wealth of petroleum under the North Sea. In the first part of the story told in this book, Denmark was the dominant power. From the sixteenth century, Sweden took the lead in wealth and power, a position it retained until the end of the twentieth century. During all that time, more than a millennium, Norway had been on the sidelines, poor, unsophisticated, irrelevant. In what is historically the blinking of an eye, it became the rich neighbour.

In May 1963, the Norwegian government issued a decree in which it claimed sovereign economic authority over its coastal sea territory. Phillips Petroleum had been seeking to commence trial drilling under the seabed, which it was then imperative to get accepted as territory under Norwegian authority. In a string of international and bilateral negotiations, it had become accepted law of the sea that states have economic sovereignty of coastal territories as far as exploitation technology allows, limited only by the midline principle by which territory is delineated by the line that divides it equally between the relevant states. In retrospect it is near-incredulous that neighbouring states and the international community would accept principles that handed a state such as Norway, which is all coast, sea territories many times its land territory. The Norwegian coast includes the archipelago of Svalbard, whereby Norway 'owns' much of the Arctic Ocean, even the tiny island of Jan Mayen deep in the North Atlantic, through which it could extend its sea territory to snuggle up to Greenland on the other side of the Atlantic. Much of the credit for this success falls to the then head of the legal division in the Ministry of Foreign Affairs, Jens Evensen. There was not much expertise available on matters concerning the law of the sea. Evensen had been an early student in America, was now a leading authority internationally, and was able to handle the relevant deliberations with foresight and skill at a time when many others were asleep in class.

SPIES

Arne Treholt (1942–2023) was a Norwegian journalist, politician and diplomat. There were other spies, including the Swede Stig Wennerström (1906–2006), a spy for Nazi Germany during the war and the Soviet Union later, but none as dashing as Treholt.

In 1967, the three Scandinavian governments had prosecuted the Greek military junta for crimes against humanity before the European Court of Human Rights, resulting in a successful conviction in 1970. Jens Evensen served as prosecutor. In this work he involved Treholt, with whom he formed a lasting fatherly friendship of collaboration. It is believed that Treholt's first KGB contact came via Greek Communists.

Evensen was a cabinet minister from 1973 to 1978, bringing with him Treholt as junior minister. He moved from a political to a non-political post in the Ministry of Foreign Affairs and served in the early 1980s as second in command in the permanent mission to the United Nations (where I knew him during my time as a UN consultant). Back in Oslo, he was arrested on 20 January 1984, at Oslo airport, on his way to Vienna with a batch of secret documents to meet his KGB handler. He had long been under suspicion and was under FBI surveillance during his time in New York. At his trial, a couple who lived down the corridor in the Treholts' fashionable apartment building, and whom they had befriended, appeared as FBI agents and witnesses for the prosecution. He was convicted of high treason and espionage for the Soviet Union and Iraq and was sentenced to twenty years in prison, serving eight. He claimed to have been serving world peace by equalising the imbalance of information between East and West.

Arne Treholt had been a golden boy of Norwegian social democracy. His father was a member of the *Storting* for the Labour Party and a minister of agriculture. Arne was the embodiment of the young, modern, progressive leftie: attractive, bright, idealistic, sporty, sociable. His treachery came as a blow to members of his circle, many of whom refused to believe the validity of the case and have kept championing his innocence. He died in Moscow on 12 February 2023.

From 1965, drilling concessions started to be awarded on terms that secured the Norwegian State sizeable shares of any profit. From 1969, oil and gas have flowed generously out of the North Sea, and revenue generously into State coffers. The petroleum sector, with all its subsidiaries in supply, logistics and infrastructure, became dominant in the national economy – and Norway a crucial supplier of gas to Europe.

The petroleum revenues were soon on a scale much beyond what could be absorbed in the small Norwegian economy. The State made itself generous, both to its own people and in international engagement, but still had loads of money on its hands that it had to find a way of managing. The solution was to establish a sovereign wealth fund through which the surplus was stored in international equity, today known as the Government Pension Fund Global. Its market value at the time of writing is approximately NOK 15,400,000,000,000, making the Norwegian State the owner of just under 2 per cent of all of the world's listed companies (including 25 per cent of Regent Street real estate in London).

Even a Norwegian author must be allowed the observation that the thread that runs through *oljeeventyret*, 'the petroleum fairy tale', is one of skill and modesty. The Norwegians have handled their windfall wealth with wisdom and competence, enjoying it, certainly, but not going overboard. This has been managed by successive governments and parliaments and with, generally, broad political consensus.

Governments both rightist and leftish have engaged internationally across a range of good causes, while also not throwing their weight around. So it is also within Scandinavia. Norway has become a high-wage magnet for labour migration from neighbouring countries, Sweden in particular, but continues to be, I think it is fair to say, a good neighbour. The Norwegians have become rich, but not, at least collectively, high and mighty towards neighbours who in earlier times may not always have granted them much esteem.

Social democracy

Scandinavian social democracy has produced leaders of eminence. In Denmark the colourful Thorvald Stauning – cigar-maker, trade unionist, charmer, hard drinker, womaniser, master of compromise, the man with the longest ginger beard in northern Europe – sat as a lone Social Democrat in a Liberal government from 1916 to 1920. He was prime minister in 1924, led his party to its best election victory ever under the slogan 'Stauning or chaos', and Denmark through the 1930s and into the war (if by then worn down by exhaustion and depression and perhaps unable to stand up to the Germany-friendly faction in the Danish leadership).

Hjalmar Branting was elected to the Swedish *Riksdag* in 1896, the first Social Democrat. He was alone until 1902, when the Social Democrats captured four seats. In 1917 he took his party into a coalition government with the Liberals, and in 1920, 1921 and 1924 formed Social Democratic minority governments, staying at the helm until he died of exhaustion at age sixty-five. Per Albin Hansson guided the country with wise flexibility through the Great Depression and the Second World War, then as head of coalition governments. Tage Erlander was prime minister for twenty-three tumultuous years from 1946 and came, eventually, to be seen as the ultimate *landsfader*, 'national patriarch'. His protégé Olof Palme was prime minister twice (until he was shot dead walking home with his wife from a cinema on the evening of 28 February 1986), taking the party back to its ideological roots and giving Sweden a distinct voice on the international stage.

Einar Gerhardsen was Norwegian prime minister from 1945 to 1963 (with two brief interruptions), and oversaw Norway's transition from wartime destruction to welfare-state excellence, like Erlander retiring into the elevated dignity of *landsfader*. Gro Harlem Brundtland was the first woman prime minister in Norway, and held the position thrice from 1981, an early trailblazer in the politics of women's equality and environmental sustainability.

The Social Democrats had entered the *Folketing* in Denmark in 1884 with two representatives (on 4.9 per cent of the vote), rising to their best election in 1935 with 46.1 per cent of the vote. In Norway they had to wait until 1903, when they won five seats (on 9.7 per cent of the vote), and until 1957 for their best election with 48.3 per cent. The Swedish Social Democrats went from 3.5 per cent of the vote in 1902 to over half of the vote in five elections (first in 1938 with 50.4 per cent and finally in 1968 with 50.1 per cent), but in most elections fell short of an absolute majority.*

These parties were to be dominant in mid-twentieth-century politics, but never hegemonic. In power they mostly presided over minority or coalition governments, although with partner-parties much smaller than themselves. The period of Social Democratic dominance lasted less than fifty years, from the mid-1930s until the beginning of the 1970s. In the most recent elections, the Swedish Social Democrats won 30.3 per cent of the vote (in 2022), the Norwegian ones 26.3 per cent (2021), and the Danish ones 27.5 per cent (2022). Since about 1970, all three countries have had shifting coalition governments, sometimes centre-right, sometimes centre-left.

The social democrats had everything going for them. Their parties sat on a foundation of class cohesion. Within a decade of workers winning the vote, they were the largest parties in their respective parliaments. From early on, the mainstream was challenged from the Left by syndicalists and radical socialists, a challenge that presented itself again in the early years after the Second World War with a relatively strong Communist presence. That challenge they took seriously, fighting it down to keep the movement as united as possible, manipulating it to insignificance with whatever means were necessary. The Labour Party, said one of its Norwegian chiefs, was never 'a damned Sunday school'.

They built an alliance of steel between the party and union branches. The parties did the parliamentary work, but with union backing and with party and union working hand in hand. No feature has been more

---

* The formal party names are *Socialdemokratiet* (in Denmark), *Det norske Arbeiderparti* and *Sveriges Socialdemokratiska Arbetarparti*.

characteristic of the Scandinavian labour movements than their success in creating organisations governed by means of (in Lenin's language) democratic centralism. The union side made itself, and has remained, not only a labour movement partner but a social partner more broadly, with an inescapable presence in the making of policy across the board and irrespective of the colour of shifting governments.

They organised culturally beyond party and union activity to create 'families' that looked after their flock from cradle to grave, establishing organisations in education, sports, song, theatre, travel. They organised women, pensioners, housing tenants, Christian socialists. They celebrated feasts together, the 1st of May importantly but also others. They organised children and youth through the year and in summer and holiday camps. They embraced the cooperative movement, in everything from daily consumption via insurance and housing associations to funeral management. They had their own newspapers, magazines and publishing houses. Authors, artists, architects and academics flocked to the cause. By 1965, the Swedish Social Democratic Party had 1.2 million members, in a population of 8 million.

The non-socialist side could match none of this. There was no class cohesion: farmers, urban academics and capitalist captains were not of the same hue. No attempt at any party political unity had any success. The social democrats could drive wedges of division into the enemy camp, which had some backing from employer organisations and from business, but nothing like the union backing on the other side. There was non-socialist cultural organisation – religious, scouting – which was often successful, but without political affiliation. The Right was neither a movement nor a family.

Socialism as an idea emerged in Europe in the second half of the nineteenth century. The goal was simple: prosperity, freedom and security for working people. The theory was simple: power sat in the ownership of capital. The liberation of workers depended on gaining control of the means of production. The social democratic way was to do this by democratic means. The working class would win political power through the vote and use that power to neutralise the force of private capital. It is in the control of capital that socialism is realised.

Hjalmar Branting defined early Swedish social democracy: fiercely socialist and fiercely reformist. It was not reform *or* socialism but reform *and* socialism. Danish and Norwegian movements were different, ideologically uncomfortable with themselves. They liked, for a while, to be radical in rhetoric but in reality gave up on socialism in any classic understanding early and easily. The Swedish social democrats did not, and continued to do battle with orthodox ideology until late into the twentieth century.

By the time the Danish social democrats were ready for government responsibility, they were pragmatically reformist. The Norwegians, however, were in a protracted identity crisis. In 1919, the Labour Party joined the Soviet-directed *Comintern*. A faction split off to the Right. In 1923 the party left the *Comintern*, drawing the rightists back in, but shedding another faction on the Left to form a Communist Party. Labour still clung to the illusion of being revolutionary. It took help from on high for them to get sorted. From 1905 to 1928 there were eleven governments, all conservative or centre-right. In 1928 another one fell. By now, the Labour Party had become the largest, with 37 per cent of the vote in 1927, the Conservatives pushed back to 24 per cent. But it persisted in pretending to be revolutionary, with a programme of orthodox socialism in which parliamentary work was secondary to direct industrial action. The leaders of the parties to the Right dithered about forming a new government. The king, Haakon VII, grasped the opportunity and called on the leader of the Labour Party. The old party leaders had not thought it possible that a revolutionary party could be invited to govern, but the king ambushed them. The Labour Party was the largest and it was constitutionally correct to call on its leader if a coalition of smaller parties was not forthcoming. The king knew exactly what he was doing. He wanted to force the hapless socialists to grow up by trapping them into government responsibility, and thereby make the party accept itself as a normal parliamentary party. The 1928 government lasted only twenty-eight days but by 1933 the Labour Party had a reformist programme, eagerly accepting government responsibility in 1935. It had taken them time, but they had joined their Danish brethren in non-ideological pragmatism. (King Haakon's manoeuvring in 1928 was the first of two occasions when he used his royal authority to assist the country, possibly decisively, at dramatic junctures, the second one being to shut down the possibility of collaborative German occupation in 1940.)

The Swedish social democrats' battle with themselves would last until the ground started to fall away from under the movement itself. The difficulty was capital. The Danish and Norwegian social democrats had resigned: regulation, yes; strategic nationalisations, yes; State investment banks, yes; worker representation on company boards, yes. But takeover of private capital as a matter of principle? No. The Swedes, however, persisted in looking for ways to gain, in the old language, control of the means of production. Scandinavian social democracy, then, was not a unified movement. Swedish social democracy was of its own kind. The Danes and Norwegians were managerial, the Swedes ideological.

In 1920, the Swedish social democrats had the first government of their own, a minority government it is true, but social democratic nevertheless. That government appointed a commission to study the socialisation of capital. At issue was to find a way of gradually shifting production capital into collective ownership. The commission worked for fifteen years. Not much came of it, but the question was kept alive. Crude nationalisation was rejected as economically inefficient – voted down in a party congress in 1932 – but the search had started for an economy that would be both well functioning and socialist.

By 1935, the labour movement, in the shadow of the Great Depression, was edging towards a deal with capital for industrial peace, resulting in the Saltsjöbaden Treaty of 1938. A subtext of that treaty, not formalised in writing (although some historians believe there was a secret protocol), was that labour and capital committed to leaving each other alone. Income, its equalisation of by progressive taxation and social policy, was fair game for labour, but capital, the ownership thereof, was a private prerogative. That was the 'historical compromise'.

It lasted through the war, but no longer. In 1944, the Social Democratic Party adopted a manifesto with three main components: full employment, fair distribution, industrial democracy, in the latter the socialisation of capital being a core component. The search for method was on again. The wartime coalition government stepped down in July 1945 and was replaced by a Social Democratic majority government which set about implementing the 1944 programme. Social reforms followed in short order, but as yet no assault on capital.

Ten years on, they were handed an opportunity via a big pension reform. A State-run basic pension had come into place gradually from early in the century. Some workers enjoyed additional earnings-related pensions, but not most blue-collar workers. Hence there was pension affluence for the few, pension poverty for the many. There was broad agreement to extend the benefit of earnings-related pensions. The non-socialists wanted a system of private and voluntary insurance. The Social Democrats wanted it obligatory and State-run. There were social policy arguments: an obligatory system would ensure that everyone was included. But there was also an argument around the management of capital. Earnings-related pensions are funded by contributions. Contributions add up to capital. In a private system, pension capital is in the hands of private managers. In a State system it is under 'collective' management. A State-run system is a way of shifting capital from private to public hands. The Social Democrats grasped the opportunity and pressed aggressively for a State solution, which after high political drama that included a manipulative referendum and fresh elections, was passed by 115 to 114 votes in the 1958 *Riksdag* (thanks to one of the non-socialists abstaining). So the 'people's pension', the final glory of the Swedish welfare state, came into being by a one-vote majority – a one-vote majority which also redistributed control of capital and took Sweden a (small) step neared to a socialist economy. It was a big victory. The Liberal Party, which had opposed the State solution, suffered a decimation of their vote in the next election. Capital did indeed add up and has been managed in a series of funds pursuing different investment profiles, including provision of high-risk State capital for Swedish business.

But that victory was not enough. In 1975, the trade union branch adopted a policy of comprehensive collectivisation of the ownership of capital, in a plan devised by the economist Rudolf Meidner. He and others thought the method had been found for gradual socialisation. It was to be done in a system of 'wage earner funds'. The party branch of the family did not like it but was highjacked. With victory in the 1982 election, it was government policy.*

There was logic behind the idea. Social democratic thinking – and the Swedes were *thinkers* in a way the Danes and Norwegians were not – was that economic security for working families depended on a robust industrial economy, which again depended on a well-functioning

---

* The prime minister to be, Olof Palme, had described the idea as 'hellish'. In the debate in the *Riksdag* ahead of the decision to establish the funds, the minister of finance, Kjell-Olof Feldt, was caught on camera having penned a poem in which he described the funds as a 'piece of damned shit... with jobs-for-the-boys for any fat-cat crony who has supported our great struggle'.

labour market. That was to be managed by way of 'active labour market policy', known as the 'Rehn–Meidner model' after the same Meidner and his colleague Gösta Rehn, another trade union economist (who had also been one of the authors of the Social Democratic manifesto of 1944). One of the merits of active labour market policy was to hold back wage inflation so as not to undermine industrial competitiveness. (Yes, social democratic thinking, including in the union branch, was that wage restraint was in the interest of the working class!) This was to be secured by offering workers collective benefits in compensation for wage moderation: full employment and social security. That worked for a while, but by the 1970s the long post-war boom had broken, bringing back unemployment, industrial unrest and a loss of competitiveness. A new deal was needed. The idea now was to offer workers another collective benefit, a growing share in the ownership of the economy. That would come about with the help of funds that would take the ownership of capital out of private hands and put it under wage-earner control, ultimately under the control of directly and democratically elected boards. Envisioned was not only a new economy but also a new polity, with economic parliaments outside the political parliament.*

After the election victory in 1982, the Social Democratic government set up five regional funds that went about buying equity out of the private economy. Their original capital came from modest earmarked taxes, enabling the funds to become profitable and self-sustaining. In his original plan, Meidner had estimated that wage-earner funds could be in control of the majority of Swedish equity in the course of a few years.

The policy was not as mad-hat as it might look in retrospect. The Swedish political economy was of its own kind, both ultra-social democratic and ultra-capitalist. Ownership of capital was highly

---

* In the early 1980s, I had a front-row seat from which to follow the unfolding drama, in the Institute for Social Research of the University of Stockholm, a stronghold of social democratic orthodoxy. Its Emeritus Professor of Labour Relations was none other than Gösta Rehn of the Rehn–Meidner model (who maintained an office in the institute after retirement, in which he partly lived). I held the professorship of welfare studies after its first holder, Sten Johansson, had become Director General of the Central Bureau of Statistics. He had published a pamphlet in 1974 under the title *När är tiden mogen?* ('When is the time right?'), meaning to complete the social democratic project by taking on capital.

concentrated in the hands of a few families, the Wallenbergs and the like. They were themselves in a sense equity-owning funds, if under private control. Competing funds under collective control might be seen as a softening-up of a monopolistic economy.

But it was a fiasco. No one, except a few diehard ideologists, was a believer. By the time it was implemented it was watered down with the rhetoric of capital ownership having been stripped out. Wage earners saw nothing in it for themselves and took no interest in any abstract share of ownership. A non-socialist government in 1991 abolished the funds, against next to no opposition. The equity they had accumulated was sold back into the private economy, slowly and carefully so as to not disrupt finance markets. The money from the resale was put into subsidised small-scale private stock investments, finally bringing some benefit to wage earners, and into various foundations in support of scientific research. The quest for a democratic socialisation of capital had come to an end.

Swedish social democrats, although ideological, were no less apt in being managerial than their fellows in Denmark and Norway. In all three countries, the period of social democratic dominance was one of industrial advancement, economic growth, full employment, better standards of living, State activism and improved social protection. The original socialist ambition was achieved. The socialisation of capital, however, failed. No viable way of democratic socialisation was found. Nor was it necessary: there was prosperity, freedom and security for working families without the means of production having been removed from private ownership. If we take the period of social democratic dominance as an experiment, it had produced a rather stunning (for orthodox socialists) outcome. Socialism was not necessary for the socialist dream to come true.

Welfare states

On 8 November 1852, a Sami riot erupted in Kautokeino in northern Norway. The local sheriff and shopkeeper were killed, the vicar whipped, others tortured and mistreated. Non-Sami Norway had been making itself felt, bringing with it a mixture of fanatical religiosity and aggressive trade in liquor. The rioters wanted to save the infidels.

The Sami had become a problem. They had not been in the past, they had been different and interesting, and were displayed to the world for their exotic dress and way of life. Now, by Enlightenment ideas of race and evolution, they were inferior and underdeveloped.

Rioters, some under the age of eighteen, were put on trial; some were sentenced to hard labour, two executed. Official Norway and Sweden had started a process of lifting the Sami out of backwardness by making them Norwegians and Swedes. Their culture was repressed, their children confined to boarding schools where they were taught in Norwegian and Swedish, languages most of them at first did not understand. This experiment in repressive assimilation lasted through most of the next century, with mainly misery to show for it.

In 1966, a group of Sami communities took the Swedish State to court over recognition of their collective ownership of land in their areas. The case finally failed in the Supreme Court in 1981. During the 1970s, Sami communities in northern Norway mobilised against incursions into their areas of hydroelectric regulation of rivers they held to be theirs, culminating in January 1981 in a spectacular act of civil disobedience by a coalition of Sami and environmentalists to disrupt construction work. The mobilisation failed in its direct purpose. But, as in Sweden, the Sami had risen. They organised. They made themselves a force others had to listen to.

Both national governments appointed commissions on Sami law that worked through the 1980s and beyond. The Sami won acceptance as indigenous peoples with minority rights. They obtained cultural recognition, specifically for the Sami languages and their use in education and public administration. In a bold innovation, Sami parliaments were established, elected by Sami voters, with legislative and administrative authority in cultural and certain economic matters. (Voting rights are obtained by Sami self-identification.) In 2006, State lands in the Norwegian county of Finnmark were transferred to an autonomous property-owning institution, bringing 96 per cent of county land into local collective ownership.

It had been a turnaround, not only in the standing of the Sami but also in governance understanding generally. Thinking had moved from social control to social integration.

Poor relief had come to Scandinavia with the Christian Church. In the Reformation it was nationalised into a State responsibility. The State outsourced that responsibility to localities which were left to manage their poor as best they could. The approach was to suppress beggary and remove the poor out of sight. Families had to take care of their own, the infirm were dispatched by rota from farm to farm or auctioned out to those charging the lowest price for their care, sometimes confined to work- or poorhouses, children to atrocious orphanages, unwanted infants left anonymously in churches or the forgotten charge of 'angel makers' (women who for a fee took charge of infants on the unspoken understanding that they were likely to vanish).

The nineteenth century was a struggle to come to grips with 'the social question'. Everyone could see that the old ways were not enough. But what to put in its place? Answers were a long time coming: for a while, mainly private philanthropy, only gradually State activism. We can divide the twentieth century in two: an initial period of learning for new ways of thinking to take hold, and a subsequent period of implementation to create a new state, the welfare state. The dividing line runs through the 1930s, with ultimate implementation after the Second World War.

The backdrop was economic growth, unexpected economic growth. The first part of the century had seen progress in spite of war and recessions. At the war's end in 1945, the expectation was bust. What instead happened, to general surprise, was unprecedented boom that went on steadily for twenty years. Also unexpected was the post-war baby boom, which blew away the old fear of population decline. The affluence which people had started to see before the war just kept on giving. From 1950 to 1970, private consumption increased threefold while public consumption reached 40 plus per cent of rapidly increasing national products. Anxiety turned to optimism.

The Scandinavians were learning about affluence. At the beginning of the century, they were among the poorest populations in Europe, certainly the Norwegians. Moving into the 1930s they were starting to have money to spend, both in private consumption and better public services. It wasn't much compared to now, but more than they had been used to. No single factor has contributed more to the making of the welfare state than crude economic growth. The welfare state was made because it became affordable.

They were learning how to use the State. In the liberalism of the early part of the century, the State was an instrument of emergency. That understanding did not survive the first half of the century; it was undermined in the management of the First World War. Here, as we have seen, the State put the economy under administration and found itself able to mobilise business and civil organisations into a hitherto unknown form of corporate public management. The liberal view that the State has to save when revenue declines was giving way to a more activist understanding that the State should step in with emergency measures, such as public works to control unemployment and social provisions to alleviate deprivation. But initially it was done with great caution: costs had to be kept down as much as possible and be covered by additional emergency taxes. Public works, for example, typically paid a bare subsistence wage, if that. But economists had started to think of ways of not only easing setbacks but preventing the cycle of boom and bust itself. That would require a different level of activism, not, for example, public works at minimum pay but at standard pay, so as to bring fresh stimulus into the economy. Outlays would not be covered by taxes but by borrowing, again for more stimulus, to be repaid out of subsequent economic growth. This is the theory we now know as 'Keynesianism', after the British economist John Maynard Keynes and his *General Theory of Employment, Interest and Money* (1936), but which was being developed ahead of Keynes by Scandinavian economists, in particular the 'Stockholm School' during the 1920s and early 1930s. That pioneering work was possible thanks to theories of interest, value and money developed by Knut Wicksell (1851–1926), who was also an inspiration of Keynes's (and an all-round radical, in opposition to Church and narrow morality, living, then scandalously, in unmarried partnership with the Norwegian–Swedish feminist Anna Bugge).

The economic thinking of the Stockholm School was absorbed by Scandinavian social democrats and went into their anti-recession policies of the 1930s. That gelled into a new acceptance of the State as an instrument of societal management. The Scandinavian States invested their new capacities in counter-recession policy with skill and energy.

They were relearning taxation. Taxes were traditionally extracted from economic activity: on land, on business by fees and tolls, in the form of manpower. Now they were reshaped to be taken out of households. Regular State taxes on income were introduced around the turn of the century (1895 in Norway, 1902 in Denmark, 1910 in Sweden). It was modest, a few per cent of income initially, and moderately progressive, so that the rich paid a bit more and the poor less or nothing. The next step was to tax household wealth, both current ownings such as housing and bank deposits and the transfer of property at sale or inheritance, again starting modestly. And the third step was to tax consumption, first in the form of sales taxes. Once introduced, household taxes were gradually extended and broadened with State taxes, municipal taxes, property and inheritance taxes, pension contributions, all at increasing rates, generally progressive, both to make taxation digestible and as an instrument of redistributing income. Sales taxes were regularised after 1945, again at first at modest rates, from the 1960s being redesigned into 'value added taxes' at steadily increasing rates; presently in all three countries the VAT rate is 25 per cent of the sale price, making it the most important single source of State revenue. The welfare state is ingenious. Households are taxed to enable governments to dispense public services back, with redistribution in the process. Those at the bottom of the income ladder pay less and get more; over time households pay while economically active and receive when not earning. It's a costly system but it pays for itself.

They were learning to understand rights. The poor had no such thing: local authorities had responsibilities, but help for the poor was at the discretion of their betters. The arrangement was also utterly disorganised, with patchworks of provisions under impenetrable rules and devoid of system, heavy on social control. Karl Kristian Steincke (1880–1963) was a Danish social democratic politician who had his formative experience in the management of municipal poor relief. In 1920 he produced a plan for a comprehensive revision of social legislation which represented a breakthrough in modern thinking. Provisions should be humane, rights-based and non-punitive. Social support should be arranged in a system of coordinated provisions. These ideas – rights, system, coordination – would be central in the rollout of welfare state reforms in the next decades. In 1929, Steincke landed his dream job of minister of social affairs and in 1933 pushed through a set of laws on social insurance against accident, unemployment, illness, invalidity and destitution which were to be a model for future reform across Scandinavia. Social provisions were not yet generous, but new principles were set in stone, specifically that of rights. The conditionality that receipt of support came at the cost of other rights, typically voting rights, would be removed.

They were learning to understand families and children. Children had been neglected, receiving only a rudimentary education and in work from a young age, with violence standard at home and in school. Families were private, insulated from public sight. In 1900, the Swedish author Ellen Key called for the new century to be the 'century of the child'. Families came to be recognised as institutions preparing the next generation of workers and citizens. There was concern about 'the population question', the ability of the population to reproduce itself. In 1934, Gunnar Myrdal, a central figure in the Stockholm School of Economics, and his wife Alva, both of the Swedish social democratic aristocracy, published a book, *Kris i befolkningsfrågan* ('Crisis in the Population Question'), which warned about the quantity and quality of population reproduction. They called for various measures of monetary and service support for parents in the job of raising children. The Scandinavian welfare state was from early on a family welfare state in which support for families and children has remained a central pillar.

EUGENICS

Concern over population quality was standard among progressive thinkers in the first part of the twentieth century. The 'population question' was not only a matter of population size but also the right kind of reproduction. In Denmark, Steincke was a proponent of measures such as sterilisation of the mentally disabled and the anti-social in the interest of genetic quality. The Myrdals advocated 'passive eugenics' to encourage good and discourage bad reproduction, and looked forward to the possibility of 'active eugenics' once science had advanced. Throughout Europe, there was concern that the working class and/or 'inferior elements' reproduced more energetically than the middle and upper classes, and that this might cause a decline in genetic quality overall. It was also part of eugenic thinking (very much so in the Myrdals' book) to improve population quality by way of better health and other provisions for mothers and children.

Selective sterilisation was a provision in Danish law from 1929, mostly on the basis of mental disability but also physical disability, alcoholism and criminality. A law of 1938 prohibited marriage for certain categories of disabled people, or allowed marriage on the condition of sterilisation. Legislation in both Sweden and Norway in 1934 enabled sterilisation of the mentally disabled, and in Sweden, on certain conditions, of sex offenders and 'vagabonds'. This classification was soon extended to vague

categories such as persons with a serious illness that might be assumed
to be hereditary, or 'obviously' unsuited or unable to manage the rearing
of children, or with anti-social lifestyles, which for men might mean
alcoholism, for women promiscuous sexual activity. Legislation made a
distinction between enforced and consensual sterilisation, a distinction
which was however blurred in practice. In Sweden, sterilisation occurred
with some frequency in the Gipsy population (as it was then known),
mostly classified as consensual.

There is much uncertainty about numbers, due to ambiguous criteria
and variable statistics. From around 1930 to about 1970, the number of
sterilisations per country per year may typically have been in the order
of 500, fewer in the years before the war, more later. Only a minority
of sterilisations may have been enforced, although nominally consensual
sterilisations may in practice have been more or less coerced.

They were learning about prevention. In poor relief, alleviation
comes after the fact to repair, or hide, damage. Now the idea grew
that damage should be prevented. Keynesianism is an economic policy
to prevent boom and bust; family policy is to invest in children for the
prevention of distress later in life.

They were learning about universality. Social assistance had been
selective, for carefully defined categories of citizens with carefully
defined needs, often reserved for the 'worthy' needy. But selectivity is
costly. It is costly in effectiveness: it is difficult to identify exactly who
is included in a theoretically defined category and to target assistance
at those deemed to be in need. It creates problems of definition: some
of those excluded are as much in need as those included. It comes
with costs in the form of stigma and shame. Inclusion and equality of
treatment were core principles in the Steincke reforms.

New ideas were bringing policy thinking generally to where the
long process of Sami policy had come specifically: from minimalist
social control to integration by way active State management. What
had been relief for this or that outcast group had become a matter of
bringing all of society together.

The hard 1930s lifted the Scandinavians into a new political culture.
There was deal-making, compromise and collaboration. There was
State activism, economic management and social reform. People,
inspired by new ideas and hitherto unknown energies, came to believe

not only in progress but in the ability to make progress. They were beginning to experience stronger States as benevolent forces dispensing, by and large, good governance. That followed through to confidence in State management. The groundwork was being laid for that elusive quality of trust between rulers and the ruled, a quality that remains conspicuous in Scandinavian State–society relations.

The progress of the twentieth century was monumental – in economic growth as never before. Equally in mindsets: democracy, rights, equality. Social democratic thinking changed profoundly. If, at the start of the century, the social democrats had a workers' paradise in mind, by mid-century their language had shifted to the *folkhem*, 'a home for all the people'. They left behind the idea of winning the class war and turned to a vision of class harmony, in another understanding of integration and universality. They went from being the workers' vanguard to making themselves the people's stewards.

Ways of living were revolutionised, and revolutionised again, from poverty towards plenty. In the 1960s and 1970s families lived immeasurably better than had those a generation or two earlier, contentedly aware of how things had improved. However, if we look back at that time from where we are today we see lives of dreariness: grey, conformist, monotonous, sparse, parochial. Only well into the post-war period came expansive modernity: popular music, colour, American films and musicals, multi-channel television, spacious living, motor cars, restaurant meals, all-year tropical fruit, foreign travel, diversity and eventually the IT revolution. Most of what we now take for granted in daily life is brand-new. Public policies played a part, but in complicated ways; it was as much a matter of social change making a new State as the new State making social change.

Industrialisation matured, with Sweden leading the way. The population shift from country to town continued, as did Nordic migration. Swedish industry was in need of a bigger workforce than the country itself supplied. An early inflow was from Finland, from where people emigrated partly for economic reasons and partly out of Cold War discomfort. That was followed by an inflow from southern Europe, in particular Yugoslavia. Later, the Scandinavian countries found themselves on the receiving end of the great global migrations. Peoples that were originally white and Protestant have become mixed in ethnicity and faith. They have reacted with a combination of generosity and meanness. They have been generous in international collaboration in order to contain the flow, and in helping those allowed in to become integrated. But they have been tight, certainly in Denmark and Norway, in accepting migration into their own territories. And, much effort notwithstanding, they have not entirely been successful with integration: ethnic tension, sometimes violent, has become a feature of public life, and immigration a disruptive issue in political life.

The welfare state has no birthday; there is no big day to celebrate. It has grown by slow and gradual trial and error, intervention on top of intervention, reform on top of reform, and reform again, never ending, still ongoing. Nor is there any precise definition of what it means; the question of what it really is can only be answered by pointing to where the ongoing process of perpetual reform stands at any given time. Democracy, standards of living and social protection have all been improved, durably we must hope, but are not at any final point. Tomorrow, the welfare state will be a different thing again, reshaped by more reforms.

A partial old-age pension had been introduced in Denmark in 1891 (for the worthy needy), and voluntary health and unemployment insurance in 1892 and 1907. The first social insurance in Norway came in 1894, against industrial accident for workers in certain exposed industries. Sweden introduced an early pension insurance in 1913, in principle covering the entire population, to yield a pension in old age or disability of up to about 10 per cent of the average industrial wage. Denmark extended its pension similarly in 1922. A means-tested pension was decided on in Norway in 1923, but its implementation was delayed until 1936 for reasons of non-affordability (although 40 per cent of the population had some municipal pension cover from around 1920). Obligatory health insurance, in Norway again, was introduced in 1909.

From these beginnings in all three countries, the State gradually imposed its will on society, sometimes as a result of general 'enlightenment', sometimes in response to labour unrest: industrial regulation and workplace inspection, regulated working hours – the eight-hour day and forty-eight-hour week – regulated holiday rights, slum clearance, school reform to equalise and extend education, specifically for girls, social recognition of illegitimate children, rights for domestic servants (six days of paid holiday a year in Denmark in 1921 but no upper limit on working hours), subsidised health and dental care, criminal reform – the death penalty was abolished – continuous tax reform, continuous extension of social insurance.

From the late 1930s there was a shift of gear and energy. The State had been a nightwatchman; now it was to be the board of directors of Nation Incorporated, after the First World War never the same, after the Second World War with new economic and ideological capacities. Thanks to economic growth and effective taxation it had money, not only income to spend but also capital to invest, which was put to work under various names: pension funds, State banks for agriculture, for districts, for innovation.

The big push for reform was not a matter of inventing new measures but of universalising what was already there in embryo and to bring things into the social democrats' beloved 'system'. Pensions, job security, sick pay, free health care, holiday rights – it was already there, but only for select groups: public-sector employees, white-collar workers, people in rich municipalities. The categories were now widened, step by careful step, to include more people, eventually the whole population, on more or less equal terms. Gustav Möller was the proud Swedish minister of social affairs from 1936 to 1951. In 1945, in preparation for the post-war push to the mature welfare state, he made a list of major social reforms in the 1930s and found that there had been thirty-two of them.

With peace, the floodgates opened. It started with family support. A child allowance was introduced in Norway in 1946 and Sweden the year after to all parents irrespective of income. It was radical: universal, rights-based, formulated to redistribute income to parents, more to those raising many children. Progress continued with steady improvements in services, notably health care and education, with free higher education up to university level. Participation in secondary schooling doubled in ten years. By 1960, there were 40,000 students in Swedish universities, up from 10,000 in 1940. There was heavy investment in schools at all levels, eventually also those for preschool children, and gradually more investment in universities, hospitals and care homes for the elderly and the disabled. Shorter working hours were introduced, longer holidays, five-day weeks, maternity leave, paternity leave. Families had more money to spend in spite of higher taxes and more leisure time in which to spend it.

All three countries enacted far-reaching pension reforms. Sweden and Norway adopted integrated 'people's pensions' in 1958 and 1965 respectively. It was a battle in Sweden, as we have seen, but easy in Norway. The Swedes had done the fighting and the Liberals in Norway were not about to take the thrashing their brethren had suffered across the border. It was mainly about coordinating and improving existing provisions and shaping the whole edifice of social protections into a 'system'. The only, if far from insignificant, innovation was the mini-socialist integration of earnings-related pensions into the State system, which had been the contentious issue in Sweden.

The push for reform took a different path in Denmark, possibly because social democracy had a weaker standing there. Family support was channelled through the tax system, with tax deductions based on the number of children; not until 1984 was it reshaped into a paid child allowance. Old-age pension provisions had been in place since 1891, and were gradually extended to a (near) universal basic pension in 1956. Earnings-related pensions, however, the ones that in Sweden and Norway had been brought into the State system, were not included. The Danes instead settled for a system in which additional pensions are handled separately, in industry schemes that enrol workers covered by relevant collective wage agreements, much as the losing side in the Swedish battle had wanted.

For workers and pensioners it does not make much difference. Everyone at retirement age gets a generous basic pension, more so in Denmark. Wage earners, all of them in Sweden and Norway and about 80 per cent in Denmark, are enrolled in additional collective pension schemes whereby they maintain in retirement their pre-retirement standard of living.

Is the Danish 'private' system less fair that the more statist systems in Sweden and Norway? The balance of opinion is that in delivery, basic and earnings-related pensions combined, they are pretty equal, with, if anything, some more inequality creeping into the Swedish system through modifications made at the end of the century. We have previously seen that socialism was not necessary for the socialist dream to come true. If we take the different pension systems in the three countries to be alternative experiments, we have reconfirmation of that conclusion. It would seem that the mini-socialism of the Swedish and Norwegian systems had not been necessary even for reasons of social policy.

*

'It took about fifteen years for Sweden to become a mature welfare state.' So say the historians Hindman, Lundberg and Björkman. It was dizzying, breathtaking, uplifting, impressive. The State in forceful action. Life was improving. Security was improving. Social integration. Class harmony. Everything was possible.

In 1965, the Swedish government committed to the building of a million new dwellings in ten years. That was active labour market policy: workers should move to where productive jobs were available. The million units were built (modern and solid but, in today's eyes, puny and the embodiment of dreary conformity). The working population relocated to industrial centres, leaving rural areas depopulated. This was not what was happening in Norway. What in Sweden was active labour market policy was in Norway active regional policy. The thinking was to maintain a dispersed pattern of population and keep the districts populated. That has proved difficult and has been only moderately successful, but there remains a difference between the two neighbours: the smaller Norwegian population is more spread out, the larger Swedish population more concentrated.

On 3 September 1967, Sweden switched from driving on the left to driving on the right. It was not popular. A referendum in 1955 had been against it. But in 1963 the *Riksdag* nevertheless decided to go ahead. At 5:50 in the morning all traffic stopped. Ten minutes later, in a countdown broadcast nationally, driving was on the other side of the road. It had been carefully prepared, in the Swedish way, including with an intensive campaign of information. A pop singer, Rock-Boris, was recruited to belt out a song that became inescapable: '*Håll dig till höger, Svensson*' ('Stay to the Right, Svensson'). It unfolded with next to no difficulty, and with next to no increase in road accidents. Nothing was beyond the State's reach.

Did it all become overwhelming? There were warnings. As the social democratic machine churned on, voices from the Right – they were labelled 'value conservatives' – shouted in the wilderness in fear of diminished individualism, efficiency, enterprise and ultimately freedom. They were ridiculed by the new establishment, but there was some truth in their despondency.

In one way, the warnings proved false. It has been standard in social thinking to fear that government-engineered social justice, however well intentioned, comes with less productivity in the economy. The Scandinavian experiment has put that dismal proposition to the test and found, in another dramatic conclusion, that it has not been borne out. The Scandinavians have invested more, and more successfully, than any other economies in social protection, and have at the same time been among the most successful capitalist democracies in terms of economic productivity and growth. The Scandinavians were never wishy-washy in social terms; they have been hard-nosed economically. It's only that they have found a way of being economical while also being generous. Economists and others who take their truth from abstract logic ahead of practical experience are in love with, as they see it, the tragedy that social justice is too expensive to be worth it. The Scandinavian story stands in glorious dismissal of that hypothesis. If you are in mastery of statecraft, you can have both affluence and justice.

But in another way those critical voices proved worth listening to. Standards improved, but in some respects social quality did not. Never have more women been housewives than in the first post-war generation, and public life was long conspicuous for the absence of women. Much of the initial generosity in social policy was built on an implicit contract of male breadwinner families with home-working women. Pressure for equal pay by gender had to wait until after the 1950s.

The weight of the tax burden doubled in twenty years. The author Astrid Lindgren wrote a fable about a country, much like Sweden, where a person, much like herself, ended up paying up to 102 per cent tax. The minister of finance, Gunnar Sträng, charismatic and exuberant, took to patronising: an author and a woman, however brilliant in her art, could not be expected to grasp the intricacies of tax rules. Astrid retorted that her numbers were solid and that it was he who was telling fairy tales – perhaps they should switch jobs? Sträng had to back down. Even the film-maker Ingmar Bergman, a social democrat by inclination but who had the misfortune of having a bit of money to manage, left the country for seven years of exile when he was caught in the dragnet of the we-know-all tax bureaucracy.

Education was advancing but the school experience was narrow and regimental. (I know, I was there.) In the provision of welfare there was uncritical confidence in planning, managerial rationalism and institutions. The ideal hospital was large and designed for factory-like effectiveness. Housing too was large-scale, much of it in apartment blocks set in environments of communal sterility. Social and health care were institutionalised, even primary health care managed from hospital settings. A heavy burden of conformity weighed down on cultural life to hold back experimentation and creativity.

Reaction set in. The system itself reacted. Collateral damage was recognised and repaired, in part by the same machinery of reform that had seemed to be out of control. The heavy hand of institutional rationality was relaxed. In health and social care there was a turn to de-institutionalisation and to home and community care, bringing care to the needy rather than the needy to care. The family doctor, modelled on the British system of general practice, came back. Confiscatory tax rates were levelled. Housing became a matter of building not only dwellings but also communities. When I see today's schooling against my own experience there is no comparison. Whereas we were made to march in rows and were disciplined top down, children now learn in participatory ways in richly equipped, colourful and broad-minded schools.

Women reacted. They organised, yet again, and in the next generation moved back into education, the labour market and public life. Soon the Scandinavian countries were the European vanguard in the emancipation of women. Gender equity became the norm in politics and government, and gradually also in business. In 2003, Norway introduced pioneering legislation to oblige listed private businesses to appoint at least 40 per cent women on boards of directors, an obligation that was realised with relative ease.

Cultural workers reacted. The genre in literature and cinema known as 'Scandi noir' emerged in response to heavy-handed social democratic complacency. The first masters were the Swedish authors Maj Sjövall and Per Wahlöö. In a series of ten 1960s and 1970s novels featuring the Stockholm detective Martin Beck, they portrayed a decent official up against a Kafkaesque monster of managerial police-state-like bureaucratic repression.

Still, the excess lingers. The suburban block housing cannot be abandoned but also not fully humanised; it is far from slummy, being well maintained and brought up to date, but remains a hard environment, sometimes stimulating ethnic tensions. The weight of conformity has not fully lifted. The Swedish author Lena Anderson, in a novel about the *folkhem*, thinks that the State that does so much for you imposes on you a burden of obedient gratitude. Writers and film-makers in the 'noir' tradition continue to portray cultures with attractive surfaces but rough, if hidden, undercurrents of violence, drug crime and perversion, in portrayals that are received as pertinent and relevant. Sweden has been the leading force in social democratic modernisation. When I lived in Stockholm in the early 1980s, I came to experience the force of it as burdensome. As a social scientist in one of the best social science institutes in Europe and a comfortably off middle-class man in one of the most vibrant cities in Europe, it should have been ideal. But I moved on and within the next couple of years became a Scandinavian emigrant. From outside I now look in, with, perhaps, some detachment. I visit often and for long periods. I see democracies I admire, systems I admire, welfare states I admire. People live well, things work, it's in good order. But it's not entirely comfortable. We Scandinavians are *so* tolerant, so open, so engaged, so advanced, so informed, so international, so solidaristic. But that's also the way we have to be. We are all one big standard mainstream.

So is it true that there is too much of a good thing in the Scandinavian welfare state? It is certainly the case that the Scandinavia that has emerged in and from the twentieth century is a good place for people to live and an attractive presence in the world. It is not unimpressive that excesses have been recognised and in large measure rectified. Prosperity, freedom and security have been spread broadly and preserved, while the dreariness of the young welfare state has been overcome in the mature one. If the Scandinavians are peoples who are not easy-going and have a streak of angst in their character, perhaps what lingers is not so much welfare state heavy-handedness as that Lutheran culture I visited earlier, that functional culture that is conducive to order and that works for the people who live under its influence, but that also comes with a burden of just slightly repressive conformity. They now have it good, those people up there in the north, but their contentment may be tempered by a touch of guilt. If so, is that also possibly to their advantage?

Continuation

Scandinavia Today

At 3:15 in the afternoon of 22 July 2011, a van drives into the compound of government offices in central Oslo. It parks at the entrance to the main building, a high-rise in modernist functionalist style with, at the top, the prime minister's office and a terrace of pride from where it was the custom to treat visiting state leaders to panoramic views of the city. A man steps out of the van, dressed in a police uniform, and walks away.

Ten minutes later a bomb detonates in the van, homemade but powerful. It blows out doors and windows in government and surrounding buildings, sets off fires and causes structural damage to the main high-rise. Eight people are killed, several hundred injured.*

The man walks to a nearby square where he has a car parked and drives west out of Oslo. An hour and a half later, he is at Lake Tyrifjorden in which sits the island of Utøya where the annual summer camp of the Labour Party's youth organisation is getting under way. He presents himself as an officer of the Oslo police, there for security following the bombing. He is heavily armed, gathers the young people around him – and sets about shooting them. Sixty-seven die of gunshot wounds, two while escaping, and more than 100 suffer physical injury (of 564 people on the island at the time). At 6:30 p.m. he is taken into police custody.

The man was thirty-two-year-old Anders Behring Breivik. He had had some engagement in Right-radical politics but was now outside any organised activity. Earlier in the day, he had posted a voluminous document entitled *A European Declaration of Independence* to 1,000 email addresses, a manifesto of rage against European integration, Islam, multiculturalism, Marxism, feminism, political correctness and other ills. He was found to be of sufficiently sound mind to be held

* The government compound is under reconstruction; the first phase, including the restored main high-rise, is due to be completed by 2025–26.

responsible for his actions, put on trial, and sentenced to indefinite confinement.

A hatred of brand Scandinavia had surfaced, strong enough for a man to set out to destroy a national command centre and eliminate a future leadership. The Norwegians reacted by coming together and affirming their values of tolerance and inclusion, much helped by Scandinavian solidarity and exemplary leadership from the prime minister, Jens Stoltenberg (later Secretary-General of NATO). The way in which the perpetrator was dealt with was a case study in correct judicial process.

It had been an attack on State and people like nothing before or since. But it was not entirely unique. There were earlier cases of domestic terrorism: the murder of Olof Palme in 1986; in 2003 the Swedish foreign minister Anna Lindh had been stabbed to death in an attack in a Stockholm department store. Scandinavia has its share of skinhead bands, gangs of neo-Nazis, hooligans, gun violence and more or less organised crime. In 2021, a Swedish rapper knowns as Einár was killed in a gangland execution in a Stockholm suburb, in a troubling case of violence-infused music that had been widely popular and highly awarded.

The American political scientist Francis Fukuyama has coined the term 'Getting to Denmark' (in his *The Origins of Political Order*). He was referring to what he thought liberal democratic capitalism should be about. He had stayed in Denmark for a while, in Århus as it happens, that same town where I started this story, and seen there, I should think, much what I saw. Well, Denmark has got to *Denmark*, and Scandinavia to *Scandinavia*, and my question has been how that has happened. Having traversed 1,200 years of history, I have picked up dribs and drabs of explanation that may make at least some sense of how so a terrible history has produced so benevolent an outcome.

That explanation starts and ends with the European influence. From the very beginning, when populations migrated north as the Ice Age came to an end, to where we are now in the shadows of the twentieth-century wars and the resulting project of European integration, pressures, influences, technologies and dangers have washed over the northern lands for the Scandinavians to absorb, react to and resist. People came from the south. Knowledge of agriculture came from the south, as did the technology that enabled the agricultural upturn from around 1200. The sail was the imported tool that made Vikings out of Norsemen. It was capital taken and traded across the Continent that enabled those Vikings to be of consequence. The early mythologies were, in large measure, a Germanic import, as were and are the Scandinavian languages. Christianity was a European import, bringing with it faith, Church organisation, the use of writing and in due course printing and publishing. The Lutheran Reformation was German, as part of the larger package of influences known as the Renaissance. The Scandinavians followed the Europeans in royal absolutism under the command of warrior kings in search of grandeur, and later into the Enlightenment, and from there gradually towards industrial economies and democratic polities. Even the welfare state, the pride of modern Scandinavia, has grown from non-Scandinavian roots: Germany's social insurance reforms of the 1880s and the British post-1945 reforms towards universality.

The European influence has come with existential enmity, from Russia to the east and Germany to the south. Ever since the Vikings were blocked out of their eastern trading routes Russia has been a menace, a menace that persists and has now brought a reluctant Sweden (and Finland) to seek protection under the NATO umbrella. Ever since Gudfred wanted to take on Charlemagne, Denmark has manoeuvred for security, and sometimes existence, against the German threat, up to the wars of the nineteenth and twentieth centuries.

The interactions with Europe have been on a one-way street, Europe the giver, Scandinavia the taker. Scandinavia is the ultimate periphery. While the Vikings moved into Europe for gain and conquest, no one in Europe saw it worth their while to retaliate, not until the Hansa for a while made themselves a military presence and established cities and trading stations of their own. European technologies and ideas have for the most part moved north with a time lag. Population and agriculture came late, Christianity came late, the use of writing came late, the mastery of trading technologies came late. Not until the eighteenth century and the Enlightenment did the Scandinavians start to catch up and make themselves more equal in Europe, such as in Swedish industrialism and across the countries in literature, music and political developments towards democracy.

Over the centuries until then, the Scandinavian quest for identity at home and presence abroad is best seen as a string of dead ends. If Scandinavia today is 'special', that is not because its long history has been 'special'. The Viking Age has had a way of impressing historians and others, but its achievements were not lasting and the whole business came to an end with not much good to show for it. The upturn of the 1200s was destroyed by the Big Death, plunging Scandinavia into distress for the next 300 years. The idea of Scandinavian unity was first manifest in the Kalmar Union, but was perverted to the opposite, to warfare, never again to succeed as more than rhetoric. The Reformation enabled royal dictatorships and resulted in the end of Norway as a kingdom. The grasp for power by Danish and Swedish kings pushed the Scandinavians into mutual hatred and more inter-family warfare. The Swedish Age of Grandeur was a waste of everyone's time, and massively of lives, livelihoods and resources. Into the twentieth century, it was only thirty-five years since Denmark had provoked a suicidal war with Germany.

The best we can say is that historical misfortune produced new awareness. Denmark and Sweden came to terms with themselves as modest kingdoms. Norway reclaimed its autonomy. The Scandinavians were finding an answer to their old question of how to be European: don't worry about it, know yourself, get your own house in order. Their new reality enabled governors to give up on lording it over the people and instead govern for and with them. At home, they reached not for union but for collaboration. In Europe, they turned from taking to contributing.

When I on that day in Århus a few years ago asked, how did it come to this, just what was it I saw? Many things, no doubt, but finally, I believe, a town, a community, a country, a region where there are no longer small-folks. The people who were left out of the telling in the *sagas* were small-folks. Most of the people who struggled and worked and soldiered and died over the following centuries counted for nothing. The majority of people, even on the threshold of the twentieth century, were still downtrodden. Their children and grandchildren no longer are. It is still the case that some have more than others, but no one is now so low as not to matter.

This revolution, far from creeping up slowly over the ages, came as an explosion over a few decades. The Scandinavia that is 'special' is, historically speaking, brand-new. Explaining that phenomenon is a matter of showing what unfolded during the twentieth century: the experience of good governance and the follow-through into cultures of trust. The force of social democratic organisation. Good, sometimes inspired, leadership. A sense of the practical in neighbourly collaboration. The instinct to moderation in political and economic life that persisted through a short, in retrospect, period of hot class conflict, and later defeated the polarisations that have come to burden some other cultures. All on the back of prosperity and democracy.

If we today try to imagine ourselves into the minds of the men and women who 100-plus years ago were marching into their new century, we will see that they had no way of comprehending what was coming. The political élites of the time, the conservatives, agrarians and liberals, could not have imagined that within thirty years they would no longer be in charge, and that the scruffy workers who were shouting abuse at them would have taken over. Nor could the socialists, who still had no other way of making themselves felt than by disruption, have imagined that power would shortly be theirs. Nor that they would use that power to build not workers' republics but *folkhem*.

And no one, of whatever persuasion, be they rich or poor, could have had any way of predicting, or even the mental apparatus to envisage, the progress of economic and technological growth that was to unfold. 'Anyone who as late as in 1945 [observed Kurt Samuelsson, writing in the mid-1960s] might have predicted what Sweden would look like twenty years later, would not have been believed and would have been thought a fantasist.' They were on their way to that progress, but that it would bring them to the standards and ways of living that were to materialise would have been utterly incomprehensible.

Is that twentieth century turnaround a social democratic story? The first answer must be 'no'. It was, again, the Scandinavian version of a greater European venture. The early-century combination of boom and bust was a European experience, as was the later triumph of growth. The rise into serious prosperity was a European experience, at least of democratic Europe. State managerialism is a European phenomenon, as is the welfare state. The discrimination of the Sami was in part a broader minority story.

But, that recognised, also 'yes'. Scandinavia is, if not fundamentally of its own kind, nevertheless different. The transition to prosperity has been from marginally more poverty to marginally more affluence. The State has been marginally more powerful, democracy of marginally better quality, social protection marginally more inclusive. The Scandinavians have been marginally lucky in that most of the margins have pulled in the same direction and in their favour. Those margins are the result, we must think, at least partially, of Scandinavian social democracy having been marginally more social democratic.

Today's Scandinavia would not be the same without the half-century of social democratic custodianship. How different we can hardly know, but it would have been different. It would be too much to say that social democracy has created modern Scandinavia, but it must be right to say that it has influenced the creation. Otto von Bismarck, the greatest of German leaders, said of statesmanship that it consists 'not in aspiring to control the current of events, only occasionally to deflect it: the statesman's task is to hear God's footsteps marching through history and to try to catch on to His coat-tails as He marches past'. That, perhaps, is what able social democratic leaders in the north have had the luck to practise. True, the Swedish ones for a while did try to control the current of events by reaching all the way for the political ownership of the economic means of production, but then overstepped and fell back to the art of the possible. Is it, perchance, that they and their comrades in Denmark and Norway have been rewarded by that same God by having their influence nudge Scandinavia, although a child of Europe, into also becoming a special child in the European family?

If the twentieth century was a period of unprecedented change, the pace of change is only accelerating.

The challenges are formidable. The world is different. Steady economic growth is no more and we are back in cycles of boom and bust. Global migrations are accelerating, bringing pressures of population movements towards affluent areas and countries. Power is draining out of the West and towards the East, China in particular, undermining democratic confidence and shoring up autocratic ideologies and practices. In 2020, the world was hit by a deadly virus that spread to become a global pandemic and put on display the vulnerability of modern interconnectedness. We are in the midst of a climate crisis which is threatening livelihoods and habitations across the globe.

Europe is different. In 2022, Russia invaded neighbouring Ukraine, angry at it being democratic and independent, taking again to raw, large-scale, barbaric war of a kind we have seen much of in this history, with one blow reconfiguring the European political and security landscape, and its cultural landscape, reigniting through Middle Europe and into Scandinavia that old fear of Russia. No single theme has run through this history more consistently than *war*. Many of us may have shared in a hope that after the Second World War we Europeans were on a path of learning to do without its ancient blight. After the fall of the Iron Curtain in the 1990s, there was hope that Russia might be included in the fraternity of peacekeepers. We were, it turned out, naïve. This book was being finished as the war was raging in Ukraine. If, until then, these 1,200 years of history might have been seen as having a happy outcome, that optimism was suddenly crushed. The Austrian author Stefan Zweig entitled his memoir of pre-Fascist Europe *The World of Yesterday*. It is difficult not to see the Russian war on Ukraine as another watershed at which the Europe we were getting comfortable with, even proud of, has become another world of yesterday.

Scandinavian democracy is different. What was once fought for is now obvious. Class reality has changed, and so has class awareness. No one takes pride in being of the working class, or any class, or even identifies with class. Social democratic force is of the past, the broad organisational families dissolved, the parties cut down to half their previous strength. Governments are coalitions, centre-right or centre-left, it does not much matter.

The cultures are different. Not long ago, the Scandinavians were emerging from poverty and started to see the possibility of prosperity. They were simple folk, they wanted decency and better lives for their children. They had a mission, soon articulated as the building of *folkhem*. They have done it. What then remains of mission? They have become sophisticated, comfortable, worldly-wise. What, they may be asking themselves, unable to find the answer, do we now want?

Norway is in need of a new economy. With global warming, the old one is to be weaned off petroleum dependency. The State's sovereign fund, which invests profits from the petroleum business, has ceased to invest in petroleum activity. It is up to the Norwegians to find the wisdom to disengage from petroleum that they were able to deploy in the engagement years. No country has in recent times been more blessed with luck. Will it be lucky again? The Swedes and Danes are not much less prosperous than the Norwegians, for all their petroleum, and are perhaps the lucky ones in not having to redesign their economies.

Scandinavia remains disjointed. The cultural divide between

Continental Denmark and the more Lutheran Norway and Sweden has not been overcome, national resentments have not fully been laid to rest. In response to the COVID pandemic, Denmark and Norway took the predictable route of State managerialism, while Sweden, of all countries, made itself the champion of *laissez-faire*. There is a divide between Denmark and Sweden in the European Union, and Norway, not yet secure enough in its independence to accept integration. But the security divide is superseded by Sweden following Denmark and Norway into NATO membership. That would have been unthinkable only a year earlier. It is not to be ruled out that Norway too may reconsider its position in European integration.

In all that is in flux, what stands firm as the core of *Scandinavia* is the welfare state. It is 'the model' that gives Scandinavia identity, that is the glue of Scandinavian togetherness, that enables the Scandinavians to present themselves to the world. In politics, where there was until recently division by class, there is now consensus. Even would-be extremists have been absorbed into the fold. Everyone is in favour of the welfare state; indeed, in political campaigns it is now the maintenance of the welfare state that defines the very purpose of government. Political disagreement is reserved for details in ways of doing it.

The man who on a day in 2011 wanted to kill *Scandinavia* didn't have a chance. Buildings and lives were destroyed, yes, but not spirit. Outsiders may think that the welfare state is a technical matter of social generosity, but the Scandinavians themselves know it goes deeper. Their understanding of State and society is underpinned by a culture of trust and collaboration. They trust each other, these people (by and large), and trust their authorities and institutions of economy and society (by and large). They are lucky. Governments dispense good governance, economies are in order, people can be confident that they matter and that things are in safe hands. If we manage to preserve our welfare-state culture, the Danes and Norwegians and Swedes may be thinking, we have what it takes to handle whatever the world throws at us. They may be right.

NOTES

14   'A ship didn't just': Pye, *The Edge of the World*, p. 70.

Chapter 1: The Vikings

18   'perhaps due to their': Frankopan, *The Silk Roads*, p. 114.

18   'an enormous influx': Winroth, *The Conversion of Scandinavia*, p. 98.

18   'multi-billion dollar': Frankopan, *The Silk Roads*, p. 116.

19   'sea-raiders': Abulafia, *The Boundless Sea*, p. xxi.

21   'between 856 and 859': Heer, *Charlemagne and his World*, p. 244.

22   'No great loss': Bishop, *The Penguin Book of the Middle Ages*, p. 60.

26   'Gradually it became clear': *The Vikings in England*, p. 16.

27   'The Scandinavians, still': Cunliffe, *By Steppe, Desert and Ocean*, p. 405.

28   'In 991, Olav Tryggvason': *The Vikings in England*, p. 17.

28   'admitted into': Stenton, *Anglo-Saxon England*.

29   'foolhardy': Fenger, *Kirker rejeses alle vegne*, p. 46.

31   'destroying the great tradition': Burns, *The First Europe*, p. 293.

34   'I may be strong': Crossley-Holland, *Norse Myths*, p. 30.

34   'a North European equivalent': ibid., p. xxxiv.

39   'favourite scholar': Nelson, *King and Emperor*, p. 10.

40   'Power was visible': Winroth, *The Age of the Vikings*, p. 105.

40   'glittering splendour': Roesdahl, *The Vikings*, p. 71.

43   'a reconstruction of Viking cooking': Serra and Tunberg, *An Early Meal*.

43   'creative in the kitchen': Price, *The Children of Ash and Elm*, p. 119.

43   'Similar estimates of population size': The Norwegian population has been estimated retrospectively from later records thanks to a high degree of stability in the location of farmsteads and a similar stability in their names, and the retrospective use this has permitted of documents relating to land transactions, tax lists and ecclesiastical and aristocratic cadasters of the late-medieval and early modern centuries, and also later parish lists. The conditions for making similar estimates for Denmark and Sweden have not been similarly present. Benedictow, 'The Demography of the Viking Age', pp. 179–81.

46   'Of the three ships': Winroth, *The Age of the Vikings*, p. 3.

46   'Most Scandinavians lived': Roesdahl, *The Vikings*, p. 4.

47   'They appeared in many guises': ibid., p. 197.

47   'gangsters': Crossley-Holland: *Norse Myths*, p. xvi.

48   'autocratic, imperial': Pye, *The Edge of the World*, p. 26.

49   'How did you win them': Crossley-Holland: *Norse Myths*, pp. 117–18.

50   'their talent': Holland, *Dominion*, p. 62.

50 'Peaceful submission was rewarded': Frankopan, *The Silk Roads*, p. 160.
50 'the violent ones': Abulafia, *The Boundless Sea*, p. 370.
51 'The natural disposition': Crossley-Holland, *Norse Myths*, p. xiv.
51 'mother of kings': and other quotes here are from Snorri, *Kringla Heimsins*.
55 'Sexually active': Friðriksdóttir, *Valkyrie*, p. 120.
55 'men were in the company': ibid., p. 6.
55 'forced exploitation': Price, *The Children of Ash and Elm*, p. 142.
55 'the great recruiting grounds': Jones, *A History of the Vikings*, p. 148.
56 'nowhere was there greater': Frankopan, *The Silk Roads*, pp. 117–18.
56 'The very word "slave"': Macintosh-Smith, *Arabs*, p. 354.
56 'Human beings were': Foot and Wilson, *The Viking Achievement*, p. 66.
56 'slave-sea': Harrison, *Sveriges historia*, p. 226.
56 'dishonourable and cowardly': Hedeager, *Danernes land*, p. 265.
57 'they would buy up': Rio, *Slavery After Rome*, pp. 30–33.
58 'Christian antipathy': Foot and Wilson, *The Viking Achievement*, p. 77.
63 'brothels were full': Holland, *Dominion*, p. 125.
64 'fills out the factual': Sophocles, *The Theban Plays*, p. 8.
65 'Germanic': Gimbutas, *The Living Goddesses*.
66 'sin and guilt': Fenger, *Kirker rejeses alle vegne*, p. 32.
66 'The classical literature': *The Cambridge History of Scandinavia*, Vol. 1, p. 520.
67 'you will find just about everything': *New York Times*, 15 August 2019.
68 'exceedingly simple': Lunden, *Norge under Sverreætten*, p. 13.
68 'His eyes burned like orange': Crossley-Holland, *Norse Myths*, p. 82.
69 'quite literally as the body': Rikhardsdottir, *Emotion in Norse Literature*, p. 77.
69 'gestures of mourning': ibid., pp. 90, 92.
70 'significantly curtailed' etc.: ibid., pp. 38, 46, 44, 45, 49, 52.
70 'Look at your beloved': ibid., pp. 104, 109.
74 'rejected books and the distinctive': Price, *The Children of Ash and Elm*, p. 194.
74 'If we were to point to': Fenger, *Kirker rejeses alle vegne*, p. 369.

Chapter 2: The First Modernisations

75 'its establishment of a community': Burns, *The First Europe*, p. 40.
76 'So in Denmark and Sweden': Almgren, *The Viking*, p. 143.
76 'few worried particularly': Winroth, *The Conversion of Scandinavia*, p. 138.
77 'through which moral authority': Burns, *The First Europe*, p. 39.
84 'boasted that he would': Heer, *Charlemagne and his World*, p. 226.
84 'twelve *primores*': Nelson: *King and Emperor*, pp. 459, 462.
88 'if he ever had it': Krag, *Vikingtid og rikssamling*, p. 191.
88 'an assortment of unidentifiable': Jones, *History of the Vikings*, p. 383.

95 'entirely Scandinavian': Winroth, *The Conversion of Scandinavia*, p. 56.
96 'A culture finds': Crossley-Holland, *Norse Myths*, p. xxv.
97 'They had no notion': Foot and Wilson in *The Viking Achievement*, p. 6.
98 'closer than an overland': Price, *The Children of Ash and Elm*, p. 197.
99 'the starving poor': Nelson, *King and Emperor*, p. 177.
100 'conquered the world': Herman, *The Viking Heart*.

Excursion: Neighbours West and East

104 'I want to buy Greenland': *New York Times*, 21 August 2019.
107 'cracked in two': Harrison, *Sveriges historia*, p. 96.

Chapter 3: The Great Transformation

115 'the most important innovation': Hørby, *Velstands krise og tusind baghold*, p. 58.
127 'whores' huts': Lunden, *Norge under Sverreætten*, p. 80.
128 'The long periods of political unrest': *The Cambridge History of Scandinavia*, Vol. 1, p. 600.
128 'from old, the monastery's peasants': Dahlerup, *De fire stender*, p. 97.
135 'absorbed its assumptions': Holland, *Dominion*, p. xxiii.
147 'When Christoffer's rule': Hørby, *Velstands krise og tusind baghold*, p. 194.
149 'the last of the Viking kings': Krag, *Vikingtid og rikssamling*, p. 239.
151 'The realm was approaching': Helle, *Under kirke og kongemakt*, p. 100.
153 'Norway as a political entity': Benedictow, *Fra rike til provins*, pp. 76ff., 336ff.
154 'one must take with lies': Åberg, *Vår Svenska Historia*, p. 96.
155 'a watershed in Swedish history': Harrison, *Sveriges historia*, p. 254.
156 'the lowest esteemed': Harrison and Eriksson, *Sveriges historia*, p. 59.

Chapter 4: Big Death, Slow Resurrection

160 'In Norway, a population of': Benedictow, *Fra rike til provins*, pp. 120–21. Harrison and Eriksson, *Sveriges historia*, pp. 33, 224. Helle, *Under kirke og kongemakt*, p. 117. Bjørkvik, *Folketap og sammenbrudd*, pp. 19–21, 25, 214. Jouko Vahtola in *The Cambridge History of Scandinavia*, Vol. 1. Wittendorff, *På Guds og Herskabs nåde*, p. 24.
161 'the state apparatus collapsed': Benedictow, *Fra rike til provins*, p. 454.
161 'Not until the second half': *The Cambridge History of Scandinavia*, Vol. 1, p. 563.
164 'There is a direct line': Harrison and Eriksson, *Sveriges historia*, p. 410.
164 'died out': Benedictow, *Fra rike til provins*, p. 455.
166 'almost miraculously': Dahlerup, *De fire stender*, p. 42.

167 'something strangely pale': Imsen and Sandnes, *Avfolking og union*, pp. 261–2.
169 'Norway was not much': ibid., p. 328.

Chapter 5: Reformation

177 'People knew that Christendom': Davies, *Europe*, p. 383.
177 'If we should try': Dahlerup, *De fire stender*, p. 151.
178 'little patience with the gentle': Davies, *Europe*, p. 484. Holland, *Dominion*, p. 298.
183 'the intellectual Catholic resistance': Rian, *Den nye begynnelsen*, p. 61.
184 'false teachers': *The Cambridge History of Scandinavia*, Vol. 2, p. 74.
185 'Swedes were at war': Aarebrot and Evjen, *Reformasjonen*, p. 88.

Addendum: The Cities

189 'By one count': Helle, *Under kirke og kongemakt*, p. 113. That count includes a good many small settlements. In another account (Lunden, *Norge under Sverreætten*), only four places in Norway grew to what might be called cities: Bergen, Oslo, Trondheim and Tønsberg. Another count again (Hans Andersson in *The Cambridge History of Scandinavia*, vol, 1) has innumerable towns in Denmark and southern Sweden in the high Middle Ages, but only ten in Norway. Yet another count has, by 1350, some sixty cities and towns in Denmark, some thirty in Sweden and about a dozen in Norway (Göran Dahlbäck in *The Cambridge History of Scandinavia*, Vol. 1).

Chapter 6: Two New Kingdoms

201 'Capitalism was starting': Wittendorff, *På Guds og Herskabs nåde*, p. 19.
203 'It is our understanding': Mykland, *Gjennom nødsår og krig*, p. 365.
205 'psychological environment of fear': Davies, *Europe*, p. 433.
213 'At the silver mines': Åberg, *Vår svenska historia*, p. 168.
215 'It is difficult to identify': Dahlerup, *De fire stender*, p. 336.
215 'culturally poor land': Villstrand, *Sveriges historia*, p. 114.
215 'danced to all over Scandinavia': *The Cambridge History of Scandinavia*, Vol. 1, p. 513.
217 'have beautiful, ancient': *The Cambridge History of Scandinavia*, Vol. 2, p. 64.
217 'completely extinguished': Åberg, *Vår svenska historia*, p. 166.
219 'If life at court': Fladby, *Gjenreisning*, p. 104.
220 'This war saw the birth': Åberg, *Vår svenska historia*, p. 180.
220 'for the next 150 years': ibid.

Chapter 7: Imperialism

221 'exceeding the production': *The Cambridge History of Scandinavia*, Vol. 2, p. 368.

221 'For most of the people': Scocozza, *Ved afgrundens rand*, pp. 269, 349.
228 Christian's 'invisible music,' recounted in Tremain, *Music & Silence*, later confirmed in musicology as summarised in Spohr, 'This Charming Invention Created by the King'.
234 'with neither will nor ability': Feldbæk, *Den lange fred*, p. 216.
238 'greatest of royal culture-vultures' etc.: Trevor-Roper, *The Plunder of the Arts in the Seventeenth Century*, pp. 10, 12, 42, 45.
240 'the love of her life': Villstrand, *Sveriges historia: 1600–1721*, p. 31.
241 'to her old methods': Trevor-Roper, *The Plunder of the Arts in the Seventeenth Century*, p. 49.
246 'a tragic being': Åberg, *Vår svenska historia*, p. 357.
248 'An estimated half a million [...] land of soldier-widows': Villstrand, *Sveriges historia: 1600–1721*, p. 165.
248 'The disasters which afflicted': *The Cambridge History of Scandinavia*, Vol. 2, pp. 164–5.
252 'The suffering caused': Wedgwood, *The Thirty Years* War, p. 7.
252 'placed ability above confession': Wilson, *Europe's Tragedy*, p. 830.
253 'The unprovisioned armies': Davies, *Europe*, p. 564.
254 'There was an explosion': Wilson, *Europe's Tragedy*, p. 784.
255 'The most awful': Rady, *The Habsburgs*, p. 141.
255 'Wherever the Swedish armies went': Trevor-Roper, *The Plunder of the Arts in the Seventeenth Century*, p. 40.
255 'the greatest collection in Germany': ibid., p. 38.
255 'The contents of monastic libraries': Wilson, *Europe's Tragedy*, p. 814.
255 'Königsmarck let his troops loose': ibid., p. 745.
256 'The question, therefore': Olden-Jørgensen, *Svenskekrigene*, p. 25.
257 'the loss of 25–30 per cent': Christensen, *Svenskekrigene*, p. 10.
261 'men and horses in heaps': ibid., p. 513.
262 'Surprisingly, 15 years on': ibid., p. 567.
265 'It was a total breakdown': Mykland, *Gjennom nødsår og krig*, pp. 431–2.

Chapter 8: A Taste of Colonialism

267 'a letter from one Peter Minuit': *The Pennsylvania Magazine of History and Biography*, Vol. 6, No. 4 (1882), pp. 458–60.
269 'The ship, *Fly*': Walvin, *Freedom*, p. 13.
270 'The Swedish East India Company': Abulafia, *The Boundless Sea*, p. 726.
272 'a man called Thormøhlen': Mykland, *Gjennom nødsår og krig*, p. 307.

Chapter 9: The Invention of Society

279 'A new kind of society': Feldbæk, *Den lange fred*, p. 205.
290 'farmer liberation': Samuelsson, *Från stormakt til välfärdsstat*, p. 58.
290 'lit by oil from': Åberg, *Vår svenska historia*, p. 352.
291 'growing masses of desperate': Samuelsson, *Från stormakt til välfärdsstat*, p. 85.

296 'Germanification': Hørby, *Velstands krise og tusind baghold*, p. 300.

300 'Children were pale': Samuelsson, *Från stormakt til välfärdsstat*, p. 148.

301 'settled down to an existence': Davies, *Europe*, p. 640.

306 'Frederik VI remained': *The Cambridge History of Scandinavia*, Vol. 2, p. 677.

309 'a strong sense of national': Dyrvik og Feldbæk, *Mellom brødre*, p. 87.

309 'in charge of governing power': Seip, *Nasjonen bygges*, p. 12.

Chapter 10: The Golden, and Not So Golden, Age

319 'The class mentalities': Hvidt, *Det folkelige gennembrud og dets mænd*, p. 150.

325 'He loved God': Seip, *Nasjonen bygges*, p. 144.

334 'Poor great Ibsen': Benestad, *Edvard Grieg*, p. 174.

351 'life-threatening brutality': Hvidt, *Det folkelige gennembrud og dets mænd*, p. 22.

358 'If it was a matter of': ibid., p. 95.

366 'short of height' etc.: Bjørn, *Fra reaktion til grundlov*, pp.130–33, 211–12, 241.

370 'Stockholm's streets did not need': Åberg, *Vår svenska historia*, p. 418.

Chapter 11: Wars and Progress

373 'pulling down mental barriers': Seip, *Veiene til velferdsstaten*, p. 19.

378 'a labour market constitution': Christiansen, *Klassesamfundet organiseres*, p. 143.

378 'an institution that with time': Andersson, *Sveriges historia*, p. 419.

378 'the end of fighting': Kjeldstadli, *Et splittet samfunn*, p. 184.

378 'historical compromise': Korpi, *The Democratic Class Struggle*, p. 47

378 'a durable and effective alliance': Christiansen, *Klassesamfundet organiseres*, p. 58, 268.

379 'shaken and shivering': Kolloen, *Under krigen*, p. 13.

404 'a damned Sunday school': so said Haakon Lie, Secretary General of the Norwegian Labour Party from 1946 to 1969, in response to later criticism that secret surveillance of Communists had been excessive and illegal.

421 'It took about fifteen years': Hindman, *Sveriges historia*, p. 604.

423 'about the *folkhem*': Andersson, *Son of Svea*.

Continuation: Scandinavia Today

429 'Anyone who as late as in 1945': Samuelsson, *Från stormakt til välfärdsstat*, p. 249

430 'to control the current of events': Davies, *Europe*, p. 760. Montefiore, *The Romanovs*, p. xxiii.

REFERENCES

Please note, these references follow the Scandinavian alphabets in which æ, ø and å (aa) are the last letters.

Abulafia, David, *The Boundless Sea; A Human History of the Oceans* (London: Allen Lane 2019).

Aidukaite, Jolanta, Sven E. O. Hort and Stein Kuhnle, eds., *Challenges to the Welfare State: Family and Pension Policies in the Baltic and Nordic Countries* (Cheltenham: Edward Elgar 2021).

Almgren, Bertil, ed., *The Viking* (Stockholm: Wahlström & Widstrand 1967).

Andenæs, Johs., *Det vanskelige oppgjøret: Rettsoppgjøret etter okkupasjonen* (Oslo: Tanum-Norli 1979).

Andersen, Kasper H., '*Da danerne blev danske: Dansk etnicitet og identitet til ca. år 1000*' (University of Aarhus, PhD dissertation 2017).

Andersson, Ingvar, *Sveriges historia* (Stockholm: Natur och Kultur 1960).

Andersson, Lena, *Son of Svea: A Tale of the People's Home* (New York: Other Press 2022).

Arendt, Hannah, *The Origins of Totalitarianism* (New York: Schocken 1951).

Aarebrot, Frank and Kjetil Evjen, *Reformasjonen* (Bergen: Vigmostad & Bjørke 2017).

Bagge, Sverre, 'The Transformation of Europe: The Role of Scandinavia' (*Medieval Encounters*, Vol. 10:1, pp. 131–65).

Bark, William Carroll, *Origins of the Medieval World* (Stanford: Stanford University Press 1958).

Benedictow, Ole Jørgen, *Fra rike til provins: 1448–1536* (Cappelens norgeshistorie, Vol. 5. Oslo: Cappelen 1977).

Benedictow, Ole Jørgen, *Plague in the late Medieval Nordic Countries* (Oslo: Middelalderforlaget 1992).

Benedictow, Ole Jørgen, 'The Demography of the Viking Age and the High Middle Ages in the Nordic Countries' (*Scandinavian Journal of History*, 1996, 21:3, pp. 151–82).

Benedictow, Ole Jørgen, *The Black Death, 1346–1353. A Complete History*, 2nd edn. (Woodbridge: Boydell & Brewer 2020).

Benestad, Finn and Dag Schjelderup-Ebbe, *Edvard Grieg: Mennesket og kunstneren* (Oslo: Aschehoug 1980).

Benum, Edgeir, *Overflod og fremtidsfrykt: 1970–* (Oslo: Aschehougs norgeshistorie Vol. 12. Oslo: Aschehoug 1998).

Bishop, Morris, *The Penguin Book of the Middle Ages* (London: Penguin 1971).

Bjørkvik, Halvard, *Folketap og sammenbrudd: 1350–1520* (Oslo: Aschehougs norgeshistorie Vol. 4. Oslo: Aschehoug 2005).

Bjørn, Claus, *Fra reaktion til grundlov: 1800–1850* (Gyldendals og Politikens Danmarkshistorie, Vol 10. Copenhagen: Gyldendal-Politiken 1990).

Black, C. F. et al., *Atlas of the Renaissance* (Amsterdam: Time-Life Books 1993).

Boggis-Rolfe, Caroline, *The Baltic Story* (London: Amberly 2019).

Braudel, Fernand, *The Mediterranean in the Ancient World* (London: Penguin 2001).

Breay, Claire and Joanna Story, eds., *Anglo-Saxon Kingdoms* (London: British Library 2018).

Brink, Stefan and Neil Price, eds., *The Viking World* (London: Routledge 2008).

Bruheim, Magnhild, *Trolldomskraft* (Oslo: Samlaget 2005).

Bull, Edvard, *Klassekamp og fellesskap: 1920–1945* (Cappelens norgeshistorie, Vol. 13. Oslo: Cappelen 1979).

Bull, Edvard, *Norge i den rike verden: Tiden etter 1945* (Cappelens norgeshistorie, Vol. 14. Oslo: Cappelen 1979).

Burns, C. Delisle, *The First Europe: A Study of the Establishment of Medieval Christendom* (London: George Allen & Unwin 1947).

Butler, Ewan, *Scandinavia: A History* (Rockville: New World City 2016).

Carlisle, Clare, *Philosopher of the Heart: The Restless Life of Søren Kierkegaard* (London: Allen Lane 2019).

Christensen, Lars, *Svenskekrigene 1657–60: Danmark på kanten af udslettelse* (Copenhagen: Kristeligt Dagblads Forlag 2018).

Christiansen, Niels Finn, *Klassesamfundet organiseres: 1900–1925*

(Gyldendals og Politikens Danmarkshistorie, Vol 10. Copenhagen: Gyldendal-Politiken 1990).

Clark, Christopher, *The Sleepwalkers: How Europe Went to War in 1914* (London: Penguin 2012).

Colley, Linda: *The Gun, the Ship and the Pen: Warfare, Constitutions and the Making of the Modern World* (London: Profile 2021).

Crossley-Holland, Kevin, *The Penguin Book of Norse Myths* (London: Penguin 2011).

Cunliffe, Barry, *Europe Between the Oceans: 9000 BC–AD 1000* (New Haven: Yale University Press 2008).

Cunliffe, Barry, *By Steppe, Desert and Ocean: The Birth of Eurasia* (Oxford: Oxford University Press 2015).

Cunliffe, Barry, *On the Ocean: The Mediterranean and the Atlantic from Prehistory to AD 1500* (Oxford: Oxford University Press 2017).

Dahl, Robert A., *On Democracy* (New Haven: Yale University Press 1998).

Dahlerup, Troels, *De fire stender: 1400–1500* (Gyldendals og Politikens Danmarkshistorie, Vol 6. Copenhagen: Gyldendal-Politiken 1989).

Davies, Norman, *Europe: A History* (London: Pimlico 1997).

Davies, Norman, *The Isles: A History* (London: Macmillan 1999).

Derry, T. K., *A History of Scandinavia* (Minneapolis: University of Minnesota Press 1979).

Draper, Nicholas, 'Capital, Indemnity and Slavery' (manuscript).

Draper, Nicholas, *The Price of Emancipation: Slave-ownership, Compensation and British Society at the End of Slavery* (Cambridge: Cambridge University Press 2010).

Dyrvik, Ståle and Ole Feldbæk, *Mellom Brødre: 1780–1830* (Oslo: Aschehougs norgeshistorie Vol. 7. Oslo: Aschehoug 1996).

Erikson, Robert, Erik Jørgen Hansen, Stein Ringen and Hannu Uusiotalo, eds., *The Scandinavian Model: Welfare States and Welfare Research* (New York: M. E. Sharpe 1987).

Ersland, Geir Atle, *Das Kaufmannshaus: Det hansiatiske kontorets rettslokale og administransjonshus i Bergen* (Bergen: Det Hanseatiske Museum 2011).

Feldbæk, Ole, *Den lange fred: 1700–1800* (Gyldendals og Politikens

Danmarkshistorie, Vol 9. Copenhagen: Gyldendal-Politikken 1990).

Feldbæk, Ole, 'The Danish Asia trade 1620–1807' (*Scandinavian Economic History Review*, 1991, 39:1, pp. 3–27).

Fenger, Ole, *Kirker rejeses alle vegne: 1050–1250* (Gyldendals og Politikens Danmarkshistorie, Vol 4. Copenhagen: Gyldendal-Politiken 1989).

Ferguson, Robert, *Scandinavians: In Search of the Soul of the North* (London: Head of Zeus 2016).

Figes, Orlando, *The Europeans: Three Lives and the Making of a Cosmopolitan Culture* (London: Penguin 2019).

Finlay, Alison and Þórdís Edda Jóhannesdóttir, *The Saga of the Jómsvikings* (translation and Introduction, de Gruyter 2018).

Fladby, Rolf, *Gjenreisning: 1436–1648* (Cappelens norgeshistorie, Vol. 6. Oslo: Cappelen 1977).

Foote, Peter G. and David M. Wilson, *The Viking Achievement* (London: Sidgwick & Jackson 1970).

Frankopan, Peter, *The Silk Roads: A New History of the World* (London: Bloomsbury 2015).

Friðriksdóttir, Jóhanna Katrín, *Valkyrie: The Women of the Viking World* (London: Bloomsbury 2020).

Fuglum, Per, *Norge i støpeskjeen: 1884–1920* (Cappelens norgeshistorie, Vol. 12. Oslo: Cappelen 1978).

Fukyama, Francis, *The Origins of Political Order: From Prehuman Times to the French Revolution* (London: Profile 2011).

Fure, Eli, *Eidsvoll 1814: Hvordan grunnloven ble til* (Oslo: Dreyers 2013).

Gaiman, Neil, *Norse Mythology* (London: Bloomsbury 2017).

Gimbutas, Marija, *The Living Goddesses* (Berkeley: University of California Press 2001).

Gøbel, Erik, *The Danish Slave Trade and Its Abolition* (Leiden: Brill 2016).

Gotaas, Thor and Roar Vingelsgaard, *Norske utedoer* (Oslo: Gyldendal 2019).

Graham-Campbell, James and Dafydd Kidd, *The Vikings* (London: British Museum 1980).

Gunnes, Erik, *Riksasamling og kristning: 800–1177* (Cappelens norgeshistorie, Vol. 2. Oslo: Cappelen 1976).

Haakonsen, Daniel, *Henrik Ibsen: Mennesket og kunstneren* (Oslo: Aschehoug 1981).

Hadenius, Stig, Björn Molin and Hans Wieslander: *Sverige efter 1900: En modern politisk historia* (Stockholm: Bonniers 1988).

Hadley, Dawn M. and Julian D. Richards, *The Viking Great Army and the Making of England* (London: Thames & Hudson 2021).

Hagemann, Gro, *Det moderne gjennombrudd: 1870–1905* (Oslo: Aschehougs norgeshistorie Vol. 9. Oslo: Aschehoug 1997).

Halperin, Charles J., *Ivan the Terrible: Free to Reward and Free to Punish* (Pittsburgh: Pittsburgh University Press 2019).

Hansen, Torkild, *Arabia Felix: The Danish Expedition of 1761–1767* (New York: New York Review of Books 2017).

Hansen, Torkild, *Coasts of Slaves* (Accra: Sub-Saharan Publishers 2002).

Hansen, Torkild, *Islands of Slaves* (Accra: Sub-Saharan Publishers 2005).

Hansen, Torkild, *Ships of Slaves* (Accra: Sub-Saharan Publishers 2007).

Hansen, Torkild, *The Way to Hudson Bay: The Life and Times of Jens Munk* (New York: Harcourt Brace 1965).

Harrison, Dick, *Slaveri*, Vol. I–III (Stockholm: Historiska Media 2006–8)

Harrison, Dick, *Sveriges historia: 600–1350* (Stockholm: Norstedts 2009).

Harrison, Dick and Bo Eriksson, *Sveriges historia: 1350–1600* (Stockholm: Norstedts 2010).

Hawes, James, *The Shortest History of Germany* (London: Old Street 2017).

Hawes, James, *The Shortest History of England* (London: Old Street 2020).

Heaney, Seamus, *Beowulf* (London: Faber & Faber 2000).

Heckscher, Eli, *An Economic History of Sweden* (Cambridge, MA: Harvard University Press 1954).

Hedeager, Lotte, *Danernes land: 200BC–700AD* (Gyldendals og Politikens Danmarkshistorie, Vol 2. Copenhagen: Gyldendal-Politiken 1988).

Heer, Friedrich, *Charlemagne and His World* (London: Weidenfeld & Nicolson 1975).

Helle, Knut, *Under kirke og kongemakt: 1130–1350* (Aschehougs norgeshistorie, Vol. 3. Oslo: Aschehoug 1996).

Helle, Knut, ed., *The Cambridge History of Scandinavia, Vol. 1: Prehistory to 1520* (Cambridge: Cambridge University Press 2003).

Herje, Torunn, Gaute Jacobsen, Endre Rustet and Hans-Jørgen Wallin Weihe, eds., *Bjørnstjerne Bjørnson: Ingen sak for liten, ingen sak for stor* (Stavanger: Hertervig 2010).

Herman, Arthur, *The Viking Heart: How Scandinavians Conquered the World* (New York: Houghton Mifflin Harcourt 2021)

Herodotus, *The Histories* (*c.*420 BC).

Hindman, Yvonne, Urban Lundberg and Jenny Björkman, *Sveriges historia: 1920–1965* (Stockholm: Norstedts 2012).

Hines, John and Nelleke IJssennagger, eds., *Frisians and their North Sea Neighbours: From the Fifth Century to the Viking Age* (Woodbridge: The Boydell Press 2018).

Hvidt, Kristian, *Det folkelige gennembrud og dets mænd: 1850–1900* (Gyldendals og Politikens Danmarkshistorie, Vol V. Copenhagen: Gyldendal-Politiken 1990).

Hørby, Kai, *Velstands krise og tusind baghold: 1250–1400* (Gyldendals og Politikens Danmarkshistorie, Vol XI. Copenhagen: Gyldendal-Politiken 1989).

Imsen, Steinar and Jørn Sandnes, *Avfolking og union: 1319–1448* (Cappelens norgeshistorie, Vol 4. Oslo: Cappelen 1977).

Isaacson, Walter, *Leonardo da Vinci: The Biography* (New York: Simon & Schuster 2017).

Iversen, Tore, *Trelldommen: norsk slaveri i middelalderen* (University of Bergen, Department of History 1997).

Jaklin, Asbjørn, *Flukten med Norges gull* (Oslo: Gyldendal 2021).

Jarman, Cat, *River Kings: A New History of the Vikings from Scandinavia to the Silk Roads* (London: William Collins 2021).

Jenkins, Simon, *A Short History of London* (London: Penguin 2019).

Jensen, Jørgen, *I begyndelsen: Fra de ældste tider til ca. år 200 f.Kr.* (Gyldendals og Politikens Danmarkshistorie, Vol 1. Copenhagen: Gyldendal-Politiken 1989).

Jesch, Judith, *The Viking Diaspora* (London: Routledge 2018).

Johnson, Steven, *The Ghost Map: The Story of London's Most Terrifying Epidemic – And How It Changed Science, Cities, and the Modern World* (London: Riverhead 2007).

Jones, Gwyn, *A History of the Vikings* (Oxford: Oxford University Press 1973).

Kaarsted, Tage, *Krise og krig: 1925–1950* (Gyldendals og Politikens Danmarkshistorie, Vol. 13. Copenhagen: Gyldendal-Politiken 1991).

Karlson, Gunnar, 'Plague without Rats: The Case of Fifteenth-century Iceland' (*Journal of Medieval History*, 1996, Vol. 22:3, pp. 263–84).

Karlsson, Svenolof, ed., *Frihetens källa: Nordens betydelse för Europa* (Stockhold: Nordic Council 1992).

Keane, John, *The Life and Death of Democracy* (New York: Simon & Schuster 2009).

Keen, Maurice, *The Pelican Book of Medieval Europe* (London: Penguin 1969).

Kershaw, Ian, *To Hell and Back: Europe 1914–1949* (London: Penguin 2015).

Kershaw, Ian, *Roller-Coaster: Europe 1950–2017* (London: Penguin 2018, published in the USA as *The Global Age*).

Kershaw, Jane, Gareth Williams, Søren Sindbæk and James Graham-Campbell, eds., *Silver, Butter, Cloth: Monetary and Social Economies in the Viking Age* (Oxford: Oxford University Press 2019).

Keynes, John Maynard, *The General Theory of Employment, Interest and Money* (London: Macmillan 1936).

King, Ross, *Brunelleschi's Dome: The Story of the Great Cathedral of Florence* (London: Chatto & Windus 2000).

Kjeldstadli, Knut, *Et splittet samfunn: 1905–35* (Oslo: Aschehougs norgeshistorie Vol. 10. Oslo: Aschehoug 1994).

Kleberg, Tönnes, *Codex Argenteus: The Silver Bible in Uppsala* (Uppsala University Library 1984).

Klinge, Matti, *The Baltic World* (Helsinki: Otava 1994).

Kolloen, Ingar Sletten, *Berre kjærleik og død: Ein bigrafi om Tor Jonsson* (Oslo: Samlaget 1999).

Kolloen, Ingar Sletten, *Knut Hamsun: Dreamer and Dissenter* (New Haven: Yale University Press 2009).

Kolloen, Ingar Sletten, *Under krigen: Vi må ikke falle* (Oslo: Gyldendal 2019).

Kolloen, Ingar Sletten, *Under krigen: Nå må vi tåle alt* (Oslo: Gyldendal 2021).

Korpi, Walter, *The Democratic Class Struggle* (London: Routledge & Kegan Paul 1983).

Kouri, E. I. and Jens E. Olsen, eds., *The Cambridge History of Scandinavia, Vol. 2* (Cambridge: Cambridge University Press 2016).

Krag, Claus, *Vikingtid og riskssamling: 800–1130* (Aschehougs norgeshistorie, Vol. 2. Oslo: Aschehoug 2005).

Lagercrantz, Olof, *August Strindberg* (Stockholm: Wahlström & Widstrand 1979).

Lange, Even, *Samling om felles mål: 1935–1970* (Oslo: Aschehougs norgeshistorie Vol. 11. Oslo: Aschehoug 1998).

László, Gyula, *The Art of the Migration Period* (London: Allen Lane 1974).

Lepore, Jill, *These Truths: A History of the United States* (New York: Norton 2018).

Lie, Haakon, *Slik jeg ser det* (Oslo: Tiden 1975).

Lillehammer, Arnvid, *Fra jeger til bonde: – 800 AD* (Aschehougs norgeshistorie, Vol. 1. Oslo: Aschehoug 2005).

Lindgren, Astrid: *Krigsdagböcker 1939–1945* (Stockholm: Salikon 2015).

Lindkvist, Thomas, 'The Making of a European Society: The Example of Sweden' (*Medieval Encounters*, Vol. 10:1, pp. 167–83).

Lockhart, Paul Douglas, *Denmark 1513–1660: The Rise and Decline of a Renaissance Monarchy* (Oxford: Oxford University Press 2007).

Lund, Niels, ed., *Viking og Hvidekrist* (Copenhagen: Reitzels 2000).

Lunden, Kåre, *Norge under Sverreætten: 1177–1319* (Cappelens norgeshistorie, Vol. 3. Oslo: Cappelen 1976).

MacGregor, Neil, *Germany: Memories of a Nation* (London: Allen Lane 2014).

Mackay, Jamie, *The Invention of Sicily: A Mediterranean History* (London: Verso 2021).

Mackintosh-Smith, Tim, *Arabs; A 3000 Year History of Peoples, Tribes and Empires* (New Haven: Yale University Press 2019).

MacMillan, Margaret, *War: How Conflict Shaped Us* (London: Profile 2020).

Magnus, Bente and Bjørn Myhre, *Forhistorien* (Cappelens norgeshistorie, Vol. 1. Oslo: Cappelen 1976).

Mansén, Elisabeth, *Sveriges historia 1721–1830* (Stockholm: Norstedts 2011).

McGuckin, John Anthony, *The Eastern Orthodox Church: A New History* (New Haven: Yale University Press 2020).

Montefiore, Simon Sebag, *The Romanovs: 1613–1918* (London: Weidenfeld & Nicolson 2016)

Moren, Gudmund, *Okkupanter: Historien om Trudel og Georg Bauer* (Oslo: Forlaget Press 2019).

Mykland, Knut, *Gjennom nødsår og krig: 1648–1720* (Cappelens norgeshistorie, Vol 7. Oslo: Cappelen 1977).

Nelson, Janet L., *King and Emperor: A New Life of Charlemagne* (London: Allen Lane 2019).

Nissen, Henrik S., *Landet ble by: 1950–1970* (Gyldendals og Politikens Danmarkshistorie, Vol 14. Copenhagen: Gyldendal-Politiken 1991).

Odelberg, Wilhelm, ed., *Guldet i flaskan* (Stockholm: Vin & Spritcentralen 1967).

Olden-Jørgensen, Sebastian, *Svenskekrigene* (Århus: Aarhus universitetsforlag 2018).

Östberg, Kjell, Jenny Andersson and Dick Harrison, *Sveriges historia: 1965–2012* (Stockholm: Norstedts 2013).

Page, R. I., *Chronicles of the Vikings* (London: British Museum Press 1995).

Parker, Geoffrey, *The Thirty Years' War* (London: Routledge & Kegan Paul 1987).

Parker, Geoffrey, *Emperor: A New Life of Charles V* (New Haven: Yale University Press 2019).

Patterson, Orlando, *Slavery and Social Death* (Cambridge, MA: Harvard University Press 2018).

Pedersen, Ole Karup, *Danmark og verden: 1970–1990* (Gyldendals og Politikens Danmarkshistorie, Vol 15. Copenhagen: Gyldendal-Politiken 1991).

Pettegree, Andrew and Arthur der Weduwen, *The Bookshop of the World: Making and Trading Books in the Dutch Golden Age* (New Haven: Yale University Press 2019).

Price, Neil, *The Children of Ash and Elm: A History of the Vikings* (London: Allen Lane 2020).

Pye, Michael, *The Edge of the World: How the North Sea Made Us Who We Are* (London: Penguin 2015).

Rady, Martyn, *The Habsburgs: The Rise and Fall of a World Power* (London: Allen Lane 2020).

Rian, Øystein, *Den nye begynnelsen: 1520–1660* (Oslo: Aschehougs norgeshistorie Vol. 5. Oslo: Aschehoug 1995).

Rian, Øystein, Finn Erhard Johannessen, Øystein Sørensen and Finn Fuglestad, eds., *Revolusjon og resonnement: Festskrift til Kåre Tønnessen* (Oslo: Universitetsforlaget 1996).

Rikhardsdottir, Sif, *Emotion in Norse Literature* (Cambridge: Brewer 2017).

Rio, Alice, *Slavery After Rome* (Oxford: Oxford University Press 2017).

Roberts, Andrew, *Churchill: Walking With Destiny* (London: Allen Lane 2018).

Robertson, Ritchie, *The Enlightenment: The Pursuit of Happiness 1680–1790* (London: Allen Lane 2020).

Rodney, Walter, *How Europe Underdeveloped Africa* (London: Bogle-L'Ouverture Publications 1972).

Roesdahl, Else, *Viking Age Denmark* (London: British Museum Publications 1982).

Roesdahl, Else, ed., *Dagligliv i Danmarks middelalder* (Copenhagen: Gyldendal 1999).

Roesdahl, Else, *The Vikings* (3rd edn., London: Penguin 2016).

Rystad, Göran, ed., *Kampen om Skåne* (Lund: Historiske Media 2005).

Samuelsson, Kurt, *Från stormakt till välfärdsstat* (Stockholm: Sveriges Riksbank 1968).

Sawyer, Peter, *Da Danmark ble Danmark: 700–1050* (Gyldendals og Politikens Danmarkshistorie, Vol 3. Copenhagen: Gyldendal-Politikken 1988).

Sawyer, Birgit and Peter, *Medieval Scandinavia* (Minneapolis: University of Minnesota Press 1993).

Scoczza, Benito, *Ved afgrundens rand: 1600–1700* (Gyldendals og Politikens Danmarkshistorie, Vol 8. Copenhagen: Gyldendal-Politikken 1989).

Seip, Anne-Lise, *Eilert Sundt: Fire studier* (Oslo: Universitetsforlaget 1983).

Seip, Anne-Lise, *Nasjonen bygges: 1830–1870* (Oslo: Aschehougs norgeshistorie Vol. 8. Oslo: Aschehoug 1997).

Seip, Anne-Lise, *Sosialhjelpstaten blir til: 1740–1920* (Oslo: Gyldendal 1984).

Seip, Anne-Lise, *Veiene til velferdsstaten: 1920–1975* (Oslo: Gyldendal 1994).

Sejersted, Francis, *Den vanskelige frihet: 1814–1850* (Cappelens norgeshistorie, Vol. 10. Oslo: Cappelen 1978).

Serra, Daniel and Hanna Tunberg, *An Early Meal: A Viking Age Cookbook & Culinary Odyssey* (Stockholm: ChronoCopia 2017).

Silver, Morris, *Economic Structures of Antiquity* (Westport, CT: Greenwood Press 1995).

Simpson, Jacqueline, *The Viking World* (London: Batsford 1980).

Smith, C. T., *An Historical Geography of Western Europe Before 1800* (London: Longmans 1967).

Sogner, Sølvi, *Krig og fred: 1660–1780* (Oslo: Aschehougs norgeshistorie Vol. 4. Oslo: Aschehoug 1996).

Sophocles, *The Theban Plays*, trans. E. F. Watling (London: Penguin Classics 1947).

Spohr, Arne, 'This Charming Invention Created by the King: Christian IV and his invisible music' (*Danish Yearbook of Musicology*, 2012, Vol. 39, pp. 13–33).

Stang, Ragna, *Edvard Munch: Mennesket og kunstneren* (Oslo: Aschehoug 1978).

Steinmetz, Greg, *The Richest Man Who Ever Lived: The Life and Times of Jacob Fugger* (New York: Simon & Schuster 2015).

Stenton, Frank, *Anglo-Saxon England* (Oxford: Oxford University Press 1947).

Stougaard-Nielsen, Jakob, *Scandinavian Crime Fiction* (London: Bloomsbury 2017).

Stråth, Bo, *Sveriges historia 1830–1920* (Stockholm: Norstedts 2012).

Sørensen, Øystein, *Historien om det som ikke skjedde* (Oslo: Aschehoug 2017).

Sørensen, Øystein and Bo Stråth, eds., *The Cultural Construction of Norden* (Oslo: Scandinavian University Press 1997).

Taylor, Barbara, *Mary Wollstonecraft and the Feminist Imagination* (Cambridge: Cambridge University Press 2003).

The Vikings In England – And In Their Danish Homeland (Exhibition catalogue, London: The Anglo-Danish Viking Project 1981).

Tremain, Rose, *Music & Silence* (London: Chatto & Windus 1999).

Trevor-Roper, Hugh, *The Plunder of the Arts in the Seventeenth Century* (London: Thames and Hudson 1970).

Try, Hans, *To kulturer – en stat: 1850–1884* (Cappelens norgeshistorie, Vol. 11. Oslo: Cappelen 1979).

Villstrand, Nils Erik, *Sveriges historia: 1600–1721* (Stockholm: Norstedts 2011).

Walvin, James, *Freedom: The Overthrow of the Slave Empires* (London: Robinson 2019).

Wedgwood, C. V., *The Thirty Years War* (London: Pimlico 1992).

Welinder, Stig, *Sveriges historia 13000 f.Kr.-600 e.Kr.* (Stockholm: Norsteds 2009).

Westad, Odd Arne, *The Cold War* (London: Penguin 2017).

Wilson, David M., *The Vikings and Their Origins* (London: Thames and Hudson 1970).

Wilson, Peter H., *Europe's Tragedy: A New History of the Thirty Years War* (London: Penguin 2010).

Winder, Simon, *Germania: A Personal History of Germans Ancient and Modern* (London: Picador 2010).

Winder, Simon, *Lotharingia: A Personal History of Europe's Lost Country* (New York: Farrar, Straus and Giroux 2019).

Winroth, Anders, *The Conversion of Scandinavia* (New Haven: Yale University Press 2012).

Winroth, Anders, *The Age of the Vikings* (Princeton: Princeton University Press 2014).

Wittendorff, Alex, *På Guds og Herskabs nåde: 1500–1600* (Gyldendals og Politikens Danmarkshistorie, Vol 7. Copenhagen: Gyldendal-Politikken 1989).

Zweig, Stefan, *The World of Yesterday* (London: Pushkin Press 2009, published as *Die Welt von Gestern* in Stockholm in 1942).

Åberg, Alf: *Vår Svenska Historia* (Stockholm: Natur och Kultur 1978).

ABOUT THIS BOOK

This is a personal book. I am a Scandinavian, both of origin and identity. I grew up partly in Oslo and partly in rural Gudbrandsdalen. I gravitated early to Copenhagen, which for us Norwegians was then the shining and exciting cultural metropole, with its taste of Continental liberalism and sophistication. Later, I lived formative years in Stockholm. My professional life has unfolded in constant Scandinavian and Nordic collaboration.

I am also a European. I have lived in Britain since 1990, and at times in Paris, Berlin, Prague and elsewhere. Since I was a schoolboy I have criss-crossed the Continent on travels. My identity is as European as it is Scandinavian. I have been a British citizen, as of 2020, during work on this project, when Norway finally accepted dual citizenship.

I cannot say exactly what made me write this history, but I think it must have something to do with my origins in the periphery and later cosmopolitanism and with an urge to get to grips with who I am and who my folks are, in this unruly territory and history that we in shorthand call *Europe*. I am one of many Europeans who are migrants. We share, I think, a wish to understand how it matters where we are from and where we have come to, and what the road has been.

In the Museum of National History in Oslo is preserved the auditorium of the old Cathedral School which Norway's Parliament, *Storting*, used for its meetings in its early years after 1814. In 1998, I was invited to give a lecture there on 'Germany and Norwegian Culture', speaking from the old parliamentary rostrum, and I well remember the solemnity of the occasion. It was on the opening of an exhibition of German inspiration on German–Scandinavian cultural links. The preparation of that lecture, and the occasion, were eye-openers for me about the historical force of those links, and it was a turning point in my European persona, from a French to a German orientation. In retrospect, it may well be that the idea for a book of this kind came out of that experience.

The first person I discussed the project with was my wife, Mary Chamberlain, who is a historian as well as a novelist, and who was at first just slightly bemused by what she heard. She has been a constant and generous companion and a sounding board on all matters historical, and other matters as well. We work together at home, each in our study, and have a wonderful symposium of writing.

Early on, I confessed my intention to Anne-Lise Seip and Øystein Sørensen of the University of Oslo, and to Haki Antonsson and Mart Kuldkepp of University College London, in conversations that laid down many pointers for the work to come. UCL has an excellent Scandinavian library which has been invaluable throughout, and I am indebted to Giulia Garoli, the area librarian. Thanks are also much due to the resources and hospitality of the British Library. UCL hosts the venerable Viking Society for Nordic Research whose excellent lectures, seminars and publications have been enormously helpful. Alison Finlay of Birkbeck College has helped on matters of early Scandinavian culture and language.

During the project, I have made contact with historians and authors far and wide to obtain from them advice, information and direction, and have been gratified by their generosity in the sharing of knowledge and experience, many reading draft materials for improvement. I wish to thank in particular, in addition to those already mentioned, in arbitrary order, Else Roesdahl, Ole Jørgen Benedictow, Nis Hardt, John Hines, Kevin Crossley-Holland, Lars Kjær (for a splendid lecture to the Viking Society for Northern Research on the enduring dream of a Danish England after 1066), Geir Atle Ersland, Svein Ivar Angell, Gad Heuman, Avi Shlaim, David Abulafia, Jane Kershaw, Sif Rikhardsdottir, Janet Nelson, Rose Tremain, Robert Evans, Margaret MacMillan, Nick Draper, Cath Hall, Erik Gøbel, Bill Schwarz, Aksel Hatland, Axel West Pedersen, Cecilia Ekbäck, Åsa Mähring (of the Stockholm City Museum, on Stockholm Old Town politics), Karen Elizabeth Lerheim, Arne Eggum, Simon Mayall (on Crusade matters) and Inge Eidsvåg.

Various friends have assisted in many ways. Pat Pearson (Connor) lent me her archive and literature backing up the 'Vikings in England' exhibition in Copenhagen, Århus and York in 1981–82, of which she was a co-organiser. Patrick Wright, Judy and Michael Cass and Geoff Haslam have been interlocutors in discussion and have generously read much draft material. So has Anders Kjølberg, friend from student days and more knowledgeable about Norse-European history than most.

I have made use of my own family history in putting the book together. Some of that has seeped into the text but there is more in the background than is visible to the reader. I have had many conversations with kinfolk, near and not so near, and what I have learned in those conversations has mattered more in this work than those I have spoken with will be aware of.

In Lillehammer in Norway, a small circle of men-friends meet regularly in what we think of as a *salong*. We are Gunnar Hagen, Ingar Sletten Kolloen, Gudmund Moren, Asbjørn Ringen, Jostein Skurdal, Harald Thoresen and myself, several of us authors. We eat well, we drink well and we enjoy robust discussion on matters of the world, including each other's works. I am in much debt to these good friends.

My agent, Peter Bernstein, has supported and guided the project from the start, with wisdom and friendship. Alan Samson commissioned the book for Weidenfeld & Nicolson, where I have enjoyed excellent collaboration with my editor Ed Lake, and briefly Maddy Price, as well as Jo Roberts-Miller in the project editorial team, Hannah Cox in production, Linden Lawson on copy editing, Natalie Dawkins on illustrations, Helen Ewing and John Gilkes on the design of maps, Hilary Bird on the index, Kim Bishop on proofreading, Elizabeth Allen on marketing, and their various W&N colleagues who have lent invaluable support

The literature I have consulted is listed in the References. It would not have been possible to write this book without being able to use the Scandinavian literature in the Scandinavian languages. I have benefited enormously from *Cappelens norgeshistorie* (fifteen volumes, 1976–1980, under the editorship of Professor Knut Mykland), *Gyldendal og Politikens Danmarkshistorie* (sixteen volumes, 1988–1991, under the editorship of Professor Olaf Olsen), *Aschehougs norgeshistorie* (twelve volumes, 1993–1998, under the editorship of professor Knut Helle) and *Norstedts Sveriges Historia* (eight volumes, 2009–2013, under the editorship of Professor Dick Harrison). *The Cambridge History of Scandinavia* (under the editorship of Professors Knut Helle, E. I. Kouri and Torkel Jansson, three volumes, two published, the final one pending) is an immense and invaluable source work. The version of Snorri Sturluson's *Kringla Heimsins* I have used is the Norwegian Gyldendal translation of 1979; the translations into English are my own. When I moved to Stockholm in 1983 I found, to make sense of the country where I was settling for a while, *Vår Svenska Historia* by Professor Alf Åberg, which I appreciated then and have appreciated again now. I have consulted rafts of works on European history, among which I pay tribute to *Europe* by Professor Norman Davies, a work of grand synthesis which has been ever helpful for the recurrent pan-European backdrop. Needless to say, the internet has been an invaluable tool: a name, a place, an event – at the press of a key multiple sources, Wikipedia and others, are at your fingertips. Danish historians (at the University of Århus) maintain an electronic encyclopaedia of Danish history – *danmarkshistorien.dk* – and Norwegian ones (at the University of Oslo) one of Norwegian history – *norgeshistorie. no* – which are treasure troves of facts and cross-references.

ABOUT THE AUTHOR

Stein Ringen is a Norwegian-British political scientist of states, governance and democracy. He has published scholarly books and other works on topics ranging from the Scandinavian welfare state via constitutional matters in Britain and the United States to dictatorship in China, and on inequality, poverty, income distribution, social and public policy and comparative government. He is Visiting Professor of Political Economy at King's College London, Emeritus Professor of Sociology and Social Policy at the University of Oxford and Emeritus Fellow of Green Templeton College, and has been an associate of Nuffield and St Antony's Colleges in Oxford. Before joining the University of Oxford he was Professor of Welfare Studies at the University of Stockholm. He has held visiting professorships and fellowships in Paris, Berlin, Prague, Brno, Barbados, Jerusalem, London, Lillehammer, Sydney, Hong Kong, Guangzhou and at Harvard University. He has held various research and government posts in Norway, including as Assistant Director General in the Ministry of Justice and Head of Research in the Ministry of Public Administration. He has been a consultant to the United Nations, and a news and feature reporter with the Norwegian Broadcasting Corporation. His journalism has appeared in the *Financial Times*, the *Washington Post*, the *Los Angeles Times*, the *South China Morning Post* (Hong Kong), *ChinaFile* (New York), *El País* (Madrid), *Aftenposten* (Oslo), *OpenDemocracy*, the *Times Literary Supplement* and elsewhere. He lives in London with his wife, the novelist and historian Mary Chamberlain.

INDEX

Page numbers in *italic* refer to the illustrations. The Danish letters æ, ø and å (aa) fall at the end of the alphabet.